R. C. Turner   R. G. Scaife

Bog Bodies

New Discoveries and New Perspectives

Published for the
Trustees of the British Museum by
BRITISH MUSEUM PRESS

©1995 The Trustees of the British Museum
Published by British Museum Press
A division of British Museum Publications Ltd
46 Bloomsbury Street
London WC1B 3QQ

British Library Cataloguing in Publication Data
A catalogue record for this book is available from the British Library

ISBN 0–7141–2305–6

Designed by Andrew Shoolbred

Typeset in Palatino by Create Publishing Services, Bath, Avon
Printed and bound in Great Britain by The Bath Press, Avon

Contents

List of Contributors

K. E. BARBER
Department of Geography, Southampton University, Highfield, Southampton SO9 5NH

E. H. BEAUMONT
St Hugh's College, University of Oxford, Oxford OX6 6LE

J. B. BOURKE
Department of Surgery, University Hospital, Nottingham N67 2UH

N. P. BRANCH
Department of Geography, Royal Holloway College, University of London, Egham Hill, Egham, Surrey TW20 0EX

C. S. BRIGGS
Royal Commission on Ancient and Historical Monuments (Wales), Crown Building, Plas Crug, Aberystwyth, Dyfed SY23 2HP

A. L. BRINDLEY
Biologisch-Archaeologisch Instituut, Rijksuniversiteit, Poststraat 6, 9712 ER Groningen, Netherlands

D. R. BROTHWELL
Department of Archaeology, University of York, Micklegate House, Micklegate, York YO1 1JZ

P. C. BUCKLAND
Department of Archaeology and Prehistory, University of Sheffield, Sheffield S10 2TN

M. R. COWELL
Department of Scientific Research, The British Museum, London WC1B 3DG

P. T. CRADDOCK
Department of Scientific Research, The British Museum, London WC1B 3DG

M. DELANEY
Department of Anatomy, Trinity College, Dublin 2

M. H. DINNIN
Department of Archaeology and Prehistory, University of Sheffield, Sheffield S10 2TN

C. R. FRICKER AND E. J. FRICKER
Thames Water Utilities, Spencer House Laboratory, Reading RG1 8DB

A. N. GARLAND
19 Mulberry Road, Newlands, Glasgow G43 2TR

R. E. M. HEDGES
Research Laboratory for Archaeology and the History of Art, 6 Keble Road, Oxford OX1 3QJ

T. G. HOLDEN
A.O.C. (Scotland) Ltd, 4 Lochend Road, Leith, Edinburgh EH6 8BR

R. A. HOUSLEY
Research Laboratory for Archaeology and the History of Art, 6 Keble Road, Oxford OX1 3QJ

D. LACY
Department of Chemistry and Physics, Nottingham Trent University, Clifton Lane, Nottingham NG1 4BU

J. N. LANTING
Biologisch-Archaeologisch Instituut, Rijksuniversiteit, Poststraat 6, 9712 ER Groningen, Netherlands

J. R. MAGILTON
Southern Archaeology (Chichester) Ltd, Westhampnett Services, Westhampnett Road, Chichester PO18 0NS

R. Ó FLOINN
Irish Antiquities Division, National Museum of Ireland, Kildare Street, Dublin 2

R. L. OTLET
Radiocarbon Dating, Downs Croft, The Holloway,
Harwell OX11 0LS

T. J. PAINTER
Institutt for Bioteknologi, Universitetet I Trondheim,
Sem Saelands vei 6/8, N 7034 Trondheim, Norway

F. B. PYATT
Department of Life Sciences, Nottingham Trent
University, Clifton Lane, Nottingham NG11 8NS

R. G. SCAIFE
Department of Geography, Southampton University,
Highfield, Southampton SO9 5NH

P. SKIDMORE
169 Carr House Road, Doncaster DN4 5DP

M. SPIGELMAN
UCL Institute of Archaeology, 31–34 Gordon Square,
London WC1H 0PY

D. M. STOREY
Department of Biological Sciences, University of Salford,
Salford M5 4WT

R. C. TURNER
Cadw: Welsh Historic Monuments, Brunel House,
2 Fitzalan Road, Cardiff CF2 1UY

W. A. B. VAN DER SANDEN
Drents Museum, Postbus 134, 9400 AC Assen,
Netherlands

A. J. WALKER
Radiocarbon Dating, Downs Croft, The Holloway,
Harwell OX11 0LS

Acknowledgements

The editors and many of the contributors wish to thank Ian Stead and the staff of the British Museum for their support in bringing this book to publication. The help and patience of Celia Clear and her colleagues at the British Museum Press is also gratefully acknowledged. The excavations at Lindow Moss in 1987 were funded by the British Museum, English Heritage and Cheshire County Council. Special thanks are due to Ken Harwood and his colleagues who work at Lindow Moss for their enthusiasm and practical help, and to Velson Horie of the Manchester Museum for providing conservation advice both on and off site. The excavations were supervised by Penny Noake and Bevis Sale.

Individual contributors would like to make the following acknowledgements. Rick Turner would like to thank the Leverhulme Trust for a grant towards his research into British bog bodies, and to Stephen Briggs, Stephen Penney, Audrey Henshall, Ed Rose, Frances Healy, Colin Richardson and others for information regarding specific discoveries. Nick Branch and Rob Scaife are grateful for Karon Oliver's and Wendy Scaife's comments on Chapter 2. Spigelman, Fricker and Fricker wish to acknowledge the support of Thames Water PLC and the Gordon Childe fund at the Institute of Archaeology, Gordon Hillman and Sue Wales for their inspiration and support and Eshetu Lemma for his help.

Brian Pyatt and his co-contributors would like to thank P. Fleming, K. Moss, M. Bawa, T. Campion and A. Bullen for their technical assistance and K. Branigan, J. Collis, D. Gilbertson and J. P. Wild for advice over the interpretation. The *Oxford Journal of Archaeology* and the *Journal of Environmental Geochemistry and Health* gave their permission to reproduce material which appeared in their original articles in these journals.

Tim Holden would like to thank Dawn Holmes, Stephen Carter, Sue College, Gordon Hillman, Camilla Dickson and John Vaughan for their help and advice: and to the SERC and the British Museum for the funding for his research. Anna Brindley and Jan Lanting would wish to record that the Irish radiocarbon dates provided by Oxford were part of a larger series of dates funded by the National Heritage Council (Ireland). The Groningen dates were provided by courtesy of the Centrum voor Isotopen Onderzoek. Maire Delaney and Raghnall Ó Floinn would like to thank Seamus Heaney and Faber and Faber for permission to produce an extract from the poem and Wijnand van der Sanden would like to thank Susan Mellor for translating his contribution.

The illustrations are all the copyright of the individual authors unless specifically stated in the captions.

Preface

Lindow Man was the archaeological find of the 1980s. No other discovery so captured the public imagination in Britain and around the world. Following his conservation, he now forms part of the British Museum's permanent collection. The inspiration behind this book was the discovery of a second, nearly complete body at Lindow Moss in 1987. This body, referred to as Lindow III, has never had the same attention as his more famous predecessor. However, in many ways, he is just as remarkable.

The earlier monograph produced by British Museum Publications – *Lindow Man: The Body in the Bog*, edited by Ian Stead, Jim Bourke and Don Brothwell – was published in 1986. It reported on the research carried out in the first 18 months after his discovery. This was to leave a number of key questions unanswered, and avenues of research unexplored. The range and types of investigation applied were to inspire the first systematic studies of bog bodies in the Netherlands and Ireland, and a more thorough review of earlier discoveries in Britain. The finding of Lindow III has provided important comparative data and a reaffirmation of the importance of Lindow Moss. This led to a much more intensive study of the peat bog than was possible due to the remarkable circumstances of the modern murder case which surrounded the recovery of Lindow I (the so-called Lindow Woman) and Lindow Man.

Research into Lindow III has proceeded much more slowly, and it is now eight years since his remains were retrieved, broken up into many pieces. This length of time has allowed for fuller consideration of the bog-body phenomenon. Twenty-seven main contributors from four countries have brought a wide range of scientific and historical expertise to this project. They have examined the bodies themselves, what they ate and how they looked. The thorny problem of what date are the Lindow and other bog bodies is considered in some detail. A more comprehensive study of Lindow Moss has reconstructed the nature of the peat bog in which they were found and the local environment in which they lived. New research has also shown how these bodies have been so miraculously preserved.

The debate is widened to consider the bog bodies recorded from Britain and Ireland as a whole and there is a review of the recent work into continental bog bodies, with the results of a research project in the Netherlands highlighted. Finally, there is a discussion of the reasons which lie behind the deposition of bodies in bogs, their social context, and how they form part of the mythological as well as historical record of northern Europe. The scope of this book is thus much wider than its predecessor and we hope that it will further illuminate the variety, complexity and wonderment of the bog body phenomenon.

R. C. Turner Cardiff   *R. G. Scaife* Southampton
March 1995

PART I

The Lindow Bog Bodies

Discoveries and Excavations at Lindow Moss 1983–8

R. C. Turner

During the 1980s, Lindow Moss, near Wilmslow in Cheshire was the scene of a succession of remarkable discoveries. On five separate occasions, the workmen at the site and the archaeologists who followed them, found well-preserved human remains. These proved to be the first British bog bodies to have been studied extensively. This opening chapter aims to tell the story of how they were found and forms the background to the other studies published in the volume.

Lindow Moss (NGR SJ 820805) was originally a very extensive lowland peat bog, covering some 600 ha (1500 acres). It was formed in a succession of hollows left by the melting ice on the southern limits of the last glaciation. Lindow is only one of a number of peat bogs which originally covered a large proportion of north-east Cheshire and the Mersey Basin (Fig. 1). The first documentary reference to the site was made in 1421 (Dodgson 1970, 230), when the right of turbary – the digging of peat for fuel – was confirmed by the lords of Mobberley and Wilmslow, the two parishes which share the moss.

The earliest description of Lindow Moss was made by Samuel Finney, miniature painter to Queen Charlotte and resident of Wilmslow, who wrote a manuscript history of the parish in the 1780s (Worthington-Barlow 1853). By his day, the moss had begun to be enclosed and drained, and only about 270 ha of the 'wild moss' remained. He recorded that:

> Accidents, as is natural to suppose are not infrequent among cows and sheep, which ranging for food, sometimes slip into the Moss Pits and trenches, and are there fastened, starved and suffo-

cated, before they can be found and relieved. Men also have found their last home upon this dreary place too in my memory. Nat Bell, and Radcliffe, returning home, loaded with ale, fell under the fatal burden and died before morning … (Worthington-Barlow 1853, 45)

Finney goes on to record the recovery of a skeleton from the sandhole in Morley Gorses just on the north-western fringe of the moss.

Lindow Moss continued to be destroyed through the cutting of peat for fuel and the reclamation of the margins for agriculture. Norbury was moved to record his observations on the site because: 'Lindow is fast being cultivated, and in a few more years all that can be said will be "This once was Lindow".' (Norbury 1884, 61)

He described the stratigraphy of the bog in some detail and particularly the forest layer to be found at the bottom. Two antiquities were found within his memory, a partly decomposed skeleton of a boar and 'a roadway made of logs of timber placed end to end, with sleepers across laid close together'. He also discussed the peculiar race of people who lived on the margins of these old commons until 50 years previously. They were buck-stealers, poachers and fishers and were expert in using the 'natural and ready products of the country' to make traps and snares, besoms, straw beehives, etc. Their ancient habits set these people apart.

The hand-digging of peat continued well into the twentieth century and Fig. 2 shows the moss in 1956. In the 1960s, a peat-extraction company was established to work the last surviving area of raised bog at Lindow Moss. This

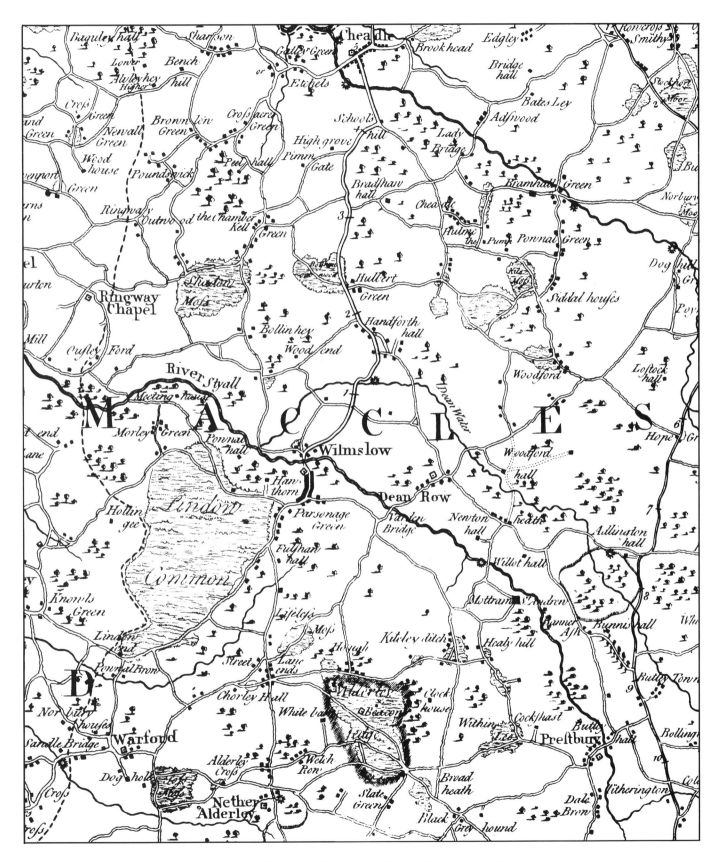

Fig. 1 Extract from Bryant's Map of Cheshire published in 1776 showing Lindow Common (Moss) and adjacent peatlands.

is the remotest part of the bog which straddles the parish boundary. It covers about 60 ha, about one tenth of the original extent of the moss. The company continued to cut peat by hand into the 1970s, after which time the first mechanical excavators were used. The present method of working involves digging long trenches or mossrooms, 7 m wide and up to 200 m long with a large 'backactor machine'. Alternate rooms are dug to a depth of 1 m at a time and the peat is stacked between them to dry out for between six months and one year. It is then loaded into trucks and run off the site by a narrow-gauge railway to the company's depot a little way off the moss (Fig. 3). The peat is tipped out on to an elevator which passes it through a shredding mill before it is despatched. It has been the men working on this elevator who found the first evidence of all the Lindow bog bodies.

The discovery of Lindow I (the so-called Lindow Woman) and Lindow II (better known as Lindow Man) have already been described in some detail (Turner 1986). However, to provide the background to the later discoveries, the salient points need to be repeated. The well-preserved head of Lindow I was found by men working on the elevator on 13 May 1983. When it was discovered, it consisted of the pliable vault of the skull which retained its outer membrane and some hair. The vault contained the decayed brain and part of the left eyeball and optic nerve were also identifiable (Fig. 4).

This find led to the solving of a modern murder. The police in nearby Macclesfield were investigating reports

Fig. 2 Hand-digging for peat on Lindow Moss in 1956. (*R. J. Haslam*)

Fig. 3 Peat extraction on Lindow Moss in 1987.

that a Peter Reyn-Bardt had murdered his wife, Malika, in 1960. He had boasted to a fellow prisoner that he had killed her, dismembered and burnt her body and buried the remains in the garden. The Reyn-Bardts had lived in a bungalow whose garden backed on to what was now the peat company's extraction site. The police had first interviewed Mr Reyn-Bardt in January 1983, but he had denied the allegations. They had excavated the bungalow's garden and found nothing. Whilst nobody had seen Malika since 1960, there was no evidence against Mr Reyn-Bardt until this well-preserved skull, identified as a 30 to 50-year-old European female by the forensic pathologist, was brought in from Lindow Moss. On being confronted with the news of this discovery, Mr Reyn-Bardt confessed to the crime.

To their credit, the police continued their investigations, excavating and sieving large quantities of peat, in the area of the likely findspot of the skull. They also involved Oxford University's Research Laboratory for Archaeology who undertook a radiocarbon dating of the skull. Just before the case came to trial in December 1983, Oxford came forward with a date of 1740 ± 80 BP, (OxA-114), some time within the Roman period. Nevertheless, Peter Reyn-Bardt was convicted of his wife's murder on the basis of his confession alone.

The second discovery was made on 1 August 1984, by the same two men working on the same elevator. This time they retrieved a well-preserved right foot, with the

ragged skin of the lower leg attached. The police were informed and took the foot away for examination. A local police sergeant tipped off Rachel Pugh, a reporter on the *Wilmslow World*. She recognised the potential importance of the find and sought my comments as the County Archaeologist. On visiting the site the next day, I was shown the peat stack from which the foot had come and walking along the adjacent uncut sections found a flap of skin protruding about 0.7 m below the surface.

Following discussions with the police and because the body of the murdered woman had never been found, it was decided to lift these remains in a single day. On 6 August, all was ready and after recording the section, the margins of the human remains were identified and the body was lifted in a block of peat, with its stratigraphy intact. The subsequent discussions which established the antiquity of the body, its excavation at the British Museum and the results of the wide-ranging investigations are well known (Stead *et al* 1986). Lindow Man had entered the world's stage as the archaeological discovery of the 1980s.

Apart from periodically monitoring the site, there was no further archaeological investigation at Lindow Moss until 1987. On 6 February the first part of the body now referred to as Lindow III was found by the men on the elevator. This was a large lump of skin which later proved to be part of the back. I was immediately called in and the police were now happy to leave this body to the

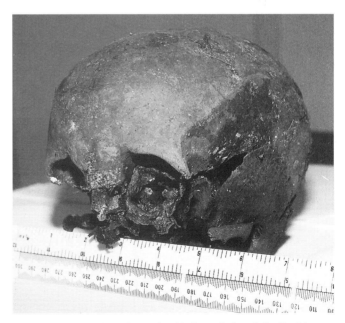

Fig. 4 The head of Lindow I. (*By kind permission of the Cheshire County Constabulary.*)

archaeologists. A team was assembled and all the peat on the elevator and within the remainder of the railway trucks parked at the depot was carefully sorted on the following day. Over 70 different pieces of this body were recovered (Brothwell and Bourke, pp. 52–8). The preservation of the tissue was as good as, if not better than that of Lindow ɪɪ, but the survival of the bone was poorer. Solid bones such as the vertebrae, phalanges and the bones of the wrist were intact, whilst the long bones were soft, like wet paper and under represented. The body must have been broken up during excavation of the peat, the subsequent re-excavation of the peat stack and the loading of the railway trucks. Two parts of the body were lifted in blocks held stable by polyurethane foam. One was a hand with several fingernails attached. The other was an intact lump of peat which contained what proved to be a leg. The stratigraphy of this piece of peat was ultimately fitted to the main stratigraphy of the moss, so fixing the position of the body in the peat sequence (Branch and Scaife, pp. 19–30).

With grant-aid from English Heritage, work continued on the site through February into March. Many tons of peat at the depot and on the moss were sorted by hand. Occasionally other parts of the body were found, including two pieces of skin from within the stack of peat on the moss. This fixed the area of the findspot to within a few metres in either direction, for the workmen showed that this stack comprised peat dug from either side. It had been piled on an apparently undug head of peat about 12 m wide and standing up to 1.2 m high.

The pressures and problems which surrounded the recovery of Lindow ɪɪ and its possible association with a modern murder were now no longer present. There was the opportunity to undertake a more considered excavation of the area of the latest body. With the encouragement of the site owners and funding from the British Museum and English Heritage, archaeological excavations took place over a four-week period in July and August 1987.

There were a number of objectives set out at the beginning of the project:

1 To relate the stratigraphy of the peat block enclosing the arm to the surviving stratigraphy on the site.
2 To show the nature of the peat bog at the time of deposition.
3 To establish the changing environment of Lindow Moss throughout the possible date range of up to 900 years given for Lindow ɪɪ.

4 To try to locate any surviving parts of the body *in situ*, or any artefacts or ephemeral structures which may have been associated with this deposition.
5 To begin to investigate the relationship between the growing peat bog and its dryland fringes. Work was concentrated on the two sand 'islands' rising above the peat bog in the hope of locating buried land surfaces and evidence for early settlement.

Figure 5 is a plan of part of Lindow Moss showing the position of the bodies, the sand islands and the excavation trenches. Trench 1 covered a 10 m length of the standing head of peat. It was centred on the findspot of the two pieces of skin found in the peat stack. The mechanical excavator has a maximum reach of about 6 m, suggesting that the body was found within a semicircle of that radius extending out from the standing 'peat' head in either direction. A 30 m length of the eastern section of the standing head of peat was drawn with the trench at its centre. It had almost no redeposited peat on the top and proved to have a highly complex stratigraphy. All the peat monoliths, bulk samples and cores were taken from this section. Within the trench the base of the spoil heap was removed. The weight of the heap had deformed and depressed the surface beneath introducing pressure cracks, which proved to run through all the stratigraphy excavated.

Below the heap were several recent features. The western half of trench 1 had been dug away by a broad W-shaped ditch running parallel to the head. It had been cut through a layer of regenerated vegetation on to the *Grenzhorizont*. This level marked the boundary between the lower, black sedge peats and the upper, brown *Sphagnum* peats. It can be identified readily throughout Lindow Moss (Fig. 6) and was found just below Lindow ɪɪ (Barber 1986). The lower limit of the excavation was set at this level, as it was likely to predate the stratigraphic position of all three bodies. Peat columns were, however, taken from below this horizon in order to investigate the earlier vegetation and environment.

Among the backfill of the W-shaped ditch which consisted of grassy clods and loose peat, was a well-preserved newspaper dated 24 May 1983, discarded no doubt, like many others, by the digger driver at the end of his working day. So the backfilling of this ditch can be dated to just 11 days after the discovery of Lindow ɪ. The workmen reported that this area of the bog had been the last to be opened up because of its treacherous nature and that it had required extra drainage to make it workable.

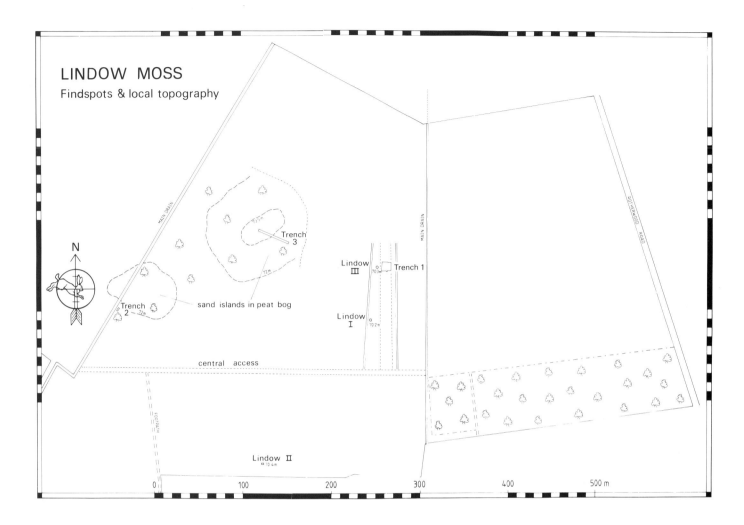

LINDOW MOSS
Findspots & local topography

N

Trench 3

sand islands in peat bog

Trench 2

Lindow III   Trench 1

Lindow I

central access

Lindow II

0   100   200   300   400   500 m

Fig. 5 Plan of Lindow Moss showing the findspots of the bodies and the excavation trenches. (*C. B. Sale*)

Fig. 6 The surviving peat stratigraphy on Lindow Moss in 1987. Note the fen carr woodland at the base of the section and the *Grenzhorizont* passing just above the mid-point of the ranging pole.

The area of intact stratigraphy within the trench was therefore reduced to 10 m by about 6 m. The top surface had a thick layer of regenerated vegetation dominated by heather (*Calluna vulgaris*). Beneath was a *Sphagnum* peat in which it was possible to see the lines of the last hand-dug peat trenches cut in this area, probably as late as the 1970s. There followed a formal excavation of the layers making up the peat bog. These consisted largely of a red–brown, *Sphagnum* peat with the species *Sphagnum imbricatum* dominant. Within the *Sphagnum* peat were thinner layers and lenses of more humified detritus peats, with a matrix of sedges and non-*Sphagnum* mosses, and a different range of macrofossils. These included the rhizomes and stems of the reed, *Phragmites*, and cotton grass, *Eriophorum* sp., indicating wetter conditions, with woody stems and roots of heather and ling (*Erica* and *Calluna*), suggesting drier patches. These features may represent the heavily compressed remains of the pools and hummocks which form the classic model of peat bog growth (Moore and Bellamy 1974).

Excavation was not straightforward. Peat bogs grow, while on more traditional archaeological sites, material is either deposited or has been dug away. Within layers of peat, lenses of the remains of the plants of one species or community can become incorporated within the steadily accumulating remains of another species or community. This situation cannot occur on dryland sites. Other problems occurred. The pressure cracks caused by the weight of the peat above, ran through the peat and led to some displacement of the stratigraphy, making it sometimes difficult to correlate layers across the cracks. Finally, some layers, particularly the more humified ones, oxidised rapidly on exposure, making colour a poor guide to establishing a consistent layer.

Fourteen different layers were recorded during the excavation, extending to a depth of up to 1 m. An important division about halfway down the stratigraphy was a thicker layer 016 of about 8 m diameter extending across most of the trench (Fig. 7). This consisted of large mats of

the woody roots of *Calluna* and *Eriophorum* in a sedge peat matrix surviving up to 0.15 m thick. Like the *Grenzhorizont*, this must represent a hiatus in active peat growth indicating local temporarily drier conditions. However, its matted and woody nature means that no solid object such as a body could have moved through it, as may have been possible in the more fluid *Sphagnum* peat.

One of the main purposes of treating the area in this way was in the hope of recovering parts of the Lindow III body *in situ*, or any associated artefacts, ephemeral structures or holes dug in the peat relating to its deposition. In this, it was unsuccessful. However, in association with the sampling for palaeo-environmental analyses which was undertaken at the same time, it has been shown how the local environment evolved over the time span when the bodies were placed in or on the moss (discussed in detail by Branch and Scaife, pp. 19–30).

During the excavation, it became clear that in the north-western part of the trench, the peat layers had slumped into a hollow formed in the surface of the *Grenzhorizont*. This hollow was up to 0.42 m deep (Fig. 8) and may have formed by the erosion of the exposed surface of the lower layer. The hollow may have been accentuated by later deformation and at this low level, pressure cracks were found which may have formed in antiquity. These features provided some evidence for earlier movement

Fig. 7 The section across trench 1, showing layer 016. The main peat monolith was taken from the right-hand end of this section.

Fig. 8 The hollow in the *Grenzhorizont* in the north-west of trench 1 (vertical scale 0.5 m).

and deformation within the peat bog. When considering the apparent difference of between 200 and 400 years between the radiocarbon dates of the bodies and the layers in which they were found (Housley *et al*, pp. 39–46), some processes whereby the bodies could have moved through the peat stratigraphy at their original deposition or later have to be identified. Buckland and Barber (pp. 47–51) discuss this in more detail.

At the same time as trench 1 was being dug, much of the remainder of the peat head was excavated by machine, under archaeological supervision. This was done in two sweeps, the first removing all the redeposited material, the second, the intact peat above the *Grenzhorizont*. Special care was taken alongside the recorded findspot of Lindow I, but almost no undisturbed peat survived at this point. Nothing was found during these operations.

As well as excavating on the peat bog itself, the opportunity was taken to look at the nearest dryland, two sand islands rising above the surrounding peat. These are about 120 m and 70 m in diameter and lie 125 m and 240 m west of trench 1 (Fig. 5). The long deep drainage ditch along the north-western boundary of the peat company's holding revealed a fine section through one of these islands and the fringes of the peat bog.

The following sequence of events was reconstructed from observations made on site. The island is a dune of periglacial wind-blown sand formed in the large hollow left by the retreating ice. During the Early Holocene, an acid soil formed on its surface. This could have supported a mid-Holocene woodland. At some point the vegetation was burnt off (possibly repeatedly), probably during its short-lived human cultivation. Rapid erosion of the soil followed and the humus and charcoal collected in pockets at the bottom of the hillslope. A podsol formed on the top of the island supporting a sandy heath vegetation similar to that surviving today on the nearby Lindow Common. Around the base of the island, fen carr woodland developed, slowly encroaching up the slope as the peat bog developed out on Lindow Moss. Eventually the fen carr was overwhelmed by *Sphagnum* peat.

A small excavation, trench 2, was laid out to look in more detail at the interface between the charcoal-rich soil and the fen carr woodland (Fig. 9). No man-made features or artefacts were found but a radiocarbon date was obtained from the charcoal in the soil of 4980 ± 70 BP, or 3030 BC, (HAR-8875). This lies in the Early Neolithic and is contemporary with the 'Elm Decline', an event recorded by pollen analysts across the British Isles (Smith 1981).

A much longer trench, trench 3, was laid out to investigate the eastern sand island. This stands a little higher than the western island, it is further out into the peat bog, and has suffered less from recent disturbance. A 2 m wide section was partly dug by machine and partly cleared by hand, for a length of 36.4 m. The trench was started on the summit of the island and ran down the slope towards trench 1 well into the margin of the bog (Fig. 10).

A fully developed podsolic soil covered the island. Within the B horizon of this podsol, a localised and thin scatter of flint was found, on which Bob Middleton has kindly reported. Twenty-nine items in all were produced on four types of flint. The raw material used was pebbles probably derived from the local boulder clay or river gravels. There was a high proportion of waste – 26 out of 29 items – indicating one or two knapping episodes on site. The implements were confined to a single flake knife, a utilised flake and a retouched lump of flint. Given the technological attributes of the assemblages, it could belong to the earlier Neolithic and be broadly contemporary with the radiocarbon date obtained from trench 2. The flints were found in an apparently undisturbed podsol, indicating that this island had not been cultivated since their deposition. So as yet, no settlement or agricultural activity contemporary with the bog bodies has been found on the fringes of Lindow Moss although the pollen evidence suggests that some cultivation was taking place.

Fig. 9 The interface between the charcoal-rich soil and the fen carr woodland in trench 2.

Fig. 10 A view up trench 3 and the eastern sand island.

This is not quite the end of the story for on 14 June 1988, the skin of the buttocks and part of the left leg of an adult male were recovered on the peat company's elevator. They derived from a peat stack some 15 m west of where Lindow II was found. On 12 September 1988, the digger driver spotted in his bucket what turned out to be the right thigh and the distal and proximal ends of the femur, close to where the finds in June had been made. Collectively these are referred to as Lindow IV. However as they represent the missing part of Lindow II, and were found close by, they must derive from the same body. The pattern of oxidation on the left kneecap suggests that this leg had been flexed while in the peat bog. Only the left foot of this body has never been found. Table 1 summarises the sequence of discovery and a full discussion of the possible relationships between the body fragments appears in Chapter 20.

Table 1   Human remains from Lindow Moss

NUMBER	DATE OF DISCOVERY	COMMENTS
I	13.5.83	Lindow Woman, cranium only
II	1.8.84	Lindow Man
III	6.2.87 and later	Many pieces from an adult male
IV	14.6.88; 12.9.88	Buttocks, left leg, etc., probably parts of Lindow Man

These final discoveries show how perspicacious the men working on the site had become, and how almost nothing seems to have gone undetected. It also shows how robust is the tissue and bone of Lindow IV, as it may have been re-excavated and restacked up to four times since being dug out in 1984. However, over the six years since 1988, no other finds have been made with the exception of a demineralised cattle bone and a piece of naturally tanned cowhide. The *Sphagnum* peat above the *Grenzhorizont* has been completely removed from the extraction site, and work has begun on the lower levels. It therefore seems extremely unlikely that Lindow Moss will produce any more bog bodies.

The Stratigraphy and Pollen Analysis of Peat Sequences Associated with the Lindow III Bog Body

N. P. Branch   *R. G. Scaife*

I Introduction

Following the discovery of the Lindow II body (Stead *et al* 1986) much interest was focused on the past environment and development of Lindow Moss, Cheshire. The discovery of most of a third body (Lindow III) in 1987 prompted the continuation of this research and a detailed archaeological excavation of part of the bog allowed systematic recording and sampling of the peat stratigraphy in the area from which Lindow III was excavated. Column samples taken from the site have been used for plant macrofossil, pollen and coleopteran analyses (Dinnin and Skidmore, pp. 31–8) with the aim of providing a detailed record of the palaeo-environment of the later prehistoric and early historic periods with special reference to the period of the bog burials.

Unlike Lindow II, Lindow III was disaggregated by the peat cutting machinery and was not *in situ* in the bog. Laboratory examination of the body remains provided a single fragment of body (part of a leg) encapsulated in undisturbed peat. This proved to be important in correlating the body with the longer, *in situ*, stratigraphic profiles described and sampled during the archaeological excavations at Lindow Moss. This paper discusses pollen-stratigraphical data obtained from analyses of the column samples of peat taken from the excavations carried out by Turner in 1987 (column I) and samples associated with the Lindow III body (column II).

II Pollen Analysis of the *In Situ* Peat: Column I

An area of six square metres of peat was excavated (trench 1) in the vicinity of where Lindow III was discovered (see Turner, pp. 10–18). The composition, physical properties and levels of humification of the peat were recorded using the Troels-Smith (1955) method for describing wet sediments and peats. This method was used to differentiate the principal stratigraphic layers to facilitate the drawing of cross-sections and plans. Two further trenches (2 and 3) and the sides of the commercial drainage ditches were also examined. An extensive sampling programme was carried out to obtain material for pollen, plant macrofossil and coleopteran analyses. Four columns of peat were taken directly from the open east-facing side of trench 1 (Fig. 7). Cores were also taken from the area surrounding trench 1 for the possible future analysis of the longer vegetational sequence at Lindow Moss.

The four overlapping columns (A1–A4) were sampled initially at 5 cm intervals over the two metres in order to produce an outline pollen diagram of the changes in vegetation and environment. Sampling at a closer interval (2.5 cm) was carried out between 160 and 70 cm. The samples were prepared using standard extraction techniques (Moore and Webb 1978) but without hydrofluoric acid treatment. The concentrated pollen and spores were stained with safranin and mounted in glycerol jelly.

Identification and counting of the pollen was carried out using Leitz Laborlux and Zeiss microscopes in the Ancient Monuments Laboratory of English Heritage. A pollen sum of 600 grains was counted at each level and resulting pollen data have been calculated as a percentage of total dry-land taxa and wetland taxa and spores as percentages of this pollen sum. The results are presented in Fig. 11. Plant taxonomy follows that of Clapham *et al* (1987) and pollen and spore nomenclature of Moore and Webb (1978).

The Macro-stratigraphy

The stratigraphy of the east-facing section used for pollen analysis is categorised in Table 2.

Table 2 describes only a small part of the stratigraphy recorded at Lindow Moss, which attained a maximum depth of 800 cm in trial boreholes. Lateral variation in the peat stratigraphy is marked and the so-called 'bacon' like

Table 2   Stratigraphy of east-facing section used for pollen analysis

DEPTH (cm)	PEAT DESCRIPTION
0–20	Disturbed peat. This was due to compaction by the heavy machinery used for peat extraction and from desiccation cracks which have occurred as a result of drainage.
20–41	Orange brown *Sphagnum imbricatum* peat (7.5YR 3/4). Nig. 2, sicc. 2, elas. 3, humo. 1, Tb 4 (subscript 1), Th+, Tl+.
41–45.5	Dark brown (7.5YR 3/4) *Sphagnum peat*. Nig. 3, sicc. 2, elas. 1, humo. 3, Tb 2 (subscript 3), Th 1 (subscript 3), Sh 1.
45.5–48.5	Dark brown–black detritus peat (5YR 2.5/2). Peat pool. Nig. 3, sicc. 1/2, elas. 0 humo. 3/4. Tb (subscript 3), Tl 1 (subscript 3) (*Calluna*).
48.5–74	Orange brown *Sphagnum* peat (5YR 4/6) Nig. 2, sicc. 2, elas. 3, humo. 1. Tb 3 (subscript 1), Tl 1.
74–81	Dark reddish brown *Sphagnum* peat (5YR 3/3). Nig. 2, sicc. 1, elas. 1, humo. 2. Tb 3 (subscript 2), Tl+, Th 1 (*Phragmites*), Sh +.
81–119	Orange brown *Sphagnum* peat (5YR 4/6). Nig. 2, sicc. 1, elas. 2/3, humo. 1, Tb 4, Tl+ (*Calluna*), Th +.
119–190	Dark reddish brown monocotyledonous peat (2.5YR 4/2) Nig. 3, sicc. 2, elas. 1, humo. 3/4. Tb 1 (subscript 4), Th 2 (subscript 3), Tl+, Sh 1.

Key   elas. elasticity; humo. humification; Nig. degree of darkness; Sh *Substantia humosa*; sicc. degree of dryness; Tb *Turfa bryophytica*; Th *Turfa herbacea*; Tl *Turfa lignosa*; YR Munsell colour chart reference

structure (Barber 1981), a complex of interweaving bands that coalesce to form level horizons, is evident (Fig. 1). Such a structure is typical of ombrotrophic peat bogs. Barber (1986) has studied the peat stratigraphy in detail considering the '... grosser manifestations ...' of stratigraphic change with regard to climatic deterioration. Further discussion of the complex arguments of bog regeneration and development are not dealt with here.

Radiocarbon Dating

Samples for radiocarbon dating were taken from the column samples after pollen analysis had been carried out. These samples comprised 2 cm thick slices of peat which were dated by the University of Belfast through the Ancient Monuments Laboratory of English Heritage. Dating of the major stratigraphical change at 120 cm was considered a priority since this possibly represents the *Grenzhorizont*. Thus, samples of peat from either side of this horizon were taken at 119–121 cm and 117–119 cm. A total of five dates were obtained for the peat sequence which has been pollen analysed from 190 cm to the top of the section at 20 cm. These produced the results shown in Table 3.

These dates show that the base of the peat sequence analysed falls within the Late Neolithic/Early Bronze Age period at *c.* 3724 BP and the top, the early Saxon period at 1488 BP, and thus spans the period to which the Lindow Moss bodies have been attributed. In the following discussion of the pollen and vegetational history, all dates are quoted as uncalibrated BP at one standard deviation unless stated otherwise.

The Pollen Stratigraphy

The pollen diagram (column ı, Fig. 11) has been divided into five recognisable pollen assemblage zones from the base of the analysed sequence at 190 cm. These are designated LIN: 1 to LIN: 5 from the base upwards. It is realised,

Table 3   Radiocarbon dates for peat samples at five depths

DEPTH (cm)	LABORATORY NUMBER	AGE BP (years)	1 SIGMA ERROR	CALIBRATED BP AT 1 SIGMA	CALIBRATED HISTORICAL AGE RANGE AT 1 SIGMA
20–22	UB-3237	1488	44	1408–1332	cal AD 542–618
55–57	UB-3238	1764	48	1731–1615	cal AD 219–335
117–119	UB-3239	2345	45	2356–2341	407–392 cal BC
119–121	UB-3240	2447	43	2712–2358	763–677 cal BC
188–190	UB-3241	3724	55	4151–3989	2202–2039 cal BC

however, that there are some metres of peat of earlier Flandrian age underlying that which is described here. These levels have not been analysed in this study and future work may redefine these pollen assemblage zones. The common names of plants recorded in the pollen diagrams appear in the Appendix on p. 30.

LIN: 1 (190–160 cm). *Quercus-Corylus* type-*Alnus*. The zone is dominated by high values of *Quercus* (to 35%), *Alnus* (27%) and *Corylus* type (50%). Other arboreal taxa include *Betula* (15%), and lesser values of *Pinus*, *Ulmus*, *Tilia*, *Fagus* and *Ilex*. *Calluna* and *Erica* are 18% and 7% respectively. Herbs include Gramineae (10%), Cyperaceae, *Sinapis* type, *Plantago coronopus* type, *P. lanceolata*, *Rumex*, *Chenopodium* type and *Urtica* type; that is, herbs possibly associated with woodland clearance and agriculture. Spores are dominated by *Sphagnum* (to 52%) with *Polypodium* (3%) and sporadic *Dryopteris* type.

LIN: 2 (160–120 cm). *Quercus-Fraxinus-Alnus-Corylus* type-*Calluna-Sphagnum*. The zone is characterised by persistently high values of *Quercus*, *Alnus* and *Corylus* type from the preceding zone. *Betula*, *Pinus*, *Ulmus*, *Tilia*, *Fagus* and *Fraxinus* are also present. The latter shows an increase between 145–125 cm associated with a peak of *Calluna*. There is some increase in the diversity of herbs and the continuation of taxa noted in LIN: 1. Wetland taxa show some increase with expansion of Cyperaceae (av. 8%) and *Sphagnum* (to 55%). Higher values of *Pteridium* are noted in the lower half of the zone.

LIN: 3 (120–55 cm). *Quercus-Corylus* type-Gramineae-*Plantago lanceolata*-Cyperaceae-*Pteridium-Sphagnum*. The zone is marked by increased values of *Sphagnum* (to 96%) with a dramatic change in peat composition and humification (reduced). The zone is characterised by some decline in the values of *Alnus* and *Corylus* type, though *Quercus* remains largely constant. Herbs are dominated by Gramineae (40%) and Cyperaceae (to 30%), but with a marked increase in taxonomic diversity. *Plantago lanceolata*, *P. media/major* and *P. coronopus* are more abundant. In addition to *Sphagnum* noted above, there is an increase in *Pteridium aquilinum* (10%).

LIN: 4 (55–35 cm). *Betula-Fraxinus-Calluna-Sphagnum*. The zone is characterised by peaks of *Betula* (10%), *Fraxinus* (4%), *Calluna* (35%) and *Sphagnum* (95%). *Pinus*, *Quercus* and *Corylus* type values are reduced from the previous zone as are percentages of herbs.

LIN: 5 (35–20 cm). *Quercus-Alnus-Corylus* type. Tree pollen becomes dominant after low values in LIN: 4. Conversely, *Betula*, *Fraxinus* and *Calluna* show some reduction. Herbs are dominated by Gramineae and Cyperaceae but also with reducing percentages.

Discussion of Vegetational History

Although the full depth of the peat bog was sampled with a Russian corer, detailed analysis has concentrated only on the upper 200 cm of peat which span the later prehistoric period; that is, those horizons which relate to the possible stratigraphic position of the bog bodies. The principal stratigraphical feature encompassed in this study of Lindow Moss is the change at 120 cm from well-humified *Sphagnum* and monocotyledonous peat to fresh, unhumified and largely *Sphagnum imbricatum* peat. This equates with the transition between pollen assemblage zones LIN: 2 and LIN: 3. Radiocarbon dating places this change between 2447 ± 43 BP (UB-3240) and 2345 ± 45 BP (UB-3239), (calibrated 2712–2358 BP and 2356–2341 BP). Evidence for this particular horizon was seen across most of the area of Lindow Moss and appears to be a major recurrence surface.

The dates obtained from Lindow Moss correlate with the pan-European *Grenzhorizont* (RY III of Granlund) discussed previously by Barber (1978, 1981, 1982). Barber (1982) suggests that for an increase in the rate of formation and number of *Sphagnum* pools to commence at the recurrence surface, a reduction of 1 °C would have to occur and this he equates with the period of gradual climatic deterioration after 2900 BP. This represents, therefore, the transition between the sub-Boreal and sub-Atlantic periods of Blytt (1876) and Sernander (1910). As shown from the discussions of Barber (1986) and Oldfield *et al* (1986), this recurrence surface is crucial to the understanding of the stratigraphical position of the human remains in Lindow Moss. This point will be further discussed in Section IV (pp. 29–30).

The base of the pollen profile examined here has been dated to 3724 ± 55 BP (UB-3241). Two pollen zones (LIN: 1–2) have been recognised above this and prior to the recurrence surface. During these zones *Sphagnum* (*S. acutifolia*) was dominant in wetter areas of pools and damper hummocks with Gramineae and Cyperaceae. *Calluna* and *Erica* (especially 180–190 cm) were probably growing on drier hummock areas. The abundance of spores of the fungal rust, *Tilletia sphagni* (Eckblad 1975;

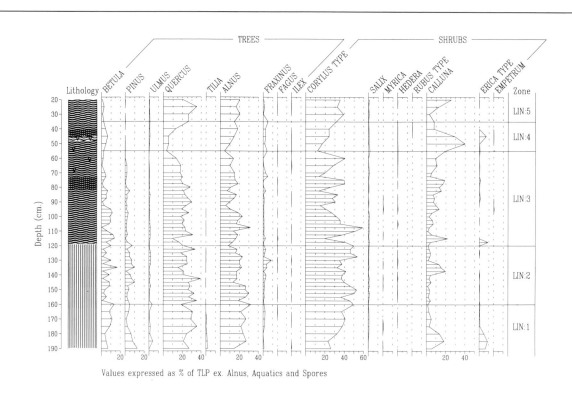

Values expressed as % of TLP ex. Alnus, Aquatics and Spores

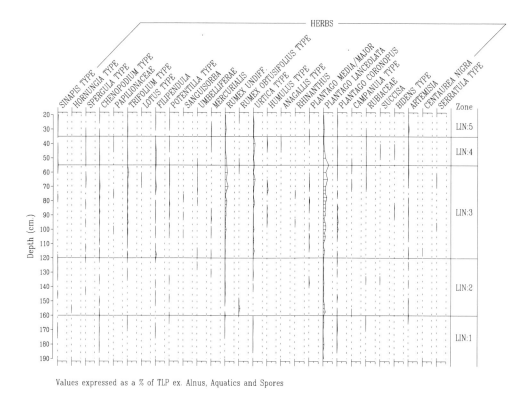

Values expressed as a % of TLP ex. Alnus, Aquatics and Spores

Fig. 11 Pollen diagram from the *in situ* peat section (column I).

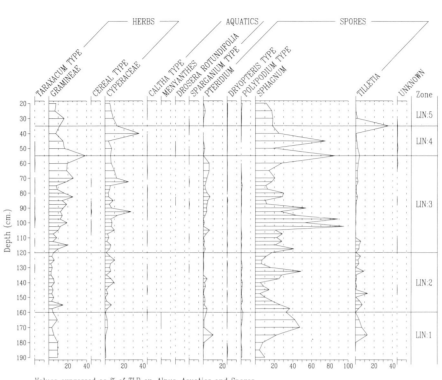

Values expressed as % of TLP ex. Alnus, Aquatics and Spores

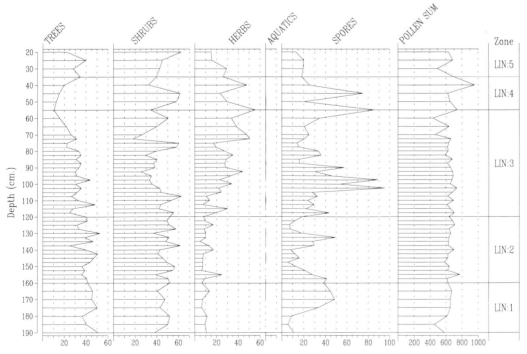

Values expressed as % of TLP ex. Alnus, Aquatics and Spores

Van Geel 1978) is also strong evidence for dominant *Sphagnum* bog. It is interesting to note that the preponderance of these fungal rust spores occurs in the pre-*Grenzhorizont* levels. As noted by Van Geel (1978, 75) this may reflect the drier character of the bog during this period or the infection of differing *Sphagnum* species. *Alnus* and *Salix* were important constituents of the arboreal flora and are also typical of wetland environments. These were probably growing in carr woodland along the nutrient-enriched marginal or lagg areas of the bog. *Salix* is generally under-represented in pollen spectra and the sporadic but continuous representation in the centre of the mire attests to its relative importance.

It is clear that the drier, adjacent land was a dominantly wooded environment perhaps with some areas of open agriculture. *Quercus* and *Corylus* were dominant throughout, but with strong representation of other woodland elements, including *Betula, Pinus, Ulmus, Tilia, Fraxinus, Fagus* and *Ilex*. Given the relatively low percentages of *Pinus* and the over-representation of this taxon in pollen spectra (being anemophilous), its presence is attributed to long-distance origins and transport. In contrast, the low values of *Tilia, Fagus* and *Ilex* are significant in relation to other arboreal taxa, e.g., *Quercus* and *Ulmus* (Andersen 1970, 1973; Tauber 1965). The occurrence of *Betula* and *Fraxinus* typify elements of secondary woodland, especially in LIN:2 where *Fraxinus* peaks with *Calluna* possibly representing a phase of woodland disturbance. The record for *Tilia* is perhaps diagnostic with relatively higher values of this taxon in lower levels becoming progressively diminished. This is reminiscent of the 'Tilia decline' described for many areas of southern and eastern England at this time (Turner 1962; Scaife 1980; Greig 1982). It is possible that this similarity resulted from increasing anthropogenic disturbance.

In conclusion, it is postulated that the region surrounding Lindow Moss was predominantly mixed woodland of open character. Openness is attested by *Ilex* and *Corylus* which require light for flowering. It is suggested that although woodland was dominant in the pre-recurrence surface period, there had been anthropogenic disturbance and secondary woodland regeneration. The presence of anthropochorous taxa, especially in LIN:2, including *Plantago lanceolata* and other herbs indicative of agricultural activity and disturbance suggests that there was continued disturbance at a local level. Archaeologically, this has been substantiated by the recovery of Neolithic artefacts from the excavation of one of the sand islands within Lindow Moss.

The recurrence surface/*Grenzhorizont* at 120 cm falls between 2447 ± 43 BP and 2345 ± 45 BP (UB-3240 and UB-3239 respectively). From these close dates, it is apparent that there was no cessation of peat growth and therefore hiatus in the stratigraphy. Conversely, the marked change to less humified *Sphagnum imbricatum* peat implies a rapid environmental change in the ecology of the bog. As noted above, this is thought to be caused by more widespread climatic deterioration during this period and correlated with the *Grenzhorizont*. The dating of this horizon has been the source of much debate. Whilst the dates provided here are commensurate with other sites throughout north-west Europe, it is probable that different sites responded to such widespread climatic change at somewhat differing periods as a function of more local climatic, hydrological and vegetational variables.

The rapid change in bog characteristics identified in the plant macrofossil assemblages is also mirrored in the pollen spectra. The dry-land vegetation continued to be dominated by arboreal taxa of similar character to those preceding the recurrence surface; that is, open canopy woodland of mixed deciduous character but with reduced *Tilia*. Pollen assemblage zone LIN:3 is especially important for two reasons. Firstly, the earlier pollen and stratigraphical analyses of the Lindow II body suggested that the body was stratified in relatively unhumified peats above the recurrence surface and at a point in the pollen diagram where there is evidence for increased anthropogenic disturbance and agriculture. LIN:3 represents the period after the recurrence surface and in which it is thought that the Lindow III body was stratified. Reasons for this hypothesis are discussed later. Secondly, this pollen assemblage zone shows a marked increase in the pollen of herbs including ruderals and segetals. This is similarly important in correlating column II with the longer sequence of column I (see Section IV, pp. 29–30).

From 120 cm in LIN:3, there is a marked and progressive increase in the diversity and percentages of many herbs. Archaeologically, this expansion correlates with the Iron Age to Romano-British period. Gramineae and Cyperaceae are dominant but may be of autochthonous derivation although at least part of the former may also derive from dry-land taxa. There is a progressive increase in the importance of disturbed and open ground herbs throughout this zone including *Plantago* spp. (especially *P. lanceolata*), *Spergula* type, *Chenopodium* type, Papilionaceae spp., *Rumex* spp., *Urtica* type, *Artemisia* and Liguliflorae. Also of note are sporadic but more abundant records of cereal type (*Hordeum/Triticum* type). This apparently reflects increased arable and possibly pastoral agricultural activity in areas adjacent to Lindow Moss. Increases in pollen of Ericaceae and spores of *Pteridium* may be indicative of soil deterioration especially on the sandy soils nearby. Podsolised soils were in evidence in sections marginal to the bog. This phase of human disturbance has similarly been identified in the analyses of Birks (1965) and Oldfield *et al* (1986) and it is now clear that there was a progressive disturbance from the Early Iron Age attaining a maximum extent during the Romano-British period. The work of Birks (1965) in a farther part of Lindow Moss similarly showed this progressive anthropogenic impact. It is likely, therefore, that the expansion of forest clearance and land use was a regional phenomenon.

The boundary between pollen assemblage zones LIN:3 and LIN:4 is drawn at a point where there is a reduction in the percentages of herbs and the taxonomic diversity noted in LIN:3. A radiocarbon date 1764 ± 48 BP (UB-3238) from this zone boundary (55–57 cm) suggests a late Romano-British date. In LIN:4, percentage values of arboreal taxa are lower than the preceding zone with the exception of *Betula* and *Fraxinus*. This perhaps represents the culmination of the agricultural phase in the later part of the Roman period. It is not clear why this should have occurred but it may be postulated that deterioration of the local sandy soils may have been responsible since podsolic soils are in evidence in the local area. This may also be substantiated by the higher values of Ericaceae also noted at this time (however, these may also be constituents of drier areas of the bog surface). *Betula* and *Fraxinus* are typical of secondary woodland colonisation. In zone LIN:5, *Quercus*, *Alnus* and *Corylus* regain their earlier importance illustrating a return to woodland dominance and reduced agricultural activity in the region. This phase of regeneration took place before the formation of the material at 1488 ± 44 BP obtained from 20–22 cm (UB-3237).

III A Pollen Section from the Body: Column II

During the examination of the Lindow III body at the British Museum (London) in December 1987, each fragment of the body was examined to ascertain whether any of the peat adhering to the body fragments was *in situ* and, therefore, suitable for pollen analysis. One fragment, recovered at Lindow Moss and later identified as part of a leg, was encased within a 25 cm block of stratified peat.

The *in situ* peat was sampled in contiguous 1 cm slices on either side of the fragment. Initially, it was not possible to ascertain which was the stratigraphical top and bottom. However, distinction was made to the vertical sense from the stratification and compaction of the peat and leg fragment. The correct top/bottom orientation became clear later, during the pollen analysis. Details of the analysis are shown in Fig. 12.

Unlike Lindow II, which was found *in situ* and thus stratified in the peat mire, the peat and body fragment represent the only available means of relating the position of Lindow III to the stratigraphy of the area excavated by Turner. The aims of studying this isolated peat fragment were threefold:

(a) To indicate whether the body was stratified in the natural peat, or whether the body was buried in a pit dug into the peat bog; a situation noted in some northern European 'bog bodies'.

(b) If the body was not placed in a pit, to correlate the pollen stratigraphies of column I and column II. It was hoped that this would determine the relative position of Lindow III in the general stratigraphy of the bog and especially relative to the excavations carried out by Turner in 1987 (see pp. 10–18).

(c) To establish the plant macrofossil stratigraphy of the peat above and below the body fragment thus providing an indication of local bog ecology in which the body was deposited. This was considered particularly important in relation to the *Grenzhorizont* and whether the body fragment was stratified in pool or hummock deposits.

A total of 22 samples taken at 1 cm contiguous intervals have been examined with pollen sums of more than 600 grains per level counted. The results of this pollen analysis are presented in Fig. 12 (a)–(c). Calculation of the pollen data follows that discussed for column I described in Section II (pp. 19–25) and facilitates direct comparison between the profiles.

The Pollen Stratigraphy

A principal concern in this analysis was to ascertain the correct top/bottom orientation of the peat profile. In reality, it was found that there is a marked similarity between the 'curves' of a number of pollen taxa in both pollen diagrams which enabled the top of the pollen diagram to be established. This has facilitated the correlation

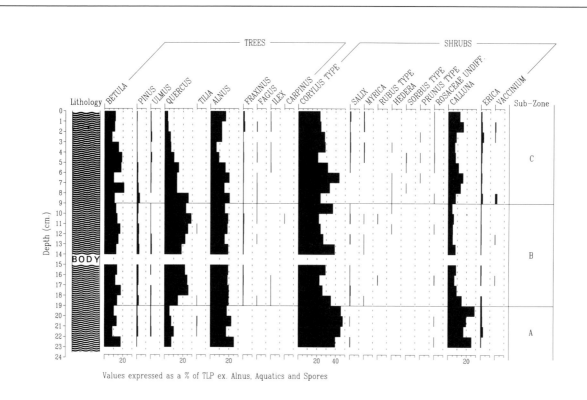

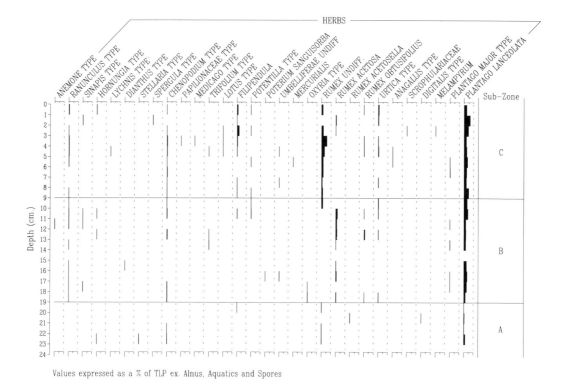

Fig. 12 Pollen diagram from adjacent to the body (column II).

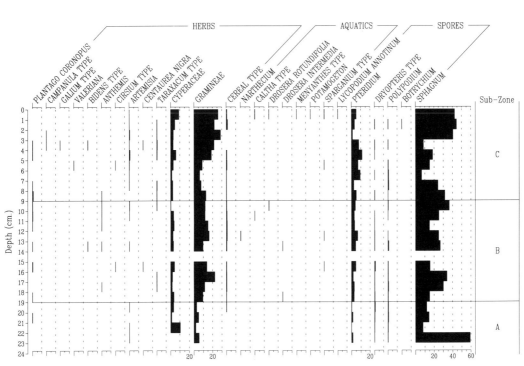

Values expressed as a % of TLP ex. Alnus, Aquatics and Spores

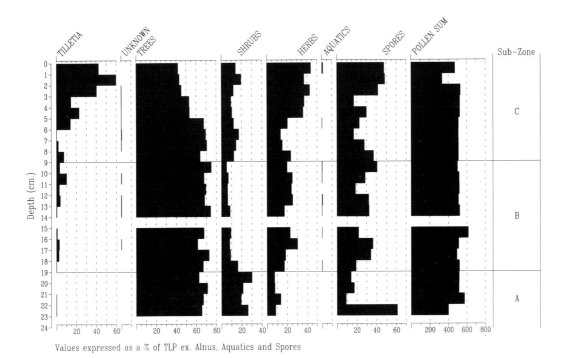

Values expressed as a % of TLP ex. Alnus, Aquatics and Spores

of this 'floating' pollen sequence within the established long profile and vegetational history described above. Furthermore, this has located the Lindow III body in the bog stratigraphy.

Three pollen assemblage zones have been recognised in this sequence. As discussed in section IV below, this entire pollen sequence falls within pollen assemblage zone LIN: 3, thus the zones described here can be regarded as pollen assemblage sub-zones. For the purposes of this discussion the changes recognised at this closer sampling interval are characterised as follows:

Pollen assemblage sub-zone A: 24–19 cm. Characterised by relatively higher values of *Corylus* type (40%), *Calluna* (26%) and *Erica* (3%) in comparison with subsequent zones. *Alnus* (to 25%), *Betula* (15%), *Quercus* (to 10%) and sporadic occurrences of *Pinus*, *Ulmus* and *Tilia* are present. *Quercus* values are lower than in subsequent levels. Herb pollen are less abundant and with less taxonomic diversity than subsequent levels. Gramineae and Cyperaceae are the principal taxa but with some *Plantago lanceolata*.

Pollen assemblage sub-zone B: 19–9 cm. This sub-zone embraces the 1 cm level in which the Lindow III body fragment was stratified (17–16 cm). It is characterised by an increase in *Quercus* to its highest values (25%) and the start of records of a number of tree and shrub taxa including *Fraxinus*, *Fagus*, *Ilex*, *Myrica*, *Rubus* type and *Hedera*, all with sporadic, individual records. *Betula* and *Alnus* remain important. There is a relative decline in ericaceous taxa (*Calluna* and *Erica*). There is an increase in herb diversity and specific increases in the percentages of *Plantago lanceolata* (to 3%), *Rumex* and Gramineae (to 25%). The records of cereal type pollen from the start of this zone should be noted. There are sporadic occurrences of *Drosera*. Spores of ferns are dominated by *Pteridium aquilinum* (to 10%). *Sphagnum* moss spores show some increase.

Pollen assemblage sub-zone C: 9–0 cm. *Quercus* progressively declines (to <5%). There is a reduction in *Pinus* to sporadic occurrences although values throughout the diagram are not regarded as of significance in the interpretation of the local flora. *Betula* (20%), *Alnus* (20%) and *Corylus* type (35%) remain dominant. Minor increases in *Fraxinus* and *Ilex* are noted and are important in making comparisons with the longer pollen sequence. There is an increase in herb diversity and increased percentages of *Erica*, *Calluna* and some herbs. *Plantago lanceolata*, *Filipendula*, *Rumex* and Compositae, Gramineae, cereal type and Cyperaceae. *Pteridium aquilinum* attains its highest values (to 15%). Spores remain dominated by *Sphagnum*.

Interpretation

One of the principal aims noted above was to establish if Lindow III had been placed in a dug pit, or placed on/into the natural surface of the moss. It became evident at an early stage of the analysis that the peat profile exhibited pollen-stratigraphical variations corresponding with column I. This showed that Lindow III was not placed in a cut trench and thus allows a more detailed correlation of the two pollen columns.

From the analysis of the *in situ* long profile, it is clear that there is a major change in bog stratigraphy at a depth of 120 cm, the start of the pollen assemblage zone LIN: 3. The transition is marked by a significant change from dark humified monocot peat to a lighter, less-humified *Sphagnum imbricatum* peat (see section II above). This horizon has been dated at 2447 ± 43 BP (UB-3240) and 2345 ± 45 BP (UB-3239) at 119–121 cm and 117–119 cm respectively. This horizon is present throughout Lindow Moss and, as in earlier work by Barber (1986), has been attributed to the *Grenzhorizont*. This is an important basic indication of the stratigraphical location from which the peat and Lindow III body fragment came. Examination of the macrofossil content and structure of the peat encasing the body fragment showed clearly that the peat was of a character typical of the post-*Grenzhorizont* stratigraphy, that is, well-structured, light, and relatively non-humified peat dominated by *Sphagnum imbricatum*.

The basal pollen assemblage sub-zone (abbreviated to p.a.s.z.) A is taken from the base of the peat block. It is unfortunate that the *Grenzhorizont* was not present in the sequence analysed here. Correlations can be made which show that the base of this peat sequence can be correlated with the few centimetres immediately overlying the *Grenzhorizont*. This and other correlations are important in locating the body in relation to the broader bog stratigraphy (see section IV). Plant macrofossil remains, spores of *Sphagnum* and pollen of sedges and ericaceous shrubs illustrate that the environment of deposition was acid *Sphagnum* bog and probably ombrotrophic. The dry-land areas surrounding the bog supported open mixed deciduous woodland dominated by *Quercus* with possibly *Corylus*. Sporadic and single occurrences of trees with low pollen production and limited dispersal, e.g. *Ulmus*, *Tilia*, *Fraxinus*, *Fagus* and *Ilex*, suggest that these also formed an important component of the local dry-land community. Although *Alnus* percentage values are relatively high, even greater values might be expected if this taxon was growing 'on-site'. As noted above in discussion of p.a.z. LIN:2 of column I, *Alnus* was important at an earlier stage in the mire's development. It is likely that water-logging which initiated rapid peat growth and change to more acid conditions reduced the area of alder dominance. It seems likely that *Alnus* was growing in areas marginal to the bog, that is, in lag areas of higher eutrophication from ground water supply and contained nutrients and higher pH.

In p.a.s.z. B, there is a significant increase in the number of herbs which are attributable to human/agricultural activity. Higher values of Gramineae, *Plantago lanceolata*, *Rumex* and the start of a continuous record of cereal type are indications of this activity. Other, less-abundant herb taxa may be referable to agricultural habitats and include Cruciferae, *Chenopodium* type, *Trifolium* type and *Anthemis* type. Although it is possible that there is greater representation of these taxa for factors such as opening of the mire or surrounding vegetation allowing pollen input to the mire, it seems more likely that we are seeing an increase in human activity in drier areas adjacent to the bog. This activity is mirrored in the p.a.z.3 discussed above and in the earlier analyses of Birks (1965) and Oldfield *et al* (1986). It is perhaps because of the opening-up of the nearby woodland for agriculture that there is a greater representation of less well-dispersed arboreal taxa on to the bog (*Fraxinus*, *Fagus*, *Ilex*). The record of this agricultural activity becomes more pronounced towards the top of this profile (p.a.s.z. C) with notable peaks in *Rumex*, *Plantago lanceolata*, Gramineae, cereal type and *Pteridium aquilinum*.

IV Correlation of Columns I and II and the Stratigraphical Position of the Lindow III body

One of the principal aims of analysing a long, *in situ* pollen profile from the area thought to have yielded the Lindow III body was to provide a detailed environmental history spanning the later prehistoric and early historic period. This profile (column I) also provides a sequence within which the 'floating' pollen sequence obtained from around the body fragment (column II) can be correlated. This section discusses the evidence from which it is suggested that the body was recovered from a layer of the peat some few centimetres above the *Grenzhorizont* dating to between 392–407 BC and AD 219–335 and possibly at a date of *c*. 300 BC (calibrated).

Methodology

Two approaches have been attempted in correlating columns I and II. First, the evidence from the pollen analysis of the Lindow II body (Oldfield *et al* 1986) and the data presented here from Lindow III (pollen column II) have shown that their stratigraphical position in the bog is associated distinctly with the earlier part of a phase of increased agricultural land use. Thus, it has been possible, by visual inspection of the pollen data and diagrams to locate the position of the leg remains in the longer vegetation and stratigraphical record obtained from column I. Second, an attempt at greater objectivity through statistical correlation has been made. These approaches are discussed separately.

Visual and Statistical Correlation

Pollen data from column II, the body section and Lindow II show that the bodies were deposited during a period when agricultural activity was gaining importance. Oldfield *et al* (1986, 84) have stated that Lindow II '... coincides with the beginning of a major phase of forest disturbance, burning, and occupation for farming...'. The same applies to Lindow III which occurs some 5 cm above the first continuous appearance of cereal type, *Plantago lanceolata* and *Pteridium aquilinum* in this short column. This corresponds with the start of pollen assemblage subzone B discussed above. Subsequently, there is a progressive increase in the percentages of these and a number of other herb taxa which are indicative of anthropogenic activity. Comparison with column I shows the greatest similarity is with pollen zone LIN:3. There are marked similarities in the occurrences and increase/decreases of a substantial number of taxa. These include the herbs: *Rumex*, *Plantago lanceolata*, Gramineae, cereal type and Cyperaceae and spores of *Pteridium* and *Sphagnum*. Other less definite correlations include *Chenopodium* type, *Potentilla* type, *Plantago media/major*, *P. coronopus* type, *Artemisia* and Liguliflorae. Similarities in the tree and shrub pollen spectra also exist; *Corylus* type, *Ulmus*, *Tilia*, *Fraxinus* and *Calluna*.

The conclusions drawn from this comparison are that Lindow III was stratified in a continuously forming peat and not buried in a trench or pit dug into the bog as has been noted in some European finds. The closest visual fit of column II into column I appears to be from a depth of about 115 cm to 80 cm. This also corresponds with the thickness of the peat associated with the body, which is perhaps fortuitous, since accumulation rates vary significantly between the differing bog habitats (pools and hummocks and differing *Sphagnum* types). This also means that column II lies above the recurrence surface attributed to the *Grenzhorizont* and within the unhumified peats of zone LIN: 3. The peat associated with the leg fragment similarly reflects the unhumified *Sphagnum imbricatum* peat and with no evidence of a more humified pre-*Grenzhorizont* material.

In order to test whether this could be substantiated statistically, a series of 'lag correlations' were carried out. Although not conclusive, the statistical analysis did illustrate a positive correlation between column II and pollen assemblage zone LIN: 3. This verifies a post-*Grenzhorizont* position for the body.

Stratigraphical Dating of Lindow III

If the above arguments are correct, the position of the body fragment in column I is thought to be at 110 cm. As noted above, a date of 2345 ± 45 BP (UB-2329) has been obtained from immediately above the *Grenzhorizont* (117–119 cm). This gives a calibrated date of 407–392 BC and is thus Iron Age (Early/Middle?). Shortly after this date, a phase of landscape disturbance was initiated, in the earlier part of which is the stratigraphical position of the Lindow bodies (II and III). Too few dates have been granted to obtain an accurate date/accumulation curve to be constructed. On the basis of the three post-*Grenzhorizont* dates obtained, however, a tentative date of between 335 and 219 BC has been interpolated.

Summary and Conclusion

A 200 cm pollen profile has been produced which spans the period from *c.* 3700 BP to 1488 BP. The pollen data illustrate that mixed deciduous woodland dominated by *Quercus* and *Corylus* was consistent throughout most of this period. Although there is evidence for secondary woodland in the lower pollen zone implying some earlier vegetation disturbance, the major phase of local and regional agricultural land use occurred from *c.* 2345 BP (*c.* 400 BC). This appears to relate to increased arable and possibly pastoral agriculture during the Late Bronze Age. This activity increased throughout the Iron

Age and into the Romano-British period until the third to fourth century AD. Subsequently, there was a cessation of agriculture at least in the local region and regeneration of secondary woodland occurred. Whether this was for cultural reasons or through natural soil degradation is unclear. At 120 cm in this profile there occurs a distinct recurrence surface which is correlated with the *Grenzhorizont* (Granlunds 1932: RY III) which has been dated to 2490–2300 BP at 1 sigma. This horizon was deemed important in the study of the Lindow II bog body (Stead *et al* 1986). During the recovery of fragments of the Lindow III body, a portion of leg was found enclosed in 25 cm of undisturbed peat. Pollen analysis of this peat and correlation with the *in situ* peat and pollen stratigraphy has enabled the stratigraphical position of the body to be ascertained. The Lindow III body was placed on the growing bog surface some 10–15 cm above the *Grenzhorizont* and not in a peat cutting. From this relationship with the bog stratigraphy and radiocarbon dates obtained, it is suggested that the remains date to *c.* 300–200 BC.

Appendix: Pollen nomenclature

Pollen nomenclature after that of Moore and Webb (1978). Plant taxonomy follows Clapham et al (1987).

POLLEN TYPE	PLANT NAME
Alnus	Alder
Anthemis type	Members of the Composites (e.g. Mayweeds)
Artemisia	Mugworts
Betula	Birch
Bidens type	Composites
Calluna	Ling
Chenopodium type	Goosefoot family
Corylus	Hazel
Corylus type	Hazel and/or Bog-myrtle (*Myrica*)
Drosera	Sundew
Erica	Heathers
Fagus	Beech
Fraxinus	Ash
Filipendula ulmaria	Meadowsweet
Hedera	Ivy
Ilex	Holly
Myrica	Bog-myrtle
Phragmites	Common reed
Pinus	Pine
Plantago lanceolata	Ribwort plantain
Plantago media/major	Hoary plantain and Rat-tail plantain
Polypodium vulgare	Polypody fern
Pteridium aquilinum	Bracken
Quercus	Oak
Rumex	Docks
Salix	Willow
Sinapis type	Crucifers and Charlocks
Sphagnum	*Sphagnum* bog moss
Tilia	Lime/Linden
Ulmus	Elm
Urtica type	Nettles and Pellitory

The Insect Assemblages Associated with Lindow III and Their Environmental Implications

M. H. Dinnin   *P. Skidmore*

Introduction

A group of peat samples was taken from, on and around the corpse with the aim of revealing information about the condition of the body and details of the immediate environment at the time of burial. A second series of samples was taken from a monolith through the peat cuttings in the location from which the body is believed to have come. The monolith was sampled at 10 cm intervals with the exception of the material around the *Grenzhorizont* at 119 cm towards the base of the column. The body is thought to have reposed just above this distinctly visible feature.

Recovery of Fossil Insect Material

Sample size varied greatly, with those immediately associated with the body being only 150–200 g, while the monolith samples were somewhat larger at 2–4 kg. The smaller samples were sorted in alcohol under a low-power binocular microscope and the insect material removed. In order to recover the fossil insects from the larger samples, it was first necessary to concentrate them. This was accomplished using the now standard paraffin floatation technique of Coope and Osborne (1968). The samples were disaggregated in warm water over a 300μm sieve and then concentrated by the addition of paraffin which adheres to the waxy cuticle of the insect exoskeletons. After the addition of cold water the paraffin was floated off along with the concentrated insect remains. After washing with detergent to remove excess paraffin, the insect portion was separated from the plant macrofossil 'flot' (in this case large quantities of *Sphagnum*). Sorting was carried out in alcohol using a low-power microscope. The disarticulated beetle remains were identified using the standard entomological keys and an extensive reference collection. Insects recovered (Table 4) are listed in taxonomic order following Kloet and Hincks (1977).

The Beetle Fauna from the Body Samples (M.H.D.)

Samples taken from the body were considerably smaller than the 3–5 kg normally required for insect analysis. As a result the amount of identifiable material recovered from the samples was comparatively low. None the less, there are sufficient species present to gain a useful insight into the nature of the contemporary environments of the bog body.

Several species of predaceous water beetle were recorded from around the body, one of which, a small species of *Hydroporus*, is notable for its rarity. The identification of *H. scalesianus* was confirmed by Garth Foster

Table 4   Insect remains recovered

Body samples

A = LW/BJ   B = LW/DV   C = Fragment 3 Peat containing skin and bone   D = AE Peat in skin contact

Monolith samples

E = 0–10 cm   F = 100–110 cm   G = 110–115 cm   H = 115–130 cm   I = 140–150 cm

TAXA	A	B	C	D	E	F	G	H	I
Coleoptera									
Carabidae									
Pterostichus sp.	1	—	—	—	—	—	—	—	—
Agonum sexpunctatum (L.)/*ericeti* (Panzer)	—	1	—	—	—	—	—	—	—
Trichocellus cognatus (Gyll.)	1	—	—	—	—	—	—	—	—
Bradycellus collaris (Payk.)	—	1	—	—	—	—	—	—	—
Carabidae gen. *et* spp. indet.	—	—	—	—	2	—	—	—	—
Dytiscidae									
Hydroporus obscurus Sturm	7	1	—	3	7	2	9	8	1
H. pubescens (Gyll.)/*planus* (F.)	4	—	—	—	—	—	—	—	1
H. scalesianus Stephens	—	—	1	—	2	2	6	9	3
Hydroporus sp.	—	—	—	—	—	—	—	—	2
Graptodytes granularis (L.)	6	1	1	2	4	3	4	6	—
Agabus bipustulatus (L.)	1	—	—	1	—	—	—	—	—
Rhantus sp.	1	—	—	1	—	—	—	—	—
Hydrophilidae									
Hydrochus sp.	1	—	—	—	—	—	—	—	—
Helophorus obscurus Mulsant/*flavipes* (F.)	16	1	1	1	—	—	—	—	2
Megasternum obscurum (Marsham)	—	—	—	—	1	—	—	—	—
Anacaena sp.	—	—	—	—	—	—	—	—	1
Laccobius striatulus (F.)	15	—	—	1	1	—	—	—	12
Helochares sp.	1	—	—	—	—	—	—	—	—
Cymbiodyta marginella (F.)	—	—	—	—	—	—	—	—	2
Hydraenidae									
Ochthebius minimus (F.)	1	—	—	—	—	—	—	—	—
Ochthebius sp.	1	—	—	—	—	—	—	—	—
Leiodidae									
Leiodes sp.	1	—	—	—	—	—	—	—	—
Agathidium atrum (Payk.)	1	—	—	—	—	—	—	—	—
A. confusum (Brisout)	1	—	—	—	—	—	—	—	—
Scydmaenidae									
Scydmaenus rufus Muller and Kunze/ *tarsatus* Muller and Kunze	—	—	—	—	—	1	2	1	1
Staphylinidae									
Xylodromus sp.	—	—	—	—	—	—	—	1	—
Syntomium aeneum (Muller)	—	—	—	—	1	—	—	—	—
Anotylus nitidulus (Grav.)	—	—	—	—	1	—	—	—	—
Stenus spp.	—	1	—	—	—	—	1	1	—
Lathrobium spp.	1	1	—	1	1	1	1	3	—
Othius spp.	—	—	—	—	1	—	—	1	—
Philonthus sp.	—	—	1	—	—	—	—	—	—
Quedius sp.	—	—	1	—	—	—	—	—	—
Aleocharinae indet.	15	5	—	1	1	1	1	4	8
Pselaphidae									
Brachygluta sp.	—	—	—	1	—	—	—	—	—
Scarabidae									
Aphodius sp.	—	—	—	—	1	—	—	—	—
Scirtidae									
Gen. *et* sp. indet (prob. *Cyphon*)	—	3	1	2	8	6	17	5	14
Elateridae									
Athous bicolor (Goeze)	1	1	1	1	—	—	1	—	1
Silvanidae									
Psammoecus bipunctatus (F.)	—	—	—	—	1	—	—	—	—

TAXA	A	B	C	D	E	F	G	H	I
Cryptophagidae									
Atomaria sp.	—	—	—	—	—	—	—	—	1
Lathridiidae									
Corticaria sp.	1	—	—	—	1	—	—	—	—
Chrysomelidae									
Plateumaris discolor (Panzer)	9	3	1	5	12	5	3	6	7
Altica britteni Sharp/*ericeti* (Allard)	3	1	—	—	3	—	1	—	1
Altica sp.	—	—	—	—	—	—	—	—	1
Chaetocnema sahlbergi (Gyll.)	1	—	—	1	—	1	2	1	1
Apionidae									
Apion sp.	—	—	—	—	—	—	—	—	1
Curculionidae									
Micrelus ericae (Gyll.)	—	—	—	2	—	—	1	—	1
Ceutorhynchinae indet.	—	—	—	—	1	—	—	1	—
Limnobaris pilistriata (Steph.)	2	2	—	—	8	5	4	3	3
Diptera									
Tipulidae									
?*Prionocera* sp.	—	—	—	—	—	—	—	1	—
Limoniine lv.	84	2	1	15	6	2	1	13	18
Pediciine lv.	1	—	—	2	3	1	—	—	—
Limnophila pup.	—	—	—	—	—	—	—	—	18
Tipulid pup.	2	—	—	—	—	—	—	—	12
Chironomidae	—	—	—	—	—	—	1	—	1
Bibionidae									
Dilophus febrilis (L.)	—	—	—	—	—	—	—	—	1
Hybotidae									
Stilpon sublunatum Collin.	—	1	—	—	1	—	2	—	—
Dolichopodidae	—	—	—	3	—	—	—	—	—
Tachinidae									
?*Phryxe* sp.	1	—	—	—	—	—	—	—	—
Hemiptera									
Lygaeidae									
Scolopostethus sp.	—	—	—	—	—	—	1	—	—
Stygnocoris sp.	1	—	—	—	—	—	—	—	—
Hebridae									
Hebrus ruficeps (L.)	—	—	—	1	—	—	—	1	5
Ulopidae									
Ulopa reticulata (L.)	1	—	—	—	—	—	—	—	—
Cicadellidae									
Aphrodes sp.	1	—	—	—	—	—	—	—	—
Psammotettix sp.	1	—	—	—	—	—	—	—	—
Gen. indet.	—	—	—	—	—	—	1	—	—
Hymenoptera									
Braconidae									
?*Clinocentrus* sp.	1	—	—	—	—	—	—	—	—
Formicidae									
Lasius niger (L.)	1	—	—	—	—	—	—	—	—
Formica ?*lemani* Bondroit	1	1	—	—	—	—	—	—	1
Myrmica ?*ruginodis* Nyl.	1	—	—	—	—	—	2	—	—
Myrmica sp.	—	—	—	—	—	—	1	—	—
Lepidoptera									
Lepidopterous pupa	1	—	—	—	—	—	—	—	—

using the elytra, thorax and metacoxal plates. *Hydroporus scalesianus* has been collected on various occasions during the last half of the nineteenth century and the early part of the twentieth century in Norfolk and latterly at Chaloner's Whin, near York (Balfour-Browne 1940). It has recently been rediscovered in Durham (Horsfield and Foster 1985), Cumberland (Bilton 1984) and Norfolk (Foster 1982; Palmer 1981) and there are records from Eire and Northern Ireland. It would seem that *H. scalesianus* may not be as rare as previously thought. Its scarcity has been attributed to a decline in suitable habitat as a result of fen drainage, disturbance and more locally through over collecting, although its small size may have resulted in it being overlooked. Fossil beetle faunas from Thorne Moors (Buckland 1979), the Somerset Levels (Girling 1976) and Church Stretton, Shropshire (Osborne 1972) indicate that at least in Pollen Zone VII(b) *H. scalesianus* was more widespread. A preference for thick mossy swamps with clear water (Balfour-Browne 1958), together with French records from woodland pools (Guignot 1933) leads Buckland (op. cit.) to suggest that the disappearance of this aspect of the fen habitat may have been responsible for the initial decline of the species before drainage took place. Fossil evidence from the Somerset Levels (Girling, op. cit) has shown that *H. scalesianus* was present throughout the hydroseral succession in both raised mire and fen habitats (see Girling 1984). The beetle's presence in Lindow Moss further demonstrates that the species is not just a fen species and that it can live in a variety of habitats.

A number of specimens of *Hydroporus obscurus* were present; this pale red species favours acid pools on peaty ground (Balfour-Browne, op. cit.) The larger species, *Hydroporus pubescens*, is widely distributed (ibid.) and is found in peaty, fresh and brackish water (Friday 1988). *Graptodytes granularis*, numerous in all the samples, frequents stagnant detritus pools and drains (Balfour-Browne, op. cit.); Harde (1984) gives slime and sludge in stagnant or slowly running water as the beetle's habitat. *Agabus bipustulatus* is extremely eurytopic and is found in a variety of wet situations, including peat bogs.

Further evidence for standing water is provided by the number and variety of Hydrophilid beetles present. Members of the genus *Hydrochus* are associated with lush vegetation growing in and around stagnant water (Balfour-Browne 1958), with species showing preferences for both acid and eutrophic water (Hansen 1987). The *Helophorus* species present could not confidently be split between *H. obscurus* and *H. flavipes*. *H. flavipes* is an acid pool species which, in the experience of Angus (1978), is the only British species of *Helophorus* found in *Sphagnum* pools, both on moors and in woodland, a preference also noted by Hansen (op. cit.). In Britain *H. obscurus* replaces *H. flavipes* in basic and neutral waters (Angus, op. cit.); this species normally inhabits temporary, shallow, eutrophic grassy pools with clayey bottoms (ibid.). The head of a beetle belonging to the genus *Helochares* could not be identified to species. *H. lividus* (Forster), *H. obscurus* (Muller) and *H. punctatus* (Sharp) live in stagnant water. The former species is restricted to the edges of acid oligotrophic pools; *H. obscurus* is a more eurytopic species and is often numerous in vegetated, neutral to basic pools and is found only occasionally in acidic *Sphagnum* pools in moorland (Hansen op. cit.). *H. punctatus* occurs in peat and *Sphagnum* pools (Friday op. cit.). *Laccobius striatulus*, abundant in one sample, lives among vegetation in shallow and slowly running water with a light, clayey bottom (Hansen op. cit.). The Hydraenid *Ochthebius minimus* inhabits both still and running water, but is most abundant in shallow, well-vegetated pools (ibid.). The larvae of the Scirtidae develop in water and therefore these beetles are tied to water to reproduce (Harde 1984). The adults are found in moss, on waterside plants and in litter; they overwinter in litter, under bark, among rush stems and in similar protected sites. They are characteristic of *Sphagnum* bogs.

The genus *Stenus* is large and difficult to identify, even when complete. The head and thoraxes proved insufficient to enable further identification. Many *Stenus* species inhabit the margins of water, be they ponds, rivers or marshes (Tottenham 1954). Likewise, the genus *Lathrobium* are associated with damp spots in a wide variety of habitats (Harde op. cit.).

The aforementioned beetles clearly demonstrate the presence of moist, boggy ground with open pools of stagnant acidic water, sufficiently disturbed to be aerated in places. The nature of the drier bog ground and landscape is revealed by another collection of beetles. Three species of predaceous ground beetle (Carabidae) are present in the body samples. A fragment of an *Agonum* thorax belonging to either *A. sexpunctatum* or *A. ericeti* was recovered. It was not possible to distinguish between the two since only a small basal fragment remained. The former species is heliophilous and is often seen running on open moist peat, sparsely covered with grass, *Carex* species and low shrubs. The latter species is more stenotopic, being restricted to ombrotrophic *Sphagnum* bogs, where it occurs in both wet *Sphagnum* areas and on drier hummocks with *Calluna* and *Vaccinium* (Lindroth 1986).

Trichocellus cognatus and *Bradycellus collaris* are also open country species living on peaty or sandy soils beneath *Calluna* and *Empetrum* (Lindroth 1974). On the continent *T. cognatus* appears to be more stenotopic, being confined to acid bogs where it is taken on moist heather-covered peaty soils (Lindroth op. cit.).

Decomposing plant remains, which would have accumulated in this environment and contributed to peat formation, support a fungal feeder community. The elytron of a species of *Leiodes* was present. This genus feeds on underground fungi and in summer swarms around sunset in forest clearings and beside water (Harde op. cit.). The two different elytra of *Agathidium* closely matched those of *A. atrum* and *A. confusum*. Both feed on fungi and are found on and behind bark in old tree stumps and in rotting branches (Peez 1971). The genus *Corticaria* are also fungal feeders and are common in a wide range of habitats.

The phytophagous component of the beetle fauna gives details of the plants present on the bog. Further evidence of an open landscape suggested by the species of *Agonum*, *Trichocellus* and *Bradycellus* is reinforced by the occurrence of the click beetle *Athous bicolor*. More specifically, *Plateumaris discolor* and their cocoons were particularly frequent in the body samples. This iridescent reed beetle feeds on *Eriophorum*, *Carex* and *Sparganium minimum* and lays eggs underwater in the roots and rhizomes of *Eriophorum* with the necessary oxygen being supplied through the plant's air channels (Stainforth 1944). The remains of the Chrysomelid, *Altica*, either *A. britteni* or *A. ericeti*, were present in two body samples. *A. britteni* feeds on *Calluna* and *Empetrum nigrum*, whilst *A. ericeti* is recorded on *Erica tetralix* (Mohr 1966). All are plants of heath or wet, boggy habitats. The larvae of the beetle *Chaetocnema* bore into the stems of plants. *C. sahlbergi* probably feeds on *Carex* species (ibid.) but other plant hosts listed include *Vaccinium* (Fowler 1890) and *Glaux maritima* (Joy 1932), the latter being a salt marsh species. Two species of weevil were present, *Limnobaris pilistriata* and *Micrelus ericae*. The larvae of *L. pilistriata* develop in the roots of *Scirpus lacustris*, with the emerging adults feeding on rushes, reeds, and marsh grasses such as the Cyperaceae (Hoffman 1950), *Scirpus* (Lohse 1983a), *Cladium mariscus* (Reitter 1916) and *Juncus*. *L. pilistriatus* appears to be rare at present having apparently been replaced by *L. t-album*, which has yet to be found fossil. The small Ceutorhynchine *Micrelus ericae* bores into the stems of *Calluna vulgaris* and *Erica tetralix* (Lohse 1983b; Smith *et al* 1985).

The fragmented thorax and front leg of the dung beetle *Aphodius* present in sample AE does not necessarily mean that there was herbivore dung in the immediate vicinity. It is more likely that the individual accidentally landed and drowned in the bog. The genus *Aphodius* are good fliers, an important ability when breeding places are patchily distributed. The beetle may have dispersed from grassland or woodland nearby and can be considered as part of the background fauna *sensu* Kenward (1975).

The beetle fauna from the peat associated with the body gives a detailed and internally consistent picture of the conditions in which the body was deposited. It clearly indicates an acid oligotrophic bog with peat and *Sphagnum*-lined pools fringed with *Sphagnum* 'lawns'. Other plants growing in and around these areas are typical of wetland communities. Various species of *Carex* and *Erica* would have grown in the wetter parts, while tussocks of *Eriophorum* and *Calluna* grew on slightly drier ground. *Scirpus* or *Cladium mariscus* may have grown in more mineral-enriched areas of the bog. The beetle fauna gives no indication that a body was present in the peat. There are no human ectoparasites, such as fleas or lice, and no carrion species. Even in winter the corpse would have soon attracted insects, particularly flies, which feed or lay their eggs in fresh or decomposing flesh. No such animals were recovered. It can only be assumed that the body was rapidly submerged, perhaps pushed under the bog surface, before carrion insects could locate and colonise the corpse.

Comparisons with Lindow II

The corpse of Lindow II retrieved from the moss in August 1984, was studied in great detail and included an analysis of insect remains by the late Maureen Girling (1986). There is considerable similarity between the faunas obtained from the two bodies. Both indicate almost identical contemporary environments. Perhaps most significantly there was no indication that either body lay on the surface for an appreciable amount of time. Neither body harboured a fauna of decomposition and they must have been rapidly submerged.

The Environmental History of Lindow Moss as Indicated by the Beetle Faunas of the Peat Monolith

Samples analysed were taken from the very top and the bottom of the monolith and from the sequence 100–130 cm, the level incorporating the *Grenzhorizont* near the body's proposed context. Immediately noticeable are the faunal similarities, both within the monolith samples and between the monolith and body samples. The sequence of monolith samples yielded only nine additional taxa and sees no significant absences; of these, five are from the most recently deposited sample (0–10 cm). The Hydrophilid, *Megasternum obscurum*, and the rove beetle, *Anotylus nitidulus*, thrive in all kinds of decaying matter, but favour plant debris and dung. Likewise, members of the genus *Brachygluta* live in decaying vegetation, humus and mossy tussocks (Pearce 1974) and require damp conditions (Harde op. cit.). *Psammoecus bipunctatus* and *Syntomium aeneum* are again damp litter species. The former beetle is a typically fenland species and is found among reeds and their debris (Vogt 1967), which have invaded the recently drained bog. *S. aeneum* is widely distributed, living in moss growing on trees, walls and in bogs and moors (Lohse 1964). These additions to the fauna do not alter the environmental interpretation arrived at from the analysis of the body samples. They act as corroborative evidence of the boggy nature of the contemporary environment.

Four of the further additions, retrieved from the lower monolith samples are perhaps not surprisingly linked with rotting vegetable matter. Sample 110–115 cm contained a *Xylodromus* thorax, a genus associated usually with mouldy hay and vegetable refuse (Harde op. cit.). A member of the genus *Atomaria* was retrieved from the basal sample (140–150 cm); these beetles are common inhabitants of rotting hay, dry dung and fungi (Lohse 1967) and occur in a variety of habitats. Elytra and thoraxes of a member of the genus *Scydmaenus* occurred in the four lower monolith samples (100–150 cm). These beetles favour mouldy residues, such as compost (Franz 1971). Also present in the basal sample were the remains of *Cymbiodyta marginella*. This eurytopic water beetle is found among vegetation in, most often, neutral to basic water, but also in acid *Sphagnum* pools (Hansen op. cit.).

The lack of significant change in species composition through the sequence of samples (including the body samples) suggests great local environmental stability throughout the period represented in the monolith. The stratigraphy is reasonably homogeneous, but a distinct Grenzhorizont at 119 cm is marked by a fibrous layer in the usually compressed *Sphagnum* layers. This drying out of the bog surface was not reflected by any change in the beetle fauna. One would expect an increase in ground beetles (Carabidae) accompanied by the replacement of hydrophilous species by those favouring drier conditions. Likewise, given time, the phytophagous component would reflect a shift from wetland plants to carr woodland as the hydroseral succession developed. Since no such obvious changes are visible it can only be concluded that this drying-out phase was too short lived to enable the relatively rapid process of colonisation by new beetle species. Alternatively, the horizon may only reflect a relatively local drying out of the bog surface as part of a dynamic process resulting in the formation of a patchwork of wet hollows and drier hummocks.

Conclusion

The beetle fauna from around the bog body suggests that the corpse was deposited in a wet *Sphagnum* bog with pools of rather acid water. These water bodies need not have been extensive since the water beetles present can be found in small, isolated pools. This water was bordered by a typical oligotrophic bog flora of cotton grass, mosses and heather. The complete absence of any carrion fauna leads to the conclusion that the body was rapidly submerged (cf. Girling 1986). Despite the stratigraphic recurrence surface, analysis of the insect assemblages above, below and around this feature revealed no appreciable change in the moisture status of the bog or any indication of climatic change.

The Diptera, Hemiptera and Hymenoptera associated with Lindow III (P.S.)

In a study based on a very small amount of non-coleopterous insect material retrieved from Lindow II (Skidmore 1986) a total absence of any necrophilous Diptera was noted. This fact was seen as entirely supportive of the view that the corpse had been submerged in wholly anaerobic conditions immediately after death. Such conditions could be expected to prevail in the peat pools so typical of lowland raised mires.

The present note concerns a very much larger quantity of insect material collected from the immediate vicinity of Lindow III, and from the body itself. The bulk of identified remains are dipterous but a small number of insects of other orders are included. A list is appended, giving the total numbers of fragments belonging to each taxon.

The material here under consideration indicates a pure bog community entirely uncontaminated by any elements associated with carrion. Furthermore, even such ubiquitous inhabitants of sodden petrifying animal or vegetable

Table 5

SAMPLES	SPECIMENS IDENTIFIED
(a) LM3. 0–10 cm	*Limonia* s. lat. 6 larval head capsules *Pedicia* s. lat. 3 larval head capsules *Stilpon sublunatum.* 1 head of adult
(b) LM3. 100–110 cm	*Limonia* s. lat. 2 larval head capsules *Pedicia* s. lat. 1 larval head capsule
(c) LM3. 110–115 cm E	*Limonia* s. lat. 1 larval head capsule Orthocladiine midge. 1 adult thoracic fragment *Stilpon sublunatum.* 1 adult head capsule and 2 thoraxes *Myrmica ?ruginodis.* 1 head capsule of adult *Myrmica* sp. 1 thoracic segment *Scolopostethus* sp. 1 pronotal fragment Cicadellid sp. indet. 1 adult facial mask and clypeus
(d) LM3. 115–130 cm	*Limonia* s. lat. 18 larval head capsules *Hebrus ruficeps.* 3 incomplete adults
(e) LM3. 140–145 cm	*?Prionocera* sp. 1 pupal respiratory horn and 2 pupal tergal fragments *Limonia* s. lat. 18 larval head capsules *Limnophila* s. lat. 18 pupal tergites Tupulid sp. 12 pupal end segments (8 males, 4 females) Orthocladiine midge. 1 adult thoracic fragment *Dilophus febrilis.* 1 adult female head capsule. Post-occipital lobes much larger than *D. femoratus* *Hebrus ruficeps.* 5 incomplete adults *Formica* sp. 1 adult head capsule (worker) ?Alysiine wasp. 1 adult head capsule
(f) LM3. Frag. 3. Skin and bones from elevator.	*Limonia* s. lat. 15 larval head capsule
(g) LM3. AE Body sample.	*Limonia* s. lat. 15 larval head capsules *Pedicia* s. lat. 2 larval head capsules Dolichopodid sp. a. 1 adult head capsule fragment Dolichopodid sp. b. 1 adult head capsule fragment Dolichopodid sp. c. 1 genital segment of male. This most resembles a *Rhaphium* sp. but cannot be related to any of the currently known British species.
(h) LM3. 39. 150B. Feb. 87 From stack on moss.	*Limonia* s. lat. 1 larval head capsule *Stilpon sublunatum.* 1 adult head capsule and 1 thorax *Myrmica ?ruginodis.* 1 head capsule of adult (worker)
(i) LM3. LW/BJ. 30.3.88	*Limonia* s. lat. 84 larval head capsules *Pedicia* s. lat. 1 larval head capsule Tipulid sp. indet. 2 male pupal end segments (as in sample 140–150 cm) Lepidopteran sp. indet. 1 incomplete pupa *Phryxe* sp. 1 fragment of adult head. This consists merely of the vibrissal angle with the facial ridges and the occipital dilation. In the chaetotactic and other details it very closely resembles members of this genus but could belong to one of the related genera. *Hebrus ruficeps.* 7 incomplete adults *Aphrodes* sp. 1 fragment of adult head capsule *?Psammotettix* sp. 1 fragment of adult head capsule *Formica ?lemani.* 1 adult head capsule (worker) *Lasius ?niger.* 1 adult head capsule (worker) *Myrmica ?ruginodis.* 1 adult head capsule (worker) *?Clinocentrus* sp. 1 fragment of adult head capsule
(j) LM3. LW/BJ	*Stygnocoris* sp. 1 head capsule and 1 pronotal fragment *Ulopa reticulata.* 1 complete forewing

matter as Sphaeroceridae and Ephydridae were entirely absent. As with Lindow II, this body lay in a totally anaerobic regime such as would occur deep in a peat pool. Buckland (pp. 47–50) notes that recent studies have shown that peat pools may survive for centuries on the surfaces of undisturbed lowland bogs and it is therefore possible that the insect fragments from around Lindow III may have long predated his 'burial'.

Two of the taxa which were positively referable to species, viz. the tiny hybotid fly, *Stilpon sublunatum*, and the *Sphagnum* bug, *Hebrus ruficeps*, are known to occur only in wet peat bogs where both may abound in wet *Sphagnum*. By far the most abundant dipterous fragments were head capsules of larval tipulids very closely resembling *Limonia* species as figured by Lindner (1959). These are detritivores, some breeding in wet organic mud. In far smaller numbers were larval head capsules of another tipulid, probably of the genus *Pedicia sg. Tricyphona*. These are predators feeding on other nematocerous larvae, worms, etc. Since head capsules of various instars (larval stages) were found, it is not possible to infer the numbers of individual specimens represented. At least two tipulids were present as pupal fragments – 18 tergal fragments of a *Limnophila s. lat.* (possibly of *Euphylidorea meigeni* (Verrall)) and a tergite and respiratory siphon of a tipuline (almost certainly a *Prionocera*). Fourteen tipulid pupal anal segments may also belong to the same *Limnophila* species. Both *E. meigeni* and the genus *Prionocera* are characteristic members of the peat mud community. The fever fly, *Dilophus febrilis*, breeds in humus soil and decaying plant matter and abounds in huge mobile swarms. It was clearly a casual intruder into the peat pool vicinity. Likewise, the ants, the lygaeid bugs (*Scolopostethus* and *Stygnocoris*) and the grass and sedge-feeding frog-hoppers presumably inhabited the drier margins of the pool. *Ulopa reticulata* feeds on *Erica* which doubtless grew on the surrounding *Sphagnum* hummocks.

List of Samples from Lindow III

Table 5 lists the specimens identified in each sample, arranged in the order used in the taxonomic list (Table 4).

Radiocarbon Dating of the Lindow III Bog Body

R. A. Housley   A. J. Walker   R. L. Otlet   R. E. M. Hedges

Introduction

The dating of archaeological finds by radiocarbon is now a very well accepted process, so much so that in many situations it has become to be seen as routine. In many situations and with certain types of sample this is often the case, but there are various types of material and burial environment where dating is not straightforward. It is our opinion that the dating of proteinaceous material from peat bogs is not without its problems and age determinations in such situations are more akin to experimental tests than are radiocarbon determinations on more established types of sample. As a result, in this chapter we devote considerable coverage to the methodologies adopted by the two laboratories (Oxford and Harwell) which participated in the dating of Lindow III – the human remains found in 1987 – as well as going to some length to discuss the technical difficulties encountered. Some of this has implications for the previous research on Lindow II (the human remains uncovered in August 1984 and popularly known as 'Pete Marsh') and so we have included the earlier findings in our general discussion. However, since neither laboratory has undertaken any new determinations on the earlier body, the overall dating situation remains as presented in the original monograph (Gowlett *et al* 1986; Otlet *et al* 1986) and in the subsequent review by Gowlett *et al* (1989).

Although both laboratories acknowledge that a major problem still exists in reconciling the two mutually incompatible C14 ages for Lindow II, we do feel that some of the problems which have been perceived in the past –

particularly concerning the difficulty in squaring the C14 evidence with stratigraphic and other relative dating means – are now less contentious than in 1986. In a sense, the work on Lindow III has partially resolved some of the dating problem of Lindow II in that the work of Buckland (pp. 47–50) has pointed to a mechanism whereby an age difference between a body and its surrounding deposits is to be expected if the absence of carrion larval infestation is to be explained. As with Lindow II, the research of Branch and Scaife (pp. 19–30) suggests the deposits surrounding Lindow III were older than the C14 age of the body. Therefore given the good laboratory agreement for the date of the human remains, and in the light of Buckland's suggestion, we are of the opinion that the difference in age between the bodies and their peat surroundings is better explained in terms of site formation processes than by chemical pretreatment problems. The C14 date of Lindow III is not fraught with the additional difficulty of understanding and resolving laboratory disagreement as occurred with Lindow II, and so the observation that there is an age difference between the surrounding burial deposits and the body is probably telling us more about events at, or soon after, the time of death than about inter-laboratory procedures. This is not to distract attention from the fact that there still is a C14 problem with the date of Lindow II. However, whether one takes the Oxford or the Harwell result, they both indicate the body is younger than the surrounding peat, consistent with the burial situation of Lindow III. In this sense the research on the 1987 finds have helped to clarify the previous work on the 'Body in the Bog'. Furthermore, now that many more bog bodies have been dated (below; see van der Sanden, pp. 146–65; Brindley and Lanting, pp. 133–6) we have a better idea of the cultural context within which to place the Lindow burials. Thus, although we do not present a new 'solution' to the question of the dating of Lindow Man, we have been able to resolve partially some of the chronological issues.

The Difficulties of Radiocarbon Dating Bog Bodies

The main problem associated with the radiocarbon dating of proteins from such environments is the danger that the extracted 'collagen' has been heavily contaminated by carbon-bearing molecules of a different age to that of the original sample. Humic-rich groundwater like that common in peat bogs contains natural tanning agents in the form of organic acids and aldehydes. These cross link to the protein to an extent which has not always been entirely appreciated. Unless steps are taken to break this cross linking and remove the contaminant, the resulting age determination may produce a biased result (the degree of bias being dependent on the difference in age of the contaminant and the amount of contamination still present). Obviously if the contaminant is the same age as the body the measured date is unchanged. It must be realised that even when steps are taken to overcome this problem it may not always be clear whether the process has been completely successful for each individual sample. A residual contamination by 10% humic material, the carbon in which is 1000 years younger, will make the C14 age 100 years too young.

Sampling

Four samples were taken from the body of Lindow III in November 1987 for radiocarbon dating. The samples consisted of two fragments of skin and two groups of bone. One piece of skin (P2256) and two rib bones (P2255) came from LW/DR, the upper part of the body, whilst another fragment of skin (P2257) and a second group of bones (P2258) came from LW/EV, the lower part. Three of the four samples (P2255, 2256 and 2258) were of sufficient size for conventional radiocarbon dating, so these three samples were subdivided in Oxford, the larger sub-samples being given to the Harwell laboratory to date. The fourth sample (P2257) was not subdivided since there was insufficient skin for a radiometric determination, so this

sample has only been accelerator dated. In Oxford all four samples were pretreated using two slightly different methods, each fraction separately dated thus producing two accelerator mass spectrometry (AMS) dates per sample, giving a total of eight AMS determinations (Table 6).

Chemical Pretreatment

As already mentioned, the preservation of bog bodies by natural 'tanning' by bog acids and related compounds poses problems for accurate radiocarbon dating, because it makes the extraction of organic materials which are native to the body much more difficult. The samples dated in Oxford were initially leached with dilute hydrochloric acid (HCl, 0.5M), to ensure that demineralisation was complete. This was followed by rinsing with distilled water, and repeated two-hour extractions with sodium hydroxide (NaOH, 0.2M) at room temperature, until the amount of coloured solution still coming off was small. Care was taken at this stage to ensure that the samples did not dissolve completely. The excess alkali was removed by rinsing with distilled water, and the samples were then either heated in milli-molar HCl at 100 °C to extract gelatin (soluble collagen polypeptides), or bleached in a 2.5% (w/vol) solution of sodium chlorite (NaOCl) at pH 3 and 60 °C, for between one and three hours. Bleached samples were rinsed with distilled water to remove chlorite, and then gelatinised. If the samples were mechanically strong and appeared to be heavily impregnated with bog organics, an alkaline extraction of the bleached collagen prior to gelatinisation was carried out using 0.1M NaOH. The next stage involved drying the crude gelatin solutions before hydrolysis (6M HCl at 105 °C) and the purification of the amino acids by ion exchange on Dowex 50W-X8. Humic cross linking should be removed by alkaline treatment, by the chlorite bleaching, and during hydrolysis to amino acids. That this process is very likely to be sufficient is demonstrated by the agreement, at least for Lindow II, between the dates for different fractions. (Compare the purified hydroxyproline fraction [OxA-783], which cannot be cross linked, with the standard pretreatment fractions [OxA-781 and 784]).

The samples dated at Harwell were given acid and alkali pretreatments similar to those used at Oxford. For the bone samples the first stage consisted of soaking in 1M HCl at room temperature for a minimum of 24 hours, followed by rinsing in distilled water. A similar treatment was used for the skin except 3M HCl was used. All

Table 6   Lindow III: the uncalibrated C14 determinations

LABORATORY REFERENCE	SAMPLE	CHEMICAL FRACTION	$\delta^{13}C$ (‰)	C14 AGE BP (±1 SIGMA)
OxA-1517	Bone (P2255) LW/DR	Amino acids from unbleached collagen	—	1740 ± 90
OxA-1518	LW/DR	Amino acids from bleached collagen	—	1750 ± 90
HAR-9094	LW/DR	Unbleached collagen	−22.8	2010 ± 80
OxA-1519	Skin (P2256) LW/DR	Amino acids from unbleached collagen	—	1850 ± 90
OxA-1520	LW/DR	Amino acids from bleached collagen	—	1700 ± 120
HAR-9092	LW/DR	Unbleached collagen	−26.9	1880 ± 80
OxA-1521	Skin (P2257) LW/EV	Amino acids from unbleached collagen	—	1890 ± 100
OxA-1522	LW/EV	Amino-acids from bleached collagen	—	1760 ± 150
OxA-1523	Bone (P2258) LW/EV	Amino acids from unbleached collagen	—	2000 ± 100
OxA-1524	LW/EV	Amino acids from bleached collagen	—	2040 ± 90
HAR-9093	LW/EV	Unbleached collagen	−22.5	1860 ± 70

Quoted $\delta^{13}C$ values are as measured. AMS measurements have been corrected for isotopic fractions using an assumed value of −21 per mil.

samples were then gently heated in NaOH (bones 0.25M, skin 0.1M) for up to ten minutes, but taking care that they did not disintegrate completely. This was followed by rinsing with distilled water until neutral (with no further colouring apparent in the solution) and a second acid rinse and final washing. The remaining insoluble fraction was filtered and oven dried ready for combustion. Weight loss in pretreatment was of the order of 80–90% for both skin and bone.

Target and Gas Preparation

At the time when the Lindow III samples were dated, the Oxford AMS system required samples to be introduced into the ion source in the form of solid carbon (graphite). Therefore after drying, the AMS samples were oxidised to CO_2, the carbon dioxide being separated cryogenically from the other evolved gases. The collected CO_2 was reduced directly to graphite, using a modification of the 'Vogel' process (Vogel *et al* 1987). Isotopic measurement of C14 was achieved using the procedures detailed in Hedges *et al* (1989).

The Harwell samples were converted in CO_2 for measurement in the miniature gas counting system described in Otlet *et al* (1983) and Otlet, Sanderson and Walker (1986). HAR-9092, the skin sample, was combusted in a tube combustion line, the two bone samples, HAR-9093 and 9094, in a miniature high-pressure combustion bomb. This latter method was preferred for the larger samples since it produces CO_2 with fewer nitrogen impurities than the tube system and is less difficult to further purify. The CO_2 produced by either method was fully purified ready for counting by thermal cycling over copper, silver and platinum at 700 °C and filled into 30 ml (70 mg carbon) size counters at 4 bar pressure. Samples were counted for between four and six weeks with data checked and dumped daily. Counting procedures were as outlined in Otlet, Sanderson and Walker (1986).

Results

All the dates quoted are uncalibrated in radiocarbon years BP using the half-life of 5568 years. At the time of measurement, Oxford was unable to measure the degree of isotopic fractionation and so no $\delta^{13}C$ have been quoted for the AMS dates. Instead an assumed value of −21 per mil (relative to PDB) has been applied. Harwell was able to measure the degree of isotopic fractionation and so the determined values are included in Table 6. By convention, all C14 results are normalised to −25 per mil, with errors quoted to one standard deviation. For the AMS dates this error term represents the laboratory's estimate for the total error in the system, including the sample chemistry. It includes the statistical precision from the number of C14 nuclei detected, the reproducibility of the mass-spectrometric measurements between different targets, and the uncertainty in our estimation of the contamination background (taken to be 0.5 ± 0.3% of the new oxalic acid [II] standard, obtained by the measurement of C14 free material). The error term on the radiometric dates from Harwell includes counting statistics of the sample itself, a factor for the reproducibility of the background and calibration samples long term, and an assessment of the errors in the sample measurement process. (This follows the method of estimating errors in liquid scintillation counting described in Otlet, 1979.)

Calibration and Discussion

The individual uncalibrated C14 measurements are shown in Table 6, with the 1 and 2 sigma calibrated age ranges being given in Table 7.

It is possible to consider the Lindow III C14 dates in several ways, and the various possibilities are presented in Fig. 13. The larger than normal variance in the AMS dataset, reflected by the 50–150 per cent greater error term, can be attributed to instability of the accelerator configuration over the two-day dating period. Unfortunately, lack of further material from several of the samples prevented repeat measurement. Therefore in this particular case it is perhaps better to place more weight on the radiometric results. However, as there is no significant age offset between the conventional and the AMS dates for Lindow III, omitting the AMS dataset does not radically alter the chronology.

So what is the most likely calendric date for the body? Table 8 lists the 1 and 2 sigma age ranges for the various possible statistical handlings of the data. The earliest 2 sigma date (c. 90 cal BC) is provided by the combined radiometric grouping, while the latest date (cal AD c. 320) comes from the AMS paired dates. If more weight is given to the radiometric dating a *terminus ante quem* of cal AD c. 225 is possibly more reasonable. The 1 sigma ranges favour a first or second century AD date for the body, although an early third century result cannot be excluded. Whether it is wise to take the interpretation further is

Table 7   Lindow III: calibrated age ranges

LABORATORY REFERENCE	SAMPLE	C14 AGE BP (±1 SIGMA)	CALIBRATED AGE (CAL AD/BC) 1 SIGMA	2 SIGMA
	Bone			
OxA-1517	LW/DR	1740 ± 90	cal AD 130–410	cal AD 70–535
OxA-1518	LW/DR	1750 ± 90	cal AD 130–405	cal AD 35–535
HAR-9094	LW/DR	2010 ± 80	165 cal BC–cal AD 70	350 cal BC–cal AD 130
	Skin			
OxA-1519	LW/DR	1850 ± 90	cal AD 30–320	90 cal BC–cal AD 390
OxA-1520	LW/DR	1700 ± 120	cal AD 170–530	cal AD 30–635
HAR-9092	LW/DR	1880 ± 80	cal AD 25–230	90 cal BC–cal AD 340
	Skin			
OxA-1521	LW/EV	1890 ± 100	90 cal BC–cal AD 230	165 cal BC–cal AD 380
OxA-1522	LW/EV	1760 ± 150	cal AD 70–430	95 cal BC–cal AD 635
	Bone			
OxA-1523	LW/EV	2000 ± 100	170 cal BC–cal AD 80	355 cal BC–cal AD 230
OxA-1524	LW/EV	2040 ± 90	200 cal BC–cal AD 55	360 cal BC–cal AD 130
HAR-9093	LW/EV	1860 ± 70	cal AD 65–235	90 cal BC–cal AD 340

Calibration according the computer program of Stuiver and Reimer (1986) [rev. 1.3] using the high-precision decadal dataset of Stuiver and Becker (1986). Age ranges are approximate after rounding to the next five calendar years.

Table 8   Calibrated age ranges for the weighted mean age values

SAMPLE GROUP (WEIGHTED MEAN)	RADIOCARBON AGE (C14 YEARS BP ± 1 SIGMA)	CALIBRATED AGE RANGE (CAL BC/AD)	
		1 SIGMA	2 SIGMA
All eleven dates	1875 ± 30	cal AD 75–210	cal AD 30–225
All four AMS weighted means	1855 ± 50	cal AD 70–230	cal AD 25–320
HAR-9092/9093/9094	1910 ± 45	cal AD 30–130	90 cal BC–cal AD 225
Four AMS pairs and three HAR-dates	1885 ± 35	cal AD 65–205	cal AD 25–230

Calibration according the computer program of Stuiver and Reimer (1986) [rev. 1.3] using the high-precision decadal dataset of Stuiver and Becker (1986). Age ranges are approximate after rounding to the next five calendar years.

unclear, and so probably the safest conclusion to make is that the body almost certainly belongs to one of three centuries, the first century BC or the first or second century AD.

How does this fit in with the stratigraphic evidence? Branch and Scaife (pp. 19–30) have been able to correlate the peat in contact with the body with the long stratigraphic sequence recovered during subsequent excavation (Turner, pp. 10–18) of the find locality. Their research, involving the correlation of the pollen from the peat associated with the leg of Lindow III and that from the trench, suggests the body came from *c*.110 cm down the stratigraphy, a position approximately 10 cm above the stratigraphic change that Branch and Scaife argues can be correlated with the Weber's (1900) *Grenzhorizont*. Interpolation of the radiocarbon dates from profile I gives a peat 'date' of *c*.2250 BP, significantly earlier than the C14 ages on the body. Although the peat in contact with the body has not been dated in the case of Lindow III, the similarity with Lindow II, where the peat was older than

Sample group (weighted mean)	Radiocarbon age (C14 years BP ± 1 sigma)	T values and confidence limits	

1   Treat all eleven dates as independent measurements

All eleven dates	1875 ± 30	T = 14.81 T < 95% confidence value (18.31)

Comment   The T value indicates the degree of variance within the dataset. The fact that the T value is less than the 95% confidence value means that the results are compatible with the samples coming from a single individual. Looking at the dataset in more detail:

2   Treat the eight AMS dates as four averaged pairs

Given that much of the pretreatment of the AMS samples was common between the pairs (the material was divided only at the bleaching step), and given that two of the pairs, OxA-1517/1518 and OxA–1522/1523, show remarkable similarity in their mean ages, it is perhaps better to treat the AMS dates as four averaged pairs:

OxA-1517/1518	1745 ± 90*	T = 0.01	
OxA-1519/1520	1795 ± 90*	T = 1.00	T < 95% confidence value (3.84)
OxA-1521/1522	1850 ± 100*	T = 0.52	
OxA-1523/1524	2020 ± 90*	T = 0.09	

(*As the date pairs are not being treated as independent measurements the error terms have not been reduced to the extent possible if they were independent)

All four AMS weighted means	1855 ± 50	T = 5.30 T < 95% confidence value (7.82)

Comment   The low T values obtained when combining the different chemical fractions (bleached *v.* unbleached collagen) shows that there is very little variance within the paired dates. One can conclude that the two chemical pretreatments have had very little effect on the obtained ages. However, the comparatively high T value (5.30) for the between pairs variance demonstrates the AMS dates are not a tight dataset, although the determinations are still within the 2 sigma confidence limits (T < 7.82).

3   Combine four AMS pairs with three Harwell dates

HAR-9092/9093/9094	1910 ± 45	T = 2.21 T < 95% confidence value (5.99)
Four AMS pairs and Harwell dates	1885 ± 35	T = 8.36 T < 95% confidence value (12.59)

Comment   The HAR- ages form a fairly tight dataset. When the AMS and the HAR- results are compared, the T value increases to 8.36 (still less than the 95% confidence limit of T < 12.59), with more of the variance deriving from the OxA- dataset. It is clear though that there is no significant systematic age offset between the OxA- and the HAR- results.

Fig. 13 Weighted mean age values and general interpretation.

the body (regardless of which set of C14 dates one accepts), is clear. There are several ways to handle this discrepancy. One is to follow standard archaeological procedure and give more weight to the stratigraphic evidence, which would place the burial in the Iron Age. Such an interpretation is still possible with Lindow III, although is harder to accept than with the previous body given the good C14 agreement of the laboratories. There is a case for examining the alternative interpretation, that the age difference between the peat and the body is a real distinction, and we should investigate how this could have occurred and whether other independent evidence supports such a conclusion.

The nature of the sediment surrounding the body has been analysed and discussed by Branch and Scaife (pp. 19–30). In addition, the examination of the coleoptera from the mire and from the body (Dinnin and Skidmore, pp. 31–8; Buckland, pp. 47–50) casts light on the conditions present at the locality at the time of burial. Both studies indicate that the body was interred in a loose liquid mud deposit. The absence of an insect carrion fauna on the body implies that it must have been pushed down under the surface and thus come to rest in peat of an earlier age. The modern presence of such pools of wet loose mud within mires is attested by Buckland, but the question of their duration is less clear (Barber, pp. 50–1). A figure of about 200 years may be a possibility; however, detailed studies are clearly needed to ascertain whether such features exist for longer periods of time. Certainly if this mechanism is to be invoked to explain the difference in age between the body of Lindow III (as well as Lindow II?) and the surrounding peat, one would have to argue for the existence of a pool which lasted c.370 radiocarbon years (2250 BP v. 1880 BP). This translates to between 300 and 600 calendar years; perhaps rather long to be explained totally by this mechanism, although data are lacking on the longevity of such pools.

But what have the Lindow III radiocarbon dates offered to our understanding of the circumstances of burial? Two things are worth reiterating: firstly, in contrast to Lindow Man, there is no dispute on the radiocarbon age of the body. Additionally, although no radiocarbon measurements were done on the associated peat around the body, the situation appears to be analogous with that of Lindow Man, namely the body came to rest in contact with stratigraphically older sediment. We would argue that this difference in age is a real archaeological problem which needs explaining. An attempt has been made to do this making use of the observations of other researchers, namely the evidence that the body must have been pushed down into sediment due to the lack of a carrion fauna; however, absence of modern studies on the longevity of analogous mire features makes proper assessment difficult. We would argue that the perceived discrepancy between the age of the sediment and the body is not so much 'a C14 problem' as an indication of the site formation processes. This is of archaeological interest and deserves further study when other human (and animal) remains are discovered in peat bogs.

So how does Lindow III fit in with the other human remains from Lindow Moss? Essentially there are four separate 'finds' of human skeletal material from the locality. The 1983 discovery by workmen of a partial cranium (to become known as Lindow Woman or Lindow I) has a radiocarbon date of 1740 + 80 BP (OxA-114). Found only a few metres away from Lindow III, given the imprecise nature of C14 dating in this instance it would be unwise to infer too much from a single date. The recovery in 1958 of a head now referred to as 'Worsley Man' has produced a similar date: 1800 ± 70 BP (OxA-1430). The difficulty of dating of Lindow II, uncovered in August 1984, has already been alluded to. The essential conflict is between two internally consistent datasets made by two separate laboratories. Harwell (Otlet et al 1986), using a small counter system, produced a weighted mean uncalibrated date of 1575 ± 30 BP for the body, the Oxford AMS system gave an age, again on samples from the body, of 1940 ± 25 BP (Gowlett et al 1986; 1989). Pretreatment was thought initially to be the problem, hence two further AMS dates were done on collagen prepared by Harwell but burnt in the Oxford combustion system. The dates obtained (OxA-787 and 788: Table 9) were not significantly younger than the Oxford determinations and thereby suggested the differing pretreatment methods were not the cause of the discrepancy.

The agreement between Harwell's dates on the peat in contact with the body (using their large liquid scintillation counters) and those done at the British Museum (the residues of which were subsequently dated by Oxford) confirmed that there was no problem in this instance between the three laboratories. The two main differences between the (uncontroversial) peat dates and those on the body are in the chemical pretreatment, and in Harwell's use of their large and small counter systems. However, although the peat dates were done in the liquid scintillation system, and those on the body in the small counter, both used the same standard, NBS oxalic acid. A subsequent intercomparison between the respective systems

Table 9 Radiocarbon determinations (BP ± 1 sigma) on human remains from Lindow Moss (excluding Lindow III)

Lindow I: partial cranium found in 1983

OxA-114		collagen from bone	1740 ± 80

Lindow II: (Lindow Man), found 1984

OxA-531	*	amino acids from hair	1920 ± 75
OxA-604	*	amino acids from bone	1850 ± 80
OxA-605	*	amino acids from soft tissue	2125 ± 80
OxA-781	*	standard amino acids	1940 ± 80
OxA-782	*	pre-bleach amino acids	1950 ± 80
OxA-783	*	hydroxyproline	1920 ± 80
OxA-784	*	standard amino acids	1900 ± 80
OxA-785	*	proline	1900 ± 80
OxA-786		collagen, Oxford preparation	1800 ± 80
OxA-787		collagen, Harwell preparation	1870 ± 80
OxA-788		collagen, Harwell preparation	1870 ± 80
OxA-789		humic (std amino acids)	2190 ± 100
OxA-790		humic (bleach)	1970 ± 80
OxA-1040	*	stomach contents	1910 ± 60
OxA-1041		humic from stomach contents	2210 ± 60
Oxford weighted mean (* dates only):			1940 ± 25
HAR-6224		wrist bone	2420 ± 100
HAR-6235a	*	leg bone	1540 ± 100
HAR-6235b	*	leg bone	1650 ± 80
HAR-6491	*	skin	1550 ± 70
HAR-6492	*	rib bone	1625 ± 80
HAR-6493	*	skin and hair	1530 ± 110
HAR-6856a	*	vertebra	1480 ± 90
HAR-6856b	*	vertebra	1610 ± 80
Harwell weighted mean (* dates only):			1575 ± 30

Worsley Man: found 1958

OxA-1430		amino acids from bone	1800 ± 70

showed no analytical discrepancy, although this situation need not necessarily have been the case when measurement took place. As far as differences in pretreatment are concerned, the fact that proteinaceous material from peat bogs is more difficult to purify than cellulose has already been mentioned, and it is conceivable that there is some factor here. However, given the peat appears older than the body, inadequate removal of the humic acids would not cause younger dates, so pretreatment is unlikely to be the problem. Therefore, without invoking an instrument error at the time of measurement we find it hard to suggest a mechanism which would affect only the Lindow Man dates leaving the known age standards and other samples unaffected.

Into what sort of general cultural framework should we see Lindow III and the other human 'burials' from Lindow Moss? This is more fully addressed by other contributors to this volume, however, on the basis of the radiocarbon dates, one could argue that all the Lindow Moss human 'burials' belong to a period of several hundred years between the first century BC and the middle of the first millennium AD. If one excludes the Harwell weighted means for Lindow II, then one could postulate that they belong to a period between the very end of the pre-Roman Iron Age and the first two centuries of the Romano-British period. This is perhaps later than many archaeologists would envisage, having been brought up on a framework of inference which tends to associate such 'burials' with the germanic rituals described by Tacitus, and the influence of Glob's (1965) *Mosefolket*. But assuming Tacitus was writing about contemporary events in the first century AD, then the possibility must exist that the same rituals continued in certain parts of the of the Western Europe underneath a 'veneer' of Roman culture. We acknowledge that from such a viewpoint, a late Romano-British (i.e. third to fourth century) date for Lindow II is hard to accommodate, but we would maintain that an early Romano-British age (or perhaps the very late Iron Age) is the most likely scenario on the basis of the (admittedly imprecise) C14 evidence.

If one accepts this generalisation, then how does such a date fit in with the other bog bodies from the rest of Britain and Western Europe? Tauber (1979) reported a number of radiocarbon measurements on bog bodies from Denmark (Table 10). Since then there have been more radiocarbon determinations on bodies from Ireland (Brindley and Lanting, pp. 133–6), the Netherlands (van der Sanden, p. 157), and from other British localities, e.g. the Cambridgeshire Fens (Healy and Housley 1992). These studies show that the bog body phenomenon first appeared in N.W. Europe in the Early Neolithic; that there was a period of activity with bodies being interred in watery graves in the later Bronze Age; but that the period from the Late Iron Age to the early Roman was particularly important in terms of the bodies recovered and dated. It is likely this partly reflects the development of many peat bogs in the later Holocene, notably the expansion of mire and blanket bogs in later prehistory (the result of climatic deterioration). But the number of Late Iron Age–Roman bodies could also reflect the amount of manual peat cutting on deposits of this age in contrast to older, less well-explored levels. In radiocarbon terms the Migration and Early Medieval periods are not well-represented. This may be due to the fact that many bogs must have had their upper layers cut away before interested antiquarians were around to record such discoveries, or museums to preserve the remains (see van der Sanden, pp. 146–65). As further bodies come to light and existing ones are investigated, the chronological background to the bog body phenomenon will improve.

Table 10   Radiocarbon determinations on other bog bodies from Western Europe

LABORATORY REFERENCE	LOCALITY	SAMPLE	MATERIAL	$\delta^{13}C$ (‰)	C14 AGE BP (± 1 SIGMA)
Britain (excluding Lindow Moss)					
OxA-2860	Methwold	2585MTW1	femur bone	−18.6	3760 ± 80
OxA-2861	Methwold	2585MTW2	femur bone	−21.8	3540 ± 80
OxA-2862	Methwold	2542MTW1	femur bone	−20.9	3580 ± 80
OxA-2863	Methwold	2542MTW2–3	femur bone	−20.7	3670 ± 80
OxA-2864	Methwold	2542MTW5	femur bone	−21.5	3650 ± 80
OxA-2865	Methwold	2542MTW7	femur bone	−20.8	3760 ± 80
OxA-2866	Methwold	2542MTW8	femur bone	−21.7	3600 ± 80
OxA-2867	Methwold	2542MTW9	femur bone	−21.5	3620 ± 80
OxA-2868	Methwold	2550MTW	femur bone	−22.1	3840 ± 80
Hv-5220	Hartlepool	—	femur bone	—	4680 ± 60
Birm-430	Quernmore	—	wooden coffin	—	1340 ± 110
Birm-474	Quernmore	—	wooden coffin	—	1300 ± 100
OxA-4286	Upware	D33835	skull bone	−20.3	1800 ± 70
OxA-4287	Burwell Fen	D33837	skull bone	−20.5	1140 ± 70
OxA-4288	Cambridgeshire Fens	D33839	skull bone	−19.9	1630 ± 70
OxA-4289	Burwell Fen	D33841	lower jaw bone	−18.8	2925 ± 80
OxA-4290	Shippea Hill	D33928, no. 1	femur bone	−20.2	3500 ± 100
OxA-4291	Shippea Hill	D33928, no. 2	femur bone	−20.2	3540 ± 85
The Netherlands					
OxA-3132	Drenthe	1981/vi-1	hair	−18.4	1870 ± 65
GrN-15458	Zweeloo	1951	skin	−21.43	1835 ± 40 ⎫ Two dates on
OxA-1722	Zweeloo	1988/iii-1	bone	(−21)	1940 ± 70 ⎭ one body
OxA-1723	Weerdingerveen	1904/vii-2a	skin	(−21)	1980 ± 70
OxA-1724	Yde	1897/vi-1	skin	(−21)	1980 ± 80
OxA-3133	Buinen	—	bone	−19.5	1990 ± 70
OxA-3131	Terhaarsterveen	1892/x-7	hair	−18.7	2025 ± 65
Ua-1500	Borger	(a), 1975	bone	−20.43	2060 ± 100
OxA-1725	Exlöermond	1914/v-1	skin	(−21)	2280 ± 75
OxA-1726	S.E. Drenthe	1962/ii-260	skin	(−21)	2300 ± 70
OxA-3917	Weerdingerveen	1992/viii-21	bone	−19.3	2940 ± 75
GrN-15459	Emmer-Erfscheiderveen	1938	assoc. wood	—	2980 ± 35
Ireland					
HAR-6909	Meenybraddan, Co. Donegal		bone	−21.5	730 ± 90
OxA-2757	Rathowen, Co. Westmeath		bone	−22.2	1295 ± 60
GrN-14758	Baronstown West, Clongownagh		skin	−24.3	1725 ± 30
GrN-153	Derrymaquirk, Co. Roscommon		bone	−21.8	2340 ± 70
HAR-6908	Gallagh, Castleblakeney		bone	−24.8	2220 ± 90 ⎫ Three dates
OxA-2923	Gallagh, Castleblakeney		bone	−20.9	2320 ± 90 ⎬ on
OxA-2756*	Gallagh, Castleblakeney		bone	−22.7	3480 ± 70 ⎭ one bone
OxA-2941	Stoneyisland, Co. Galway		bone	−21.7	5170 ± 90 ⎫
OxA-2942	Stoneyisland, Co. Galway		bone	−21.3	5270 ± 80 ⎪ Four dates on
OxA-2943	Stoneyisland, Co. Galway		bone	−20.0	5180 ± 80 ⎬ one bone
OxA-2758 *	Stoneyisland, Co. Galway		bone	−22.6	6200 ± 80 ⎭
Denmark					
K-1396	Huldremose, Randers		skin	—	1920 ± 100
K-2132	Møllemose, Hjørring		skin	—	2030 ± 100
K-2812	Haraldskær Mose, Vejle		assoc. wood	−26.8	2400 ± 80
K-503 *	Grauballe, Viborg		tissue	—	1640 ± 100 ⎫ Two dates on
K-3117	Grauballe, Viborg		tissue	—	2030 ± 55 ⎭ one body
K-2876	Elling Mose, Viborg		tissue	−24.5	2170 ± 55 ⎫ Two dates on
K-2877	Elling Mose, Viborg		assoc. skin cape	−22.2	2120 ± 55 ⎭ body and cape
K-2814A	Tollund, Viborg		tissue	−21.1	2200 ± 55 ⎫ Two dates on
K-2814B	Tollund, Viborg		tissue	−20.7	2130 ± 50 ⎭ one body
K-1395	Borremose, Ålborg 1947		tissue	—	2380 ± 100
K-2108A	Borremose, Ålborg 1948		tissue	—	2560 ± 100 ⎫ Two dates on
K-2108B	Borremose, Ålborg 1948		tissue	—	2480 ± 100 ⎭ one body
K-2813	Borremose, Ålborg 1946		tissue	−20.1	2600 ± 80

Publications: *Archaeometry* **31** (2), 20–34; *Archaeometry* **34** (1), 141–59; *Archaeometry* **36** (2), 337–74; *Antiquity* **66**, 948–55; *Kuml* 1979, 73–8; *Radiocarbon* **34** (3), 292–5.

* Dates thought to be an unreliable estimate of the age of the body. Assumed $\delta^{13}C$ are enclosed by brackets, e.g. (−21).

Two Views on Peat Stratigraphy and the Age of the Lindow Bodies

A: Peat Stratigraphy and the Age of the Lindow Bodies

P. C. Buckland

The initial study of Lindow I and II immediately introduced problems over dating. The head, Lindow I, provided a single date within the Roman period, while the several dates from Lindow II ranged from early in the Iron Age to the post-Roman period. Dates from the enclosing peat, however, were remarkably consistent in suggesting an Iron Age date for Lindow II (Gowlett *et al*; Ambers *et al*; Otlet *et al* in Stead *et al* 1986). Stead (in Stead *et al* 1986), in his overall assessment of the find, influenced by the seemingly incontrovertible palaeobotanical evidence (Barber; Oldfield *et al*, in Stead *et al* 1986), and the apparent pre-Roman Iron Age context of the few dated Danish examples (Parker Pearson 1986) was inclined towards the earlier date, centring on *c*. 300 BC. The dating problem has only been partly resolved by the larger number of additional dates (Gowlett *et al* 1989; Housley *et al*, pp. 43–6) and a date range at least for Lindow II, of 2 BC–AD 119, covering the Late Iron Age and first part of the Roman period, appears confirmed; Lindow III may belong to later in the Roman period (Housley *et al*, pp. 42–5). Figure 14 provides a summary of all the relevant dates. The reluctance to place the finds within the Roman period is at least partly the result of interpretation of the killings as either human sacrifices or official executions rather than ritualised murders (Stead, in Stead *et al* 1986). Buckland, Housley and Pyatt (1994), however, have recently drawn attention to the relative inability of archaeological paradigms to incorporate examples of aberrant behaviour fortuitously surviving in the stratigraphic record. Ritual murder outside the norms of the state, like the pseudo-masonic activities of the notorious Victorian murderer of prostitutes in London, Jack the Ripper, remains a possibility. Accepting this *caveat* would remove the apparent archaeological constraint on the dating and it becomes easier to examine the evidence at face value: the enclosing peat is demonstrably much older than the bodies and explanation has to be sought in purely taphonomic terms rather than doubting the geochronological evidence.

The stratigraphic context of Lindow II is evident from the field observations, with no question of intrusion by deliberate burial (Stead *et al* 1986, Figs 41–42). The body lies at the base of a horizon described as 'pool mud'. Barber, unaware of the other lines of evidence, was asked to assess (in Stead *et al* 1986) the potential maximum rate of burial of the body by peat growth. The fossil insect faunas from both bodies, however, provide unimpeachable evidence for immediate covering of the victims (Girling; Skidmore, in Stead *et al* 1986; Dinnin and Skidmore, pp. 31–8), excluding all aerobic decay processes. If later events have led to the dissociation of the bodies from their primary context on the surface of the bog, the forensic entomological evidence, particularly that of Diptera, would remain evident on, and in, the bodies.

One process whereby the corpses might be divorced

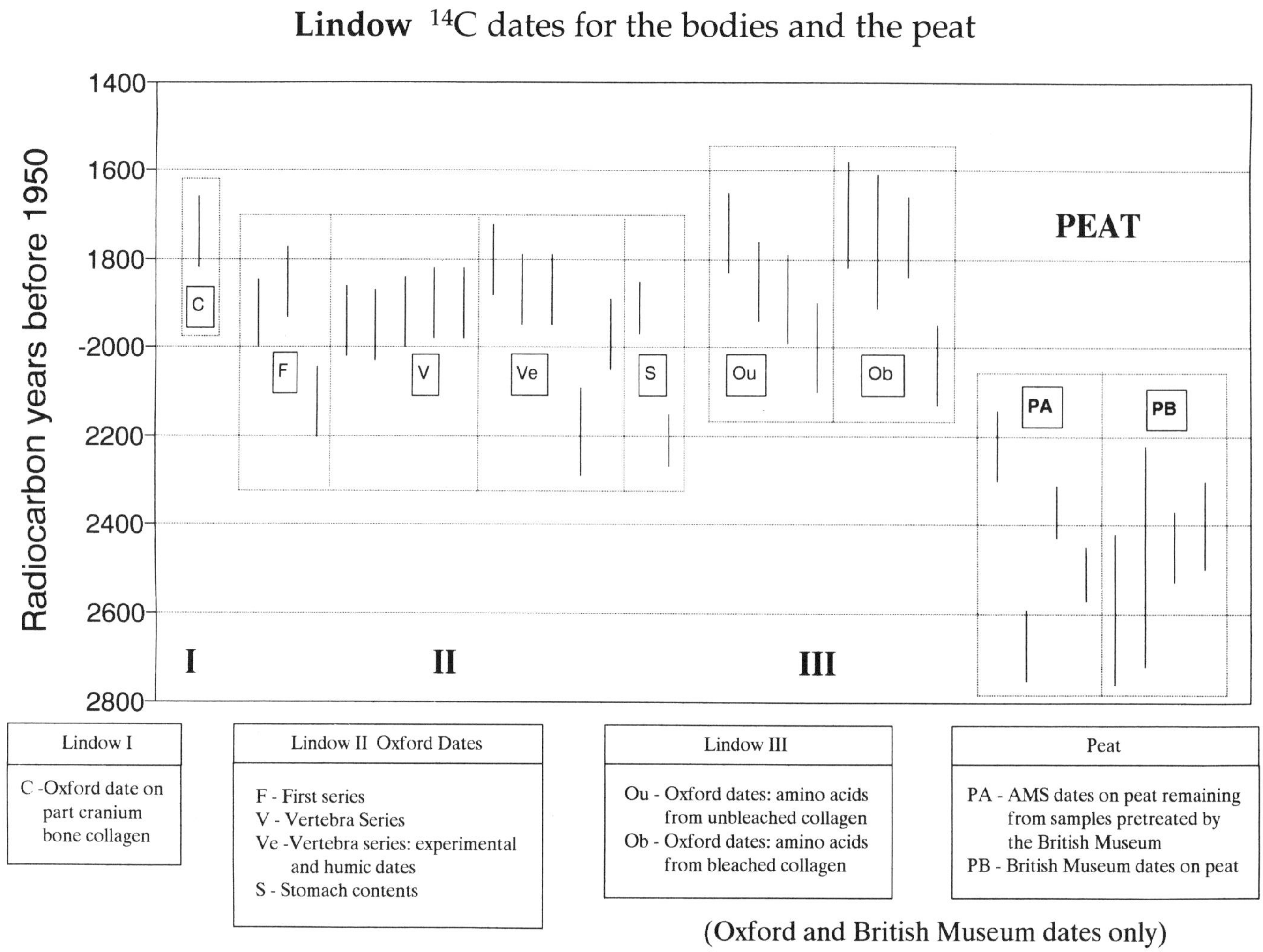

Lindow ^{14}C dates for the bodies and the peat

Fig. 14 Diagrammatic representation of the Lindow radiocarbon dates. (*P. C. Buckland*)

from their primary context and which might be difficult to recognise in the attenuated stratigraphy of a largely drained peatland, is that of bog burst. In 1535–7, Leland described the catastrophic collapse of part of Chat Moss: 'For Chateley Mosse that with breking up of abundance of water yn hit did much hurt to landes therabout, and rivers with wandering moss and currupte water.' (quoted in Gorham 1953)

Chat Moss lies some 18 km north-west of Lindow and was similarly a lowland raised mire. The scale of destruction is better indicated in a 1771 account of a similar event on Solway Moss, Cumbria:

The enormous mass of fluid substance moved slowly on, spreading itself more and more as it got possession of the plain. Some of the inhabitants,

through the terror of the night, could plainly discover it advancing like a moving hill . . . . One house after another, it spread around – filled and crushed into ruin; just giving time for the terrified inhabitants to escape. Scarce anything was saved, except their lives: nothing of their furniture: few of their cattle. (Gilpin, quoted in McIntire 1940)

The inundation eventually covered over 200 hectares (500 acres) of farmland to depths in excess of 12 m (op. cit.). In blanket bog on slopes, such events, caused by heavy rain, may lead to the translocation of entire areas of peat, but in lowland raised mire bursts must relate to the collapse of the water-saturated dome. Such structures no longer survive in lowland England but nineteenth-century accounts of Thorne Moors in South Yorkshire speak of the central dome of the raised mire expanding annually in winter to obscure the view of Crowle church from Thorne, across the otherwise flat terrain of the Humberhead Levels (Parsons 1877). Whether catastrophic collapse takes place under wholly natural conditions is debatable. The description of Solway Moss as being retained by a 'peat wall' (McIntire 1940) suggests that inadvertent peat cutting, without suitable provision for drainage of the core, may have led to the disaster. Such events seem likely to have resulted in large scale disruption of peat stratigraphy and its is improbable that the problems with the Lindow Moss dates can be explained in this way.

Explanation must therefore rely upon a re-examination of the nature of peat accumulation and the relationships between hummocks and pools on the bog. The lack of evidence for insect degradation of the corpses indicates that both were immediately submerged. Whilst the surface of any 'pool' between hummocks may have open water, beneath it may lie a considerable depth of organic mud, with varying degrees of plant macrofossil preservation and containing a fossil insect fauna indicative of both acid water and limnic mud, as well as those taxa associated with the adjoining hummocks and some adventitious individuals (see Dinnin and Skidmore, pp. 35–6).

Interpretation hinges upon the age and relative permanence of pools on raised mires and this has been the subject of much debate (Foster and Wright 1990). The prevailing orthodoxy of shallow pools and hummocks replacing each other as the bog grows upwards (cf. Moore and Bellamy 1973), propounded by Osvald (1923) was supported by most ecologists, but, in a stratigraphic test of this regenerative complex theory, Walker and Walker (1961) failed to find support for the model. Although hummocks did occasionally rise from the sites of pools, autonomous degeneration of hummocks did not appear to occur. In a more extended study, Barber (1981) related changing pool and hummock patterns to climate, although allowing for some autogenic factors in bog growth. Accepting that Lindow II had been placed in a pool, he (Barber 1986) in his interpretation of the plant macrofossils, particularly the bryophytes, suggested that the body would have become covered by unconsolidated *Sphagnum* mats at the rate of about 30 mm per year. In most circumstances, however, a corpse rapidly acquires a characteristic fauna of decay, an aspect widely researched in forensic entomology (cf. Smith 1986); it has to be emphasised again that the total submergence in anaerobic conditions of both bodies was immediate after death. In

such circumstances, the question remains whether the discrepancy in ages between bodies and peat are merely a reflection of the age of the pool.

Barber (1994), whilst recognising that some large pools may have extended lives, has shown that many smaller examples are short-lived. Moore (1977) found that the larger pools on Claish Moss in Argyll may have lasted for about 5000 years and, in a more detailed radiocarbon-dated study, Foster and Wright (1990) have shown that the pools on Hammarmossen and Nittenmossen, in central Sweden, are permanent features of the bogs' development, originating shortly after mire initiation and persisting for several thousand years. By their very nature, large pools are areas of low productivity and low accumulation, relative to adjacent hummocks and *Sphagnum* lawns (cf. Clymo 1991), and work by Johnson and Dammen (1991), examining experimentally the processes of decay of *Sphagnum*, indicates that *S. cuspidatum*, associated with pools, breaks down more rapidly than *S. fuscum* on the hummocks. Moore (1991), in reviewing this research, also notes that the hummock-forming *S. magellanicum* also appeared more resistant to decay. Differential rates of accumulation and decay therefore provide mechanisms whereby the smaller pools, once initiated, may last for extended periods, varying in size in response to climatic and hydrological factors, until finally overgrown by lawns and hummocks. At Lindow, *S. cuspidatum* occurs in the pool peat surrounding Lindow II, but the remainder, like much of the lowland Holocene peat record in Britain, is dominated by *S. imbricatum*, now virtually extinct outside the uplands (Dickson 1973; Stoneman *et al* 1993).

Lowland bogs may differ from those in the wetter, cooler uplands. Lindsay and others' (1988) map of pool forms on bogs does suggest that the more southerly mires are characterised by smaller, perhaps more ephemeral pools, yet England has no extant lowland raised mires and the sample is, of necessity, small and western. Cartographic evidence implies a degree of permanence on at least one site analogous to Lindow, if the place-name itself, *Llyn Ddu*, the black pool, does not necessarily imply a distinctive feature of the bog. The 1853–4 Ordnance Survey map of Thorne Moors in South Yorkshire shows over one hundred pools of varying size remaining on the already partly drained bog. The first published reference to them appears in Casson's (1829) description of Thorne and the last seems to have been drained in the 1960s (Limbert 1987). A description by Hatfield (1866) could apply equally to an undrained Lindow:

The pits on Thorne Moors. ... were deemed by the superstitious to be bottomless. They are certainly most treacherous, for the Sphagnum has so encompassed the margin that, unless the mass of moss and other fibrous vegetation have accumulated to a considerable thickness, extending partly across the water and, in several instances, entirely over it.

The permanence and former size of these pools is further evidenced in a manuscript account of *c.* 1745 by George Stovin:

Blackwater: now called wild Pitts. – there is many of them upon these moors of an oval form for the most part. about 14 yards Deep, and always full to the Top. in dry or wet seasons and never overflow. the water Black. Some of y^m 100 yards about.

Without drainage, the Thorne pools could well have continued far beyond their 215 years of recorded existence. The deep pools at Thorne perhaps have more in common with those of the Baltic bogs studied by Foster and Wright (1990), a connection recently made on invertebrate grounds by Eversham, Skidmore and Buckland (1995), than with upland Britain, but their permanence is relevant to Lindow, where shallower pools, largely infilled with thixotropic organic mud, provide the context for at least Lindow II. Limnic mud, accumulating in the base of the pools, would maintain its stratigraphic integrity. The intrusion of a large body, however, could easily lead to extensive disturbance. In one of the few areas of uncut bog remaining on Shetland, sheep occasionally become enmired in such pools and sink rapidly into the mud, leaving only the end of a mandible or hoof protruding (Fig. 15).

Fig. 15 The context of the Lindow bodies? Remains of a sheep enmired in the limnic mud of a peat pool, Heogel of the Moor, North Mainland, Shetland.

In cold weather in particular, a human body deliberately pushed down into such a 'pool' would be unlikely to break the surface again, as the processes of decay, which would normally liberate gases to buoy up the corpse, would be inhibited by the low temperatures. At Lindow, the internal consistency of each set of radiocarbon dates can be explained *only* if the basal deposits of the 'eyes' in the bog, into which the victims were pushed, were at least three hundred years older than the event. Later compaction, when the limnic mud would be compressed to less or an equal thickness to the adjoining peat, would obscure all traces of the deed.

B: Peat Stratigraphy and the Lindow Bog Body: a Reconsideration of the Evidence

K. E. Barber

Studies of peat stratigraphy and macrofossil analysis have advanced materially in recent years, but there are still a number of misconceptions abroad which I have done my best to correct (Barber 1994). I consider that the arguments put forward in the present volume by Buckland are unsatisfactory in the face of the field stratigraphic and macrofossil evidence from Lindow Moss. The purpose of this note is to reiterate and emphasise this evidence and to put forward a more parsimonious explanation of the state and date of the body which is in accord with the 1986 evidence.

At the time of writing the 1986 report (Barber 1986) I

was unaware of the insect evidence for the rapid entombment of the body, and the controversy over the different radiocarbon dates, on the body and on the peat, seemed capable of resolution with more work. Asked by the first editor, Ian Stead, to estimate how quickly the body could have been covered by growing *Sphagnum* moss, I quoted the kind of maximum growth rate commonly reported in the bryological literature of some 3 cm per year. Clearly this would have been inadequate to prevent the development of a rich invertebrate fauna on the corpse.

There is no doubt from the stratigraphic drawing in Stead *et al* (1986, Fig. 41) that the pool peat recorded is of a type and depth which are commonly seen in the lowland raised bogs of Britain and Ireland. Though they may be laterally extensive, these are shallow features in the peat, generally of some 5–10 cm depth, representing original water depths of about 10–20 cm. *Sphagnum cuspidatum* is the main coloniser of such pools and does not colonise deep pools (Boatman 1983) and the peat formed over the last 2500 years has not been subject to much compaction to judge by bulk density measurements. The pools may be of open water in winter and after rain, but by late summer they are often full of the more hygrophilous bog-mosses. The pool peats that result are composed of the remains of *Sphagnum cuspidatum* and less often *S. auriculatum* (= *S. Subsecunda* in Barber 1986), usually coated with the remains of algae. Laid down in the shallow pool at the end of each growing season in felted layers they form a very distinct type of peat. This was the field evidence recorded by Richardson and Yates, as reported in Oldfield *et al* (1986) and evident in the two monoliths which I sampled for vegetative macrofossils.

Some confusion may have arisen by the use of the term 'pool mud' to describe the pool peat in Fig. 41, but there is in fact no distinct algal mud layer (Barber 1986, 89) which would indicate a deeper, more long-lived pool. Such habitats do exist on British bogs, particularly in the north and west of the country (Boatman 1983; Moore 1977) but they are less common in lowland bogs. Where they have existed, algal pool muds of 1–2 cm thickness and more are typical and broad shallow pools may display such yellow-green muds in their central parts (Barber 1981, 84–105). At Lindow, however, the evidence of the Cladocera and the Chironomidae also points to a shallow pool (Dayton 1986), and there is therefore no justification for the arguments concerning deep pools advanced by Buckland (pp. 49–50).

Macrofossil analyses (Barber 1986, Fig. 44) completely bear out the field interpretation and the samples are archived in the collection of the Palaeoecology Laboratory at Southampton. Below the level of the pool the peat is dominated by *Sphagnum imbricatum*, the major peat former of the Late Holocene (Stoneman *et al* 1993; Barber *et al* 1994) which has, in the past, inhabited a wide niche with respect to water level. At Lindow, to judge from the associated assemblage of cotton sedge and lesser amounts of heather and cranberry, and the relatively low humification, it was growing in a lawn community and the surface of the bog was only slightly undulating. A small hummock developed from this surface and the pool superseded this with no evidence at all of any hiatus – this is common in lowland English bogs (Barber 1981; Smith 1985; Wimble 1986) – and the only slightly humified peat of the pool is succeeded by the sort of infill sequence common in many other bog profiles.

Buckland's discussion of bog bursts, the now falsified cyclic regeneration theory of Osvald (Barber 1981; Backeus 1991), and the age and longevity of raised bog pools is misconceived and does not relate directly to the actual evidence at Lindow. There is no evidence of bog bursts at Lindow Moss and I have recently dealt with the other matters elsewhere (Barber 1994) and will not rehearse the detail here. To reiterate therefore, the clear evidence from Lindow Moss is for a shallow pool stretching right across the peat section and forming in response to the effect of climatic deterioration on an ombrotrophic (rain-fed) bog, in accord with the Phasic Theory (Barber 1981).

How then can the dates for body and peat, and the state of decay of the corpse, be reconciled, given the shallowness of the pool? The simplest explanation is surely that the body was inserted into the upper layers of the bog. The felted pool peat could easily have been cut into and rolled back like a carpet, the mat of bog moss interlaced with cotton sedge roots and shoots being quite coherent – one can do this today on intact bogs. The body could then be laid on the exposed surface and the upper peat rolled back over it. This would create minimal disturbance to the stratigraphy and its contained biota and be exceptionally difficult to detect, even if the excavators were expecting and looking for it. Indeed, after 1500 or more years of further peat accumulation and the recent draining of the bog, it would in my opinion (and experience of working on disturbed peat sections) be impossible to detect.

The Human Remains from Lindow Moss 1987–8

D. Brothwell   J. B. Bourke

Following the publication and exhibition at the British Museum of human remains from Lindow Moss in 1986, there was only a short time gap before further specimens began to appear in February 1987 (Turner, pp. 10–18). Two major groups of human remains were found. The first consisted of about 70 pieces of soft tissue and bone recovered from already excavated peat, from a location about 50 m north of the presumed findspot of the Lindow Woman (now referred to as Lindow I). These were recovered during February and March 1987. The second group consisted of part of the buttocks, the skin of a leg and some associated skeletal material recovered on two other occasions, in June and September 1988, at a point about 15 m west of the findspot of Lindow Man (now referred to as Lindow II). These additional groups are referred to as Lindow III and Lindow IV respectively.

Taphonomic Aspects

The material was received in the British Museum Conservation Department in a moist condition. However, in the case of both groups of material, the human remains were likely to have been excavated and stacked in peat on more than one occasion before being loaded into railway trucks and on to the peat company's elevator where most were ultimately recovered. This peat processing had led to some drying and had probably initiated a second phase of decomposition.

Thus, while the larger pieces of leg (Lindow IV) were comparable in preservation to the Lindow II body, the smaller jaggedly torn pieces were very dark, very soft and

exhibited what might be described as a 'seaweed' texture (Figs 16–24). Given the location of the finds, the similarity in preservation and the complementary nature of the anatomy, Lindow IV is considered to be part of Lindow II, and is referred to as the latter throughout this chapter.

Fig. 16 Low-magnification view of part of a distal phalange from the Lindow I/III body, displaying variable preservation.

Because the varying degrees of preservation of the soft tissue were clearly influenced by environmental conditions following accidental exposure, such features could not be used as a clue to how many individuals might be represented by the remains. It should also be noted that the condition of the bone fragments, either partly contained within soft tissue or separated accidentally by the peat cutting and subsequent hand sorting, varied from dark, soft, crushed pieces hardly recognisable in morphological terms, to largely intact pieces. In the case of the distal and proximal femur fragments from Lindow II, bone size and shape appear to be quite unaltered.

Softening of the bones due to decalcification was not the only factor causing at times their collapse. While, at a macroscopic level, the bone surfaces could appear to be in perfect condition, microscopically there could be evidence of considerable damage. Figures 16 and 17 show two views of a distal hand phalanx from body III. The low-magnification view displays some intact areas of periosteum, but also zones of fragmentation with deep cavities. There is, therefore, not only decalcification of the bone, but also subsequent localised decay of the collagen infrastructure. This same kind of decay was also present on some exposed bones and teeth in Lindow II.

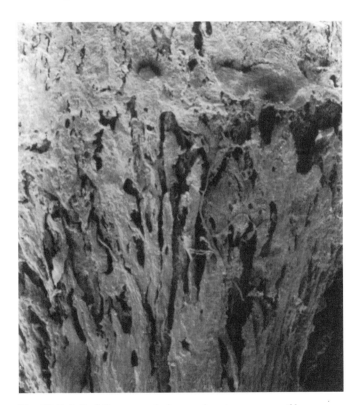

Fig. 17 Detail of the same phalange, showing an area of bone surface disintegration (× 170 approx.).

Soft Tissue Remains

About seventy separate pieces of human body were brought to the British Museum Conservation Department for study during 1988 and later. In fact, as these samples were cleaned and investigated, they separated into a larger number of separate pieces. All the material was noted and given separate registration codes for archival purposes. As in the case of the previous Lindow finds, these were stored wet at a low, but not tissue-freezing, temperature. Preservation in the Lindow bog, with its anaerobic, anti-microbial environment, contributed to by tannins, sphagnan and other factors, would appear to have resulted in the survival of soft tissues especially near the body surface. The internal organs were generally not identified, except for restricted areas of intestinal tract. Limited amounts of muscle remained, for instance in relation to a series of vertebrae. Although the epidermis appears to be generally missing, areas of palm and sole prints could still be discerned on one or two fragments.

The identification of a number of the fragments to regions of the body was problematic. The association of fragments of bone enabled positioning in some cases. Identification of fingers, knee, scrotal region and heel, provided the kinds of detail which helped to gradually piece together at least one substantial body (Fig. 18). Unfortunately, although quite a few pieces could be positioned tentatively into limbs and trunk, good links between torn surfaces of tissue were very few indeed.

Skeletal parts, often crushed and incomplete, which were associated with soft tissue and assisted in identification, included the right iliac blade; part of the left side of the sacrum; part of the left ischio-pubic region; the very distal ends of the right tibia and fibula (in association with the talus); fragments of left tibia, calcaneum and talus; crushed mid-shafts of both forearms; a crushed left humerus shaft; a very incomplete right knee (tibia, fibula and soft tissue); and parts of the left tibia and fibula shafts with soft tissue. Added to this list are the bones described in more detail separately. In the case of the well-preserved proximal and distal ends of a femur and associated soft tissue from thigh and buttocks, this was clearly indicative of a separate body, very probably Lindow II (Fig. 18). Before considering the number of bodies represented by all these pieces, a number of larger soft-tissue fragments and better preserved bones might be listed, in particular:

1 The probable second, third, fourth and fifth thoracic vertebrae. The second and third are in correct alignment

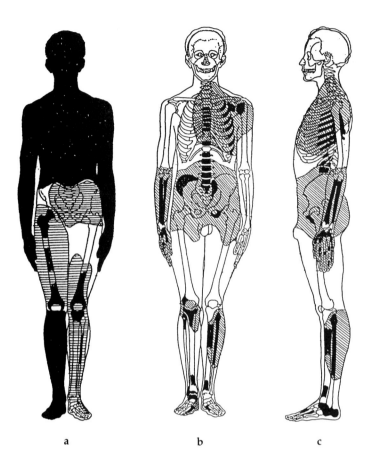

Fig. 18 Tentative positioning in body diagrams of the human remains from Lindow Moss.
a) Outline in black of the known parts of Lindow II, together with the new finds, Lindow IV, which may belong to the body. The bones are in solid black and the soft tissue is hatched.
b) and c) Front and side views of the bones (black) and the soft tissue (hatched) tentatively identified as belonging to Lindow I/III. Note in the side view, the forearm and hand are as of the right side.

but the fourth is displaced. The fifth aligns approximately with the fourth. The cause of this misalignment was unclear at first but delineation by radiology indicated post-mortem damage. There is a compressed anterior and posterior thoracic cavity which did not contain intra-thoracic contents. The lower part, folded back upon itself, was eventually straightened out and further investigated, following radiography.

2 A large mass of tissue comprising five lumbar vertebrae and some associated soft tissue, with skin overlying it. Radiological examination was undertaken.

3 A large piece of skin with part of the pelvis attached to it; this was shown to be the right anterior superior iliac crest. Transillumination shows some patterning of the skin which required opening out and photographing in the appropriate manner, in order to look for impressions of ribs, etc.

4 A considerable mass of tissue, when examined, showed the lower part of the oesophagus, the stomach, the first part of the duodenum, the greater omentum and part of the transverse colon. The distal antrum and the first part of the duodenum contained a certain amount of luminal content which was recovered for further analysis. There was also some colonic content adhering to the transverse colon.

Three other pieces of colon with adherent faeces were also present (Fig. 19); it is uncertain which part of the colon these pieces come from. Some residual 'slurry' was also retained.

5 A substantial amount of the skin of the right hand, comprising the palmar and dorsal aspects of the hand; the main palm prints were visible. No digits are present and much of the soft tissues have been lost as well as the bones (Fig. 20).

6 A talus and the skin of a heel (side not obvious), with some dermatoglyphic ridging still discernible on this dermal fragment (Fig. 21).

7 Five finger nails, being separately identified as pieces of tissue, were cleaned for identification. It was significant that, as in the case of Lindow II, close examination of

Fig. 19 Specimen FC. Lindow I/III. Fragments of colon, with lumpy faecal material visible.

Fig. 20 Specimen BQ. Lindow I/III. Two views of a very damaged hand, before and after cleaning.

Fig. 21 Specimen EB. Lindow I/III. Soft tissue in the region of a heel, with associated bones.

Fig. 22 Specimen DG. Lindow I/III. Damaged foot with some evidence of the base of the toes.

one of them revealed a neatly cut and rounded nail end, with no evidence of deep scratching to the nail surface. This provides evidence from the hands that the two Lindow individuals were unlikely to have been involved in rough manual labour to the extent that it would have left evidence in the condition of the nails.

The isolated bones

Of the better-preserved bone fragments and whole bones available for study, 25 are listed here for particular comment.

1 Parts of two vertebrae (LW/GE and LW/CS) from the lower thoracic region. In both cases, there is a deep horizontal groove on the abdominal aspect of the vertebral bodies. This was first suspected of being evidence of crush fracturing in life, but on later consideration of X-ray and surface evidence, it was concluded that the damage was related to stresses and collapse sustained during peat cutting. However, it is suggested that the 'sharp' margins of the centrum in one, and very early osteophyte development in the other, argue for an age of the individual of probably more than 35 years.

2 A flattened fragment of bone representing the inferior angle of the scapula blade (LW/EN). The blade is quite thick and robustly made, suggesting maleness.

3 Probably six right carpal bones, a hamate, capitate, trapezoid, trapezium, scaphoid and triquetral. The latter could in fact be a damaged proximal metatarsal. All the joint surfaces are normal. The bones may well belong to the same right hand.

4 A complete first metacarpal (thumb) of the right hand. The proximal and distal joints are normal. Metacarpal length, as defined by Von Bonin (1931) was 49.4 mm. Applying the stature regression formulae provided by Musgrave and Harneja (1978) for metacarpal lengths, a very tentative stature estimate of 178.5 cm is obtained.

In the case of right metacarpal five, the joints are again normal. Applying the appropriate stature regression formula to the length of 55.5 mm gives an estimated stature of 174.9 cm. Considering both of these stature estimates as tentative figures, an average would be 176.7 cm (with the error of this estimate being perhaps of the order of 4 cm). This individual (Lindow I/III) was therefore probably taller than Lindow II.

Parts of two other metacarpals were present. In the case of the right second, only the proximal and distal

ends remain (joint surfaces normal). In the case of metacarpal four, the proximal half is present but damaged.

5 There are five hand phalangeal fragments of normal appearance. One is a proximal II, one a piece of proximal III, a whole middle phalanx of IV, the proximal part of mid-phalanx V and proximal phalanx V.

6 Of special note are two very small, but mature hand phalanges, which represent either a congenitally deformed digit or a very small supernumerary digit. The middle phalanx is like a thick button, no more than 5.4 mm in length and 7.5 mm in maximum width. The distal phalanx is nearly equally diminutive, being 9 mm in length and 8.5 mm in maximum width. Whether these represent a deformed finger in a five-digit hand, or an extra reduced digit, the individual clearly displayed a noticeable congenital deformity (Figs 23 and 24).

In considering the nature of the deformity indicated by the two minute finger bones, two alternative congenital conditions need initial consideration. Firstly, it is reasonable to ask if the two bones represent a localised brachydactyly, restricted to the thumb? This seems less likely, as conditions such as 'stub thumb' result in shorter but usually much broader bones, whereas the Lindow phalanges are very small in all dimensions.

The most likely explanation is that the bones represent an example of pre-axial polydactyly associated with the thumb. In life, these minor congenital conditions can be fairly concealed or noticeably bifid, depending on the size of bones in the extra digit and the degree of separation from the normal part of the hand. Figure 24 shows in diagrammatic reconstruction the most likely form the Lindow anomaly would have

cm

Fig. 23 Evidence of polydactyly in Lindow I/III. Two small extra phalanges.

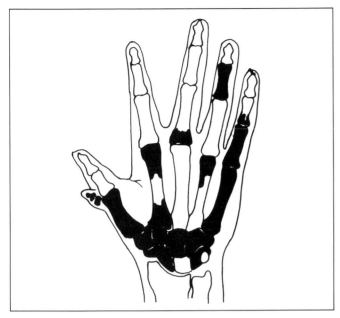

Fig. 24 Identifiable right hand bones of Lindow I/III, in semi-schematic outline. Bones present are in black, including the tentative positioning of the congenital abnormalities of the thumb.

taken. It is interesting to note that polydactyly of some form is relatively common in human communities, although probably displaying regional variation in incidence, from 0.16% in Europeans to 1.7% in an African sample.

7 Parts of three metatarsals (2L, 1R) appear to have been separated from soft tissue. The first metatarsal (big toe) is a robust bone of 62 mm in length and 20.7 mm distal articular width. The joint surfaces are normal. There is a fairly large mid-shaft nutrient foramen.

8 The only other bone worthy of comment is the right femur, associated with the thigh of possibly Lindow II (LX/AJ). All the previously noted bones are likely to be associated with Lindow I/III or both numbers separately. The well-preserved parts of the femur consist of the proximal and distal thirds, the mid-shaft area having been crushed. The proximal end is free of tissue except in the region of the quadratus femoris insertion. There is a shallow concavity in the region which can display Allen's fossa. The maximum width of the femoral head is 46.1 mm. The distal end is free of soft tissue, except for limited areas of cartilage on the articular surfaces. The bicondylar breadth is 83.5 mm. Neither proximal nor distal articular surfaces display any osteoarthritis changes. However, on the lateral condyle, there are shallow depressions covering an area about 13 mm in diameter and extending into the bone.

This anomaly does not appear to be post-mortem damage, in which case it may be an early stage of osteochondritis dissecans (indicating earlier joint trauma).

Unusual Bone Erosion

An unexpected finding, as a result of X-raying the bones of the hand of Lindow III and part of the newly discovered femur of possibly Lindow II, was an unusual form of erosion. In the case of the carpals, metacarpals and phalanges, the radiographs (Fig. 25) revealed what looked like punched-out lesions. In some bones, there was a single zone of rounded bone loss and in others, multiple rounded zones of loss. In the case of the femur (Fig. 26), rounded zones of rarefaction were not so clear but nevertheless did extend from the damaged shaft towards the distal articular surface of the bone.

Had this kind of bone loss been present in a living Lindow individual, some form of multiple destructive tumours within the bone would have been a possible explanation. However, in view of other post-mortem decay and erosions occurring in the bog specimens, there is little doubt that the holes are post-mortem too, and represent interesting pseudopathology.

The Question of Numbers of People

The material which has been studied since 1987 has presented us with some formidable problems of identification. What emerged from a detailed consideration of every fragment and an attempt to piece together as much as possible, is that there are parts of at least two individuals (Fig. 18). These may be considered as follows:

1 Parts of the thighs, buttocks and left lower leg, in a better state of preservation than the majority of other pieces. These specimens (LX/AD, LX/AJ and LX/AA) represent areas of the body which are not duplicated in Lindow II. The associated pieces of femur are from an adult, well-built male, and it thus seems likely that these pieces also belong to Lindow II.

2 The remaining fragments can be placed in various parts of another body without overlap, although there is no certainty that only one other body is represented. Fragments can be associated with both legs and arms, much of the trunk – including segments of the vertebral column, the soft tissue extending as far as the neck. But there is no clear evidence of the head. Parts of the scrotal area would indicate that the individual was a male.

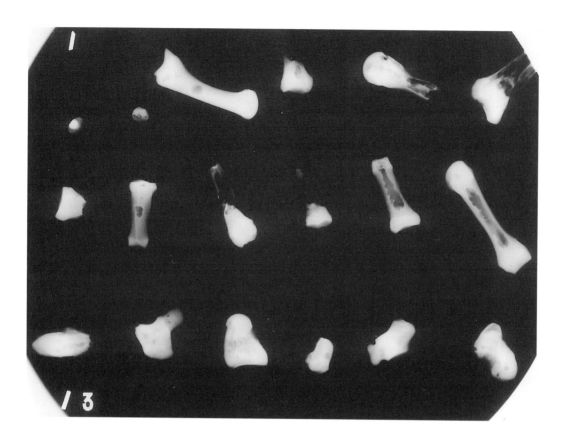

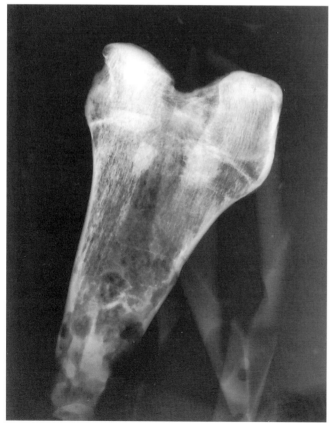

Fig. 25 Radiographic detail of the hand bones of Lindow I/III, revealing unusual erosions.

Fig. 26 X-ray of the distal right femur of Lindow II, displaying some 'globular' erosion. (*Courtesy of Janet Lang, British Museum Radiography Unit.*)

The question now arises as to whether this second body is associated with the head of Lindow I? There is certainly compatibility as regards body parts, but the sex of Lindow I was originally considered to be female (Brothwell 1986). Sexing an incomplete skull is not easy, however, and it could be that what remained of the cranium was not markedly masculine. Until other techniques are devised to check this sexing further, there will remain this uncertainty as to whether there is now evidence for at least Lindow I, II and III, or whether the new evidence merely consolidates Lindow I and II. Because of the remaining uncertainty, we have described the new remains as Lindow I/III and II.

ADDENDUM: Extracting DNA from Lindow Man's Gut Contents. Modern Technology Looking for Answers from Ancient Tissues

M. Spigelman   C. R. Fricker   E. J. Fricker

The recent development of the polymerase chain reaction (PCR) by Mullis and Faloona (1987), may be the major technical advance in molecular genetics of the past decade. Its importance lies in the ability to amplify traces of DNA, either fragmented or intact, by a simple technique. By its use we can amplify in a few hours over a million copies of a piece of DNA of 50–2000 or more base pairs. In theory a single target molecule in a complex mixture of DNA and other substances can be amplified and analysed. The important reagents are two single-strand oligonucleotides (primers) synthesised to be complementary to known sequences of the DNA of the organism being sought. Figures 27, 28 and 29 show the sequence of the PCR reaction.

Ancient microbial DNA was first successfully extracted from bones afflicted with *Mycobacterium tuberculosis* by Spigelman and Lemma (1993), finding ancient DNA in bones from Europe, Turkey and pre-European-contact Borneo. More recently, Salo *et al* (1994) have again repeated the experiment using identical primers, only this

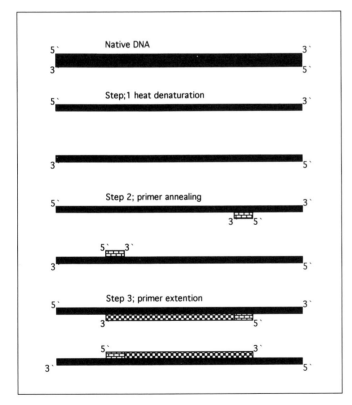

Fig. 27 First cycle of the polymerase chain reaction. The polymerase chain reaction takes place in the same tube in three steps formed by one external variable, i.e. the temperature. Step 1 involves the highest temperature in the reaction and melts the double-stranded DNA into single strands. In Step 2 the temperature is lowered and the two oppositely directed oligonucleotide primers anneal to complementary sequences on the target DNA, which acts as a template. Step 3 takes place also at lower temperature and the primers are extended from the 5' to 3' direction in the presence of Taq DNA polymerase. (*By kind permission of John Wiley & Sons Ltd.*)

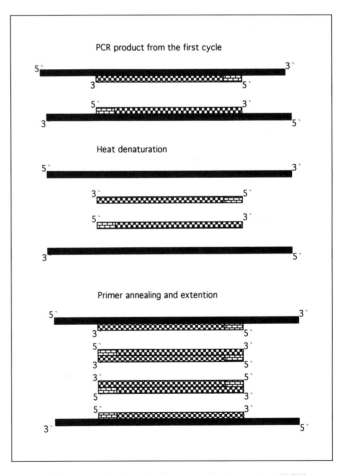

Fig. 28 The accumulation of polymerase chain reaction (PCR) products. The exponential increase of the PCR products is 2^n, where n is the number of cycles. During the first and the second cycles the DNA increase is as shown, from two chains to four chains. More than a million copies will be produced in 20 cycles. (*By kind permission of John Wiley & Sons Ltd.*)

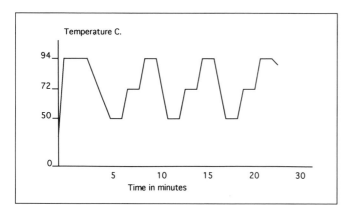

Fig. 29 Temperature profile. A typical temperature profile of the polymerase chain reaction (PCR) at 94 °C (denaturing), 50 °C (annealing) and 72 °C (extension) temperatures. Usually the first denaturing step is done for a longer period (5 min) compared to the subsequent steps (2 min). At the end the PCR cycles the annealing temperature is held for a further period (5 min) to complete the reaction. (*By kind permission of John Wiley & Sons Ltd.*)

time extracting the DNA from the lung tissue of a Peruvian mummy about 1000 years old. *Mycobacterium tuberculosis* was chosen because it leaves morphologically identifiable lesions, as well as having a thick protective wall thus increasing the chances of its ancient DNA surviving. *M. leprae* was the next target organism for the same reasons and *M. leprae* DNA has been successfully isolated from a bone from AD 600 (Rafi *et al* 1994).

With the success of these experiments, we become convinced that other containers could well exist that would preserve ancient DNA in a similar manner. Palaeofaeces were considered a likely prospect and a joint project between scientists working at Thames Water Plc and the Institute of Archaeology, University College, London, was commenced to try and extract ancient bacterial DNA from samples of palaeofaeces. Our aim was to develop a technique, by which any sample suspected of being faecal could have tests run to determine its veracity. A number of tests exist which can help identify faecal material, but until now none has been scientifically specific.

The hypothesis for our experiment is that the most common bacterium in all mammalian faeces is *Escherichia coli* and should a specimen have this, its faecal origin is proven. Furthermore, the mammalian gastro-intestinal tract sheds its mucosal cells on a weekly basis, and thus if human DNA can also be found in this tissue, then it may well be described as human faeces; particularly if it were excavated in a context which raised this possibility. In bog bodies or mummies, gut contents can often be extracted, and thus can be attributed with certainty, so this type of specimen appeared ideal to test our theory.

There is, at times, controversy in establishing faecal and human origin to a coprolite specimen. A number of tests exist, e.g. reconstitution with trisodium phosphate, and the smell and colour associated with this. The appearance of the specimen in animal and human stools has distinct morphological differences (Holden (*b*) 1990, pp. 9–12). The presence of faecal alkaline phosphatase is limited to specimens in which the enzyme is not deactivated. In the case of coprostenol, a heat-stable sterol found in the faeces of mammals and some birds, thin layer chromatography has been used to identify it in faeces (Hoskins and Bandler 1987). This method has recently been used to confirm the faecal origin of suspected coprolitic material (Wales and Evans forthcoming). Also, the presence of the eggs of *Trichuris* and/or *Ascaris* in heavy concentrations is regarded as suggestive of human palaeofaeces. Indeed, Jones (1983) excavated a stool from an Anglo-Scandinavian layer at York and found concentrations of up to 88,000 eggs per gram of both organisms. All these tests are not fully specific, and all require further confirmation for certainty of diagnosis. That DNA persists in faeces has been shown by experiments on the excrement of brown bears where Hoss *et al* (1992) have identified the species DNA and dietary plant DNA.

Our initial experiment has concentrated on the extraction and identification of *E. coli* DNA from the gut content of Lindow Man (as internally the stomach and upper small intestine were well preserved. The gut contents of Lindow II has been analysed by Holden (1986) and Scaife (1986). We feel that post-mortem migration would have allowed the small intestine contents to be colonised by *E. coli* from the colon. Ostinga (1993) raised the possibility that DNA is destroyed by the acidic conditions in bogs. We feel that whilst PCR technology is, in theory, exquisitely sensitive and specific, many problems arise when this method is used to detect DNA in environmental samples. Similarly, detection of DNA in faecal material is difficult because of inhibitors present in the sample, which include humic acid and several types of metal ions. Consequently there is much research needed on the development of methods to overcome these problems.

Early experiments involved attempts to detect *E. coli* DNA from freshly voided stools. We used a primer set which amplifies a 154 base pair region of the *uid* A gene from *E. coli* and a further set which amplifies a 264 base pair region of the 1*ac* Z gene. The *uid* A gene is common to virtually all *E. coli* strains (Fricker and Fricker 1994) while the 1*ac* Z gene, which is present in most *E. coli* strains, is also present in most strains of the *Enterobacteriaceae*. Using these two primer sets we have shown that *E. coli* can be accurately identified. All such attempts to use PCR directly on these samples were unsuccessful and only when *E. coli* was added at a concentration of 10^5 per ml were we able to detect the presence of *E. coli* specific DNA. This result was not surprising and we therefore studied the literature to identify possible methods to 'purify' the DNA prior to testing by PCR. Some of the most widely used methods for environmental samples include the use of gel filtration which separates molecules on the basis of molecular size. Whilst this method is useful for the detection of intact nucleic acid where the size of the genome is known, it cannot be used for the detection of 'ancient DNA' which may be fragmented into pieces of variable size. Our efforts to identify a suitable method for sample preparation prior to PCR were therefore concentrated on methods that were not based on molecular size.

A method based on the purification of DNA using guanidinium isothiocyanate and adsorption of the DNA on to silica particles as described by Hoss and Paabo (1993) was used in the first instance. However, with this method we were unable to amplify DNA from *E. coli*. This method was an adaptation of that of Boom *et al.* (1990) which was used successfully by Spigelman and Lemma (1993). We thus resorted to this method with only minor modifications, and were able to amplify DNA successfully from *E. coli*. The bands obtained on gel electrophoresis were extremely faint and barely visible to the naked eye. However, after double amplification, using the same primer set, the bands were clearly visible.

The implications of our studies are that DNA can at times be identified in bog remains. Developing a technology to isolate ancient DNA from these remains may give us an insight into ancient diseases, particularly the many diarrhoeal disorders that are reported in ancient texts. Polio and the plague leave no recognisable remains but are passed in the stools, and thus might leave evidence. Even with the initial DNA experiments on bone, we can now state that TB pre-existed European contact in both the Americas and Asia, a fact which until now was a matter of controversy (Ortner and Putschar 1981).

Mobilisation of Elements from the Bog Bodies Lindow II and III and Some Observations on Body Painting

F. B. Pyatt   E. H. Beaumont   P. C. Buckland   D. Lacy
J. R. Magilton   D. M. Storey

Summary

As part of the study of the bog body Lindow III, recovered from Lindow Moss, Cheshire, samples of skin together with associated peat were examined by means of electron probe X-ray microanalysis. The investigation revealed an excess of aluminium, silica and copper, together with traces of titanium and zinc. These elements are interpreted as residues of clay-based copper and other pigments applied to the skin of the individual. A comparison of the geochemistry of the bog bodies II and III is presented together with a consideration of the mobilisation of elements from bodies to the bog environment. The literary evidence for the use of body paint among the Britons is reviewed in the light of these analyses and the interpretation of classical references in terms of woad-painted Britons is questioned.

Introduction

The publication of the results of the examination of Lindow II presents a wealth of detailed information upon both the body and its environment of deposition (Stead et al 1986). The present study reports further investigations of the geochemistry of skin and bone fragments together with associated peat. The skin samples of Lindow III were obtained from the shoulder region, whilst those of Lindow II were from under the right side of the body, i.e., from the arm region. Bone samples of Lindow II were obtained from the upper right orbit. Some of the results are more fully reported in Pyatt et al (1991a, 1991b).

Lindow III

In view of Ross and Robins' (1989) claim for an Irish origin for Lindow II, examination of the chemical composition of the tissue offered the possibility of narrowing down the geographic origin of this individual, particularly in view of the proximity of Lindow Moss to the important metalliferous veins of Alderley Edge, where several minerals, especially copper, have been mined, probably since the Bronze Age (Carlton 1979; Craddock and Gale 1988). In addition, there have been frequent attempts to examine diet in past populations by means of trace element studies (cf. Gilbert 1985; Francalacci 1989; Lambert et al 1984, 1989; Waldron 1987). Most such research has inevitably been based upon bone from burials, with the attendant problems of the migration of ions into and out of the medium (cf. Bethell and Carver 1987).

In common with Lindow II (Girling 1986; Skidmore 1986), the insect evidence from Lindow III (Dinnin and Skidmore, pp. 31–8) includes no carrion elements which implies that the body was submerged, deliberately pushed under peaty mud immediately after death, rather than thrown into an open pool, an interpretation which the chironomid and cladoceran faunas from Lindow II would also support (Dayton 1986). Both bodies showed no evidence for associated clothing, although it should be noted that some vegetable fibres, such as linen, are unlikely to survive in recognisable form in acid bog conditions. A fragment of fox fur was found around the left arm (McCord 1986).

In Lindow III, the skin from the shoulder had been tanned to a deep brown colour and, though flexible, was tough and bark-like in texture. Bourke (1986) described the skin of Lindow II as 'having the feel of soft leather'. However, whilst preservation has reduced pliability in the latter find, their microscopic structure is essentially the same. The whole of the epidermis (which in the shoulder is likely to have been less than 0.3 mm thick) is lost and only dermal fibres are preserved.

The living human dermis consists of felted collagenous connective tissue with elastic fibres, blood vessels, lymphatics and nerves lacing through it. Microscopic examination of the skin sample indicated that, in Lindow III, as in Lindow II, only the network of collagen fibres remains, effectively 'tanned' by the acid peat water. These are very densely packed on the upper surface, which has a pitted appearance, due presumably to dermal papillae, which bound this layer to the epidermis, and to the intrusion of hair follicles, although no hairs, in the samples, were preserved. In the deeper dermis, the fibres are loose in texture, where they presumably surrounded subcutaneous fat deposits. Their appearance here is not unlike suede leather (Pyatt et al 1991a).

The chemical composition of Lindow II was examined by Connolly and others (1986). Samples of bone, hair and nail were studied, along with the associated peat, utilising a similar technique, X-ray energy dispersive microprobe analysis, to that employed in the current study. This method, although destructive, employs only small samples of materials. Connolly and his co-workers noted that the preservation of animal tissue within peats depends upon three prerequisites: 1) virtually anaerobic conditions; 2) a lack of putrefactive bacteria; 3) a highly acidic aquatic environment, with a complex and variable mixture of constituent organic acids. It was stressed that the cellular structure of Lindow II had been destroyed and this was attributed to a combination of osmotic and other physical effects of waterlogging, together with enzymatic, microbial, and other chemical degradation processes.

Similar research does not appear to have been published from the well-known bog bodies from Denmark (Glob 1971), although Hancock and others (1989) have discussed these processes in relation to human bone from a Florida peat bog.

Lindow II

Although Stead (1986) concluded: 'Palaeobotanists have presented a convincing argument suggesting that he (Lindow II) met his death around 300 BC', the greater number of dates now available (gazetteer, pp. 205–34, and Gowlett et al 1989) would suggest that there are problems with the peat stratigraphy (Buckland, pp. 47–50) and a date closer to, or within, the Roman period is the more probable.

The bodies, however, have spent nearly 2000 years immersed in the bog and their preservation involved changes in the physical and chemical composition of some tissues. Pyatt et al (1991b) noted that the skin is remarkably well preserved, but it is the dermis, rather than the epidermal cells, which survives. The basal layer of the human epidermis consists of thin-walled cells, the stratum Malpighii, from which the keratinised upper layer, the stratum corneum sloughs off during life. The thin-walled cells would rapidly decompose and their contents dissolve in the acidic environment. Then the remaining epidermis separates from the underlying layers and putrefaction is consequently accelerated. No trace of epidermis was found in the skin samples of Lindow III examined (Pyatt et al 1991a) and, in Lindow II, Connolly (in Stead et al 1986) found epidermis preserved only in the thickened friction ridges on the soles of the feet. The preserved dermal structure is non-cellular and the collagenous connective tissue remains intact, if altered by the humic acids of the bog. It is stained brown, but retains some flexibility. Internally most soft tissues have been reduced by putrefaction and enzyme activity to an unrecognisable state, apart from the stomach, jejunum and duodenum which may have been 'fixed' due to their acid nature. Whilst secretions from the small intestine are slightly alkaline, Lucas and Mathan (1989) gave the pH of such mucosal surfaces as 5.8 ± 0.09 in normal human patients. The acidity preserved their contents – probably the remnants of an unleavened cake made of ground wheat and barley (Holden 1986).

The bones of Lindow II have altered both physically and chemically. Normal bone owes its tensile strength to its organic matrix of collagen fibres and its hardness to the inorganic bone salts. The mineral component, mainly of calcium and phosphate, makes up two thirds of the weight of the bone or half its volume. In Lindow II, demineralisation caused the bones to become 'plastic' as it is mainly the flexible collagen fibres that remain. Thus distortion and compression have occurred to some extent throughout the skeleton. This is normal in an acidic environment and the skulls of Carboniferous vertebrates, where peat has been compressed to form coal, have often been reduced to two dimensions by plastic distortion without any cracking of the individual bones (Beaumont 1977). In Lindow II the skull has twisted and the long bones of the limbs have become very thin and compressed.

Three samples obtained from Lindow II were investigated to determine which elements had persisted in the skin and bone following a period of about 2000 years burial in an anaerobic bog environment. Furthermore, the condition of tissue such as bone was examined and a comparison made with Lindow III. Previous work on Lindow II had included a test for the dye indigotin, the colorant in woad, with negative results (Taylor 1986).

The potential ways by which a body may accumulate heavy metals are indicated in Fig. 30.

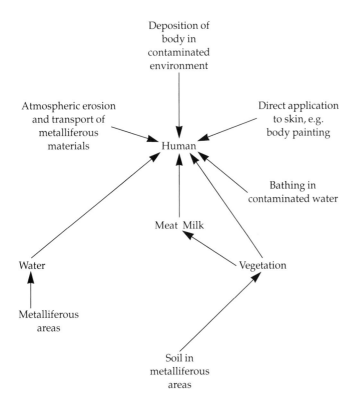

Fig. 30 Routes of cations (for example Cu) from the environment to the human body.

Experimental Procedure

Skin from the shoulder region of the body (Lindow III) was provided for analysis and a sample of the enclosing peat was also examined; both had been stored in ethanol since excavation. Hair was absent from the sample examined and there was a considerable degree of surface abrasion due presumably to damage during excavation. In section, it exhibited a homogeneous appearance and only limited structural detail was apparent. Samples of skin (under right side of body – from arm), and bone from upper right orbit of Lindow II were also examined. Samples were mounted on to 13 mm diameter carbon stubs and were secured by conductive carbon cement. The material was given a light coating of carbon in a Nanotech coating unit to eliminate problems caused by electrostatic charges. The samples were placed in a Cambridge Stereoscan 600 and analysed by electron probe X-ray microanalysis with a Link System 860 series 2 computer, using a ZAF-4 program. On each sample, suitable areas (10 000 μm^2) were selected for analysis using the microscope VDU and then analysed at a magnification of $\times$ 500 for 100 seconds of live time at 25 kV. In the process of X-ray micro-analysis, an electron beam strikes the solid specimen and a number of interactions occur including the production of X-rays. These are detected by a lithium drifted silicon detector and are thence passed on to a multi-channel analyser.

The technique is described in detail by Pyatt and Lacy (1988) who noted that the quantitative accuracy of this technique on biological material may be restricted to c. 10% relative of the true value. The results are presented as percentages and refer to elements from sodium and above in the atomic series. The problem of converting the percentage results into units such as mmol/kg or parts/10^6 is due partly to the nature of biological material, where carbon, oxygen, nitrogen and hydrogen are well represented, and partly to the type of detector which cannot detect these light elements. The detection limit for the electron probe X-ray microanalysis (Link System 860 series), for the cations investigated, is approximately 0.1%; this value constitutes the Minimum Detection Limit (MDL) and the achieved confidence level was 95%. The data, however, show all the important trends in a *comparative* or relative sense and hence may be compared in this way with other published work. The results expressed (Tables 11 and 12 and Fig. 31) are the average from a minimum of five replicates in each case. For comparative purposes, skin samples were ashed in a muffle furnace to

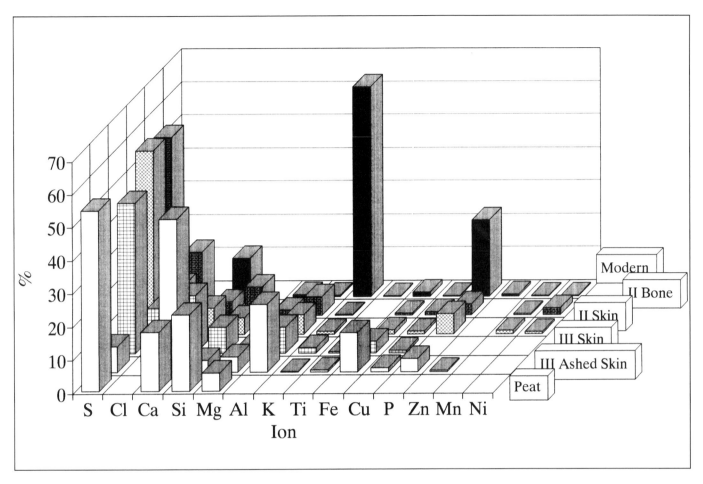

Fig. 31 Ionic composition of tissue samples obtained from the bog bodies Lindow II and III. (*P. C. Buckland*)

Table 11 *Element composition (%) from samples of tissues derived from Lindow III. (Results obtained from at least ten replicates)*

ELEMENT	SKIN	ASHED SKIN	PEAT
Mg	2.1	4.5	5.3
Al	7.7	20.3	—
Si	7.8	3.5	22.8
S	45.2	7.7	54.3
Cl	13.7	—	—
K	1.5	0.2	—
Ca	17.3	46.0	17.6
Ti	0.4	0.4	—
Fe	3.5	11.7	—
Cu	0.8	1.2	—
P	—	4.0	—
Zn	—	0.4	—

Skin (10): S>Ca>Cl>Si>Al>Fe>Mg>K>Cu>Ti
Peat (4): S>Si>Ca>Mg
Table modified from Pyatt *et al* (1991a).

Table 12 *Element composition (%) from samples of tissue derived from Lindow II. (Results obtained from five replicates)*

ELEMENT	SKIN	BONE	PEAT AND HAIR
Mg	1.1	1.6	1.4
Al	5.8	5.6	3.6
Si	5.0	8.4	10.8
S	55.4	53.7	28.7
Cl	14.7	19.2	21.2
K	0.7	0.1	1.4
Ca	7.9	4.2	22.6
Ti	—	—	—
Fe	1.1	0.6	4.6
Cu	0.8	1.0	1.4
P	6.0	3.2	1.0
Zn	—	—	—
Mn	0.9	0.3	1.0
Ni	0.6	2.0	2.4

LIII (Skin) S>Ca>Cl>Si>Al>Fe>Mg>K>Cu>Ti
LII (Skin) S>Cl>Ca>P>Al>Si>Mg>Fe>Mn>Cu>K>Ni
Table modified from Pyatt *et al* (1991b).

destroy organic matter and the residues similarly ana-lysed. Peat from immediately adjacent to the body was air dried and processed in order to obtain some idea of the geochemistry of the enclosing medium.

Discussion

Twelve elements were recorded from Lindow III; of these, ten occurred in the skin samples and only four were present in the peat adjacent to the body.

Connolly and others (1986), using the same techniques on Lindow II, found that sulphur was present as a major component, with far lesser quantities of phosphorus, cal-cium, aluminium, silicon, chlorine and potassium. They concluded: 'the spectrum of elements identified in the bone sample from Lindow Man reflects more or less pass-ively the inorganic composition (with respect to these elements) of the surrounding peat'. The bone had there-fore reached an approximate equilibrium with the enclos-ing medium. The nail and hair, however, show a less balanced range of ions, which at least partly reflects the primary composition. Lindow III's skin sample similarly shows a massively enhanced sulphur content, a feature of the prevailing environmental anaerobiosis and the simi-larity of calcium concentration between tissue and peat indicates the mobilisation of calcium from the body into equilibrium with the enclosing peat; magnesium, iron, copper, and titanium were also identified.

Phosphorus was absent from the skin sample of Lindow III (Table 11 and Fig. 31) – it would have migrated out from the skeleton during the process of leaching and equalisation with the enclosing peat, and part could have been redistributed irregularly through the skin, q.v.. The larger sample, used for ashing, may have provided a better overall image of the composition of the tissue, although it also led to the total loss of chlorine.

As would be anticipated in a raised bog environment (Barber 1986) relying upon rainwater for its maintenance (Moore and Bellamy 1976), the peat has a low diversity of ions and the relatively high silicon content must reflect a combination of inorganic aeolian input (SiO_2 – quartz) to the bog surface, perhaps related to local forest clearance (Oldfield *et al* 1986), and phytoliths from higher plants in the succession. Similarly, magnesium probably derives largely from chloroplasts in the vegetation. The metal ions, copper and zinc, might initially suggest a connection with metalliferous veins, particularly copper minerals, along Alderley Edge (Carlton 1979). This metal might be

expected to have a significantly raised frequency in local streams draining from the Edge, as well as in the veg-etation of soils derived from the mineralised Triassic sandstone. Both metals, however, are essential to animal life and a wide range of tolerance to them is to be found (Venugopal and Luckey 1978). Titanium, however, is not a necessary nutrient but is a frequent background com-ponent in vegetation, although it is unlikely to accumulate in animal tissue as experiments show that most would be rapidly lost after ingestion by excretion; its presence in the tissue in both the skin and ashed skin sample is enigmatic and its absence in samples derived from Lindow II, may suggest a significant difference between the individuals. The results from Lindow II are presented in Table 12.

Ground water movement within the bog leads pro-gressively towards equalisation between the ion content of the body and the enclosing peat; in a raised bog situ-ation it seems unlikely that much elemental concentration into the body will occur. This is evidenced by the action of calcium where the concentration in the body is markedly depleted and, in the case of Lindow III skin, approaches the value in the encompassing medium (Table 12).

The bone samples obtained from the upper right orbit of Lindow II contained appreciable quantities of sulphur, phosphorus, calcium, aluminium, silicon, chlorine, and potassium (Table 12 and Fig. 31), results similar to those reported by Connolly and others (1986). Similarly, there is an extremely well-defined peak of sulphur content (53.7%) and clear evidence of demineralisation. However, in this investigation the presence of additional, clearly defined, cations was also noted; these were magnesium, iron, copper, manganese and nickel. The scanning elec-tron micrograph (Fig. 32) illustrates the structure of the

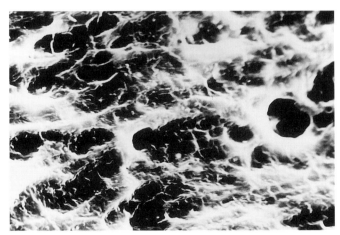

Fig. 32 Scanning electron micrograph of bone from the upper right orbit of Lindow II.

bone in part of the upper right orbit. The spongy (cancellous) bone has retained its structure without undue distortion and part of the Haversian canal system is still recognisable. However, the structure is maintained due to the collagen component rather than the mineral elements which have been mobilised, as internal decomposition proceeded, and thence migrated to the medium surrounding the body.

Analysis of the skin samples obtained from under the right side of the body (from arm) revealed the same 12 elements (Table 12 and Fig. 31) as found in the bone sample from the upper right orbit. It should be noted that Pyatt *et al* (1991a) determined only ten elements in comparable samples obtained from the skin of Lindow III. Phosphorus, manganese, and nickel were peculiar to Lindow II, whilst the skin samples of Lindow III, unlike those obtained from Lindow II, contained titanium. The skin from the two individuals differs in both the concentrations of the various elements and also in the concentration ranking. From Tables 11 and 12 it can be seen that the elements in Lindow III skin can be ranked:

$$S>Ca>Cl>Si>Al>Fe>Mg>K>Cu>Ti$$

whilst those in the skin from Lindow II are ranked:

$$S>Cl>Ca>P>Al>Si>Mg>Fe>Mn>Cu>K>Ni$$

Migration of Elements

The problem of migration of metal and other ions in organic sediments remains incompletely understood. It is probable that the processes of preservation of the body have led to considerable cation exchange over a period approaching 2000 years. The processes can lead to some migration of metal ions but the scale of elevation of metal ions within the body is greater than anticipated when compared with modern samples. These are perhaps better explained in terms of clay mineralogy and pigment rather than in terms of diagenesis; the problems, however, merit further investigation, including similar studies of other bog bodies.

Chemical 'Fingerprints'

The destructive nature of the analysis precludes the study of samples from elsewhere on the bodies but, overall, Lindow II and Lindow III appear to have somewhat different chemical 'fingerprints'. This may be the result of dietary differences, perhaps a result of being native to different geochemical provinces (Pyatt *et al* 1991a).

However, additional data would be necessary to develop constructively this speculation. Whilst differences may have existed in life, they could also be affected by differential degrees of elemental leaching, a result of slightly differing depositional environments within the bog, or a significant temporal difference in the date of their death. This, however, appears improbable. A further explanation, derived from the hypothesis put forward by Pyatt *et al* (1991a) would be that Lindow II and Lindow III had a different chemical composition to pigments applied to their respective bodies, thus it is conceivable that they utilised different metal-element-based paints in the decoration of their bodies for battle and recognition purposes. As the pigments are not likely to have been applied generally, but rather in discrete patterns and motifs, it is hardly surprising that differences exist and caution in the interpretation of trace and major element data from less well preserved inhumations is advised.

Elements in the Skin Samples Obtained from Lindow II and III

The percentages of the various elements occurring in the skin samples of Lindow II and Lindow III are very different (Table 12). Thus, for example, the skin of Lindow II has less magnesium, aluminium, silicon, potassium, and far less calcium and iron; no titanium, but more sulphur and chlorine, than detected in the skin of Lindow III. The amounts of copper, likely to be the prime base of the pigment, are comparable in the skin from both bodies. Lindow II, unlike Lindow III, has skin containing or contaminated with (as also noted in the bone sample derived from the upper right orbit) phosphorus, manganese, and nickel. Both manganese and nickel may be traces after iron in the body paint but the elevated phosphorus may derive from the calci-apatite of the bone. The total number of elements in the skin of Lindow III was found to be ten, whilst twelve were noted from Lindow II; they share nine in common. In the absence of a technique able to provide a complete elemental body scan, it is impossible to determine to what extent these differences may be explained by differential rates of weathering or leaching of elements or indeed, other processes occurring after death.

Elements in Peat and Hair Samples

Samples of peat and hair (Table 12 and Fig. 31) obtained from below the right shoulder and cheek of Lindow II contained the same 12 elements as noted in the skin and bone samples. The hair was heavily contaminated with peat and it was not possible to separate the hair out to facilitate separate analyses. The silicon content was enhanced, which is probably due to sources such as the decomposition of diatom frustules, phytoliths, etc. Calcium also was very well represented (22.6%) as compared with the bone sample from the upper right orbit (4.2%); this is probably indicative of the mobilisation of calcium from the body into the surrounding acidic medium. Values of chlorine, iron and nickel were elevated (Table 12) while the percentage content of aluminium, sulphur and phosphorus were less.

Comparison of this sample with the Lindow III peat sample is difficult as the materials are not strictly comparable; these samples lacked the hair which permeated through the Lindow II samples. However, it may be noted (Table 12) that the peat in close proximity with the body of Lindow III was found to contain only four elements whilst that peat and hair mixture associated with Lindow II contained twelve. The elements were also ranked differently.

Lindow III: S>Si>Ca>Mg

Lindow II: S>Ca>Cl>Si>Fe>Al>
              Ni>Mg>Cu>K>Mn>P

Although the order in neither case was identical to that found in the appropriate adjacent skin sample (Tables 11 and 12) it is apparent that there is a clearly defined relationship between the geochemistry of the skin and the enclosing peat; in the absence of a more detailed study, an otherwise general chemical homogeneity of the peat as a whole has been assumed.

Movement of Bodies

As discussed elsewhere (Buckland and Barber pp. 47–51) the body dates of Lindow are not the same as the stratigraphy and it is conceivable that the bodies have moved relative to the stratigraphy. Thus, whilst a comparison of the chemical ions within the peat immediately adjacent to the body with peat samples further from the body would be useful, this was not attempted. It would be very difficult to trace similar horizons across the bog to obtain peat samples which were certainly contemporaneous with the body from non-adjacent locations.

Fig. 33 Skin sample from Lindow II examined by means of the scanning electron microscope.

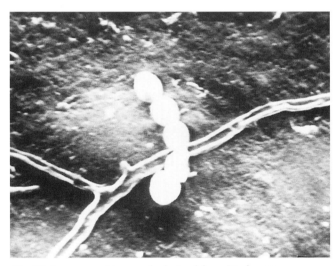

Fig. 34 Spores on skin sample derived from Lindow II

Decomposer Fungal Hyphae

Samples of skin (under right side of the body – from the arm) of Lindow II were also carefully examined under the scanning electron microscope (Figs 33 and 34). The skin sample was found to be covered by a network of ramifying tubes which probably represent the remnants of the mycelia of ancient decomposer/saprophytic fungi – the chains of spherical structures are possible fungal spores such as chains of condiospores; they were not found to be viable – the material had been preserved in alcohol. It should be stressed that both the fungus and the spores may have existed in the peat and simply have become adpressed to the body of Lindow II. It is also conceivable that the fungus represents a far more recent invasion of the body tissue – perhaps directly after exhumation.

Interpretation

Movement of Elements between the Body and the Peat

The Lindow bodies, in a raised bog with limited input of nutrients by rainwater might seem to provide a useful baseline for examination of the potential of dietary reconstruction from animal remains by way of their geochemistry. Whilst loss of ions from the bone and tissue has been demonstrated, there would have been little available to move into the bodies, the concentrations of heavy metals in modern peats being a result of atmospheric pollution since the Industrial Revolution (Livett *et al* 1979; Jones 1987).

The leaching of ions from the bodies, however, is likely to have taken place at different rates. Livett and others (1979) note that zinc is more easily leached than lead in an acid bog situation and it is therefore difficult to be certain that all ions had reached an ambient state at the time of recovery.

Element Content of Lindow as Compared with Modern Human Tissue

Since the figures cannot be converted directly to whole quantities, comparisons have to be made on a ratio basis and the required standard of an average composition for human tissue is difficult to arrive at, in that modern samples are heavily influenced by metal emissions from vehicle and industrial sources, metals incorporated in insecticides and other substances consumed inadvertently, and other casual influences.

An 'average' overall composition for man is provided by Mason (1960) and it is immediately apparent that in comparison with other metal ions, the copper concentrations in Lindow III and Lindow II are markedly elevated. Initially this may appear to result from ingestion of food grown on soils with a high copper concentration or similarly contaminated water in the area of mineral veins along Alderley Edge (Fig. 30), which would support the hypothesis of a local origin for Lindow; however, other inconsistencies in the ion content are far less easily explained in this way. Aluminium is present only as a trace in modern tissue and has been implicated in Alzheimer's Disease; it is toxic at high concentrations (Venugopal and Luckey 1978). In Lindow III, its concentration is also very high, relative to other elements. These elements cannot be regarded as components of normal skin tissue, nor the result of movement of ions in from the surrounding peat. It is probable that this composition is better explained in terms of an original application of a foreign substance to the surface of the skin, which penetrated by way of the pores.

Preferred Interpretation: Application of Mineral-rich Pigments to the Bodies

The aluminium and silicon concentrations seem best explained in terms of clay minerals, present in metacolloidal form, the base of which is a hydrated aluminium silicate essentially providing a base to which pigment could be added. The copper component might then represent pigment, in the form of finely ground ore, either of the oxides, Cu_2O, cuprite, which would yield an intense red, CuO, tenorite, a black, or the carbonates, $CuCO_3.Cu(OH)_2$, malachite, a bright green, $2CuCO_3.Cu(OH)_2$, azurite, an intense blue. The artificial pigment, Egyptian blue, $CuCaSiO_4$, used during the Roman period in wall paintings (Biek 1982) and earlier in the manufacture of faience beads (Newton and Renfrew 1970) and glass, is also possible. Copper sulphate ($CuSO_4.5H_2O$) also occurs as a natural mineral, chalcanthite, in the weathering zone of copper lodes and can be manufactured by boiling the oxide or carbonate ores with pyrites (FeS_2); its solubility renders it less likely to be represented in the tissue.

Other ions also may relate to paint on the body. Zinc is often associated with copper mineralisation and iron would also be expected. The presence of titanium is best explained either by its occurrence in the clay or by detrital grains of ilmenite ($FeO.TiO_2$) or rutile (TiO_2) associated with ochre pigment. The lack of titanium from samples of Lindow II and the differing percentages of some of the elements may indicate different pigments. It appears probable that Lindow III had been at least partly painted with a clay-based pigment, in which the iron and copper provided the basic colourants. Previous attempts to locate dyes on Lindow II were restricted to a search for vegetable substances, the notorious woad (Taylor 1986), rather than mineral ones, but the green fluorescence, noted on the fox hair band around the arm (Priston 1986), may also be a result of copper enrichment.

Thus, from the data obtained which examines the percentage concentrations of the various elements present, along with their ranking, it is suggested that the elements which were present on the skin in enhanced concentrations were not derived from atmospheric pollution nor as a result of accumulation through trophic levels. The authors suggest that the elements, present after 2000 years, represent the remnants of metalliferous pigments applied to the skin of the individuals while alive. Such pigment applications would enable individuals to recognise each other in various situations and would be of enormous benefit.

Archaeologists have devoted considerable energies to attempts to reconstruct diet from human bone composition (e.g., Antoine *et al* 1988; Price *et al* 1985; Lambert *et al* 1984), yet there remain serious problems in interpretation of data from modern material, where the additional problems of ion exchange with the encompassing medium are absent. McKenzie (1979) noted a lack of correlation between levels of zinc in hair and other tissues and Petering and others (1971) suggest that comparison of metal concentrations should be restricted to individuals of the same sex and of a comparable age band. This alone should be sufficient to cause concern over fossil data and the problem is further exemplified by the work of Cornelius (1973), who showed that variation in hair treatment and water were sufficient to preclude its effective use of its trace element content in forensic science. Hancock and others (1989) have further warned against the uncritical use of bone analyses for archaeological dietary studies. The hypothesis of body paint on Lindow III and Lindow II raises another possible source of problems, since the metals from any pigments are likely to concentrate in the bone. Ochre and other pigments, presumably for cosmetic use, are known from at least the Middle Palaeolithic onwards (Wreschner 1976) and the ritual employment of body paint is widespread in human societies. Taken with the contamination problems from both substrate and metal artifacts in graves, it raises further doubts over the validity of some geochemical studies devoted exclusively to bone.

Painted Warriors in the Written Sources

The popular image of Ancient Britons as painted warriors stems undoubtedly from Caesar (*De Bello Gallico* V.14), although there are other allusions in ancient sources. Caesar's reference forms part of a digression on the geography and ethnography of Britain (V.12–14) which interrupts the account of his second invasion of the island and which, in a modern translation (Handford 1951), is not unreasonably treated as an extended footnote. Some of the information is admitted by Caesar to be hearsay, and some is checked by personal observation; it reads as if a gloss has been added to information initially compiled before the British expeditions. Section 14 may be translated as follows:

By far the most civilised are those living in Kent, a purely maritime district, whose customs differ little from those of the Gauls. Most of the peoples of the interior do not sow corn but live on milk and meat, and dress in skins. All the Britons stain themselves with *vitrum* which gives a blue colour and a wilder appearance in battle: they let their hair grow long and shave every part of the body except the head and upper lip. They have wives shared between sets of ten or twelve men, especially between brothers and between fathers and sons: those born from these unions are considered the children of the man with whom the woman first slept.

Of this section the first sentence is probably based on personal observation. The second must rest on oral or written information. It is plainly incorrect – there is ample archaeological evidence for the cultivation of cereal crops – and is suspiciously similar to his description of the Germans, as if stock phrases to describe the more uncouth barbarians are being employed. The sentence about the Britons dyeing themselves with *vitrum* presents several problems. It says quite specifically that custom applies to all Britons, that is including the civilised Cantiaci as well as those of the interior, but no other reference to blue-painted warriors is found in Caesar's campaigns: had he encountered them in battle, they would surely have been mentioned. The custom of shaving the body, if it is not listed as simply another strange habit, is a non-sequitur unless, in an expanded form, the sentence originally explained that the Britons, like the Germans, wore garments which left most of their body bare. The allegation of polyandry in the final sentence may simply be a 'bad rumour' (Thomson 1948, 153) part of a stock of ethnographic commonplaces (Goodyear 1970, 9) since, as Killeen (1976) has pointed out, Herodotus (iv.104; iv.172; iv.180) describes similar practices elsewhere. Cartimandua's rejection of Venutius for Vellocatus (Tacitus, *Histories 3*, 45) may, however, reflect such a custom, which may have survived later among the Picts (Bede, *H.E.I.I.*). In summary, section 14 of Caesar seems to consist of an introductory sentence based on personal observation, followed by notes of uncertain provenance which, if at all reliable, could refer to a period long before the mid-first century BC.

Caesar may have provided the inspiration for two early imperial poetic allusions to painted Britons, one by Propertius (*Carmina II*, 18B, 1–4) and the other by Ovid (*Amores II*, 16, 39), but whilst Propertius refers merely to 'painted Britons', Ovid speaks of *viridis Britannos*, contrasting with Caesar's *caeruleum colorem*. Pomponius Mela (*de Chorographia III*, 6,51) in his section on Britain seems to be quoting an independent source. He writes:

Fert populos regesque populorum, sed sunt inculti omnes, atque ut longius a continenti absunt, ita aliarum opum ignari, tantum pecore ac finibus dites – incertum ob decorem an quid aliud – vitro corpora infecti.

This translates as:

[Britain] bears peoples and kings of peoples, but all are uncivilised, and the farther away they are from the continent, the more they are unacquainted with its other blessings: so much that, rich only in live-stock and their territory – it is uncertain whether as an embellishment or for some other reason – they dye their bodies with *vitrum*.

Pliny (*Nat.XXII*,ii), in a section discussing the uses to which plants may be put, provides another reference to Britons staining themselves, and is the only author to state that a vegetable dye was employed:

… similis plantagini glastum in Gallia vocatur, Britannorum coniuges nurusque toto corpore oblitae quibusdam in sacris nudae incedunt Aethiopum colorem imitantes.

This translates as:

There is a plant like a plantain called *glastum* in Gaul; the wives and young women of the Britons, having stained the whole of their bodies with it, so that they resemble in colour the Ethiopians, process naked at certain religious ceremonies.

Martial, writing at the end of the first century AD, also refers to sky-blue Britons. In an epigram to *Claudia Rufina* (XI, LII), the wife of a friend, he begins:

Claudia caeruleis cum sit Rufina Britannis edita, quam Latinae pectora gentis habet!

This translates as:

Claudia Rufina, though she is sprung from the sky-blue Britons, how she possesses the feelings of the Latin race!

The rest of the short poem is flattering, as in an earlier address (IV, XII) thought to be to the same woman, and the mention of her sky-blue ancestors is perhaps better seen as a joke rather than as a jibe.

Later references to the custom of body painting are all specific to northern Britain, where the practice may have lasted longest. Herodian, writing of Septimus Severus'

adversaries in Scotland, says: 'They mark their bodies with various figures of all kinds of animals and wear no clothes for fear of concealing these figures'. (*Herodian III*, 14,7)

He is the only author to use a verb which means 'tattoo' rather than 'stain', indicating that the effect was produced by puncturing the skin. The term *Picti*, first used of a confederation of tribes in Scotland in two of the *Panegyrici Latini* (VIII(V), II,4 and VI(VII)7,2) in the late third and early fourth century, is often taken as a descriptive, purely Latin term, meaning 'the painted men'. Earlier, the word is used by Virgil, for example, as an adjective to describe certain northern tribes (*Aeneid IV*, 146; *Georgics II*, 115), although never as a proper name. It may alternatively be a latinised native name – the native name in the Early Christian period was Cruithni, perhaps from P-Celtic **Pretani*, meaning 'the tattooed people' (Rivet and Smith 1979, 281) – or a Pictish word of unknown meaning.

Vegetius (*De Re Militari IV*, 47) describes scouting craft of the Classis Britannica as *picti*, saying that the sails and ropes of the ships, the sailors' uniforms and their faces were dyed the colour of the waves for camouflage. Bede (*H.E.I.I.*) records a tradition that the Picts came from Scythia, and Scythians, alone with the Dacians and Sarmatians, were well known to classical writers for their tattoos. Gildas (*De Excidio Britonum*, 19) refers to the Pictish custom of fighting naked, but says nothing of stained or tattooed bodies, and there seem to be no echoes of the practice in Irish mythology or in the Welsh legends known as the Mabinogion.

There appears to be little to be gained from epigraphic sources. Viridius, attested at Ancaster, Lincs, to whom Trenico set up an arch (Whitwell 1970, 125–6), but otherwise unknown, may be 'The Green Man' since *viridis* is a loan word in British, becoming *gwyrdd* in modern Welsh (Jackson 1953, 268), or his name may be Celtic meaning 'lively, vigorous, virile', although there are no derivatives in medieval or modern Celtic languages. The former interpretation could hint at an agricultural deity, but it is not impossible that he was a green-painted Celtic warrior.

* *Glasto* becomes *glas* in the modern insular Celtic languages (cf. Jackson 1953, 533); woad is *glasrac* in Scottish Gaelic and, despite the difficulties, the traditional translation of the word may be correct. Ekwall (1960) prefers this root for the place name, Glastonbury, first found in the form Glastingoea in 704, yet, surprisingly, the Welsh form of the name Ineswytrin, presumably by back-translation, appears to derive from Latin *vitrum*; the abbeys of both Glastonbury and Muchelney in Somerset were major producers of woad during the medieval period (Godwin 1978, 159). That woad was grown also in Early Christian Ireland is suggested by the story of Cormac Mac Airt's overturning of the judgment of Lugaid Mac Con, who had pronounced sentence on a woman whose sheep had eaten the queen's crop of woad (O'Grady 1892).

Pliny, the only author to specify that a plant dye was used, says that *glastum* resembles the plantain, *Plantago*, so named in Latin because its leaves look like the sole of a foot, planta. *Glastum* is invariably translated as woad, although the leaves of the latter do not resemble those of a plaintain and yield a blue dye, whereas *Aethiopum colorem* would suggest dark brown or black. Such a colour could have been produced by crushing woad leaves, but the Gaulish word *glastum* implies a green, blue or grey colour, the name presumably being bestowed on the plant on account of the colour of dye it produced. It is just possible that the Celts believed that Ethiopians *were* blue. In the Irish story 'The Intoxication of the Men of Ulster' King Conchubur's fool Rómit Rigóinmit is described as 'balding, with short, black hair, bulging, great eyes – one bright – in his head, and a smooth, blue, Ethiopian face' (Gantz 1981, 208).

Perhaps Linnaeus (1753) was a little unsure of the term *glastum* when searching Pliny's *Natural History* for a generic name for the group of plants into which he wished to classify woad. The word which he adopted, *isatis*, occurs three times, twice in Latin and once in Greek. The two former occurrences (*Nat.* (26) 39; (27) 84) describes seaweeds as 'like isatis' and are of little value in identifying the plant; the other indicates that the plant grows in woods, which presumably explains Linnaeus' use of the term.

Caesar's word *vitrum*, usually 'glass, crystal' in Latin presents greater problems, but has been translated as woad since the sixteenth century (Golding 1565), when the plant was a popular source of a blue dye (Thirsk 1985). Pomponius Mela uses the word, as does Pliny on two occasions, but a re-examination of Pliny's use raises considerable doubts as to whether 'the notorious British woad' (Wild 1970, 81) is intended. The first reference (*Nat.* (34) 123): '*color (atramenti sutorii) est caeruleus vitrumque esse creditur*', appears in a passage describing the natural occurrence of copper sulphate, the mineral chalcanthite, in Spain and is better translated as 'is often taken for glass'. The second usage (*Nat.* (35) 46): '*aut cretam Selinusiam vel anulariam vitro inficiunt*', is obscure, since both *creta Selinusia* and *creta anularia* are unknown, but, by analogy with the former reference, (blue) glass may be intended. Further reinforcement for the term *vitrum* referring to a copper-based pigment lies in Pliny's use of the word *caeruleum* (*Nat.* (33) 162), the colour of Caesar's Britons, to describe what is clearly the mineral azurite used in paint. Similarly Ovid's (*Amores II*, 16, 39) *viridis Britannos* are better understood in the context of a copper, perhaps

malachite, pigment, although this interpretation would perhaps imply that his primary source was not Caesar.

The latter references to north Britons give no hints as to the likely dyestuffs employed. The Picts may have been the last to practise what had once been a widespread British custom – the word Britanni may actually mean 'tattooed folk' (Rivet and Smith, 1979, 281) – or theirs may have been an independent tradition. Herodian is the only author to mention tattooed designs; Pliny, Caesar and Pomponius Mela appear to be describing the application of a single colour over the whole body.

There is, however, a series of Late Iron Age coins from northern Gaul apparently showing facial paintings or tattoos (Thomas 1963, 92), although these may be no more than an expression of Celtic artist's exuberance in wishing to leave no portion of the coin undecorated.

The archaeological record adds little to what can be gleaned from Pliny. The Tyrolean Ice Man, a mummified corpse released by a glacier in the Oetztaler Alps, discovered in September 1991 and dated to the Chalcolithic on the basis of his copper axe, has tattooed lines and a cross on his back and legs (Höpfel *et al* 1992). More elaborately tattooed pieces of skin come from the fifth century BC chieftains' graves in the Altai Mountains of southern Siberia (cf. Rudenko 1970, figs 53 and 54). Needham and Bimson (1988) have recently published a pellet of Egyptian blue from a Late Bronze Age site at Runnymede on the Thames and this could have been employed in body painting; they suggest that other finds may have been overlooked. Analysis of Roman wall-painting pigments (Biek 1982) shows the frequent use of Egyptian blue, which need not have been imported. Copper-based pigments used in dyeing are likely to have also been missed in archaeological contexts, but Wild (1970, 120) notes the use of copper, perhaps applied by means of a lactate, in the dyeing of a piece of felt from a site in Basel, Switzerland.

The evidence for woad in prehistoric Britain is scanty and most references, for example the frequent comments upon woad-painted warriors (e.g. Cunliffe 1974, 307; Webster 1980, 78) can inevitably be traced back to often rather colourful interpretations of the doubtful passage in Caesar. Originally a plant of southern Russia and the Caucasus (Godwin 1978, 159), the earliest British record is seeds from a Late Iron Age or early Roman pit at Dragonby, Humberside (van der Veen *et al* 1993). Finds from medieval England and Ireland are noted by Hall (1992). On the Continent, it is recorded from the Danish Roman Iron Age (Wild, pers. comm: Korber-Grohne, 1987) and four cloth samples from Hallstatt, Austria, were dyed with blue indigotin, probably from woad (Ryder 1993, 312). However, its relative scarcity and therefore value in the north may be suggested by the inclusion of its seeds in the ninth century female royal burial in the Oseberg mound, in southern Norway (Holmboe, 1927). Taylor (1989) has recently reviewed the evidence for the use of woad in his discussion of textile dyes from Coppergate, York, and the plant has also been identified from Anglo-Scandinavian deposits on the site (O'Connor *et al* 1984).

Carus-Wilson (1967, 216) is more careful than most in her discussion of woad and suggests that it had been grown at least since the Saxon period, although it was also extensively imported from France. The frequent wars with France and the eventual loss of English possession on the Continent led to a demand for increased local production, which appears largely to have ceased (idem, 36). In the early 1540s, when supplies from France and the Azores were cut off, French refugees introduced its cultivation to England and it thrived to the extent that it threatened to replace grain as a cash crop, leading to its banning in 1585 and restriction on its growing until 1601 (Thirsk 1985), by which time it had begun to be replaced by imported indigo. It is in this context that the assumption that a blue colour had been obtained from woad by Caesar's adversaries begins to make sense.

The surviving sculptural evidence of Celtic warriors, either as gods or on Roman triumphal monuments, appears to provide no evidence of body decoration, although such is as likely to have been painted on the sculpture as on its original. If Stead's (1985, 31) reconstruction of a warrior with elaborately painted body art is to be accepted, an important corollary is the recognition of suitable equipment for the preparation and application of paint to the body. Jackson (1985) has drawn attention to a peculiarly English group of small bronze pestle and mortars which are found in Late Iron Age and early Roman contexts, but, without an unequivocal male context, these and other cosmetic or toilet sets tend to be inevitably regarded as women's possessions.

In the area of the Hunsruck-Eifel culture, however, toilet sets, comprising tweezers, 'nail-cleaners' and 'ear-scoops', occur exclusively in men's graves (Haffner 1979, 29). In England, from the Iron Age, only two cosmetic elements are known from male graves: one, possibly a 'nail-cleaner', was recovered from the Late Iron Age Welwyn Garden City burial (Stead 1967) and a further piece comes from the Queen's Barrow at Arras (Stead 1979, 84). Other examples are either from unsexed or female graves. There are few burials with a range of grave goods known from Britain outside of the Welwyn and Arras groups, however, and even less where the sex of the individual is known. From the end of the Iron Age or early Roman period, a cosmetic set is associated with a (?) male cremation at the King Harry Lane site, St Albans (Stead and Rigby 1989, 104).

Conclusion

The recognition of what potentially represent mineral-based paints by X-ray microanalysis, probably using iron as well as copper pigments, on the fragments of the bodies from Lindow Moss, raises a number of problems, not the least of which is the possibility that body decoration was a widespread phenomenon in prehistory, with all its attendant problems in the interpretation of trace element analyses from less well-preserved burials. The tradition, current at least since the sixteenth century, of woad-painted Britons is open to considerable doubt and the plant, *Isatis tinctoria* L. is first recorded from the Anglo-Saxon period in East Anglia. Classical authors note body painting and/or dyeing among both warriors and women and the Lindow evidence might extend this to the priestly caste. The Romans, however, clearly regarded it as an archaic and barbaric practice, sometimes referring to it in the context of criticism of female use of cosmetics. If, as several classical authors maintain, the Celts habitually fought naked, then distinctive painted designs on the body would have been the one means by which the tribal affiliation of individuals could be recognised in the mêlée of battle. It remains to be seen whether it will be possible to reconstruct any patterns on the Lindow bodies. It is believed that the nature of body painting, rather than diet, of Lindow II and III, was different. It is conceivable that Lindow II and III were indeed natives of different areas and so were decorated accordingly.

ADDENDUM: Copper in the Skin of Lindow Man

M. R. Cowell   P. T. Craddock

Introduction

The continuing study of the bodies from the Lindow Moss has produced many interesting insights. Among them is the suggestion by Pyatt *et al* (1991a and pp. 69–70) that the Lindow II and III bodies had been painted with a copper pigment. They analysed specimens of skin from these bodies and both were considered to have elevated levels of some elements, notably copper and aluminium for example, although the general pattern of inorganic components differed between the two individuals. The investigation was based on the analysis of single samples of skin from the two individuals: the arm of Lindow II and the shoulder region of Lindow III. Peat and bone samples were also analysed. The suggested explanation for the apparently higher levels of copper and other elements (e.g. aluminium, silicon, titanium, etc.) was that both bodies had been painted with a copper-mineral-based pigment in a clay-based ground.

However, as Pyatt *et al* (pp. 69–70) admit, equating the enhanced copper levels with a pigment is far too simplistic since there are other contributory factors to consider. Not least among these are the copper content of the living human body and the possibility that different parts of the body post-mortem differentially concentrated or retained any copper that might be present in the environment.

The two skin samples analysed by Pyatt *et al* (ibid) were from areas of the bodies which might be expected to be pigmented if body painting had been practised. Unfortunately they did not analyse skin areas where pigmentation would not be expected – which could then be used as a control to confirm the validity of the elevated concentration levels.

Since parts of the Lindow III body are still available at the British Museum, we sought to examine this latter aspect by analysing fragments of skin from the left heel (two samples), palm of the right hand and a finger (possibly also from the right hand) which we considered were unlikely to have been painted deliberately and therefore constituted controls. Part of the torso was sampled which, assuming that painting had been applied to the body, might reasonably be expected to have been pigmented. If the copper content was the same all over the body this might suggest that the copper had been absorbed naturally, but if it was markedly higher in the torso areas then an application of paint would be a possibility.

Because of the poor state of preservation of the torso parts, the anatomical location of the sample taken cannot be defined and hence it does not necessarily correspond with the sample examined by Pyatt *et al* (ibid). However, it was considered to be as representative as possible of the surviving torso areas which could have been painted. A sample of peat adjacent to the body when recovered was also obtained as an environmental control, although it must be emphasised that its long-term association with the body parts involved cannot be guaranteed.

Analytical Procedure and Results

The intention in this investigation was to determine the copper content of the skin and peat samples since this element seemed the most relevant in a reappraisal of the possibility of body painting.

An initial examination was carried out by non-destructive, energy-dispersive X-ray fluorescence. This technique is surface specific and reasonably sensitive for copper and offered a suitable qualitative analysis of the skin surfaces. Copper was detected specifically in the torso parts and indicated that further quantitative analyses were justified. These were carried out by atomic absorption spectrometry, using a conventional instrument which requires solution samples.

Most of the samples examined (except one of the heel samples, LW/EB, which has been freeze-dried) have been stored wet. After removal of excess water, they were air dried for 48 hours at room temperatures, and weighed. They were then ashed at 900 °C and the residue extracted

Table 13   Atomic absorption analyses of skin and peat samples from Lindow III

DESCRIPTION	DRY WEIGHT (mg)	COPPER (µg/g ± precision)
LW/EB heel	79	4 ± 2
LW/BW l.heel	113	2 ± 2
LW/DG palm	63	10 ± 2
LW/CC finger	51	<2
LX/AJ peat	69	6 ± 2
LW/DR torso	74	36 ± 4

with 5 ml of concentrated nitric acid while being heated on a hot plate at 80 °C for about 15 minutes. The extracts were diluted to fixed volumes with deionised water and analysed by atomic absorption spectrometry using standard procedures. The results are shown in Table 13.

Discussion

Clearly, the copper content of the torso skin sample is somewhat higher than that of the other skin samples and also the peat sample. This is broadly in support of the results obtained by Pyatt *et al* although the actual values strictly cannot be compared since their data are not expressed in the same form (the data here are concentrations in the original skin samples as opposed to normalised partial analyses by Pyatt *et al*). The difference between the torso sample and the other, *control*, samples is statistically significant. We suggest, however, that it is not of sufficient magnitude to provide convincing evidence that the copper was deliberately applied as a paint, especially as the epidermis, which was the original surface of the skin and would have carried the putative paint, is lost.

It is relevant in this context to consider the copper content of modern man, which averages 100–120 mg in 70 kg, or about 1.5 µg/g whole body (Eastman 1985), and also to note that copper is not distributed evenly throughout the body. It is apparent that most of the *control* skin samples and even the environmental background peat contain rather more copper than the average whole body content. This elevated skin content may be at least partly explained by the substantial, and possibly selective, loss of organic body weight through decay, leading to a preferential enhancement of the inorganic components. The equivalent levels in the peat also suggest that some equilibrium has been established between body and peat. However, since information on the movement of ions within the peat bog is lacking, it is not clear if copper has moved from the peat into the body or vice versa.

Given such uncertainties, the moderately higher concentrations observed on the torso would be explained equally well by factors other than deliberate application.

The Last Meals of the Lindow Bog Men

T. G. Holden

Introduction

The idea that important archaeological data regarding past diet could be obtained from human faecal debris including the gut contents of well-preserved ancient human bodies is not a new one. Analyses of samples of food residues from the human gut were undertaken as early as the beginning of the century with publications by Jones (1910), Netolitzky (1911; cited by Wilke and Hall 1975). Warren (1911) and Young (1910), from Britain, North America and North Africa. Research expanded in the 1960s and since that time has played an important role in palaeodietary studies, especially in parts of the world where preservation of organic material by desiccation occurs naturally. For a recent review of the potential and practice of such analyses, see for example, Fry (1985), Hillman (1986), Holden (1994). Early attempts at scientific analyses of the macroscopic food remains from northern European bog bodies included those by Netolitzky (1936) on a body from Assen, Holland and that by Brandt (1950) on a body from Borremose, Denmark. It was, however, probably the results from the well-publicised Tollund and Grauballe men from Denmark by Helbaek (1950; 1958) which most fired the imagination and revealed the potential of such samples for illuminating aspects of diet and other important elements of prehistoric life. Since then, new discoveries and awakened interest in old ones, have resulted in the publication of more data relating to the 'bog body phenomenon' in northern Europe (Brothwell *et al* 1990a, 1990b; Liversage 1985; van der Sanden 1990; Stead and Turner 1985; Stead *et al* 1986). The analysis of

the intestinal contents has formed one of the principal components of multidisciplinary projects which have developed around these bodies and an ever-increasing corpus of knowledge is accumulating. Notable analyses include those from Dätgen, Germany by Martin (1967); Zweeloo, Netherlands (van der Sanden 1990); Huldremose, Denmark (Brothwell *et al* 1990b; Holden, forthcoming) and from Lindow, Britain (Hillman 1986; Holden 1986).

This chapter presents the results from newly analysed samples recovered from the alimentary canals of two of the Lindow bog bodies. A number of samples from the badly disturbed gut of the Lindow III body are discussed and further samples from different areas of the intestinal tract of Lindow Man (Lindow II) presented, so adding to those previously published.

Lindow II

A preliminary analysis of a sample from the fundus and body of the stomach has already been made by Hillman (1986) and Holden (1986). These analyses indicated that the major part of the meal was made up of a cereal component. The bran (testa and pericarp) of wheat or rye and the chaff of barley were reported as being the most dominant components of the food debris. Chaff fragments further indicated that both emmer (*Triticum dicoccum* Schübler) and spelt (*Triticum spelta* L.) wheats were also present and it is considered likely that much of the cereal bran identified as wheat/rye probably belonged to one or the other of these wheat species. Minor contaminants of the cereal food consisted of fragmentary seeds of several common weeds of cultivation along with other organic and non-organic inclusions which were considered to have been consumed accidentally.

Sufficient length of the gut survived in the severed torso to enable the taking of further samples from distinct areas of the upper parts of the intestinal tract. By so doing, it was hoped that it would be possible to identify compositional changes indicative of different meals eaten in the last few hours before death. Of the samples provided for analysis, four, including that presented earlier from the fundus and stomach, proved to be suitable for detailed study. These were:

LP/EE	gastric content 4.3 g (fundus and body of the stomach)
LP/EF	antrum content 2.2 g (stomach)
LP/EL	small intestine 5.8 g
LP/EN	upper small intestine 6.8 g
Note:	Weights = wet weight

Each of these samples was subjected to the separation and sorting techniques outlined in Holden (1986). The small sample size and fragmentary nature of the remains precluded the application of any system of empirical quantification; the results are therefore presented as a four point subjective scale in Table 14 (+ = rare, ++ = occasional, +++ = common, ++++ = abundant). Nomenclature follows that of Clapham *et al* (1987).

Lindow II – Results

As can be seen from Table 14, in terms of the major constituents, i.e. the bran of wheat/rye and the chaff of barley (lemma and palea), the composition of all four samples proved to be in close agreement. It is, therefore, likely that they all derived from the same meal. The minor variations of the less commonly occurring components such as the highly fragmented weed seeds (Fig. 35, nos. 1 and 2), charred organic debris (Fig. 35, nos. 3 and 4), moss

Table 14   *The composition of samples from Lindow II. Naming conventions follow Clapham* et al *(1987)*

SPECIES	COMMON NAME	PLANT PART	LP/EE	LP/EF	LP/EL	LP/EN
Wild Plants						
Sphagnum sp.	sphagnum moss	leaf	++	++	+	++
Brassica sp.	cabbage family	testa fragment	+			
Chenopodium album L.	fat hen	nutlet fragment	+	+	+	+
Umbelliferae indet.	carrot family	fruit	+			
Polygonum cf. *lapathifolium*	pale persicaria	nutlet fragment	++	+	++	+
Fallopia convolvulus (L.) Á. Löve	black bindweed	nutlet fragment	+		+	+
Polygonum indet.	knotgrass family	nutlet fragment	+		+	
Rumex sp.	dock	nutlet fragment	+	+	+	+
Alnus sp.	alder	charcoal			+	+
Calluna vulgaris (L.) Hull	heather	leaf	+			
Galeopsis cf. *tetrahit* agg.	common hemp nettle	nutlet fragment	+			
Lapsana communis L.	nipplewort	achene	+			
Bromus sp.	brome grass	bran fragments	++	++	++	++
Avena sp.	oat	bran fragments	+	+	+	
Fungi indet.		hyphae and spores	+	+	+	+
Charred indet.			++	++	++	++
Cereals						
Triticum spelta L.	spelt wheat	glume base	+			
		rachis fragment			+	
Triticum dicoccum Schubler	emmer wheat	glume base	+			
Triticum sp. (glume wheat indet.)	wheat	glume			+	+
cf. *Triticum* sp.	wheat	glume/rachis	+	+	+	+
Triticum/Secale sp.	wheat/rye	bran (testa/pericarp)	++++	++++	++++	++++
Hordeum sp.	barley	rachis fragment			+	+
Hordeum sp.	barley	lemma/palea	++	++	++	++
Hordeum type	barley type	bran fragment	+	+	+	
Hordeum/Secale sp.	barley/rye	rachis internode	+		+	
Cereal indet.		chaff indet.	+++	+++	+++	+++
Other						
Animal hair			+	+		
cf. Animal connective tissue			+			
mineral indet.			+	+	+	+

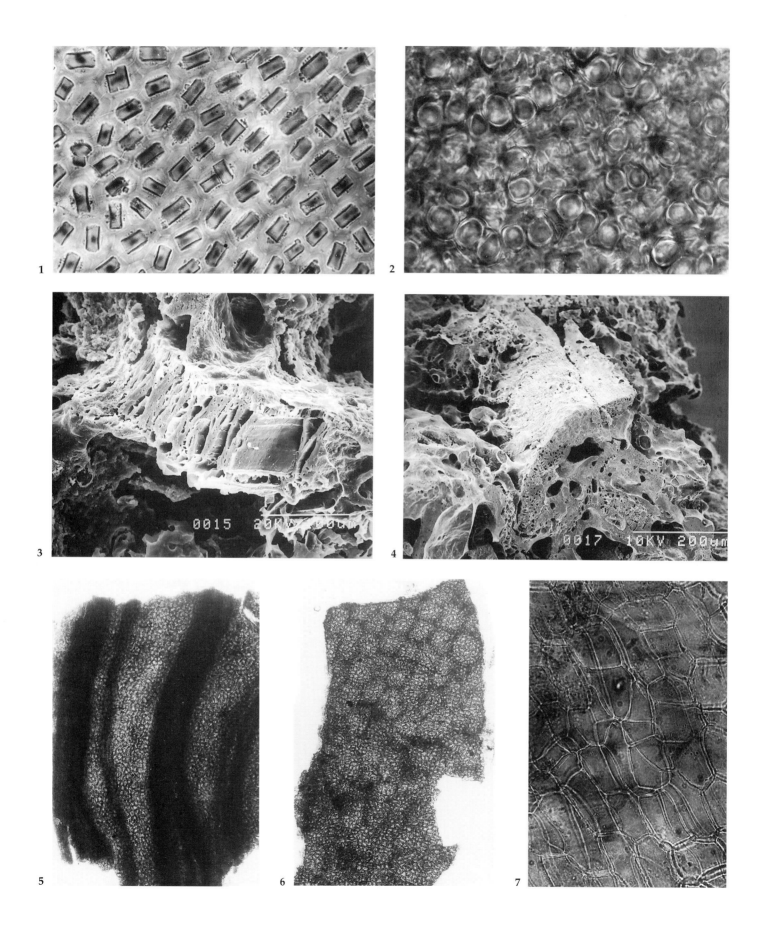

leaves, fine animal hair and mineral fragments would appear to be of little significance.

Information relating to how the food was prepared has been given in the discussions by Holden (1986), Hillman (1986: 109), Robins *et al* (1986) and Sales *et al* (1990). The size of the fragments of the wheat/rye bran and the associated weed seeds were consistent with their having been finely milled. The fragmentation of the barley chaff was more compatible with its having been prepared by crushing or using a technique such as pearling, which would leave a proportion of the chaff adhering to the grain. This implies that it was a hulled variety.

At present it is not possible to state whether the barley and wheat fragments were prepared together or whether they were prepared separately but eaten together as different parts of the same meal. The data provided by ESR (electron spin resonance) by Robins *et al* (1986) and Sales *et al* (1990) indicated that the wheat chaff component had been heated to a temperature of 200–250 °C for a relatively short period of time. This suggested that this wheat, at least, could not have been prepared by boiling as, for example, a gruel, since this would have produced a maximum temperature closer to 100 °C. A combination of the poor rising qualities of the cereals used (barley, emmer and spelt) have been used to suggest that they were probably eaten as an unleavened bread or griddle cake. Small fragments of alder charcoal probably represent adherent traces of cooking fuel while burned fragments of food may support a rapid cooking theory. They were, however, so small (little more than 2–3 mm across) that it would seem just as likely that they were the burnt residues of previous meals picked up from the baking surface or cooking utensils. This being the case, the charred part of the meal is unlikely to have been of any special significance. No starch grains were noted in any of the samples.

Fig. 35 Light micrographs (LM) or scanning electron micrographs (SEM) of food fragments.
1) LM of testa of *Galeopsis* sp. (hemp-nettle) from gut of Lindow II (× 325).
2) LM of nutlet fragment of *Fallopia convulvulus* (L.) Á. Löve (black bindweed) from the gut of Lindow II (× 325).
3) SEM of unidentified charred food debris from the gut of Lindow II.
4) SEM of unidentified charred food debris from the gut of Lindow II.
5) LM of a fragment of testa from *Corylus avellana* L. (hazel) from the gut of Lindow III (× 325).
6) LM of a fragment of testa from *Raphanus* sp. (radish) from the gut of Lindow III (× 85).
7) LM of a fragment of grass testa, probably *Hordeum* sp. (barley) from the gut of Lindow III (× 325).

Lindow III

Of the more than seventy fragments of the Lindow III body recovered, several of the larger pieces were evidently parts of the thorax and abdomen. The peat-cutting machinery had so disturbed the body that when recovered, the vertebrae and intestines were positioned towards the outside of the mass of tissues. In spite of this, it was possible to determine the orientation of the larger pieces and to identify lengths of the gastrointestinal tract. Samples were removed from various parts of this and the surrounding areas but in most cases the disturbed nature of the body meant that few of them could be considered as well-sealed or uncontaminated. The following samples were studied in detail:

LW/EW	cf. faeces 5.5 g
LW/EX	cf. faeces 4.3 g
LW/EY	intestinal contents 3.6 g
LW/FG	colonic content 5.9 g
LW/FH	colonic content 2.4 g
LW/FJ	colonic content with adherent faeces 12.8 g
LW/FO	rectal passage 1.1 g
LW/FP	stomach wall 4.4 g
LW/FR	stomach contents 3.0 g
LW/FS	duodenal wall 13.77 g
LW/FT	duodenal contents 0.7 g
LW/FU	transverse colon and adherent faeces 26.8 g
LW/FW	gastrointestinal debris 8.6 g
Note:	Weights = wet weight

Lindow III – Results

The initial results were disappointing, with many of the samples yielding no identifiable food debris. Samples, such as LW/EW, LW/FR and LW/EX, which were thought to originate from the gut, proved to be made up of a compacted but seemingly amorphous, brown organic 'silt' from which no evidence of cellular plant material, other than the occasional *Sphagnum* moss leaf, could be extracted. My only explanation for these is that they possibly represent faecal debris from a totally non-fibrous meal such as eggs, cheese or other meat products, in which case the sample would be dominated by colonic bacteria. Alternatively, and more probably, they represent the highly degraded and compacted remains of body tissues or food debris. Chemical analysis of these samples probably represents the only way of resolving this question more fully.

Only two samples, from the intestinal (LW/EY) and the colonic (LW/FJ) areas of the gut yielded identifiable food debris. These were, however, clearly contaminated by adherent stem and leaf fragments of *Sphagnum* moss from the surrounding peat. Unfortunately, the nature of this contamination, poor preservation, small sample size and the fragmentation of the debris, made detailed quantification impractical. A four-point subjective assessment of the composition identical to that used with the Lindow II body was therefore made. The results are presented in Table 15.

The intestinal and colonic contents showed close agreement in their composition but did not lend themselves to a high level of interpretation. As with the Lindow II sample, the diversity of food remains was not high, but this time they were dominated by fragments of the testa and brown inner layer of the pericarp of *Corylus avellana* L. (hazel nut, Fig. 35 no. 5). The size of the hazel fragments were consistent with their having been eaten raw or following a coarse preparation technique such as crushing or pounding. Also present, but in lesser quantities were fragments of cereal bran which, even though badly degraded and lacking the distinctive transverse cell layer, were identifiable as that of either wheat or rye (*Triticum/Secale*). The small size of the cereal bran fraction was indicative of it having been finely milled. Rare testa fragments of a type which includes barley (*Hordeum* type, Fig. 35, no. 7) were also recovered as were occasional fragments of the seeds of a number of common weeds of cultivation such as pale persicaria (*Polygonum* cf. *lapathifolium*) fat hen (*Chenopodium album* L.), brome grass (*Bromus* sp.) and wild radish (*Raphanus* sp., Fig. 35, no. 6). These species all have relatively robust or resistant outer coats and tend to survive well in waterlogged archaeological deposits. They therefore probably represent only that small portion of the last meal that survived to the present day in an identifiable form.

Discussion

The Cereal Component

The cereal component of the gut samples generally fall into line with our understanding of the development and geographic distribution of cultivated plants from the Iron Age/Roman period in Britain (e.g., Greig 1991; Jones 1981). However, a discussion of some of the more important points regarding the identification and survival properties of the different species would seem appropriate.

Unfortunately, it is usually not possible to identify most cereal crops to the level of species from the remains of the bran alone, especially where preservation is poor. With wheat and rye, for example, if preservation is good and distinctive cell layers of the pericarp (one of the outer layers of the bran) survive in good condition, then extreme forms can be distinguished. However, under more usual conditions of preservation these and other potentially identifiable layers do not survive, leaving the two superimposed layers of the testa (seed coat) as the only remaining evidence. Such fragments are very distinctively that of rye or wheat but the surviving anatomy is not sufficient to enable the separation of these two species. Similarly, with species such as barley and oats, the cell patterns on fragments of the testa and pericarp are not sufficient to distinguish cultivated forms from their wild relations or even, in some cases other genera. Because of

Table 15   The composition of samples from Lindow III. Naming conventions follow Clapham et al (1987)

SPECIES	COMMON NAME	PLANT PART	LW/EY	LW/FJ
Wild Plants				
Sphagnum sp.	sphagnum moss	leaf	++++	++++
Raphanus sp.	wild radish	seed fragment	+	
Chenopodium album L.	fat hen	nutlet fragment	+	++
Polygonum cf. *lapathifolium*	pale persicaria	nutlet fragment	++	
Corylus avellana L.	hazel	testa and endocarp	+++	+++
Juncus sp.	rush	seed		+
cf. *Bromus* sp.	brome grass	testa	+	+
Charred fragments indet.			++	++
Cereals				
Hordeum type	barley type	testa	+	+
Triticum/Secale sp.	wheat/rye	testa	++	++
Other				
Mineral indet.			+	+

this, it was often only possible to categorise cereal remains into broad taxonomic groups unless identification was supported by evidence from other more diagnostic cereal remains. The examples from the Lindow II samples were a case in point. Evidence for both emmer and spelt wheat were positively identified on the form of the remaining glume fragments. This implied that the wheat/rye category of bran was in fact also derived from one or the other of these two wheat species.

With barley there is a similar taphonomic problem related to the identification of poorly preserved remains. There is a very obvious difference in the quantity of barley type bran fragments recovered and the quantity of chaff fragments identified. This is particularly clear in samples from the Lindow II body as shown in Table 14. Occasional fragments of the testa with the distinctive, brick-like cellular arrangement of the testa (see Holden 1986; Dickson 1987) were identified as compared with large quantities of cereal chaff, some of which consisted of the basal part of the lemma and adherent rachilla. This worrying disparity can be explained only by the differential survival properties of the two different parts of the plant. Dickson (1989, 138) has demonstrated experimentally the fragile nature of the cell structure in barley, which becomes very degraded as a result of pearling followed by boiling. In spite of this, fragments matching the structure of barley were recovered regularly, but at a consistently low level. This implies that certain areas of the testa survive more readily than others or that processing, such as pearling, has removed a large proportion of the identifiable bran. There is a clear gap in our understanding of the taphonomic processes involved during the preparation and digestion of barley and there is scope for further experimental work in this area of research.

The testa of oats was also present in small quantities from Lindow II though they, too, were highly degraded. In such cases, the difficulty in recognising the largely diaphanous bran among the mass of other organic material may mean that they are under-represented in the species lists. It would seem likely that oats were, in fact, being grown in parts of Britain during the Iron Age (Jones 1981, 108) although the evidence tends to suggest that they did not become an important cereal until the Saxon period (Green 1981). There is no evidence to suggest that oats were a major part of any of the last meals and it is more likely that they represent the remains of tolerated crop contaminants rather than deliberate additions to the meals analysed here.

The Weed Seed Element

One of the most noticeable features of the Lindow samples was that the diversity of the debris is significantly less than their Danish counterparts from Grauballe, Tollund and Borremose (Brandt 1950; Helbaek 1950; 1958) and much more in keeping with those from Zweeloo (van der Sanden 1990a; b) and Assen (Netolitzky 1936). These latter samples were dominated by major cereals, common millet (*Panicum miliaceum* L.) and barley respectively, with much lesser quantities of non-cereal seeds. The samples analysed from the Huldremose bog body (Brothwell *et al* 1990; Holden forthcoming) lie somewhere between these, having a relatively low diversity of species but with an estimated third of the original meal having been made up of the seeds of corn spurrey (*Spergula arvensis* L.).

In the samples from Lindow II, Lindow III and the Zweeloo body, weed seeds generally played only a minor part in the last meals. Remains of *Bromus* sp., *Brassica* sp., *Raphanus* sp., *Polygonum* sp., *Rumex* sp. and *Galeopsis* sp. were, however, all present in trace quantities. These are all common weeds of agriculture and are probably best interpreted as minor contaminants of the cereal element with little dietary significance. One exception to this is the quantity of blackberry pips recovered from the gut of the Zweeloo body, which were most probably a genuine part of the last meal.

Other Components

The Lindow III samples yielded amounts of the testa of hazel nut (*Corylus avellana* L.). That hazel nuts were being exploited should be of no great surprise since they would have been plentiful in northern Europe at this time and must have been used as a welcome supplement to the agricultural staples. Their presence in the vicinity of Lindow Moss has been confirmed by pollen analysis (Branch and Scaife, pp. 19–30). Unfortunately, even though the nuts are only seasonally available, their storage properties are good, so their identification from the gut of Lindow III cannot be used as an indicator of the season in which they were eaten.

There was evidence of meat consumption in very few of the samples. This was in the form of small fragments of largely structureless, rubbery material with a distinctive glossy appearance under light microscopy. They were thought to be fragments of elastin-rich tissue such as tendon or cartilage which tends to have good survival properties (Holden 1994). One or two individual hairs were recovered from samples from Lindow II. These were small, with very delicate scale patterns but it is unlikely that it will be possible to make a species identification of these (Holden 1986, citing Priston pers. comm.) Whether such animal hairs were the remains of a meal or a contaminant of food was impossible to say.

Two other classes of debris were assumed not to have been deliberately consumed. The first of these were contaminants from the bog itself in the form of *Sphagnum* moss leaves and stem fragments. In the case of Lindow III the majority of contamination occurred after the disturbance of the body in recent times. With the Lindow II body, however, the moss leaves were recovered from within the compacted faecal matrix with little chance that post-depositional contamination had occurred. These *Sphagnum* leaves were therefore probably ingested with drinking or cooking water taken from the bog environment. Fragments of grit were possibly the result of contamination during the preparation of food, using primitive grinding equipment from which tiny stone fragments became detached.

Summary

The results of the analyses presented here have revealed that the main constituents of the gut contents of the Lindow II bog body were a mixture of emmer and spelt wheats and barley, which had probably been prepared as an unleavened bread such as a griddle cake. The Lindow III bog body on the other hand seems to have consumed a quantity of hazel nuts and a smaller amount of wheat/rye. In both cases the minor constituents such as seed and charcoal fragments were considered to have been incidental contaminants deriving from the weeds associated with a cereal crop and other elements incorporated during food processing or cooking. In all probability the debris do represent the last meal of the individuals. Samples from the small intestine and stomach of Lindow II for example, were almost identical, indicating that if any residual debris from previous meals were present it was either minimal or of exactly the same composition as the last meal.

There is nothing regarding the composition of these last meals to indicate that they had any special significance, ritual or other, relating to the death of either man. This anticlimactic conclusion does, however, serve to highlight the varied manifestations of the bog body phenomenon when compared with the more diverse assemblages recovered from the Danish bodies. Is it possible that the Danish examples from Borremose, Tollund, Grauballe and Huldremose reflect a more fragile agricultural system commonly beset by crop failure and that the weed seeds represent attempts to stretch failing supplies of cereal grain? There is plenty of ethno-historical evidence to suggest that this practice was commonplace in many parts of Europe. If this is the case, it would be tempting to try to link the ritual killings from Denmark with years of particular famine. The less diverse plant assemblages recovered from other parts of Europe, however, suggest that this is probably too simplistic to explain all of the available information. In any event, it does appear as though certain trends are beginning to manifest themselves and it can only be hoped that as the present database is enlarged, the relevance of these trends may become clearer.

Pollen Analysis of the Lindow III Food Residue

R. G. Scaife

Introduction

Nineteen samples were examined from faecal, colonic, gastro-intestinal, duodenal and rectal residue. These were taken in conjunction with sampling for plant macrofossils (see Holden, pp. 76–82) with the aim of elucidating the dietary characteristics of Lindow III and to compare with those results obtained from the stomach and intestinal contents of Lindow II (Scaife 1986).

Methodology

Samples of 0.5–1 g were prepared by deflocculation in boiling 8% potassium hydroxide and by acetolysis in sulphuric and glacial acetic acid (1:10), the latter being less harsh than the more commonly used Erdtman technique. As no inorganic material was present, hydrofluoric acid treatment was not required. The concentrated pollen was stained with safranin and mounted in glycerol jelly. Examination and identification of the extracted pollen was carried out at magnifications of ×400 and ×1000 with the aid of phase contrast. Taxonomy follows that of Clapham *et al* (1987). Samples examined comprised the following:

LW/EW	? faecal material; 3 samples
LW/EX	? faecal material
LW/FG	colonic content; 2 samples
LW/FJ	colonic material; 3 samples
LW/FM	colonic content
LW/FO	rectal passage

LW/FP	stomach wall; 2 samples
LW/FR	stomach contents
LW/FT	wall of duodenum
LW/FU	transverse colon and faecal debris
LW/FV	transverse colon
LW/FW	gastro-intestinal debris; 2 samples

Because of the severe disruption of the body of Lindow III, several of the samples analysed have suffered from contamination by pollen and spores from the surrounding peat, thus making interpretation impossible. This was due to the fragmentation of the body by the mechanical peat cutter. Of the 19 samples examined, 13 proved to have pollen but, with the exception of 3, these were contaminated. Absence of mire taxa (especially *Sphagnum*, Gramineae and Cyperaceae) provided a good indication of those uncontaminated samples. Furthermore, samples LW/FJ (one of three), LW/FV and LW/FT contained no pollen. Of the remaining samples, those taken from the colon (LW/FM, LW/FG, LW/FJ) and a (?) faecal sample (LW/EW), contained the only pollen which could be attributed to food/faecal remains.

It can also be noted that in samples contaminated from the surrounding peat, there was little or no evidence of mixing with pollen of palaeodietary significance. Pollen of undoubted palaeodietary origin was in general sparse in all samples and only relatively small counts were obtained. In many cases the grains, largely the cereal pollen, were degraded, which contrasts with the fine preservation experienced with pollen obtained from Lindow II (Scaife 1986). These pollen data are presented in Table 16.

Table 16 Pollen recorded in the gut contents of Lindow III

| LINDOW III | COLONIC | | | | FAECAL | |
SAMPLE	FM	FJ	FJ	FG	FG	EW
Betula	—	—	—	—	1	—
Quercus	—	—	—	—	—	1
Alnus	1	2	—	—	—	—
Corylus	1	—	1	—	4	3
Calluna	1	1	—	—	—	—
Trifolium type	—	—	—	—	1	—
Hornungia type	—	—	—	1	—	—
Spergula type	—	—	—	2	—	—
Chenopodium type	—	3	—	—	4	—
Sanguisorba officinalis	—	—	—	—	1	—
cf. *Hypericum*	—	—	—	—	1	—
Rumex	—	—	1	1	—	—
Polygonum persicaria type	—	—	1	—	—	—
Campanula type	—	—	—	—	1	—
Anthemis type	—	—	1	1	—	—
Bidens type	—	—	1	1	—	—
Liguliflorae	—	—	1	1	—	—
Gramineae	—	1	1	4	2	—
Cereal type	15	6	33	38	50	1
Indeterminable	—	—	—	1	2	—
Pteridium	—	—	1	1	—	1
Sphagnum	1	—	—	—	—	4
Trichuris	—	—	28	—	—	—
Charcoal	—	—	—	—	*	—
Phytoliths	—	—	—	—	*	—

Discussion of Results

It is now recognised that pollen which has become incorporated in food and drink and subsequently ingested may readily pass through the digestive system with little alteration. The pollen taphonomy may, however, be complex. Pollen may derive from a number of sources including the deliberate use of flowers in teas and medicines, secondary incorporation of pollen derived from crop plants themselves and their associated weed floras and from a wider region (the background component) ingested in food or drinking water. Whilst cultivated and natural seed and vegetative crops in general, undoubtedly formed an important part of the diet, the use of floral elements of plants may also have been an important component of liquid and solid foods. Thus, pollen recovered from human and animal palaeofaeces and internal digestive organs may provide valuable evidence of diet which may corroborate or add to knowledge gained from plant macrofossil studies.

There are now numerous studies on palaeodiet dating back to the pioneer work of Laudermilk and Munz (1938) who recognised the existence of pollen in coprolites (palaeofaeces) of prehistoric creatures. Martin and Sharrock (1964) showed that palynological study of human palaeofaeces from the arid area of Glen Canyon, Utah, USA could provide evidence of the diet of the Pueblo Indians. This study proved especially useful in identifying the use of flowers as well as seeds which are more frequently found in palaeobotanical studies of palaeofaeces. A more detailed review and appraisal of these and later researches has been given previously (Scaife 1986).

A detailed examination of the stomach and intestinal contents was carried out on Lindow II with plant macrofossils studied by Hillman (1986) and Holden (1986) and the pollen by Scaife (1986). The latter palynological investigation illustrated clearly a diet composed largely of farinaceous products, which was confirmed by the macrofossil analyses. In addition, there were herbs and weeds associated with cereal crops which, along with the cereal pollen, were probably trapped in the husks of the cereals remaining through crop processing, food production and ingestion. There was a notable presence of *Viscum album* (mistletoe) pollen about which there has been much speculation as to Druidical practices. It is perhaps more likely that mistletoe was used for medicinal rather than ceremonial purposes (Scaife 1986, 131).

These data contrasted strongly with those obtained from the study of, for example, Grauballe Man, which had little cereal pollen and high frequencies of weed pollen. With the discovery of Lindow III, the opportunity presented itself for comparison of the final meals of the two Lindow bodies.

Samples obtained from the colon yielded the most significant results (LW/FM, LW/FJ, LW/FG). As with Lindow II, the dominant pollen taxon was cereal type which formed 75–80% of the total pollen in these samples. Determination to *Triticum/Hordeum* type was made on the basis of size, pore/annulus size and columellate structure. This is in accord with Holden's (p. 80) identification of *Hordeum* sp. and *Triticum* sp. testa fragments in samples LW/EY and LW/FJ. The dominance of cereal pollen, as in the case of Lindow II, suggests that the final meal(s) was farinaceous and possibly unleavened bread (Hillman 1986).

In addition to cereal pollen, there are sporadic occurrences of pollen of weeds which were undoubtedly associated with the cultivation of the cereal crops. These typically include Cruciferae (*Hornungia* type), *Spergula* type (possibly *S. arvensis*), *Chenopodium* type (goosefoots and oraches), *Rumex* (docks), *Polygonum persicaria* type

(Persicaria) and Compositae (*Anthemis* type, *Bidens* type and Liguliflorae). As noted, it is most probable that these taxa and the pollen of cereals became trapped in the husks of the cereal inflorescences and were later incorporated into the finished food.

Holden (pp. 76–82) has recovered a small number of seeds of typical weeds of cultivation including *Polygonum* cf. *lapathifolium* (pale persicaria), *Chenopodium album* (fat hen), *Bromus* (brome grass) and *Raphanus* sp. (radish). These are all comparable with the pollen record and are also seen as aberrant inclusions in the final meal(s) of Lindow III. However, unlike Lindow II, no 'unusual' taxa such as mistletoe and possibly black bryony were recorded which may have been ingredients of herbal or medicinal drinks, or even plants of Druidical significance!

Sporadic occurrences of tree pollen and herbs unlikely to have been associated with arable habitats are also present, but in small numbers. These taxa which include the trees and shrubs: *Betula* (birch), *Quercus* (oak), *Alnus* (alder), *Corylus* (hazel) and *Calluna* (ling) may be contaminants from the peat surrounding the body fragments. Alternatively, they may be from regional pollen rain becoming incorporated into food and/or drinks. This remains unclear since the pollen data presented by Branch and Scaife (pp. 19–30) show similar taxa in high frequencies during the period at which burial in the bog took place.

Parasitology

During pollen analysis of Lindow III, and as with Lindow II (Jones 1986), ova of the intestinal parasite *Trichuris* were found. Although detailed size measurements were not carried out, it is likely that these ova are of *T. trichiura*, the human whipworm. It should be noted, however, that *Trichuris suis*, the whipworm of pigs, has also been found in human beings (Jones 1986). Ova were most abundant in LW/FJ (sample 2) from the colon. Ova of the maw worm (*Ascaris lumbricoides*) were, unlike Lindow II, not found in these recent analyses.

From this, it can be concluded that both Lindow II and III were infested with parasitic intestinal worms. It is difficult to assess the severity of these infestations since these nematodes produce great numbers of ova and light infestations may not have been harmful. There has, in recent years, been substantial archaeological evidence showing that whipworm and maw worm were common in prehistoric and later communities in Europe (Pike and Biddle 1966; Szidat 1944, in Jones 1986; Greig 1981). It is also interesting to note that the Danish, Grauballe and Tollund bog bodies also contained ova of *Trichuris trichiura*.

PART II

Other Bog Bodies

Chemical and Microbiological Aspects of the Preservation Process in *Sphagnum* Peat

T. J. Painter

Why do bodies, and other biodegradable things, get preserved in peat? To answer that question properly, it is necessary first to ask several more. Why does peat exist at all? Why do *Sphagnum* mosses grow, year after year, upon the dead remains of previous generations, while deriving little, if any, sustenance from them (Clymo and Hayward 1982)? Why do these residues decay so slowly, when a heap of grass clippings, for example, will rot so quickly that it becomes hot?

Many traditional uses of *Sphagnum* moss and peat point to an antimicrobial property. Bandages made from dried *Sphagnum* have been used in folk medicine since the Bronze Age, and they were used extensively as field dressings during the First World War. Research at London's Royal National Orthopædic Hospital (Stanmore) has recently confirmed that they do indeed have a better wound-healing effect than ordinary cotton bandages (Varley and Barnett 1987). In past centuries, seafarers took peat-bog water with them on long voyages, because they had found that it would stay 'fresh' much longer than ordinary spring or well water. This almost certainly means that algae grew much more slowly in the bog water (Sharp 1979).

Sphagnum peat is highly valued in horticulture because it can be stored indefinitely without becoming mouldy, infested with nematodes or insects, or smelling unpleasant. When mixed with an equal proportion (or less) of farmyard manure, it neutralises the odour so completely that the mixture can be used as a potting compost for indoor plants. When used as a soil conditioner, that is, to conserve moisture in the soil, it has the considerable advantage of decomposing much more slowly than humus from higher plants (Puustjärvi 1976).

In the discussion that follows, an attempt will be made to explain these facts, and to suggest some additional reasons why bodies sometimes do not get preserved in peat, apart from the obvious one that they may have decomposed before being submerged in bog water. Preservation in peats derived from mangroves and sedges will also be mentioned, and contributions made to the current discussion on possible sources of error in radiocarbon dating, adipocere formation, and the conservation of bodies in a condition suitable for display, once they have been found.

The 'Sphagnol' Hypothesis

It is natural to suspect that *Sphagnum* mosses contain some kind of antimicrobial substance, especially as similar inferences have proved correct before. For example, woods of trees of the family Cupressaceae, which include cypresses, junipers, incense cedar (*Calocedrus decurrens*) and western red cedar (*Thuja plicata*) resist decay because they contain potent fungicides called *thujaplicins*, as well as bactericidal substances such as *p*-cresol and derivatives of thymol (Hegnauer 1962). It is likely that the resinous exudates of these trees and shrubs, or the fragrant oils distilled from their leaves, were among the materials used to mummify bodies in ancient Egypt. (The written accounts are vague, obviously because plant taxonomy was not very advanced during the second and third millennia BC. The use of 'cedar oil' is explicitly mentioned

(Harmer 1979), but this does not necessarily mean that it came from the genus that we now call *Cedrus*.)

It is important to emphasise that one is looking for a constituent of *Sphagnum* that can be extracted by a mild procedure that would not change it chemically. Powerful disinfectants can be prepared from peat, as they can from coal, by pyrolysis (dry distillation) at high temperatures (Fuchsman 1980), but this obviously explains nothing about the preservative properties of peat in its natural state.

The 'sphagnol' hypothesis is this sort of muddle. The name 'sphagnol' was first given by Czapek (1913) to an unidentified crystalline phenol obtained by boiling *Sphagnum* moss with caustic soda in a pressure cooker. There is virtually nothing in vegetable matter that would not be changed in some way by this treatment, and Czapek made it clear that he thought sphagnol was a degradation product of a cell-wall polymer. He did, however, report that it had bacteriostatic and fungistatic properties, and this statement has subsequently been cited out of context.

The notion that sphagnol is the antimicrobial substance in *Sphagnum* moss and peat is now so popular that it is reported as a fact by the *Encyclopædia Britannica* (Sharp 1979). Later research has already shown, however, that sphagnol was an artefact of the method used to prepare it, and that it is not present in the living moss or in peat, except perhaps in trace amounts that could have no significant effect upon microbial activity (Rudolph and Engmann 1967; Rudolph 1972). Living *Sphagnum* mosses do contain 1–2% of phenolic compounds, which they release, in part, into the ambient water, but their bactericidal potencies are too low to be significant at the concentrations in which they are estimated to occur in bog water (Wilschke *et al* 1989; Painter 1991).

The distinguished soil microbiologist Selman Waksman (Nobel Prize, 1952) vigorously contested the notion that peat possessed any significant antimicrobial activity, after finding 10^7–10^8 cells per gram (dry weight) of aerobic bacteria, microscopic fungi and actinomycetes in the surface layer of a lowmoor peat bog. Deeper down, where the conditions were anoxic (oxygen-lacking), 10^4–10^6 cells per gram of anaerobic bacteria were found (Waksman 1930). Although these figures are very low compared with the 10^{10} cells per gram that may be found, for example, in a rotting heap of grass (Kononova 1961), they are hardly evidence of toxicity; they could be due simply to a lack of nutrients.

Aerobic v. Anaerobic Bacteria as Agents of Decay

The fact that there is virtually no molecular oxygen below the top 30–50 cm of a peat bog does not mean that there would be no decay. On average, anaerobic bacteria are just as effective as aerobic ones in breaking down the proteins in animal remains and the polysaccharides in vegetable ones, because these are hydrolytic reactions that require only the presence of water. Likewise, fats can be hydrolysed to give glycerine and long-chain fatty acids, but further breakdown of the latter entails repeated oxidation.

Even oxidative reactions can be carried out by anaerobic bacteria, but only by reducing other substances such as carbon dioxide (to methane), sulphate (to sulphur or hydrogen sulphide), or nitrate (to nitrogen or ammonia). When these are lacking, or when the bacteria derive too little energy from the oxidation to meet their metabolic requirements, the reaction will not go, and incompletely oxidised substances accumulate as end-products.

Typical end-products of the anaerobic breakdown of cellulose are lactic acid, succinic acid, ethyl alcohol, and short-chain fatty acids. Those from proteins include short-chain fatty acids and toxic, foul-smelling amines such as putrescine, cadaverine, and skatole. The long-chain fatty acids released by hydrolysis from fats and waxes can be reduced when they are unsaturated, but instances of their oxidation under anoxic conditions are rare. Sulphur-metabolising bacteria in marine sediments provide one exception to this rule (McInerney 1988).

Lignin and humic acids are polymers that anaerobic bacteria find it particularly hard to cope with, probably because their breakdown entails oxidative steps right from the beginning. Some researchers claim to have observed a very slow breakdown, with release of carbon dioxide and methane, but others have been unable to confirm this (Colberg 1988). Ancient, waterlogged woods, which seem at first sight to have been 'preserved' in anoxic sediments, often prove to be no more than a fragile honeycomb of lignin, from which the cellulose and hemicelluloses have been hydrolysed selectively away. It would, therefore, be correct to state that the anoxic conditions in a peat bog contribute to the preservation of lignin and humic acids, and also of the fatty acids liberated from fats and waxes, but not of the bodies or the carbohydrates in plant residues.

Acidity as a Disinfectant

Another theory that has gained wide acceptance is that preservation is due to the acidity of peat-bog water, combined with the anoxic conditions beneath the surface layer. It is based essentially upon the well-known fact that foods can be preserved by pickling in vinegar (and usually also salt) at a pH of about 2.5. This kind of preservation makes use of the fact that anaerobic, putrefactive bacteria (such as *Clostridium*, for example) usually grow best under nearly neutral conditions (pH 5.5–7.5). Acid-tolerant strains are known, but they do not usually mean trouble in the kitchen.

The acidity of peat has, however, been exaggerated, possibly because of a misconception that will be explained in the next section. It is necessary to distinguish between two different kinds of peat. Lowmoor peat (fens) as its name implies, is flushed continuously by groundwater that has run off from higher terrain, and is buffered by the salts (especially calcium bicarbonate) dissolved in it. Its pH is typically 5.5–6.5 (Waksman 1930). This is close to the *optimum* pH for growth of most normal strains of putrefactive bacteria. It is also a typical pH range for unpolluted rainwater, and for many kinds of soil that have rich microbial floras and no preservative properties.

Highmoor peat (blanket bog), on the other hand, is watered almost exclusively by precipitation. Its pH is typically 3.2–4.5, with most readings close to the average of 4.0 (Waksman 1930; Clymo 1984). The acidity arises because *Sphagnum* mosses contain a cation exchanger which absorbs the cations of salts dissolved in rain water, liberating mineral acid (Clymo 1963; Brehm 1970, 1971; Clymo 1984). The cation exchanger is the holocellulose, which is the total polysaccharidic fraction of the cell walls of the moss, consisting of cellulose, hemicellulose and pectic acid (Schwarzmaier and Brehm 1975; Painter and Sørensen 1978). The traces of salts in rain water originate mainly from the oceans and deserts, from which they are swept up by strong winds. They consist mainly of the chlorides of sodium and magnesium, and hence the acidity is due mainly to hydrochloric acid.

Intermediate between these two extremes is the special case of 'raised' bogs on low terrain. As the name implies, the surfaces of these bogs have grown up above the level of the surrounding land. That part of the peat which lies above the upper limit of the water table resembles highmoor peat in that it is watered mainly by rainfall. In periods of dry weather, however, groundwater rises by capillary action to replace water lost from the surface by evaporation, like oil climbing the wick of a lamp. It is hard to give a statistically reliable average, but the present author has never found a pH lower than 5 in this sort of lowmoor peat. Lindow Man, Tollund Man, and Grauballe Man were found in peat of this kind (Turner, personal communication).

Even in highmoor peat, however, acid-tolerant bacteria, both aerobic and anaerobic, have been found (Waksman 1930; Waksman and Stevens 1929). It is worth remembering that most wines and ciders are produced by anaerobic fermentation at pH 3.0–3.8. The special strains of yeast that do this are, of course, genetically adapted to grow on fruits and their juices; most yeasts, like most bacteria, grow best under neutral conditions. It should not, therefore, be a surprise to learn that millions of years of natural selection have likewise ensured that peat bogs have their own, special, microbial floras, uniquely adapted to exploit whatever opportunities for growth they offer.

Attention is drawn to a special, microbiological investigation of Lindow Man's body, and samples of peat associated with it (Ridgway *et al* 1986). The most prominent micro-organisms were bacteria of the genus *Pseudomonas*. These are typical saprophiles, widely distributed in soils and water, and capable of adaptation to both aerobic and anaerobic growth. They were evidently growing on nutrients derived from the peat or the bog water, but not from the body.

Sequestration of Multivalent Metal Cations

One of the most consistent observations on bog bodies is that they are extensively decalcified. The British Museum's previous report is especially clear on this point (Connolly *et al* 1986). In exceptional cases, the bones have dissolved completely (Coles and Coles 1989; Ross and Robins 1989). Everybody knows that vinegar softens and dissolves fish bones as well as preserving the flesh, so the inference in the minds of the discoverers must have seemed quite compelling: peat-bog water is acidic, and quite strongly so.

There are, however, other substances in peat that will decalcify bones and teeth much more efficiently than a trace of acidity. *Sphagnum* holocellulose will sequester calcium and other multivalent metal cations with high selectivity compared to monovalent cations such as sodium (Smidsrød and Painter 1984). It will do this at any pH above 3, but it does so most efficiently at pH 7

(Andresen *et al* 1987). The anionic groups that take part in this binding are concentrated in polysaccharidic chains that are chemically related to pectic acid, but which also contain building units of an unusual keto-uronic acid, namely 5-keto-D-mannuronic acid, which is abbreviated to 5KMA.

In the living moss, the pectic acid is chemically linked, through its 5KMA units, to the other cell-wall polysaccharides in the holocellulose (cellulose and hemicellulose), and also to lignin. As the dead moss is slowly transformed into peat, these chemical linkages are gradually broken by a reaction known as 'autohydrolysis', and the pectic acid, still containing most of the original 5KMA units, is released in soluble form (Painter and Sørensen 1978; Painter 1983a, 1983b, 1991). The properties of this polysaccharide are so different from those of ordinary pectic acid that it has been given a special name, *sphagnan* (Painter 1991).

Sphagnan is the refined and concentrated form of the cation exchanger in *Sphagnum* holocellulose and the living moss, and it has the same affinity for calcium and other multivalent metal cations (Fig. 36). Because of its content of 5KMA it is, however, an unstable substance – most keto-acids are unstable. Under mildly acidic conditions, and especially in the presence of ammonia or an amine, it is slowly converted into a brown, anionic polymer that is familiar to everyone, namely, aquatic humus or humic acid (Painter 1983b, 1991). [Note: When completely neutralised, humic acids should, strictly speaking, be called 'humates', but it is more convenient to call them 'humic acids' all the time, and to specify the pH separately. In peat with a pH range of 3.2–6.5, they would be only partly neutralised.]

Humic acids also sequester multivalent metal cations. They do this so efficiently under mildly acidic, neutral, or even alkaline conditions, that they will even erode and dissolve rocks (Kononova 1961). Bog bodies are permanently immersed in a solution containing sphagnan, intermediates in the conversion of sphagnan into humic acids, and the humic acids themselves. There can be no doubt that this is why they are decalcified. Decalcification is not evidence of acidity, and in fact the sequestering properties of these polymers would be impaired by too much acidity.

Humic Acids as Regulators of Microbial Growth

Micro-organisms cannot grow without trace elements (micro-nutrients), which include multivalent metal cations such as those of copper, iron, manganese, molybdenum and zinc. Since these are sequestered by *Sphagnum* holocellulose, sphagnan, and humic acids, it is to be expected that microbial growth in peat would be suppressed. With one soil bacterium that has a special requirement for calcium ions (*Azotobacter vinelandii*), it was found that both sphagnan and aquatic humus from peat inhibited growth very strongly (Painter 1991).

It should be emphasised that this kind of bacteriostatic activity does not kill the cells, and that when the supply of essential cations exceeds the capacity of the humic acids to bind them, they grow quite normally. When the cations of toxic metals such as cadmium and lead are present, a little humic acid can even stimulate growth by sequestering them selectively (Prakash *et al* 1973; Steinberg and Muenster 1985). Low concentrations of humic acids can also stimulate growth by acting as a carrier for iron (Foster *et al* 1991), but there is general agreement that high concentrations (relative to the concentrations of essential cations) are inhibitory. The ancient mariners' belief in the 'keeping' properties of bog water was well founded!

These findings raise an interesting question: does *Sphagnum* peat, in its natural state, ever become so saturated with essential, multivalent metal cations that this kind of bacteriostatic activity ever ceases to operate? Could this explain why the bones of some bodies dissolve, leaving some soft tissue intact, while the soft tissues of others decay completely, leaving only the bones? Ross and Robins (1989) have commented interestingly on this paradox, describing the outcome of any bog burial as a 'lottery'.

Only the first of these two questions can be answered here. It is a fact that *Sphagnum* mosses do not normally accumulate on fertile terrain. They specialise in growth under conditions of extreme nutrient limitation. Such is the extent of this adaptation that the growth of most *Sphagnum* species is actually inhibited by even moderate concentrations of calcium ions (Brehm 1970; Clymo and Hayward 1982). Some ombrogenous (rain-fed) peats seem to have a considerable surplus of cation-binding capacity down to depths corresponding to an age of 2500 years or more (Mattson and Koutler-Andersson 1955).

Once the peat has been formed, the agricultural, industrial, and dam-building activities of Man could, of course, intervene to change this picture. For example, it is unlikely that peat watered by run-off from agricultural soil would preserve a body buried in it today.

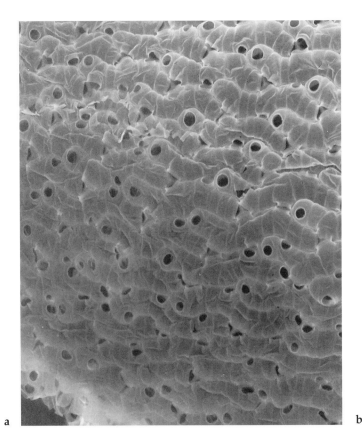

a

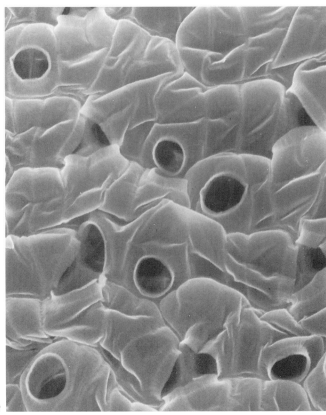

b

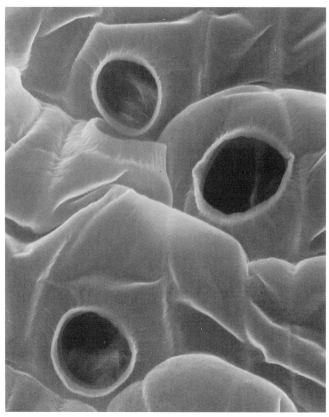

c

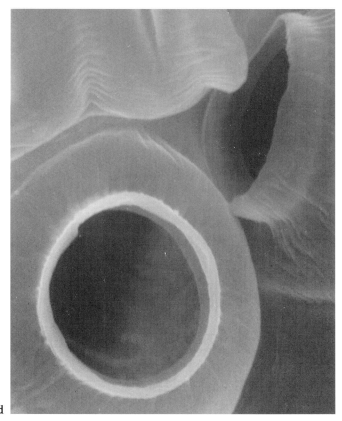

d

Possibilities for Tanning by Polymeric Polyphenols

Another consistent observation on peat-bog bodies is that the best-preserved parts are the connective tissues, and especially the skin. In these tissues, the collagen fibres are remarkably intact, and they seem to be *tanned*, as in leather (Connolly *et al* 1986). Bourke (1986) likens the skin of Lindow Man to soft, suede leather.

It is natural to suspect that peat contains a vegetable tannin of the type used traditionally in the leather industry. These materials are polymeric polyphenols, and are familiar to everybody from their mouth-drying, astringent taste in cheap red wine, over-brewed tea, and the skins of all fruits – especially the rind of the pomegranate.

Polyphenolic tannins are widely but not equally distributed in the vegetable kingdom. They occur most abundantly in the bark, leaves and heartwood of woody dicotyledons ('dicots') such as acacia (bark, 36%), eucalyptus (bark, 40%), mangrove (bark, 46%), oak (bark and wood, 15%), and sumac (leaves, 25%; galls, 64%). Their proportion is generally somewhat lower in woody monocotyledons ('monocots') such as hemlock (bark, 15%), larch (bark, 12%), and spruce (bark, 16%). In herbaceous (non-woody) dicots, which include most of the vegetables used as food, it is much lower (1–3%), and in herbaceous monocots, which include the cereals, reeds and other grasses (Poales), as well as sedges and rushes (Cyperales), it is usually insignificant. In *Sphagnum* mosses, polyphenolic tannins are completely absent (Hegnauer 1962).

It should be emphasised that all of the plants just mentioned, including *Sphagnum*, contain other kinds of phenolic compounds that do not tan. Only a special kind of polymeric (or oligomeric) phenol will bind to the collagen fibres of skin in such a way as to protect them from microbial attack, toughen them physically, and stabilise them to heat (which would convert untreated collagen into gelatin) (Fig. 37).

What is it, then, that tans the bodies? Barber (1986) has provided an excellent account of the vegetation at Lindow Moss during the period 615–60 BC, based upon the identification of the fragments of plants found preserved in the peat. During this period as a whole, the only woody dicots were heather (*Calluna vulgaris*, order Ericales, also called 'ling') and the cranberry (*Vaccinium oxycoccus*, order

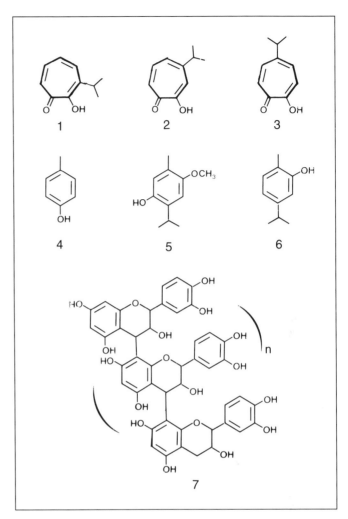

Fig. 37 Antimicrobial substances in vascular plants. Fungicides: 1) α-thujaplicin; 2) β-thujaplicin; 3) γ-thujaplicin. Bactericides: 4) *p*-cresol; 5) *p*-methoxthymol; 6) carvacrol. Tannins: 7) general formula for a polyphenolic tannin of the type found in heath plants (Order Ericales).

Ericales). Both plants contain polyphenolic tannins, as expected (Hegnauer 1966).

In a 15 cm thick band of peat surrounding Lindow Man, *Calluna* was absent, but fragments of *Vaccinium* were stated to be either 'rare' or 'occasional'. The rest of the peat was dominated by *Sphagnum*, especially *S. imbricatum*, but fragments of the cotton sedge (*Eriophorum vaginatum*, order Cyperales) in different samples were stated to be 'absent', 'rare', or 'occasional'. A report on the chemical composition of this and other *Eriophorum* species makes no mention of the presence of polyphenolic tannins, as expected for a sedge (Hegnauer 1963).

Could these rare or occasional trailing stems of cranberry have supplied enough tannin to preserve the body?

Fig. 36 Four scanning electron micrographs of a delignified leaf of *Sphagnum*, showing the hyaline cell-walls in which sphagnan is located: a) × 230, b) × 1155, c) × 1680, d) × 3380. (*S. Herzberg*)

Woody dicots grow much more abundantly than this on other kinds of soil, including that of many cemeteries, without imparting any preservative properties to them. Probably more animal remains would be found preserved in soil if polyphenolic tannins did not oxidise so easily, with loss of their tanning properties; this would also occur in the oxygenated, surface layer of a peat bog.

One exception must, however, be noted: preserved bodies have been found in mangrove swamps, in a special kind of peat formed from mangrove leaf litter (Coles and Coles 1989). Mangroves are unique in that their senescent leaves, which drop continuously, rather than seasonally, on to the mud below, are rich not only in polyphenolic tannins, but also in salt. Indeed, about 40% of their dry weight is sodium chloride.

Two pieces of direct evidence likewise oppose the idea that polyphenolic tannins contribute significantly to the preservation of bodies in *Sphagnum* peat. Direct, chemical tests on samples of soft tissue from Lindow Man gave negative results (Omar *et al* 1989). The significance of this observation is unfortunately diminished by the possibility than any polyphenols initially present could have changed chemically during 2000 years of interment.

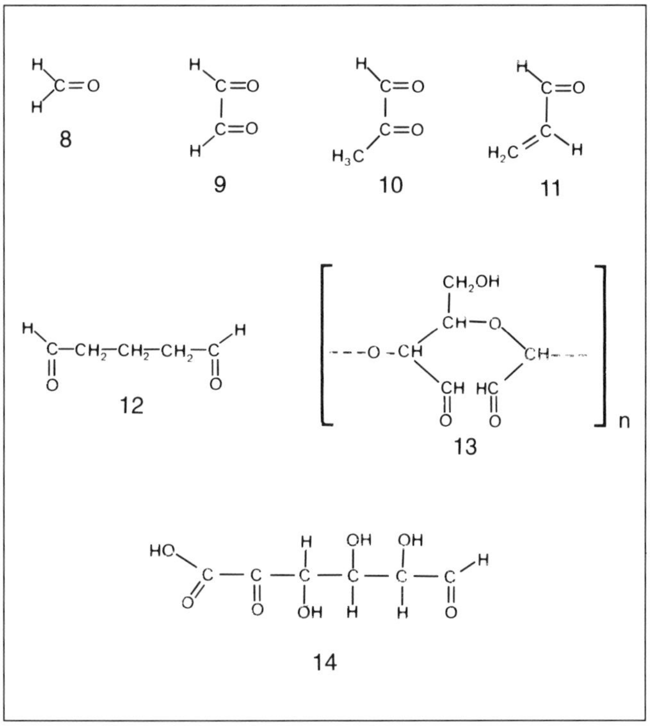

Fig. 38 Highly reactive carbonyl compounds capable of tanning collagen, preserving other proteins, and inactivating enzymes under mildly acidic conditions: 8) formaldehyde; 9) glyoxal; 10) pyruvaldehyde; 11) acrolein; 12) glutaraldehyde; 13) dialdehyde starch; 14) 5-keto-D-mannuronic acid.

The other piece of evidence is the colour of the bodies. Leathers produced by conventional vegetable tannage are light, brownish-yellow, brownish-orange or brownish-red ('tan', or 'tawny', in fact). In contrast, the bodies are roughly the colour of black coffee – all well-authenticated, modern reports affirm that this is the case. The only apparent exception is Grauballe Man, which is stated to have been only partly tanned upon discovery (Coles and Coles 1989). Lindow Man became lighter in colour upon freeze-drying (Omar *et al* 1989), but coffee and humic acids also do this when they are freeze-dried. It is a purely physical phenomenon, resulting from the special, reflective properties of the surfaces created by freeze-drying.

A final word is needed about sedge peats, especially as they often form strata in and under *Sphagnum* peats. Pure sedge peats do not seem to preserve bodies. In Great Britain, at least, all bodies found in sedge peats are represented only by bones (Turner, pp. 115–7). If a report were to be obtained of the discovery of soft tissue in sedge peat, it would be necessary to question whether the peat was entirely free from *Sphagnum*. Sedges can evidently preserve themselves without any help from *Sphagnum*, but this is almost certainly because they contain silica, which creates a physical barrier to microbial attack (Hegnauer 1963). The silica dissolves under alkaline conditions, so that peat formation by sedges would be promoted in acidic environments.

Tanning by Sphagnan

Leather can be formed by many other kinds of organic compounds besides polymeric polyphenols. In theory, any compound containing a reactive carbonyl ($>C=O$) group should tan under mildly acidic conditions. In the leather industry, formaldehyde, glyoxal, pyruvaldehyde, glutaraldehyde, acrolein, and periodate-oxidised starch ('dialdehyde starch') are all used (Fig. 38) (Gustavson 1956; Nayudamma 1979; Clark and Courts 1977).

Dialdehyde starch is especially interesting, because it is a polysaccharide into which numerous reactive carbonyl groups have been introduced artificially by selective oxidation. Sphagnan already contains reactive carbonyl groups in its 5KMA residues, and is therefore a naturally-occurring tanning agent of the same kind. It is very unusual for naturally-occurring polysaccharides to contain keto-sugars, but *Sphagnum* is an unusual plant. It is believed from fossil discoveries to have separated from the mainstream of evolution sometime in the Permian Period, 220–280 million years ago, when, instead of developing roots, it specialised in absorbing nutrients through its leaves (Andrews 1961).

Chemically speaking, 'aldehyde tanning' consists in the building of polymeric 'bridges' between the free amino ($-NH_2$) groups on different collagen molecules, rather like threads of spider's silk stretched between the twigs of a tree. When the tanning agent contains two or more carbonyl groups in the same molecule, the 'bridges' themselves may be 'bridged', and a kind of 'cobweb' develops. If one now thinks of the molecules of proteolytic enzymes as flies, one has a simple picture of how aldehyde tanning prevents decay.

There is a lot of empty space in the 'cobweb', and leathers produced by aldehyde tanning alone are correspondingly porous. They are soft and turgid when wet, but shrink markedly and become hard on drying. Chamois leather, used for washing windows, is produced by formaldehyde tanning. Leather produced by tanning with sphagnan would be even more hydrophilic (water-attracting) and lipophobic (fat-repelling) than other aldehyde leathers, because sphagnan is chemically related to pectin, which has a high affinity for water.

Experiments on the tanning of pigskin (chosen because of its similarity to human skin) have confirmed these expectations, and have shown as well that the leather produced is dark brown, like the bodies. This very dark, coffee colour is so characteristic of tanning by sphagnan that one could confidently assert that any body of a different colour must have been preserved in some other way.

The colour is the product of a 'Maillard', or 'melanoidin' reaction. This is a well-known, but complex, chemical transformation that occurs whenever reducing carbohydrates, and certain other aldehydes and ketones, react with proteins, amino acids or other amines under mildly acidic conditions (Maillard 1916, 1917; Ellis 1959). The pigments in soya sauce and black treacle are authentic products of a Maillard reaction.

Preservation of Non-collagenous Tissue

The word 'tanning' implies the conversion of hide into leather, so it may be incorrect to apply it to proteins other than collagen. Sphagnan does, however, react with other proteins by the same mechanism, and with the same effect of protecting them from microbial attack. In this section we consider other water-insoluble proteins such as myosin, the principal fibrous protein of muscle.

It is seldom realised that the preservation of fish and meat by 'smoking' (exposure to wood smoke or treatment with an oil condensed from wood smoke) is identical in principle with aldehyde tanning. Wood smoke does contain phenolic compounds with antimicrobial properties, but the most active preservatives are a group of at least 133 different aldehydes and ketones referred to in the industry as 'carbonyls'. These include formaldehyde, glutaraldehyde and acrolein, three of the aldehydes actually used in leather manufacture. In addition, smoke contains formic, acetic and many other organic acids that would catalyse the reaction with protein (Maga 1988).

Fish skins contain collagen, and readers will have noticed that the skin of a smoked cod is quite leathery after cooking, whereas that of a fresh cod is little more than a soft, gelatinous film. Ordinarily the fish muscle is only superficially 'tanned', long enough to preserve it for a few months, but when fish is smoked for too long by mistake, it becomes brown and tough all through. This product would undoubtedly 'keep' for years, but it would be useless as food, because the protein would have become just as resistant to the body's digestive proteases as to microbial ones.

The non-collagenous tissues of Lindow Man had decomposed much more than the connective tissues (Connolly 1986), and in Damendorf Man they had dissolved completely, along with the bones, leaving only skin and hair (Coles and Coles 1989). This must be partly because the sphagnan in the bog water took longer to reach them; it is a fairly big molecule, and it diffuses slowly.

It should be noted, however, that the degradation of animal tissues that commences immediately after death has nothing to do with invasion from without by microorganisms in the first instance. It is caused by a special group of digestive enzymes contained in cell organelles called 'lysosomes'. In living tissues, these serve to remove dead or damaged cells, so that they can be replaced by new ones. Lysosomes are present in all the tissues of the body, including the skin, but they are most abundant in the cells of organs such as the liver, pancreas and kidneys; it is therefore to be expected that these would be the first to disintegrate after death. Interestingly, the embalmers of ancient Egypt must have known from experience that these organs would disintegrate first, because otherwise it is hard to explain why they used to remove them, and preserve them separately in jars (Harmer 1979).

In some bog bodies, such as the one found at Scaleby (Cumbria, UK), internal connective tissues such as the intestines and ligaments have been tanned and preserved, while the skin has decayed (Turner 1988). This is unlikely to have a natural explanation, because the collagen in these tissues is essentially the same as that in skin. Possibly the victim had died in a fire which had selectively gelatinised the collagen in her skin. The custom of burning heretics and witches at the stake, and of burying their remains dishonourably on waste land, may explain other discoveries of this kind.

Tanning as a Source of Error in Radiocarbon Dating

The chemical linkage formed by the Maillard reaction between sphagnan and tissue proteins is stable to acids and alkalis. A part of the sphagnan molecule which is not involved directly in carbohydrate–peptide bonding can be hydrolysed away with hot, dilute mineral acid, but a substantial part remains that will withstand prolonged boiling with concentrated acid (Painter 1983b, 1991).

Since sphagnan is soluble in water and the movement of water in ombrogenous peat is predominantly downwards, this could result in the transfer to the body of carbon fixed by photosynthesis at a later date. It would be unsafe to assume that the problem can be circumvented by measuring the radioactivity of hydroxyproline isolated from the body's collagen (Gowlett *et al* 1986), because this amino acid also occurs in several plant glycoproteins (Lamport 1973; Allen and Neuberger 1973) which could have become bound to the sphagnan nearer the surface of the bog, before it had migrated downwards and reacted with the body's collagen.

In the author's opinion, it would be logically safer and practically simpler to measure the radioactivity of cholesterol, extracted, for example, from residual brain tissue. Peat does not contain cholesterol, but it does contain β-sitosterol and β-sitostanol, and simple procedures for isolating these in crystalline form have been described (Fuchsman 1980). These materials should be suitable for radiocarbon dating of peat samples, because they are highly insoluble in water, and unlikely to migrate from one part of a bog to another (Fig. 39).

Tanning as a Cause of Adipocere Formation

Turner (1988) following Thomson (1984), defines 'adipocere' as a 'condition where the tissues (of a bog body) are converted into a mixture of soaps, fatty acids and volatile substances, which exude on to the body surface'. In a report on Meenybraddan Woman, Omar *et al* (1989) state that 'there were deposits of adipocere distributed over the body and under the skin. Adipocere is produced by the prolonged storage of animal fat under anaerobic, cool conditions'.

Certain fish, such as salmon, mackerel and herring, become oily when smoked. The oil does not come from the smoke (cod and haddock do not become oily when smoked) but from polyunsaturated fat stored in the muscle. It gets physically squeezed out as the muscle contracts. The contraction is due partly to the loss of water by evaporation, but also to the cross-linking of the myosin fibres by the carbonyl compounds in the smoke.

In leather manufacture, the hide is always de-fatted before tanning (Nayudamma 1975). If this step were to be omitted, the leather produced would exude fat for a long time afterwards. The present author has confirmed this by doing experiments with chicken skin (chosen for its high fat content). The exudation occurred both with sphagnan and with a polyphenolic tannin as the tanning agent.

In the anoxic region of a peat bog, the exuded fat would be broken down to a limited extent by anaerobic bacteria. The initial reaction would be hydrolysis of triglycerides to give first diglycerides, then monoglycerides, and finally glycerine and long-chain fatty acids. At the pH of the bog (probably 5–6), the latter would be present partly as soaps. The bacteria would then ferment the

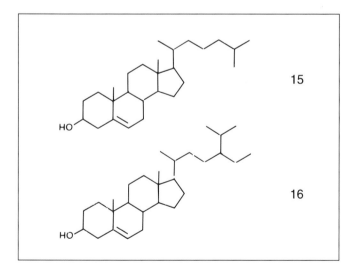

Fig. 39 'Signature' molecules whose identities reveal their origins: 15) cholesterol is found only in animals; 16) β-sitosterol only in plants. Both are insoluble in water and resistant to biodegradation under anoxic conditions, though they may be partly reduced by anaerobic bacteria to β-cholestanol and β-sitostanol, respectively. β-sitosterol has been found intact in very old peat (*Fuchsman 1980*).

glycerine, with the formation of volatile, short-chain fatty acids such as acetic and propionic acids, but they would not break down the long-chain fatty acids (McInerney 1988).

It has been suggested (Thomson 1984) that adipocere contributes to the preservation of the bodies, but the facts listed above indicate that adipocere formation and preservation are two separate consequences of tanning.

Binding and Inactivation of Soluble Proteins and Enzymes

The binding of soluble (globular) proteins such as serum albumin, gelatin and haemoglobin, and of enzymes such as pepsin, trypsin, amylase, pectinase and cellulase by *Sphagnum* holocellulose, has now been observed in the author's laboratory. Once bound, the enzymes lost their activity completely in about 3–10 days at 20°C, whereas in aqueous solution they were considerably more stable. *These observations imply that any enzyme secreted by any micro-organism into the ambient water would become trapped and inactivated on the surface of the insoluble fragments of* Sphagnum *in peat, and prevented from attacking its substrate.*

The enzymes would include proteases capable of hydrolysing the proteins in animal remains and woollen artefacts, and the cellulases, hemicellulases and pectinases that hydrolyse the polysaccharides in wooden artefacts and the remains of higher plants, as well as the cell walls of *Sphagnum* moss itself. This implies that the bio-degradation of *any* polymeric substrate (that is, molecules that are too big to be ingested whole by bacterial cells) would be suppressed in peat, even when it cannot be tanned.

The binding and inactivation of water-soluble enzymes do not, however, occur so rapidly as to preclude any possibility of decay in *Sphagnum* peat. Moreover, enzymes bound to bacterial cell walls can also act on polymeric substrates. It is quite clear that bio-degradation does occur, very slowly, in peat (consider the case of adipocere, for example). Collagen and keratin (the fibrous protein in hair, wool and nails) seem to survive particularly well because they are protected in several different ways.

Sequestration of Amino-nitrogen

In both its soluble and insoluble forms, sphagnan will undergo a Maillard reaction, not only with soluble proteins and enzymes, but also with simple amino acids, and even with ammonia, to give dark brown, nitrogen-containing polymers that are more or less as resistant to microbial attack as is leather. These bio-resistant, brown polymers make up the humic fraction of peat.

The fate of humic acids in both soil and aquatic environments has been extensively investigated, and it is established that they can be broken down, extremely slowly, by aerobic bacteria and moulds, but only when these are supplied with additional nutrients, including an alternative source of carbon and, of course, molecular oxygen (Schnitzer and Khan 1972). This explains why peat does not become mouldy unless it is mixed with some other kind of organic matter.

It is, on the other hand, extremely doubtful whether humic acids can be broken down microbiologically without oxygen, as noted on p. 89 (final paragraph). The very existence of peat is evidence in itself for this, and in addition there are the bodies. This means that the anaerobic bacteria in the anoxic region of a peat bog are starved of amino-nitrogen. There is nitrogen there, but it is 'sequestered' in a form that is inaccessible to the bacteria. Probably some of the bacteria survive by fixing atmospheric nitrogen dissolved in the bog water; *Clostridium*, a strict anaerobe, is known to do this. Others probably get nitrogen by reducing nitrate and nitrite (originating from thunderstorms) to ammonia inside the cells; some *Pseudomonas* species can do this.

The capacity of peat to sequester amino-nitrogen is, of course, limited. Treatment of peat samples from the Ramma bog (Sweden) with an excess of ammonia, followed by an acid wash (to remove ammonia bound as ammonium ions only) increased the nitrogen content, on average, from about 1% to 4% of the dry weight of the peat (Mattson and Koutler-Andersson 1955). The nitrogen content of peat from unpolluted bogs seldom exceeds 2%, so it is unlikely that the saturation limit is ever reached in the natural situation. When peat is supplied with groundwater that has run off from agricultural soil, however, it must sooner or later become saturated with nitrogen and other nutrients, and then it could not be expected to have any preservative properties.

Problems for Museums

In the light of the information now available about the mechanism of tanning by sphagnan, it is possible to comment briefly on the methods that have been used to conserve the bodies after they have been found. For displaying purposes, some kind of drying is necessary. The problem is how to avoid the shrinkage, hardening, cracking and crumbling that this would lead to unless the interstitial water in the skin and other soft tissues is replaced by some other substance. This should be a non-volatile fluid, wax or jelly with lubricating and shock-absorbing properties.

In leather manufacture, oils are used, either alone or in combination with soaps or other detergents. Fish oils, such as cod liver oil or sardine oil, are especially favoured, because their high content of polyunsaturated fatty acids leads to their polymerisation inside the leather. This prevents them from oozing out again, as often happens with cheap leather. Vegetable oils, including safflower, castor, palm and groundnut oils, are also used (Nayudamma 1979).

The exceptionally hydrophilic (lipophobic) properties of skin tanned with sphagnan have already been mentioned, and consistently with this it was found to be virtually impossible to impregnate sphagnan-tanned pigskin with any kind of oil, either alone or as an emulsion in water containing Cetavlon (a cationic detergent). Tollund Man's head was treated with a solution of paraffin wax in toluene (Omar *et al* 1989), but this could have done little more than provide a superficial film of wax.

Grauballe Man was re-tanned with oak bark, which contains a polyphenolic tannin. This is interesting, because tanning with polymeric polyphenols is different in principle from aldehyde tanning. Whereas aldehydes and ketones build 'bridges' between the occasional, pendant amino-groups on collagen fibres, polymeric polyphenols fasten themselves on to the main polypeptide chain, rather like caterpillars clinging to a twig with all their legs. They are also bulky molecules, so they fill up more of the interstitial spaces in the skin, giving a fuller and firmer leather that shrinks less upon drying. It still hardens upon drying, however, and is normally oiled to prevent this. Grauballe Man was oiled with a mixture of glycerine, lanolin, and cod liver oil, with Turkey Red oil as a detergent (Omar *et al* 1989).

Because the different tannins bind to different parts of the collagen molecules, they are not mutually exclusive. A leather that has been well tanned with an aldehyde will still bind a polyphenolic tannin, and vice versa. Indeed, 'multiple tanning' is the rule, rather than the exception, in modern leather manufacture (Nayudamma 1979). Most polyphenolic tannins are soluble in water, and compatible with hydrophilic tannins like sphagnan.

Unfortunately, however, there is a limit to the value of what can be learned from the principles of leather technology, which are based upon experience with the hides

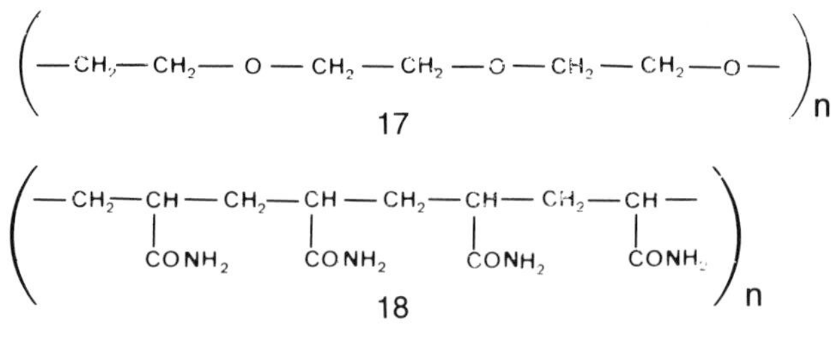

Fig. 40 Hydrophilic, non-biodegradable polymers potentially suitable for the conservation of tissues preserved by sphagnan: 17) polyethylene glycol; 18) polyacrylamide.

of recently slaughtered animals. Over a period of centuries, irreversible changes occur in all proteins. Two processes, known as *denaturation* and *racemisation*, respectively, are particularly significant, as they lead to a weakening of the forces that bind the separate protein molecules together in fibres, and hence to a loss in mechanical strength. They would be retarded by tanning, but not prevented.

Lindow Man was immersed for ten weeks in a 15% solution of polyethylene glycol (PEG 400) in distilled water, and then freeze-dried (Omar and McCord 1986). PEG is a hydrophilic substance, and is therefore preferable to oil or paraffin wax as a filler and lubricant for tissues tanned by sphagnan (Fig. 40). The most serious problem would be to ensure that the tissues are fully and uniformly impregnated with sufficient PEG to prevent undue shrinkage upon drying. Impregnation of a body would be easier and more complete if the filler could be applied as a monomer and polymerised *in situ*, in analogy with the fish oil favoured by leather technologists. PEG is made by polymerising ethylene oxide, but this reaction is unsuitable because an alkaline catalyst is needed.

Acrylamide, on the other hand, can be polymerised in aqueous solution, just by shining a light on it. The product, polyacrylamide, is a hydrophilic, non-biodegradable polymer somewhat similar in properties to PEG (Fig. 40). By adding a cross-linking agent, jellies can be prepared, and by varying the proportion of the cross-linker, these can be made to vary in consistency from that of a soft table jelly to that of a tough rubber.

Conclusions

1 The low density of bacterial cells in the anoxic region of a *Sphagnum* peat bog is due to deprivation of essential

metal cations and amino-nitrogen. Both kinds of nutrient are sequestered by a pectin-like polysaccharide (sphagnan) in the cell walls of *Sphagnum* mosses.

2 Bodies are preserved in *Sphagnum* peat partly because they are tanned by sphagnan, and also because sphagnan reacts with the digestive enzymes secreted by putrefactive bacteria, immobilising them on the surface of *Sphagnum* fragments in the peat, and causing them to lose their activity. Wooden artefacts and the remains of higher plants are also preserved for the latter reason.

3 Because of the solubility of sphagnan in water, collagen and other proteins in preserved bodies could bind sphagnan photosynthesised at a different, and normally later, period in history. This could lead to errors in radiocarbon dating unless a tissue component, such as cholesterol, which does not bind sphagnan, is utilised.

4 Adipocere is fat, squeezed out of the tissues of a bog body by the tanning process, and then partially hydrolysed and fermented by anaerobic bacteria.

5 The chemical nature of the tanning brought about by sphagnan is such as to allow severe shrinkage upon drying, followed by hardening and cracking. It also gives the tissues a hydrophilic (water-attracting) quality, which resists impregnation by hydrophobic (water-repelling) oils and waxes. Impregnation with a hydrophilic polymer such as polyethylene glycol should give the best protection against shrinkage upon drying, but impregnation would be easier to accomplish if the polymer could be applied as a monomer, and polymerised *in situ*.

Recent Research on the Lindow Bodies in the Context of Five Years of World Studies

D. Brothwell

It is important to view the current research on the human remains from Lindow Moss in relation not only to other European bog bodies, but also to studies which have been carried out in general on better-preserved human remains. The literature as a whole on these special burials is becoming voluminous and my concern here is not to review all of it, but instead to place current research on the biology of the Lindow people (referred to here as Lindow I, II and III, as this is the common usage in the literature) against a background of work on other such remains over approximately five years – or in fact since the previous Lindow monograph was published (Stead, I. M. *et al* 1986; *Lindow Man: The Body in the Bog*. British Museum Publications). In so doing, it can be seen that bog body studies have by no means lagged behind in advancing research on the biology of people from the past. Inevitably, progress is variable, with research problems slowing work in one aspect but with clear advances on another front. There is no doubt that studies on the Lindow humans have helped to advance standards of investigation generally on such ancient remains.

Bodies from Contrasting Environments

Before his death, Alfred Dieck had revised his estimate of the number of European bog bodies at over 1860 (Verlaeckt, personal communications). The numbers actually preserved in museums are not easy to estimate, but many of those that are preserved are in need of re-evaluation. The CT scan study of the Danish Huldremose woman, recently undertaken by Bennike and Boesen, Department of Radiology, University of Copenhagen, is a contribution to such restudies. Northern Dutch specimens have also received new detailed attention (van der Sanden 1990), as reported on here (pp. 146–65). In Ireland too, in addition to the studies on the Meenybraddan body reported on pp. 123–32, the Castleblakeney Man, a near contemporary of Lindow II, is currently being reinvestigated (described in Ó Floinn 1992). Human remains from the Great Bog of Ardee (donated to the Royal College of Surgeons of Ireland in 1849) and from Baronstown West (Ó Floinn 1991) are also likely to be investigated soon. This new bog body research impetus in Europe is likely to result in yet more tissue sampling and further investigations elsewhere.

Preservation of human bodies in dry, hot environments results in different but still variable preservation. Without doubt, Latin-American archaeology continues to discover more material of this kind than is appearing in other arid environments; thus, previously discovered material is being reinvestigated in Peru, Bolivia, Colombia and Chile.

Internal organs need not always be well preserved in these dry climates, although gut contents may be very good – even producing unusual surprises. Holden (1991), for instance, describes mollusc radulae and acarid mites from palaeofaecal material from ancient Chilean bodies. Somewhat surprising is the fact that two mites turned out to be new species (Baker 1990).

Since the first publication of the Lindow finds, the English edition of *The Greenland Mummies* has appeared, making the data easily accessible (Hansen *et al* 1991). This study set high standards for the investigation of naturally freeze-dried bodies, and it is clear from current studies on the frozen Neolithic body from the Alps (Höpfel *et al* 1992; Spindler 1994) that the accepted investigation procedures are being followed and even improved upon. Less well known is the fact that frozen bodies have been found over a period of decades in the high Andes. Of these, the body of a child with rich grave offerings, from Cerre el Plomo in Chile, is best known. All deserve further study.

Finally, there are the unexpected examples of well-preserved soft tissue, as in the remarkable corpse from a Han dynasty tomb in China (Wei 1973) and the preserved tissue from a Japanese feudal lord (Yamada *et al* 1990), both probably influenced in their preservation by mercury or mercurides associated with the burial.

All of these studies, on the Lindow people, bog bodies in general, desiccated and frozen human remains, over the past few years provide a new impetus to develop a blueprint, an overall methodology, for the examination and analysis of such well-preserved remains. We are by no means ready, when the next body appears, to put into action an agreed set of investigatory procedures; but at least with each collection of studies and with each investigation, the blueprint is nearer to becoming a reality.

Dietary Studies

The remains of food in part of the intestinal tract of Lindow II has already received detailed study by Holden (1986). The identification of very damaged fragments of gut in the newer finds, enabled further studies on food residues to be undertaken again by Holden (pp. 76–82). However, owing to the torn and incomplete nature of the gut tissues identified, contamination by peat flora was considerable. Fortunately, this post-burial mixing could be distinguished from the *in vivo* contamination of the cereal crops (wheat, rye and barley) by weed seeds. In comparison with other recent European bog studies, the Lindow bodies would seem to suggest low dietary variation. Admittedly, these last meals may have more ritual significance than dietary, although the degree of variation

in the European evidence as a whole may argue against such a conclusion.

During the time of the Lindow discoveries and research, other gut studies were being undertaken. These have included chemical analyses, not only of faecal remains (Moore *et al* 1985), but of residues in pottery (Needham and Evans 1987). The chemistry of foods is a complex research area, and no less so with ancient human remains, where different environments may lead to the variable survival of food components. Identifications from pottery residues or coprolites have included olive oil, beeswax, fish oil and animal fats (Wales and Evans 1988). As yet the prospects for the study of the faecal chemistry of bog bodies, as opposed to say, the food chemistry of dried South American bodies, is largely unknown. It is clearly an interesting line for future investigation.

From Conventional Radiography to CT Scans

The Lindow investigations have been lucky in being able to call on sophisticated scanning techniques to explore inner details of the human remains. In particular, computed tomography (CT) scans are proving of particular value. Not only the Lindow specimens, but also the Meenybraddan (p. 127) and Huldremose (p. 100) females were studied by this means. Soft-tissue detail of bog bodies can be extremely good and, for instance, in the case of the Meenybraddan woman, detail of the convolutions and possibly some internal cerebral structures could be discerned by CT scan. In the case of the Huldremose woman, the fine detail of the lower intestinal tract enabled a small trapdoor to be cut precisely over one section of the gut which was clearly positioned near to the abdominal wall, so that faecal material could be sampled for food analysis (Brothwell *et al* 1990).

Innovations developing in association with computed tomography are also permitting three-dimensional surface reconstruction of inner organs and tissues, such as the skull (Vannier *et al* 1985; Pahl *et al* 1988). The most recent application of this technique has been to the Neolithic frozen body from the Alps (Nedden and Wicke 1992). The problem in applying such reconstruction innovations to bog body material is that, so often, shrinkage or distortion has modified the original morphology. In all the older discoveries, drying has caused changes, and this is a problem even in the case of freeze-dried Lindow II. Where material has dried out to some extent, as in the case of various Dutch and Danish bodies, van der Sanden has questioned the possibility of rehydration and restoration (personal communication 1988). This may not be as easy as it sounds, and currently there is experimental work being carried out in Ireland with a view to establishing a procedure – if at all possible – for at least restoring skeletal tissue from bogs to their original size.

Another problem, revealed in the case of Lindow II, is that distortion of the head has occurred as a result of some skeletal decalcification and burial pressure. Reconstruction from CT scan data would thus be of doubtful value unless some means could be found to correct for post-mortem distortion – a mathematical challenge yet to be taken up!

Forensic and Pathological Aspects

The examination of the Lindow II body stimulated much speculation as to the cause of the man's death. Some considered it merely an extravagant 'mugging', others a special ritual murder. The range of trauma suggests that this was not of an 'accidental' nature, although the author is reminded of a suicide reported by Smith and Fiddes (1955), in which the man displayed three separate bullet wounds, an incised wound to the throat (and four smaller incisions), an incised wound to the wrist, and a deep rope impression on the neck. The author hastens to add that the Lindow II individual could not have produced all of his injuries in a suicide bid!

Clearly, forensic investigations of such remains are important, and other studies recently have helped to emphasise the need for the restudy of earlier material. In the case of the well-preserved, and now dried, Huldremose woman from Jutland, new studies are clearly worthwhile (Brothwell et al 1990). Pseudopathology included long-bone bowing due to post-burial pressure of stakes across the body and the peat cutter's damage to the right hand. The woman had, however, certainly received multiple cuts to her body before death, or at least before burial. Her hair had also been cut off. Apparently pseudopathology is also to be seen in the left foot of the prehistoric Castle-blakeney body at the National Museum in Dublin. Here, there appears to be a severe dislocation at the ankle.

In contrast to such evidence of potential forensic interest, there is far less information on the pathology of the ancient individuals established some time prior to death. Intestinal parasites, as revealed by worm eggs, have been found in various bodies, and are well discussed from wetland, arid and frozen remains. Probably the most ante-mortem pathology has been revealed in recent years in the preserved bodies from South America. The serious

health conditions identified include tuberculosis, but the most surprising demonstration has been of a possible trypanosomal condition which is indicative of Chaga's disease (Rothhammer et al 1984).

Trace Element and Other Chemical Studies

During the period of the Lindow studies, and in fact extending back over the past 20 years, there have been various investigations on the chemistry of ancient human remains. These have been particularly concerned with differences in bone chemistry and their possible associations with diet (see Price 1989), although there have been recurring warnings of post-depositional, or diagenetic, changes in archaeological material (Nelson and Sauer 1984).

The discovery of the Lindow bodies has, without doubt, provided some stimulus for the study of further aspects of ancient body chemistry. In particular, Pyatt and his colleagues (pp. 62–75) have considered various elements in the skin, bone and surrounding peat of both Lindow II and III, keeping in mind the possibility of interchanges between body chemistry and burial micro-environments. Nevertheless, they argue that the 'chemical fingerprints' of Lindow II and III have value, provided interpretations are cautious. They noted that the skins of these two individuals differed in the concentrations of certain elements and their ranking, and they suggested that the differences might be linked to dietary differences (associated with different geographical and geochemical provinces). They also tentatively suggested that certain elements represented the residues of clay-based pigment emulsions, maybe applied as distinctive body decoration.

As is the pattern of science, data provided by one researcher may spark off questioning in another. Thus, the suggestion by Pyatt and colleagues that the copper in the Lindow body pigment may have caused the green fluorescence seen in the fur arm band on Lindow II, has been challenged by Smith (forthcoming). But the hair of Lindow II has no copper, so the green fluorescence must originate from some other fluorophore or possibly as a result of anaerobic changes to the hair keratin by acid hydrolysis.

Finally, it is worth pointing out here that Lindow II contained endogenous cholesterol but no adipocere (Evershed and Connolly 1988). In contrast, the Meeny-braddan and Huldremose women displayed considerable amounts of adipocere on arms, breasts, abdomen and legs. What is the significance of such differences in bog bodies?

On the Molecular Biology of Ancient People

Since the beginning of the discoveries of human remains at Lindow Moss, there has been an escalation of interest in the occurrence of DNA in human remains. This is indeed an exciting new line of investigation, of forensic as well as archaeological interest (Hagelberg *et al* 1991; Paabe 1986). Other molecular information may be equally revealing in the future. Human lymphocyte antigens (HLA) have been detected in Palaeo–Indian material from Florida (Lawler *et al* 1991) and in the naturally freeze-dried Eskimo bodies from Greenland (Hansen and Gürtler 1983). Employing a different technique, ELISA, the occurrence of haemoglobin has been confirmed in bones from various sites and a well-preserved Guanche body (Smith and Wilson 1990), but of course the confirmation of the occurrence of normal haemoglobin is a long way from establishing the ancient occurrence of abnormal haemoglobin.

While it is good to be optimistic at this stage in such enquiries, there is clearly a need for caution as well. To begin with, not all burial environments are conducive to the preservation of DNA and other molecular evidence. Peat bogs seem to be generally detrimental to the preservation of DNA. There is also the problem of sample sizes when considering aspects of Holocene population genetics. Furthermore, what do we yet know about the degradation of DNA and of the potential for contamination at a site or in the laboratory? Where DNA is needed only to provide a simpler presence or absence result, then these studies may indeed by very rewarding. If we employ polymerase chain reaction specifically to identify, say, the mycobacteria of tuberculosis in a bone specimen suspected of indicating that disease, then indeed we have a powerful tool to investigate further the history of human disease.

Worsley Man, England

A. N. Garland

Over the past three centuries, the remains of over 220 individuals, ranging in completeness from a single bone to a complete body with soft tissue and bone, have been recovered from peat deposits from some 170 sites in Great Britain and Ireland (Turner, pp. 205–20 and Ó Floinn, pp. 221–34). Very few have undergone extensive examination. Large numbers of skeletal remains survive in various museums and anatomical collections, but remains from bodies where tissue survived are very rare.

On 18 August 1958, a human head was recovered from a peat bog in Worsley Moss, Lancashire, England (general grid reference: SD70SW). A rather fruitless five-day police search of the surrounding 252 acres (100 ha) of the moss ensued, in the hope of finding further remains. A search of the register of missing persons was also carried out, but again, without any success.

On the following day the remains were examined by Dr A. St. Hill of Liverpool University, who thought that the remains were those of a 'male, between the ages of 24 and 40, that it might have lain there for less than a year and that certain features suggested an Oriental origin'. Dr G. B. Manning, a Home Office pathologist at Chorley, examined the remains on 24 August and he formed the opinion that 'the remains were those of a male aged about 40, the lower jaw was fractured and that the head may have lain in the peat for less than a year'. However, after more detailed examination, which included radiology and chemical tests, he finally concluded that 'death took place between 100 and 500 years ago' (*Leigh, Tyldesley and Atherton Journal* 24 October 1958). Manning also stated that peat was a fine preservative and there were bodies 2000 years old found in peat bogs, showing that he was aware of the Danish finds before the *Bog People* was published in English (*Bolton Evening News* 17 October 1958).

These results were presented at the subsequent coroner's inquest on 17 October, and because the cause of death could not be established, an open verdict was returned. The remains were returned to Dr Manning for further examination and were subsequently transferred to the Museum of the Pathology Department of the Manchester Medical School where they were mounted and placed in a Perspex box.

Early in 1987, a multidisciplinary team was assembled with the aims of reviewing the 1958 findings in the light of modern medical technology, to study the preservation of the soft tissue and bone, to attempt to establish the manner and cause of death and to look for signs of heavy metal intoxication.

Anthropological Examination

The specimen consisted of a skull, the mandible, the first cervical vertebra, half the body of the second and a considerable amount of overlying soft tissue. The skull appeared to have suffered much post-mortem damage and many of the bones of the cranium had been put together in their correct anatomical position with wire staples. Because of this damage it was not possible to make any accurate or sufficient metric measurements of the skull.

On the basis of current anthropological criteria (Workshop of European Anthropologists 1980; Krogman and Işcan 1986) the skull was assessed to be that of a male. When viewed from the front (Fig. 41), it was possible to see a partial metopic suture running upwards from the

Fig. 41 Frontal view of the skull and soft tissue.

Fig. 43 Detail of the right side of the head showing the deformed ear and beard hair.

Fig. 42 Right side of the skull and soft tissue.

Fig. 44 The skull viewed from above showing the evidence for the wounds.

nasion, and a fracture extending downwards through the right side of the body of the mandible and into the empty socket for the lower right canine tooth. Nothing of note was observed on the left side of the skull. An occipital view of the skull revealed a lambdoid ossicle in each of the lambdoid sutures; the left measured 30 × 24 mm, the right 12 × 12 mm.

Attached loosely to the right side of the skull was an irregular mass of brown-coloured soft tissue (Fig. 42) in which the right ear was discernible, but shrunken. Hair of a brown/reddish colour was present on the beard area and in front of the ear (Fig. 43). The hair in this area was not neatly trimmed. A laceration, approximately 28 mm in length, extended upwards behind the ear. Examination of the wound margins, using a dissecting microscope,

Fig. 45 The soft tissue from the base of the head, showing the cord projecting on the left side (see arrow) and the severed vertebrae.

revealed a laceration with irregular edges and displacement of hair follicles into the wound.

When the skull was viewed from above (Fig. 44) it was possible to see numerous fracture lines running through the frontal and parietal bones. There were features suggestive of a depressed fracture in the region of the bregma, where skin and bone fragments were seen lying underneath the inner table of the skull.

When the skull was viewed from below it was possible to see the first two cervical vertebrae, and that the body of the second had been transected by a sharp cut. The two vertebrae were surrounded by an amorphous mass of dark-brown, soft tissue (Fig. 45). Embedded inside this tissue was a twisted cord (see arrow on Fig. 45) which, when traced, appeared to encircle the soft tissue of the neck and extend upwards between the soft tissue and bone of the right side of the face.

Radiological Examination

In the first instance, plain radiography of the skull was attempted. However, because of the severe demineralisation of the bones and the problem of superimposition of the structures, it was decided to examine the head by computed tomography in the Department of Diagnostic Radiology. Sections were obtained through the skull at 3 mm intervals and three-dimensional reformations were performed using the available software. The bone structure was best visualised at a window level and window width, usually employed to look at lungs.

The radiological pictures obtained revealed there to be several deficits within the skull vault, mainly over the vertex. The right orbital wall was absent, so too were the greater and lesser wings of the sphenoid bones bilaterally and also the right zygomatic bone. No soft tissue was seen within the skull. The fracture of the mandible, described earlier, was visualised, but it was impossible to suggest radiologically whether this or the damage to the skull vault had occurred ante, peri or post-mortem.

Examination of the Dental Remains

Two teeth were present in the jaws; the upper right second molar and the lower right first molar. The empty tooth sockets of the maxilla and mandible indicated that the subject possessed the complete adult permanent dentition of thirty-two teeth during life. Further investigations were undertaken by Mr N. P. Chandler in the Department of Conservative Dentistry, Manchester University Dental School, and his report provided the following information.

The appearance of the sockets suggested that the missing teeth were lost post-mortem. Both alveolar arches were well formed and it was unlikely that the teeth were crowded. The sockets indicated that the third molar teeth were full erupted and this suggested that the individual was over 18 years of age.

Both teeth had assumed a dark brown/black colour and had lost their entire enamel surfaces. Some loss of dentine and cementum had also occurred, and the teeth appeared small in consequence. There was no evidence of dental caries on examination of the remaining dentine of the teeth, and no evidence that periodontal disease had affected the alveolar bone. No abscessing or other dento-alveolar pathology was evident on macroscopic examination. The number of teeth, the absence of occlusion and the loss of enamel made an estimation of the subject's age on the grounds of attrition impossible.

Radiographic examination of the dental remains included:

1 Orbiting panoramic view (Cranex).
2 Periapical view of the upper right second molar.
3 Intraoral xeroradiographs of the mandible (Xerox 110).

Radiography of the dental remains proved difficult, and it was not possible to achieve film contrasts used in routine dental diagnosis. Special screens were employed for the extra oral views, and for xeroradiography the generator was adapted to 40 kV in an attempt to improve image contrast.

The views obtained showed no evidence of supernumerary teeth, retained roots or other dento-alveolar pathology. The intact lamina dura of the alveolar bone confirmed that post-mortem loss of the missing teeth took place and suggested that the root formation of these teeth had been completed. Radiologically, both teeth appeared to be of less than average size. They were devoid of enamel and some loss of cementum and dentine had occurred. The dental pulp appearances were those of an individual aged between 20 and 30 years.

Energy Dispersive Electron Probe Analysis (EDAX)

Specimens of skin, hair and cord, measuring approximately 10 × 5 mm were removed from the remains and were mounted on to a stub and carbon coated. The analysis was carried out using a Cameca/Link System instrument by Mr T. Hopkins, Senior Experimental Officer in the Department of Geology, University of Manchester. The spectra obtained from the specimen of skin demonstrated the presence of sodium, chlorine, silicon and lead. The principal peaks found on examination of the hair were for chlorine, calcium and sulphur. These results should be compared with those from Lindow II and III (Pyatt *et al* pp. 62–75). The spectra obtained from the twisted cord from the neck region showed the presence of chlorine, in particular, and traces of sodium, silicon and sulphur. No iron or copper was detected.

Histology

The following specimens, measuring approximately 10 × 10 mm, were taken for histological examination: soft tissue and hair from the face, soft tissue and bone from the neck, a fragment of the ear and a piece of twisted cord from the neck. The soft tissue specimens were rehydrated, processed, sectioned and stained as described by Garland (1989a). The piece of bone was processed by embedding in LR white resin, sectioned and stained as described in Garland (1989b). Both the soft tissues and bone sections, when stained with toluidine blue or Giemsa, turned a green/yellow colour. Histological examination revealed the following:

1 Skin: Disorganisation of the micromorphology. The epidermis was absent but there was a residual supporting matrix which consisted almost entirely of collagen fibres.
2 Ear cartilage: A lack of chondroid tissue, but metachromasia was present in the amorphous structure. Metachromasia is a property whereby tissues change the colour of staining dyes due to the presence of numerous acidic groups in the tissue structure.
3 Cord: It was not possible to say whether the cord from the neck was made of tendon or sinew. However, the tissue was of animal origin rather than plant.
4 Bone: Well preserved, although demineralised. No osteocytes (bone cells) were found, but inclusions of plant material, probably *Sphagnum* were seen lying among the trabeculae. No evidence was found of local histological destruction as a result of bacterial/fungal invasion of the bone.

Radiocarbon Accelerator Dating

A piece of skin, measuring approximately 30 × 20 mm, was removed from the right side of the face and submitted to the Radiocarbon Accelerator Unit of the Research Laboratory for Archaeology and the History of Art, Oxford, for the purpose of dating by accelerator mass spectrometry. Dr R. Housley reported the date, in uncalibrated radiocarbon years, to be 1800 ± 70 years BP (OxA-1430); that is, Romano-British and potentially contemporary with Lindow II and III and its significance is discussed in more detail in Housley *et al* pp. 39–46.

Conclusions

The remains of Worsley Man are an important survivor of the tissued bog bodies from Britain. The head is that of a man, aged 20–30. Severe demineralisation of the bone elements and dentition was apparent, both radiologically and histologically. This means that it cannot be demonstrated whether the injuries noted were committed before, immediately after or some time after death. However, it can be shown from the remains of Worsley Man's head that he had received injuries sufficient to fracture the top of the skull, had had a cord tied around his neck, and that his head had been severed from his body at the second cervical vertebra. A police search of the area of the bog where it was discovered failed to produce any further remains of the body. A single radiocarbon date has been obtained which indicates that the victim came from the Romano-British period.

There are some obvious comparisons to be made between this find and Lindow I and II. The sites are quite close together, about 20 km apart. Their radiocarbon dates may be contemporary. A similar range of tissue has been retained and the condition of the bone is analogous. Potentially, the causes of death are paralleled in the Lindow bodies, with perhaps blows to the head, garotting and decapitation being represented. Further research work is still possible into Worsley Man, including a more extensive study of the cord, the determination of the blood group and the analysis of the surviving hair, but this preliminary report confirms the significance of the discovery.

Recent Research into British Bog Bodies

R. C. Turner

Introduction

Lindow Man was hailed as Britain's first bog body to put alongside the discoveries made famous by P. V. Glob's book, *The Bog People*. For British archaeologists, anatomists and a range of other specialists, this find presented an opportunity to study a body as well preserved as Denmark's Tollund and Grauballe Man. Somehow, earlier discoveries of this type from the British Isles, often no less remarkable, had been ignored or overlooked. Yet continental researchers were aware of these earlier discoveries. Glob's book quoted figures of 41 bog bodies from England and Wales and 15 from Scotland. These were derived from a catalogue assembled by a German archaeologist, Alfred Dieck, over a lifetime of research (Dieck 1965). Included in this catalogue was every reference he could find to the discovery of any form of human remains in any type of peat deposit. He recognised that these discoveries belonged to many periods and were to be found in peat bogs for a variety of reasons (Dieck 1963; Dieck 1986).

Dieck's catalogue, with a number of discoveries gathered independently from the antiquarian literature by Stephen Briggs, was to form the basis of the gazetteer and discussion of British bog bodies in the Lindow Man monograph (Briggs and Turner 1986). This article showed that the discovery of human remains in peat was widespread across the British Isles and instances had been recorded since the seventeenth century. There had been a number of bodies whose preservation had been as complete as that of Lindow Man. The gazetteer from Britain produced totals of 85+ individuals from 50 sites in England and Wales, and 36+ individuals from 16 sites in Scotland. This was significantly higher than figures that Dieck had published in 1972 of 51 and 10 respectively (Dieck 1972), revised to 68 and 17 in 1986 (Dieck 1986). It is now clear that in collecting his information for the British Isles, Dieck did not rigorously check his sources or seek out corroborating evidence, so a number of the entries in his catalogue have had to be dropped. The same has been true for one or two items in the 1986 gazetteer.

Six years have now passed since the publication of that gazetteer. The discovery of the Lindow bodies has stimulated further research by several people into British bog bodies. The number of discoveries has not changed dramatically (the gazetteer on pp. 205–220 now has totals of 106+ individuals for England and Wales and 34+ for Scotland), but what has greatly improved for some of the important discoveries is the documentation contemporaneous with the finds. The remains of some bodies have also been located and some of them have been radiocarbon dated. In three cases in England, clothing and artefacts associated with three of the bodies have been traced to local museums. The discovery of Lindow III has provided important comparative material and the excavation of the timber alignment at Flag Fen, Peterborough (Pryor 1991) has produced prehistoric human remains associated with a huge votive deposit of other objects.

Nevertheless, the picture remains incomplete. Of the twenty-two bodies from England and Wales reportedly discovered with tissue and bone surviving, only parts of four survive to be studied. Those which produced only skeletal remains have survived better, with remains of over 56 individuals represented. Eleven bodies had some sort of clothing associated with them but there are remains from only three. Ten discoveries had potentially dateable artefacts associated with them of which six items have survived. The written sources can also be very limited in the range of data that they include. The best sources are those that are contemporary with the discovery and contain eye-witness accounts. Details can be shown to change in subsequent descriptions and in some cases different bodies can be confused. Each discovery needs to be taken on its merits.

With these caveats in mind, some attempt will now be made to group and quantify the discoveries when presenting the evidence and results of new research from Britain. It is easiest to review the discoveries from England and Wales by grouping them under broad types of peat deposit, as this affects the character of preservation of the remains (Painter, pp. 88–99) and to some extent may be an indication of date. Many earlier finds are not accurately located so they may not easily fit into this classification.

The finds from Scotland form a very different set to those from England and Wales. The best preserved and best documented of all seem to be post-Medieval in date, despite deriving from a wide range of peat deposits, distributed across the whole country. Nevertheless, these finds are a reminder of the diversity of the bog body phenomenon and raise a whole series of questions that should also be asked of some of those finds from England and Wales.

When reading this chapter, reference should be made to the gazetteer at the end of the book, for further information on each discovery and for bibliographic references.

England and Wales
Intertidal Peats

Fluctuations in sea-level since the last glaciation have produced very complex sedimentary sequences around the coastline of England and Wales (Tooley 1978a). At periods of relatively low sea-level, peat-forming plant communities have grown in areas which previously, and then subsequently, were covered by the tide. The peat bands are now revealed on beaches and mudflats, or are encountered during the construction of sea defences or dockworks. These bands are usually heavily compacted by the sands or silts which have accumulated above them. They are generally late prehistoric in date with significant episodes of relatively low sea-level recorded in the Neolithic and Bronze Ages.

Peat deposits of this nature have produced remains of nine or ten human bodies. All are skeletal and their distribution can be traced on Fig. 46. The only dated example is from Hartlepool Bay (14/1 in the gazetteer, p. 209). A radiocarbon sample taken from cleaned but untreated bones produced a date of 4680 ± 60 BP (Hv-5220). The body, found in 1972, was a partly disarticulated skeleton of a man aged about 25–38 of short, stocky build. There was evidence for two head injuries and a broken rib, but all these had healed during his lifetime. The burial was extended, implying an inhumation. The immediate area produced a struck flint, but finds of flint, wooden objects and a roughed-out Neolithic axe have been made elsewhere from this peat shelf (Tooley 1978b).

The contexts of the other bodies in this group are not as well reported. The find from Aberavon, Mid-Glamorgan

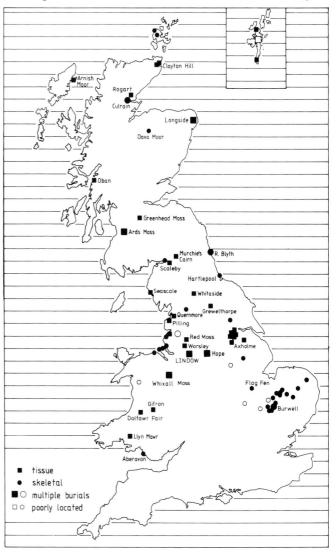

Fig. 46 Distribution map of bog bodies found in Britain.

(65/1) consisted of two bones of the skull associated with the sacrum of an Irish elk found during dock works in a band of peat, 0.8 m thick, below 4.5 m of sand. By implication this may also have a Neolithic date. Similar circumstances surround the bodies found at Gladstone Dock, Liverpool (22/1), Gloucester Road, Birkdale (20/1) and Leasowe Embankment (12/1), all found in peat bands below deep layers of blown sand during construction works.

Dove Point, Meols (11/1) is close to the group of three just described from the north-west of England. This site on the foreshore at the end of the Dee Estuary, produced a remarkable range of finds during the nineteenth century, eroding out of the peat alongside a natural creek. These ranged in date from late prehistory to the Norman Conquest, with a particular concentration of Dark Age objects. The faunal remains were less well recorded. In general, human remains were 'of less frequent occurrence, but skeletons in whole or in part are occasionally found, not at the site of the ancient burying ground, but protruding from the black earth' (Hume 1863, 348).

From across the estuary at Prestatyn came two more bodies (61). One (61/2) was an infant burial surrounded by an oval fence of eight oak stakes forming an enclosure 1.5 m long by 0.8 m wide. The burial can be shown to be late Iron Age on stratigraphic grounds (Blockley 1989, 20–3). The other body from Prestatyn (61/1), the skeleton of a women (found in 1924), is unlocated and not dated. With the addition of two skulls dredged from the bed of the River Blyth (50/1, 2), this makes a total of ten bodies recorded from intertidal or formerly coastal peats. The extent of the prehistoric exploitation of the marshlands, in which this peat formed at times of relatively low sea-level, is only now beginning to be identified. Extensive surveys in Essex (Wilkinson and Murphy 1986) and in the Severn Estuary in Gwent (Bell 1991) – where an isolated skull was recovered from a peat section at Goldcliff in 1993 – have shown exploitation at different periods from the Mesolithic onwards with evidence of settlement at levels now covered by every tide. The circumstances, where known, of the deposition of human bodies in these locations seem to imply inhumation and perhaps they should be compared with those contemporary bodies from the East Anglian Fenland, to be described below.

Upland or Blanket Bog

This is a smaller group to which only seven bodies from six sites can be assigned. The area covered by blanket bog in England and Wales exceeds that of lowland peats, so the number of human remains per unit area is far smaller than for the other types of peat described in this summary. Five of these bodies are inhumations. They include the man and woman from Hope in Derbyshire (19), who died in 1674, a crouched body found within a stone cist at Murchie's Cairn, Cumbria (15/1), and bodies within wooden coffins from Maes-y-Pandy, Gwynedd (64/1) and Quernmore, Lancashire (15/1). The last of these bodies still survives. It was found at the base of the blanket peat and on top of the underlying boulder clay, at a height of 290 m AOD. The wooden coffin carved out of a whole log was cut into a lower and upper half. All that survived of the body were quantities of hair and 14 nails. There were two pieces of a folded woollen cloth originally 1.5 m square and three whitish feathers. Radiocarbon dates of 1340 ± 100 BP (Birm-430) and 1300 ± 100 BP (Birm-474) were obtained from the two halves of the coffin.

The survival of only the human hair and fingernails shows the peculiar qualities of this peat bog, whilst the woollen shroud is the only complete woven garment surviving from an English or Welsh bog body. Ryder (1977, 178) has reported on the cloth:

> The cloth had a ginger–brown colour similar to the natural brown of prehistoric sheep, but microscopic examination showed that only the coarse fibres had natural pigment. The finer fibres must originally have been white (or have been dyed) but now had the yellow–brown discoloration common in archaeological material.

Reconstruction of the burial shows that the shroud was torn so that the feet were bound separately, with the body lying across the diagonal of the main piece. The coffin was too small to contain an adult. The place at which the body was found is a natural vantage point where an early twentieth-century watchtower was erected and a modern car park has been built. This dominating position may explain why the burial took place here.

The remaining bodies in this group came from the Pennine Moors of North Yorkshire. One found in Whitaside in 1797, (56/1), was subsequently reburied in Grinton-in-Swaledale churchyard. The same fate awaited the body from Grewelthorpe Moor found in 1850 and reburied in Kirkby Malzeard churchyard (55/1). What was remarkable about this latter discovery was the clothing in which he was found.

> The robes were quite perfect and the material tough – having been tanned and preserved by some natural agency. The toga was of a green

colour, and some of the dress of scarlet material; the stockings of a yellow cloth, and the sandals cut out in a beautiful shape – like those found in the Thames some years ago – and were likewise finely stitched (Heslington, 1867).

It was only the hasty reaction of the local policemen that retrieved the stockings and sandals from the souvenir hunters. Parts of the left shoe and a woollen insole survive in the Yorkshire Museum and have been the subject of a reappraisal (Turner *et al* 1991). The nailed shoe is typical of Roman *calceus* construction (Fig. 47). The diamond pattern of the thong slots on the upper sole is a feature of northern Britain, and with a single exception from London, unknown in southern England and on the continent. This would give a date range for the shoe of the first to third century AD, when compared with similar shoes from dated contexts.

The insole is also typical of the production of spinners

Fig. 47 The surviving sock and shoe from Grewelthorpe Man, now in the Yorkshire Museum.

and weavers of the northern Roman provinces. It has been cut down from a larger garment, perhaps a cloak, and is now the peat-brown colour typical of clothing retrieved from these situations. However, there is no reason to disbelieve the original description. Dyestuffs can sometimes survive in these environments. Contrasts in colour survive in many of the Scottish finds of clothing (see below). There are more exceptional circumstances as for example with the Roman Iron Age, female, bog body from Lønne Hede in south-west Jutland, Denmark, where the formerly vivid colours are unmistakeable even now (Munksgaard and Ostergaard 1988). This again demonstrates that minor variations in bog chemistry can preserve things in unusual ways (see Painter, pp. 88–99).

None of these upland bodies would seem to be the victims of foul play or have any of the attributes of ritual sacrifices. They would appear to have died of natural causes, perhaps from exposure in some cases, and be buried with different degrees of formality in what where by chance peat bogs.

Lowland Raised Mires

It is finds from these peat bogs that cause the greatest excitement. The preservation of a wide range of tissue as well as bone often had a striking effect on the finder, and allows a greater degree of analysis of each body. Lowland raised mires are not evenly distributed across England and Wales. They occur in all the northern counties of England with particularly large areas in Lancashire and the Mersey Basin, and extend into the midland counties of Cheshire, Shropshire and modern Humberside, where the Isle of Axholme, Thorne Waste and Hatfield Moors now form the largest complex of raised mires surviving in Britain. Wales has the largest intact mire system at Cors Goch and the largest single dome at Cors Fochno, both in north Dyfed, as well as a ring of smaller sites fringing the uplands of the centre of the country.

In southern Britain, only the Somerset Levels had any extensive area of peat bogs of this type but all the *Sphagnum* peat has been cut away and much of the area is under an agricultural regime. In their unreclaimed state, lowland raised mires could cover very extensive areas. Chat Moss, Greater Manchester, is estimated to have been c. 11 000 acres (4400 ha) in size in the seventeenth century whilst some of the small kettlehole raised mires of Cheshire and north Shropshire are only a few acres in size.

From the evidence in the gazetteer it can be suggested that there may have been 27 bog bodies recorded from this type of peat bog. Some locations are uncertain and some descriptions are contradictory. In some cases, the description of the preservation of the body implies it was deposited within *Sphagnum* peat. The descriptions extend back into the seventeenth century (e.g. de la Pryme 1694; Leigh 1700). Both these authors imply that the discovery of well-preserved human remains was widespread if not commonplace at this time. De la Pryme ends his description of a body from Hatfield Chase: 'Though these things may seem strange, yet many authors have yet related the same' (de la Pryme 1694, 275). Leigh reports in his *Natural History of Lancashire, Cheshire and the Peak District* how 'sometimes in mosses are found human bodies entire and uncorrupted' (Leigh 1700, 65).

The seventeenth century was the period when, with the help of Dutch engineers, attempts were made to drain the major wetlands of the Fenlands, Isle of Axholme and South Lancashire. It also corresponds with the growing scientific awareness represented by the formation of the Royal Society. It is, therefore, perhaps not a coincidence that the earliest descriptions come from that period. However, most of the remaining bog bodies in this group were found by men digging for peat by hand right up to the middle of the twentieth century. The right of turbary, the cutting of peat for fuel, is widely documented from the medieval period onwards. Where lowland raised mires existed they were often divided into a number of parishes, and peat provided an alternative to increasingly precious woodland as a source of fuel. As they were at the top of the sequence, *Sphagnum* peats were the first to be cut and were also the best for burning. For bodies found during peat-digging to get into the archaeological record, someone with a scientific or antiquarian interest, normally a doctor, clergyman or squire, had to be close at hand and any description they made be published in a local newspaper, journal or diary. These factors have probably greatly reduced the number of descriptions now available for study.

The distribution of the bodies in this group is given in Fig. 48. Since 1986, new information has come to light and, more importantly, more human remains and artefacts have been available for study. Most important of these are the Lindow bodies and Worsley Man which have been described in detail already in this volume. Reports of three bodies found in the nineteenth century in Whixall Moss, Shropshire (51), have recently been unearthed (Turner and Penney 1996). Whixall Moss still covers some 700 acres (280 ha), and was originally similar in size to Lindow Moss. The first report was of a male body found in 1889. This consisted of a nearly complete skeleton with

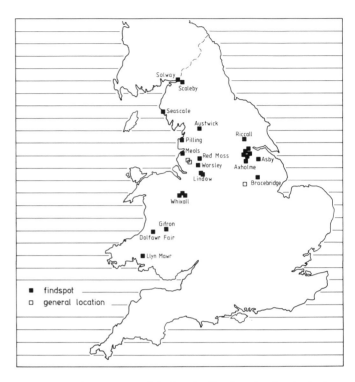

Fig. 48 Distribution map of the bog bodies from lowland raised mires.

some hair and small bits of flesh adhering to the skull; the ribs and legs were partly covered with flesh. The body lay flat, face downwards and there was no trace of clothing. The feet were missing. The stratigraphic position was accurately described. There were three broad layers in the peat, the topmost brownish grey, the second much darker and the third perfectly black. The body lay at the junction of the second and third layer. Recent research has accurately dated the junction between the first and second layer to within the first two centuries AD whilst the lower junction is probably Bronze Age in date (Twigger and Haslam 1991).

This discovery prompted two earlier finds to be brought to light. Some 20 years previously at about 183 m from the find described above, two men 'found the remains of a young man, in a sitting position, over a three-legged stool and partly covered with a leather apron'. Some 12 years previously the remains of a young woman had also been found. Both these last two bodies were reburied in Whitchurch churchyard. The fact that the finders could confidently age and sex these bodies implies that they were well preserved.

From Cumbria are two bodies of equivalent type. In Scaleby Moss (16/1) in 1845, George Hogg

... came to the remains of a human skeleton buried about eight or nine feet beneath the surface, and closely embedded in the lowest stratum of black peat. The skeleton was wrapped in what appears to have been the skin of a deer and has evidently formed a garment ... This garment has been composed of different pieces united by seams ... The whole was bound together by thongs of strong leather. (Turner 1989, 1)

Apart from the skeletal material, only the hair, the brain and some ligaments survived. A later source says that a stick, three feet long and twelve inches in circumference, was found gripped in the bony hand.

The stratigraphic position of this body, like the first body described from Whixall Moss, is well down the sequence of the raised bog. Both are certainly below the *Sphagnum* peats which form above the *Grenzhorizont*, a stratigraphic indicator of the early first millennium BC (Barber 1986), and are potentially in peats formed in the Neolithic or Bronze Age. This lower stratigraphic position is confirmed by the very partial preservation of the tissue, unlike those bodies recovered from *Sphagnum* peats. Despite the problems associated with equating the stratigraphic position of bog bodies with their apparent date of deposition, these bodies from Scaleby and Whixall Mosses are significantly earlier than those from Lindow and Worsley. They could equate with the Neolithic date obtained for the body from Stoneyisland Bog, Ireland (Brindley and Lanting, pp. 133–6) or the Middle Bronze Age date of the body from Emmer-Erfscheidenveen, Netherlands (van der Sanden, pp. 161–2). The latter body was also found wrapped in a leather cape.

Cumbria has produced another bog body, this time from the south-west of the county. It was found in Seascale Moss (18/1) in 1834, while peat-digging (Turner 1990).

... about one foot from the surface, he discovered a substance which resembled in shape part of the human form, and on further inspection found the remaining parts of a body. From the length of time which it had laid in the earth, however, the bones were mouldered to dust, but the mosswater had acted, it is evident, as a preservative to the skin, and gave the hands the appearance of a pair of fine leather gloves: the nails continuing on the fingers. The left ear and the feet are quite perfect, part of the scalp had the hair upon it, and the chin showed a vestige of the beard ... A walking stick of hazel was lying by its side.

The presence of a stick alongside the body is reminiscent of the Scaleby Moss find and the body from Castleblakeney, Gallagh, Ireland (Ó Floinn, pp. 139–40).

The most interesting group of bodies come from what is now Humberside, an area formerly divided between Yorkshire and Lincolnshire. A succession of peat bogs surround the Humber Estuary: Goole Moors, Thorne Waste, Hatfield Chase, Isle of Axholme and Asby Moor. In all there were seven different well-preserved bodies recorded as found in this area in the seventeenth and eighteenth centuries. New information has come to light about two of them. The Spalding Gentlemen's Society was founded in 1720 and is the second oldest society in Britain to be devoted to antiquarian interests. Its detailed minute books record discussions on an extraordinarily wide range of objects and discoveries from all over the country. Two bog bodies are described. The earliest of these was found in 1724 (29/1):

Mr Downes acquainted us that about 5 instruments of a sort of Bell Mettle found in Asby Moor near Brigg in ye County abt. 3 months agone. Also the Skeleton and Skin of a Man found upright in the same moor by one John Luipton, a Quaker and Many Oaks and Firrs Large and Firm. (*Minute Book of 1724*, f. 86, see Turner and Rhodes (1992)).

Accompanying this note is a sketch of a double-looped axe, presumably of Late Bronze Age type. This body was inaccurately located at Spalding in the earlier gazetteer of bog bodies (Briggs and Turner 1986, 184).

The minute books also provide some information on the woman's body found on Amcotts Moor (30/1) in 1747. The body was found by a man digging for peat, when his spade cut through the toe of a left shoe. Dr Stovin, a local antiquarian, quickly organised a further exploration which led to the excavation of the body. It proved to be a woman, lying on her side in a crouched position, naked except for her sandals. Stovin sent one of her hands and her right shoe to the Royal Society who illustrated the latter in their transactions (Fig. 49) and who also passed them on to the Society of Antiquaries. This prompted the artist and antiquary, George Vertue, to write to the editor of the *Philosophical Transactions*. He noted the shoe was of ox-hide and had been cut from a single piece of leather. He concluded, by comparing it to the few known parallels, that it was Medieval in date.

The discovery was brought to the attention of the Spalding Gentlemen's Society. Their minute book for 24 September 1747 described the shoe: 'She had sandals on,

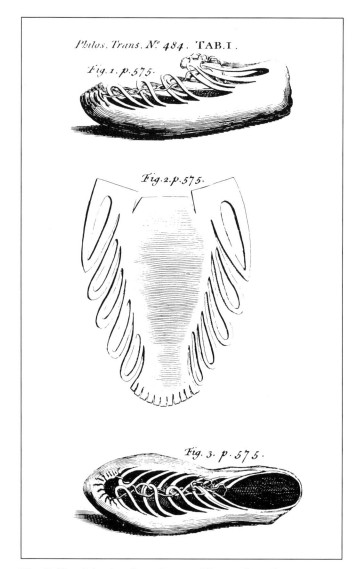

Fig. 49 The right shoe from Amcotts Woman (from the *Philosophical Transactions* of the Royal Society).

Fig. 50 The left shoe from Amcotts Woman, now in the Spalding Gentlemen's Society Museum. (*M. Rhodes*)

laced at the Top of the foot having a seem at the heel, sewd with a throng of the same hide. 5 loops cut in the whole leather on each side, and 2 small ones at the Toe, so that it drew up the Toe like a purse mouth.' Among other antiquities found by Stovin on the moor were 'some Brass British Celts (as called), a Dart and Two Daggers, so ye Dr. doubts not this was a British Lady'.

Ten years later the Society was presented with the left shoe by Charles Amcotts, on whose manor it had been found. By unexpected and great good fortune, this shoe has survived, and is displayed in a cabinet in the Society's museum (Fig. 50). It still shows the damaged tip caused by the labourer's spade over 240 years ago, at the moment of the body's discovery. The rediscovery of the shoe has allowed its style and date to be reconsidered (Turner and Rhodes 1992). The Amcotts shoes are typical of one-piece shoes found throughout the northern provinces of the Roman Empire, in having a semicircular heel shape, a back seam and a series of side loops to accommodate the lacing.

The date of the Amcotts shoes rests on the unusual form of the side loops which face forward and were formed by slitting and expanding a leather tab. The toe tabs are another rare feature, with parallels coming from groups of shoes in West Yorkshire and isolated examples in London. Toe tabs are also present on native shoes from Denmark, North Germany and along the Roman *limes*. The style and construction of the shoes indicate a late third to fourth century date. Amcotts Woman is therefore the first body in this group to be independently dated, not relying on radiocarbon dating, a method which has been shown to have inconsistencies when applied to bog bodies.

Despite this new information, the group of bog bodies from lowland raised mires is hard to analyse. The only bodies from which parts survive are from Lindow Moss (13) and Worsley Moss (26/1) (perhaps just three individuals). The shoe from another body, Amcotts Woman, is available for study. These each give a date ranging from the early first century to the fourth century AD. All could derive from the Romano-British period. For the rest, reliance has to be placed on the original descriptions. The jet and amber beads recovered with the head of Pilling Woman (24/1), (Edwards 1969) are probably Bronze Age in date. The stratigraphic descriptions and the character of the preservation of one of the bodies from Whixall Moss and the body from Scaleby Moss suggest Bronze Age or Neolithic dates. The only other inference that can be drawn is that where the bodies are very well preserved they must have been deposited in a *Sphagnum*-dominated peat bog. These are likely to be Iron Age or later.

Cause of death is by no means clear in all cases. There are several decapitations. Lindow I, Worsley Man, Red Moss (21/1), Pilling (24/1), Gifron (66/1) and possibly Llyn Mawr Farm (62/1). There are two headless bodies, Lindow III and Dolfawr Fair (63/1). The only evidence for hanging or nooses occurs with Lindow II and Worsley Man. In no other case is the cause of death known.

Fenland Peats

The group is a geographical entity rather than a group from a specific type of peat environment. It includes remains of bodies from the Lincolnshire, Cambridgeshire and Norfolk Fenland and isolated finds from other peat deposits in the East Anglian counties. With over 57 individuals, from the English and Welsh population of 106 plus finds, this area dominates the statistics. However, as a group there is less to analyse than for those already described. With one exception, all the finds are skeletal. This exception is an otherwise unsubstantiated description of a body found in Burwell Fen (2/1) sometime in the middle of this century.

> He stood upright in his dug-out canoe. His lank black hair dropped to his shoulders. His peat-dark skin was still stretched over the bones of his face. The eyes had gone but the eye-sockets were dark with mystery. He was clad in a long leather jacket, belted, with garters round his legs and the right arm was raised as though about to cast a spear. That body of the unknown hunter, the nameless warrior had been preserved in the peat for uncounted aeons of time. It crumbled to dust in the sharp Fen air (J. W. Day, in Clarke 1971)

Though Rainbird Clarke and J. Wentworth Day were present at this discovery, nothing from this find seems to survive. The canoe, though reported to be in the Downing Street Museum, Cambridge, has never been accessioned there. It is hard to imagine that this story was invented though it may well have been embellished. Potentially, one of the most important British bog bodies is known only from this description.

One early description of human remains from peat in this area is known. This is the body from West Tofts, Norfolk, (35/1), found in 1720 in an oak coffin. The skeletal remains were associated with '30 small beads, a black face of Lancashire coal, a golden funnell and a cypher ... The cypher and beads are of a blue colour' (Norfolk SMR no. 5137 from original MS). The rest of the finds are reported from the second half of the nineteenth and twentieth centuries. Many of these are fragmentary, with skulls and mandibles over represented. There are few exhaustive contemporary descriptions as with those from other types of peat and many were uncovered by machine, dredgers or the plough; so their original position within the stratigraphy is inaccurately known.

Where this group does differ significantly from the others is in the survival of a high proportion of skeletal remains. Of the 57 individuals recorded in the gazetteer, remains survive from 48 of the bodies. The largest collections are in the Sedgwick Museum, Cambridge, the Norfolk Museums Service and the British Museum (Natural History). Healy and Housley (1992) have looked in detail at a number of finds from the parishes of Southery (42) and Methwold (39, 40 and 41) in the Norfolk Fens. Fourteen individuals were represented including 'Nancy', the Southery Fen female, found in association with an Early Bronze Age jet bead necklace and bronze awl, and a number of skeletons recorded by the local archaeologist, Frank Curtis, during drainage works.

Healy and Housley wished to relate these finds to the dense, Early Bronze Age occupation on the Fen edge, which followed the Fen Clay marine transgression now dated to 2800–2140 BC at nearby Feltwell Common. Nancy had been recovered in peat immediately above the fen clay equating the stratigraphic position to the associated artefacts. The Oxford University Radiocarbon Accelerator Unit dated nine femurs from the 14 individuals recorded. The whole series of dates falls within the Early Bronze Age with the mean dates ranging between 3840–3540 BP and the calibrated range with 95% confidence limits being 2570–1685 BC.

These newly dated bodies were all found in Methwold parish in four locations. Three locations imply the burial of family groups together (Norfolk SMR 2542 (i) consisted of a man and two adult women, children of about 7–8 and 11 years and an infant. 2542 (ii) consisted of a man and two children of about 6 years old, and 2585 of a probable woman and two children of about 10 years old.) Each group of bodies had isolated artefacts found with them but they may have been carried or worn by one of them in everyday life. All the groups had been disturbed when found but in the only case where sufficient survived *in situ* for a plan to be drawn, the impression was of chaos. However, the one isolated body, site 2550, consisted of a skeleton of a woman lying on a regular setting of wood, implying a more deliberate deposition. Healy argues that these discoveries may represent a contemporary treatment of the dead not previously recognised in the Early Bronze Age with the groups being the victims of epidemic or accident, or deriving from the repeated use of particular (marked ?) locations.

The distribution of human remains from the Fenland is by no means even, but a similar concentration of human remains occurs at Burwell Fen, Cambridgeshire (2). Over and above the description given at the beginning of this section is a very extensive collection of skeletal material. Up to 12 different skeletons were discovered by peat diggers in the late nineteenth and early twentieth centuries and these were collected by T. McKenny Hughes who probably paid a reward for each find made. Skulls and mandibles make up almost the whole collection and there is little to suggest that whole skeletons were found together or in groups as at Methwold. The only finds with any provenance are D.33838 and 33840 in the Sedgwick Museum, which have an associated note saying: 'Portions of 2 skulls and a long bone found in 1884 in Burwell Fen, at a depth of 4 feet in the same deposit as roots of shrubs and trees occurred', and a letter written in 1919 describing an unabraded flint tool associated with these finds. All are young or mature adults and some show the heavy tooth wear found on the Methwold adults.

What is remarkable about Burwell Fen is the range of other animal and bird skeletons that were found at the same time. The list includes wild boar, otter, beaver, auroch, brown bear, wolf, roe and red deer, sea eagle, crane, mute swan, ducks, geese, bitterns and razorbill. The most dramatic discovery was a complete skeleton of an auroch, *Bos primigenius*, with a Neolithic axe lodged in its cranium (Hughes 1896; Burleigh *et al* 1982), though some doubt has been cast on the authenticity of the pole-axed auroch (Healy, personal communication).

The impression given by this remarkable assemblage is of a natural animal trap, perhaps used or modified by man to catch game. However, it is hard to see how the human skeletal material fits in. If these were bodies accidentally mired during hunting, then whole skeletons would have been expected to occur. Perhaps they represent a modified form of funerary practice, as suspected at Methwold, and it would be interesting to see the results of a programme of dating to discover if the Burwell Fen material is contemporary. McKenny Hughes (1916, 29) reached the conclusion:

Human bones have not been very often found in the Fen, and when they do occur it is not always easy to say whether they really belong to the age of the peat in which they are found or may not be the remains of someone mired in the bog or drowned in one of the later filled-up ditches. That they have long been buried in the peat is often obvious from the colour and condition of the bone.

The most important discovery of human remains from the Fenland in recent years was made at Flag Fen, near Peterborough. Linking the Late Bronze Age wooden platform at Flag Fen to the dryland field system on the Fengate is an alignment of timber posts running for over 1 km in a straight line. Excavation of part of this alignment on the Fengate Power Station site in 1989 (3) revealed a remarkable collection of finds (Pryor 1991, 105–18). A 150 m length of the alignment, up to 8 m wide, exposed nearly 800 wooden posts. From within and around the post alignment, and particularly concentrated on its south-western side, came a remarkable series of objects of Late Bronze Age to Early Iron Age date, *c.* 1200–300 BC (Coombs 1992). Just over 300 pieces were recovered, the majority of bronze. The commonest types were pins, rings and ornaments, with the greatest weight of metal being in weapons, swords, dirks, daggers and a rapier. Tools were rare but included a group of twenty tanged chisels, punches and awls, perhaps an individual craftsman's kit, and a pair of shears in their wooden box. Many of the items were deliberately vandalised or broken, but as they were found together then they must have been dropped or placed in the water from a boat or the alignment itself.

In addition to this range of votive metalwork were bones, including seven dog burials and parts of at least three human skeletons. One complete body was found at about 10 m distance on the north-western side of the posts, and some distance away were two thigh bones of a fairly tall person. Within an area of posts was a group of loose human bones associated with a broken shale bracelet and a boar's tusk. As yet these bones have not been dated but they are assumed to be contemporary with the metalwork assemblage.

Pryor argues that the wooden platform at Flag Fen may have carried halls or public buildings and the post alignment was constructed to mark a boundary when the water level had risen making the platform buildings unusable. The platform and the alignment were the sites of a variety of ritual and religious functions, because of their position at the edge of the cultivated land, the open Fen and the ever-rising sea. The majority of the metalwork lay on the landward side of the alignment and so may have been offerings of thanks or asking for good fortune or the commemoration of particular events or people. The human remains lay on the opposite side and may reflect tension or crisis, perhaps sacrificed in fear of the rising sea-water which threatened their lands and homes (Pryor 1992).

Scotland

There is much less to add to the earlier summary of Scottish bog bodies (Briggs and Turner 1986, 151–2). As a group they cannot be subdivided by type of peat bog, as the information available does not make this possible. The available data range is also very narrow. Potentially the earliest finds came from Stirlingshire, where several skeletons were said to have been found in *c*. 1830, buried in peat and associated with bronze celts and other implements. A search of the Royal Commission's archives has failed to produce any evidence for a Bronze Age metalwork hoard, or of human remains from a Stirlingshire peat bog. Nothing can also be added to the descriptions of burials in monoxylous oak coffins from Longside (67) and Oban (81). So there is no certain evidence of any prehistoric bog bodies from Scotland, though the votive deposition of metalwork is well established (Clarke *et al* 1985).

All other Scottish discoveries are likely or known to be medieval or post-medieval in date. Two sites produced groups of bodies, six at Culrain, Ross-shire (69) and twelve at Bressay, Shetland (78). These are likely to be victims of an epidemic or a disaster, such as the shipwreck in the case of Bressay. Three bodies seem to be murder victims. At Quintfall Hill, Caithness, the skull showed the mark of a heavy blow. The late seventeenth-century body at Greenhead Moss, Lanarkshire (80/1) had cut marks on his shoes and cap. From Arnish Moor, Lewis (81/1), a partial skeleton was recovered in 1964, partly clothed. The bones were reduced 'to the consistency of rubbery sea-weed'. It proved to be the body of a young man of about 20–25, no more than 1.6 m tall. He had died following blows to the head.

He was wearing a woollen undershirt, shirt, thigh-length jacket, stockings and a bonnet. No shoes survived but these may have dissolved away. Within the clothing was a striped woollen purse containing a wooden comb, a piece of oak, horn spoon, two quills and three strands of wood (Fig. 51). The finders were paid a reward of £30 for the clothing. The style of this clothing suggested a late seventeenth- or early eighteenth-century date, though 'there are obvious difficulties in applying criteria derived from the wealthy to the ragged garments from an area remote from the fashionable centres of Europe' (Bennett 1975, 178). Bennett linked this body to a long-established story of a murder at this spot.

The contents of the Arnish Moor purse are very similar to the contents of the pockets of a man found at Gunnister, Shetland (Fig. 52). In one of his pockets was a spare woollen cap wrapped around a horn spoon, in the other a small horn and knitted purse with three low-value late seventeenth-century coins, one Swedish and two Dutch. A stick lay across the legs and a wooden tub, a wooden knife

Fig. 51 The contents of the purse of the man found in Arnish Moor, Lewis. (*By kind permission of the National Museums of Scotland.*)

Fig. 52 The clothing recovered from the burials at Barrock Fell, Arnish Moor and Gunnister. (*By kind permission of the National Museums of Scotland.*)

Fig. 53 The body from Clayton Hill, Caithness, when found. (*By kind permission of the National Museums of Scotland.*)

Fig. 54 The jacket from Clayton Hill when conserved. (*By kind permission of the National Museums of Scotland.*)

Fig. 55 The linen tunic from the body from Rogart, Sutherland. (*By kind permission of Lord Strathmore and the National Museums of Scotland.*)

handle and two tablets of wood were at his feet. There were also two lengths of woollen cord. The two collections of objects may be all that a poor traveller of the day would carry, suggesting in the case of Gunnister (76/1) and perhaps Clayton Hill (70/1) – Figs 53 and 54 – and others, that these men died of exposure in winter and were buried on the spot, as at Hope in Derbyshire (19).

One significant new discovery from Scotland has not yet been fully published. This was found at Springhill, Knockan, in the parish of Rogart, Sutherland (72/1) in 1875. The police report of the incident states that the following was found:

> ... ten pieces of human bone, a coarse linen shirt or shift, and a small bag containing some home-spun linen thread, and further, on this date, there were found at the same place, two pieces of coarse linen ... which had apparently been used as stockings, as a shoe was found attached to one of the pieces, also some decayed bones. The bones had the appearance of being those of a grown-up person.

Subsequent correspondence reveals that two round stones were laid over the legs which pointed in an easterly direction. The costume is now in the Royal Museum of Scotland having previously hung in Dunrobin Castle. The shift or tunic consists of a body made of a single piece of coarse linen joined on the right side and with an opening for the neck (Fig. 55). The sleeves are of different cloth and of two pieces each. The design can be compared with the thirteenth or fourteenth-century tunic from Bocksten, Sweden and related finds (Nockert 1985). There is no buttoning, cuffs or other adornment. The shoes are also of a primitive type being one-piece moccasins, hand stitched and with a few simple hobnails. This is potentially the earliest complete costume from Scotland and from any British bog body and needs expert study before a high medieval date can be confirmed.

The Nature of the Sample

Peat bogs still form a significant part of the British landscape. At 1 582 000 ha or 5.8% of our land area, the United Kingdom is the country with the ninth largest area of peat in the world (Fig. 56). However, the rate of loss of peat bogs and in particular the lowland raised mires has been very dramatic. It is estimated that 96% of the raised bog existing in Britain in 1850 has been lost. For the Lancashire Mosses, it has been shown (Pearce 1990) that there were nearly 11 000 ha of raised bog at the end of the seventeenth century of which less than 1% is left. In the Fenland, only

very isolated pockets such as Wicken Fen retain their natural vegetation and the famous Holme Fen post driven into the ground, level with the then surface in 1852, now stands 4 m above ground level due to peat shrinkage (Pryor 1991, 18).

The loss of blanket bog has been less dramatic, but 50–70% of all new forestry in Scotland up to 1978, was carried out on peat soil, a process dramatically speeded up in the 1980s (Pearce 1990). It has, therefore, taken around 300 years of peat cutting, drainage, agricultural improvement and forestry largely to obliterate a natural resource accumulated over about 7000 years. It is against this background that the discoveries of human remains in peat bogs should be set.

There are now sufficient numbers of finds from England and Wales to consider some simple statistical analysis. However, the nature of the information about each discovery is very different and often very partial. When compared with the wealth of data available for the Lindow bodies and those discovered or investigated in modern times from the continent, most other finds are disappointing. The validity of any statistical comparisons, such as those undertaken by van der Sanden on the better preserved Dutch bodies (see pp. 146–65), has to be questioned. From the sample of 106 plus bodies in the gazetteer, 22 bodies are recorded to have had tissue surviving. Parts of only four of these bodies are known to survive, the two bodies from Lindow Moss, the head of Worsley Man and the hair and fingernails of the Quernmore Burial. Seventy-two bodies are reported as being represented by skeletal remains only, of which the remains of 56 are known to survive. For the remaining ten bodies no accurate indication is given. Sixty-one of the bodies are described as adult and only 14 as young adults or children. Relatively few have had their sex identified though 27 are described as male and only 13 are described as female. So there is a strong bias towards adult males being represented by this phenomenon.

An attempt has already been made to link the bog bodies to the type of peat deposit from which they derived. Summarising those figures again: 10 come from intertidal or coastal peats, 7 from upland or blanket bogs, 27 plus from lowland raised mires, and 57 plus from the Fenland, where a variety of peat bogs were to be found. These totals are not a reflection of the relative areas of the different peat deposits in England and Wales which are ordered in the following way: upland or blanket bog, the Fenland, lowland raised mires, and intertidal or coastal peats. The type of peat bog and the stratigraphic position

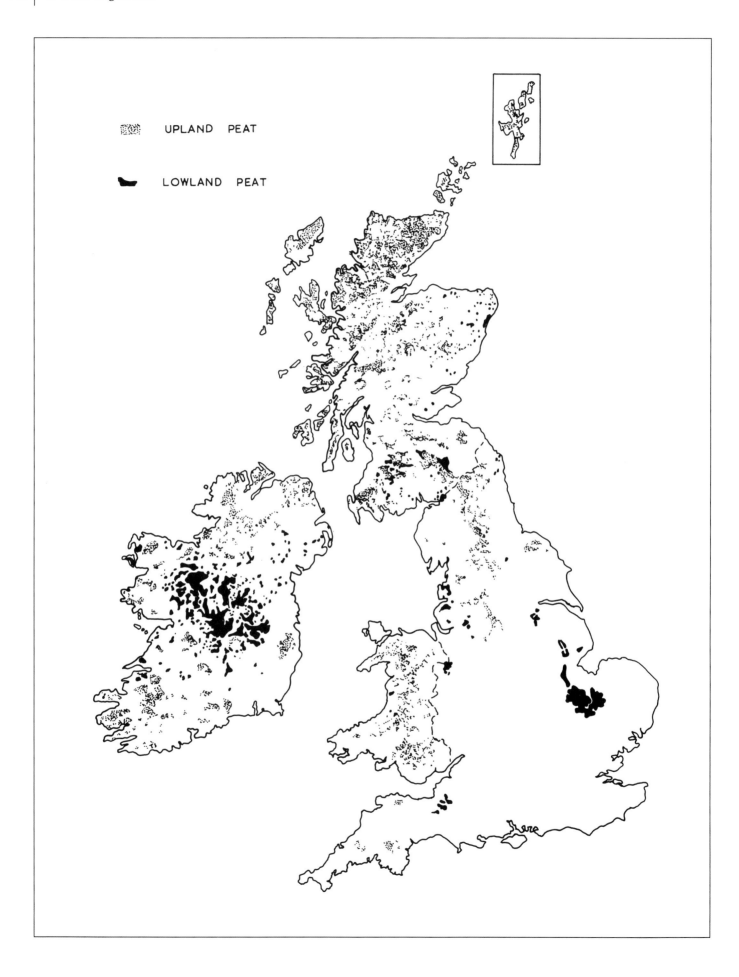

UPLAND PEAT

LOWLAND PEAT

within certain types of bog does affect the nature of the preservation of the body and any associated artefacts. The figures for the bodies are given above but some consideration can also be given to the associated artefacts.

Eleven of the bodies were found in association with clothing or woven cloth. Variations in bog chemistry can lead to the partial survival of different types of garment. Where tissue survives, then so does woollen cloth. However, linen and other fibres may decay. Untanned skin or fur will also survive where tanned leathers, particular oak-tanned leathers, may not. Consequently, the surviving items of clothing associated with bog bodies may not fully represent those in which they were buried. Of the early bodies reported from England and Wales, only Grewelthorpe Man and one of the finds from Burwell Fen were found fully clothed, though the latter description remains unsubstantiated. Most remarkably, the clothing from Grewelthorpe Man retained its colours, whilst most other bog clothing is stained from a yellow to red-brownish colour, though patterns may still be discerned.

The two seventeenth-century bodies from Hope were buried in their clothes. The body from Scaleby was wrapped in a leather or deerskin cape whilst one of the Whixall bodies is described as wearing a leather apron. Shoes were found on Amcotts Woman, two of the bodies from Hatfield Chase and near to the body from Austwick Common. Lindow Man had a fox-fur band around his left arm. The woman's head from Pilling Moss was wrapped in a woollen cloth and the Quernmore burial in a woollen shroud. This is a very impoverished collection to set alongside those from Scotland (Henshall 1952) and Ireland (Ó Floinn, pp. 137–45, 221–34), and insufficient survives for the sort of detailed analyses and intercomparisons being undertaken on the continent (Hald 1972 and 1980; Groenman–Van Waateringe 1991).

Wooden artefacts also will normally survive even when the bodies are represented by skeletal remains only. It is therefore surprising that only eight bodies have been associated with wooden objects. The bodies from Quernmore, West Tofts and Maes-y-Pandy were found in oak tree-trunk coffins, whilst one of the Methwold bodies lay on a platform of logs. The baby's body at Prestatyn was enclosed by a stake fence. Sticks were held or found alongside the bodies from Scaleby and Seascale and one of the Whixall bodies was said to have been found close to a three-legged stool. None of the bodies was staked down in

the bog like 'Queen Gunhild' and others in Denmark (Glob 1969, 74) or in the Netherlands (van der Sanden 1990, 86–9).

Even more disappointing is the number of bodies reported as associated with potentially datable metal, pottery or bone artefacts. There are ten sites where direct associations can be made and so some idea of date can be given. Most of these come from the Fenland. At three of the four sites in Methwold parish, Norfolk, the individual or groups of bodies each had associated artefacts. Site 2542 (i) produced a copper alloy awl of Early Bronze Age type, and 2542 (ii), two flint scrapers. Site 2585 yielded a bone pin. Subsequent radiocarbon dating confirmed that all these sites were Early Bronze Age in date (Healy and Housley 1992). From the nearby Southery Fen, the female skeleton had a necklace of eight fusiform jet beads and a bronze awl or pin, also of Early Bronze Age date (Clark 1933).

From the Late Bronze Age, came the finds from Soham Fen, a necklace of jet beads and spacers and a socketed chisel-like axe associated with a skeleton (Fox 1923, 55) and at Flag Fen, the group of loose human bones was found with a smashed shale bracelet and boar's tusk. The burial in an oak coffin at West Tofts, Norfolk, was associated with about 30 small, square irregular blue beads, a face carved in black Lancashire coal (shale ?) and a golden funnel. From the descriptions and sketches made in 1720, Clarke suggested that this burial might be related to the Wessex Culture of the Early Bronze Age (Clarke 1971).

Away from the Fenland, artefacts are almost unknown. The only equivalent discovery was the woman's head from Pilling, Lancashire which had a necklace of two strings of jet beads. On one link the beads were about half an inch long and cylindrical and on the other the beads were irregular with a large round amber bead at the centre. From this description, Edwards (1969) believed this find to be Bronze Age in date. The final item in this group may be more fanciful, for a man and a horse in complete armour are said to have been found in Solway Moss, Cumbria by peat-diggers. They are believed to have fought in the battle there in 1542.

This dated group of bodies came almost exclusively from the Bronze Age and the items associated with the bodies are usually personal adornments. The frequency of jet and shale objects may be coincidence but is higher than that for burials on dryland sites. None of the potential sacrifice victims of the Iron Age or Roman period was associated with readily datable artefacts.

Given the rate of loss of peat deposits described at the

Fig. 56 The distribution of upland and lowland peat in Britain and Ireland. (*After Pearce 1990*)

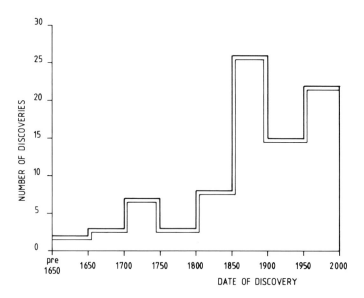

Fig. 57 The frequency of discovery of human remains in peat in England and Wales.

beginning of this section, it is interesting to look at the frequency of discovery or reporting of bog bodies from England and Wales (Fig. 57). The bulk of the finds were made after 1850. This includes nearly all the Fenland material and reflects a growing interest in physical anthropology and the active collecting policies of the University of Cambridge and the Norwich Castle Museum. Finds made before 1850 are often the most interesting discoveries. For them to have been recorded, a local person had to become involved, usually a vicar, doctor or squire with antiquarian or natural history interests. Their notes or correspondence then had to be published or have found its way into archive collections, to be rediscovered during the coarse of modern research. Inevitably, the numbers of bodies reported must be only a percentage of those discovered and that percentage will be lower the further back in time they were found. However, given the relatively slow rate of the rediscovery of these earlier reports since 1986, it is probable that a high percentage of those bodies that were reported have now been found. Therefore, the sample of bodies available for consideration is not likely

to increase dramatically, though knowledge of individual discoveries may be refined further.

Despite all the problems with the data, the bog body phenomenon in Britain is now firmly established. The pattern of distribution across northern Europe first identified by Dieck has been accepted by British archaeologists. However, the recent research outlined above shows that British bog bodies occur over a wide period of dates and in different depositional environments. A relatively small proportion of the total are likely to date from the Iron Age and Romano-British periods and even fewer of these seem to have had obvious signs of a violent or ritualistic death and are thus comparable with the Lindow bodies. Nevertheless there is a core group of bodies from the northern half of England and Wales which have these characteristics and can be compared with the much larger numbers of finds of this type from Denmark, north Germany and Holland (see Fig. 48 for their possible distribution).

Whilst ritual sacrifice represents the most appealing and popular explanation, the other bodies described here are no less interesting. The finds from Methwold, perhaps paralleled by those from Burwell Fen, may represent a previously unrecognised funerary practice. The association of human remains with the dog skeletons and wide variety of weapons, tools and personal adornments found alongside the post alignment at Flag Fen, may betray a different form of ritual from that undergone by the Lindow bodies. The inhumations in peat, either in wooden coffins or out in the coastal peats, are distinct forms of burial. The more recent bodies from Hope in England, and those from Scotland, remind us that peat bogs are hostile places where death by miring or exposure in winter may have been commonplace. They are also remote places where murder victims could be hidden in comparative safety.

Each bog body should therefore be judged on its merits. Given the partial and often unsubstantiated information that exists for these finds, great care should be taken before drawing inferences from the population as a whole. Nevertheless British bog bodies include some wonderful discoveries which have been unjustifiably ignored by archaeologists for so long.

A Bog Body from Meenybraddan Bog, County Donegal, Ireland

M. Delaney   R. Ó Floinn

*'and I rose from the dark
hacked bone, skull – ware,
frayed stitches, tufts,
small gleams on the bank.'*

'Bog Queen' by Seamus Heaney,
North, Faber, 1975

Introduction

On 3 May 1978, farmer Frank Battles and his neighbours were hand-cutting turf on bogland at Meenybraddan, Inver, Co. Donegal, situated mid-way between Ardara and the village of Inver, when they uncovered a human body under one metre of virgin turf. The precise location details are: td. Meenybraddan, par. Inver, bar. Banagh, O.S. 6 inch Sheet 83, 40.6 cm from W.; 24.0 cm from S. National Grid Ref. G 793 869. The woollen cloak and the body are preserved in the National Museum of Ireland where they are registered respectively 1978:341a and b.

The discovery was reported to the Chief State Pathologist, Dr John Harbison, two days later and was investigated by him and Mr R. Ó Floinn of the National Museum of Ireland on 6 May. The body was extended and was wrapped in a woollen cloak which was used as a shroud (Fig. 58). It lay on its back, the head lying at a depth of 88 cm below the surface of the bog. The feet lay 15 cm below the level of the head. The body was oriented north west/south east with the head in the north west.

Meenybraddan lies in the centre of an extensive area of upland bog covering some 400 km². This particular stretch of bog was first cut in 1942 and the present bank only three to four years before the discovery. The bog was at least 2 m deep in the vicinity of the find. An examination of the area immediately surrounding the body yielded no evidence of wooden stakes, brushwood or stones. The find was located some 300 m from the Ardara–Inver road and about 60 m to the west was a gravelled track which is known locally as an old bog road from Dunkineely to Glenties.

The body was that of a woman aged 25–35 years and when examined on 6 May, measured 1.50 m in length. There was no evidence of trauma or pathology. She had been buried naked apart from a cloak which had been adapted to form a shroud. There were no other associated artefacts, nor was there any sign of a pit or grave dug into the turf. The body was well preserved although the feet had been damaged. This was due to the fact that in the previous year's cutting, the face of the bank stopped just short of the area of the feet and in the intervening period this part of the body had dried out. The remains were removed to Dublin where they were stored in a freezer until 1985 when a full examination of the body was begun. The cloak was conserved in the National Museum of Ireland.

Fig. 58 Bog body wrapped in its woollen shroud, May 1978. (*National Museum of Ireland*)

This was the first well-preserved bog body found this century in Ireland and the opportunity was taken to undertake a full scientific investigation of the remains. The discovery of Lindow Man in 1984 and its subsequent investigation acted as a catalyst to the examination of the Meenybraddan find and aspects of the investigations were interrelated and the latter was, in fact, conserved in advance of the Lindow find in order to test the effects of freeze-drying.

Sequence of Events

May 1978

3 The body was discovered at 1.30 p.m. It was raised and taken to the Shiel Hospital in Ballyshannon. Later in the afternoon the body was unwrapped by Garda Cormack of Mountcharles Garda Station.

5 Superintendent T. Murray of Ballyshannon Garda Station informed the State Pathologist's Office and the National Museum of Ireland.

6 Dr J. Harbison, State Pathologist, his assistant Mr C. Driver and Mr R. Ó Floinn, Assistant Keeper, Irish Antiquities Division, National Museum of Ireland, inspected the body and the findspot.

Dr Harbison took X-rays of the body with a portable machine. Later that evening the body was removed to Dublin and placed in a freezer in the City Morgue.

May 1985

23 The body was examined in the City Morgue. Present were Dr J. Harbison; his assistant, Mr C. Driver; Dr I. Stead of the British Museum; Dr D. Brothwell of the Institute of Archaeology, London; Mr J. Bourke, surgeon from University Hospital, Nottingham; Prof. G. F. Mitchell, formerly Professor of Quaternary Studies, Trinity College, Dublin; Mr R. Ó Floinn and Mr V. Butler of the National Museum of Ireland and Dr M. Delaney.

Because of deterioration as the body defrosted it was brought to a body fridge in St James' Hospital, Dublin and stored at a temperature of −4°C.

June 1985:

3 A CT scan was carried out in the Richmond Hospital Dublin by Prof. M. Ryan and his assistant Mr J. Attard.

6 A further examination was carried out in St

James' Hospital Morgue by Dr Harbison with a view to autopsy. Dr H. Barry, Senior Lecturer, School of Dentistry, Trinity College, Dublin was present and examined the teeth.

Superficial examination only was carried out and an endoscopy was arranged. Mould was observed on the body at this time.

13 An endoscopy was performed in St James' Hospital by Prof. J. S. Pritchard, Gastroenterologist, Dept of Clinical Medicine, Trinity College, Dublin.

As further deterioration was noted, it was decided not to proceed with invasive procedures and the body was again frozen and stored in a freezer in Dr Harbison's office.

July 1985

22 The body was removed and transported to the British Museum by Ms M. McCord of the British Museum Organics Conservation Department. In transit, the body was wrapped in a survival blanket and placed in a specially constructed crate containing dry ice.

23 The body arrived in the British Museum Conservation Department, Organics Section Laboratory. It was removed from the box still wrapped in the survival blanket and was placed in a chest freezer.

26 The body was unwrapped and examined in the presence of Mr S. Omar and Ms M. McCord of the Conservation Department and Dr M. Delaney. It had suffered no damage in transit. It was then replaced in the freezer.

August 1985

23 Thawing commenced in the Conservation Laboratory.

28 Thawing was completed.

29 Autopsy was performed by Mr J. Bourke, Dept of Surgery, University Hospital, Nottingham. This was necessary in order to remove interval organs before freeze-drying.

30 Impregnation with PEG was started.

November 1985

11 Conservation completed.

May 1987

28 Body returned to National Museum of Ireland.

Specialist Reports

1 At the original examination at the Shiel Hospital, Ballyshannon Dr. John Harbison, Chief State Pathologist, made the following observations (see Figs 59 and 60):

Position: The body was extended lying on the back. The head was turned to the left with the chin resting on the left clavicle. The right arm was resting along the right side with the hand on the front of the upper right thigh. The right elbow was slightly flexed and the forearm was pronated. The wrist was relaxed. The fingers were flexed at the first interphalangeal joint, so that the

Fig. 59 Body after the removal of the shroud, May 1978. (*National Museum of Ireland*)

Fig. 60 Detail of the face, May 1978. (*National Museum of Ireland*)

second and third phalanges were folded under the first.

The left upper arm was lying by the left side, the forearm was lying across the upper abdomen at a little less than a right angle. The forearm was pronated and the wrist relaxed, the hand almost touching the right forearm and the fingers bent as in the right arm. The shoulders were slightly raised. The legs were extended and lay parallel to one another.

Preservation: Much of the soft tissue had been preserved. The scalp and hair were well preserved on the right side which had been uppermost in the bog. The face was moderately well preserved. The hair appeared wavy and of moderate length. The eyelids, eyelashes and eyebrows were all present, with the suggestion of some tissue remaining in the socket,

visible in the slight gap between the upper and lower lids.

The skin was breaking down over the right zygoma. The cartilage and skin over most of the nose were missing and overgrown with turf. The lips were also infiltrated with bog plants and the bottom lip was in a better state than the top. There was no enamel on the teeth but the dentine remained. The skin was well preserved over most of the torso and especially on the back, which was downmost in the bog. It had broken down in patches to display adipocere, muscle and tendon.

The skin had broken down in the abdominal region and was much infiltrated by plant and bog material. However, skin did extend to the top of the legs where it rapidly disappeared. Both the forearms and the legs were reduced to bone. The legs retained some muscle and tendon. The fingernails were well preserved *in situ*. Some damage had been done to the feet and the phalanges and toe nails were absent.

Preservation of the skin seemed to be best where there was underlying soft tissue rather than bone. Adipocere was well preserved. It also seemed to provide protection to the underlying tissues.

The bones were all demineralised, and were soft and pliable. The internal organs seemed to be preserved but collapsed and shrunken. The whole body was stained dark brown. The soft tissue areas which were downmost in the bog seem to have been the best preserved, but also seem to have been the most demineralised.

2 Report by Prof. Max Ryan, Professor of Radiology, Royal College of Surgeons in Ireland, assisted by Miss Una Kinsella and Mr Joe Attard, Senior Radiographers, Beaumont Hospital, Dublin on the radiographs and CT scan:

Plain Radiographs

Skull: No fracture can be identified. The shrunken brain surrounded by air is well seen. The convolutional markings are clearly identifiable as also are the cisterns. The ventricles are small and distorted and there is a suggestion of some air within them. This is most obvious in the anterior horns. The trigonal region of the lateral ventricle may be represented.

In the lateral projection of the skull, there is a well-defined opacity over one of the orbits. It is not certain if this is part of the orbit or a foreign body which could have been inserted at any time after death.

Chest and abdomen: These are grossly distorted by marked increased soft tissue density surrounding air-filled spaces. An unusual linear shadow with a convoluted margin projected over the peripheral part of the right chest cavity could be due to thickened pleura. A fairly well-defined area of increased density projected over the medial aspect of the left lower thoracic region extending from the level of the fourth to ninth vertebra could be due to the heart and aorta.

A more homogeneous density is clearly defined on the right side between the chest and mid-abdomen, extending from approximately the level of the eighth to eleventh thoracic vertebra. This is probably due to the liver. The kidneys could not be identified with certainty.

Spine: The disc spaces are remarkably dense. Close analysis shows that this is mainly in relation to the annulus fibrosis with relative radiolucency of the nucleus pulposis. The vertebral bodies show marked diminution in density but there is no vertebral collapse. No bony injury can be identified.

Pelvis: There is a remarkable homogeneous sclerosis of the femoral heads and proximal femoral shafts. The pelvis otherwise appears normal except for some increased density projected over the medial aspect of the iliac bones. This could be due to the thickened skin of the buttock rather than to bone change.

Shoulders: There is also marked sclerotic reaction in relation to both humeral heads and to the adjacent humeral shafts.

Left forearm: The left forearm lying across the left abdomen appears normal. No fractures are seen.

Computerised Tomography

Extensive computerised tomographic images were made of the skull, chest and abdomen. The body was scanned with a second-generation CT scanner and recorded on magnetic tape – now obsolete. The resolution is poor compared with the currently used fourth generation scanners.

Skull: The skull and facial bones are very distorted. No fracture is visible in the skull vault but there are two unusual sclerotic foci not identifiable on the plain radiographs. The brain is shrunken and surrounded by air. The differentiation of grey and white matter can be identified with the dense brain stem extending into the spinal cord. The gyri and sulci are clearly seen.

The most interesting feature noted is the marked increased density of the spinal cord. There is a clear transition from increased density of the round cord to the less dense, smaller conus medullaris and cauda equina. The vertebral bodies show remarkably diminished density and the increased density of the annulus fibrosis is clearly seen.

Chest: There is gross distortion of the thoracic cavities, with shrinkage of both lungs surrounded by what appears to be dense pleura. In the left para-vertebral region there is a dense homogeneous opacity which is most likely due to the heart and aorta.

Just below this level there is a homogeneous density situated posteriorly but extending across the anterior aspect of the spinal column. This is most likely due to shrunken liver. Immediately below this region on the left side posteriorly there is a further homogeneous density with fairly well-defined margins which is most likely due to the spleen.

Summary: Examination of the bones indicates that this is the body of a young, fully developed adult. No evidence of bone trauma or degenerative disease is seen.

3 Report on the teeth by Mr Hugh Barry, Senior Lecturer and Consultant in Oral Surgery, Dublin Dental Hospital and Trinity College, Dublin:

In order to gain access to the teeth it was necessary to dissect away some of the bog plants which had invaded and partly replaced the circum-oral tissues. The mandible was slightly dislocated due to post-mortem events: the maxilla was distorted due to softening and buckling. There was virtually a full dentition present, the third molars being fully erupted. The teeth were black in colour and were flexible.

There was no contact between adjacent teeth (absence of contact points) and there was complete absence of tooth enamel. This almost total decalcification was a result of the prolonged contact with the acid environment of the bog. Radiographic examination of three teeth – the upper right central incisor and first molar and the lower right third molar, illustrated the degree of the decalcification.

Assessment of the age at death of the individual was difficult due to the absence of the enamel which provides the most sensitive indication of tooth wear. The first molars showed moderate wear of the dentine, while the third molars showed little or no wear. The probable age of the individual at death was 25–35 years.

4 Report on the endoscopy performed by Prof. J. S. Pritchard, Dept of Clinical Medicine, Trinity College, Dublin:

Dr Harbison made a transverse incision in the left hypochondrium (upper abdomen) and the endoscope was inserted there. The incision was extended across what was essentially bog material for further endoscopic and naked eye examination.

The interior of the body was very well preserved. The tissues were moist and much less stained than the external tissues. They were a greyish colour. The membranes were all very thin, but not particularly fragile. Individual organs were difficult to identify as they had either collapsed, shrunken or been squashed flat according to the various processes during the time in the bog. The room to manoeuvre was also limited so that minimum damage would be done.

The upper left abdomen was examined first. Little was identified here but samples were taken from areas which could have been stomach or intestinal lumens. The liver was identified in the right hypochondrium (upper abdomen). It was dark in colour, granular in texture and was shrunken. The pelvis was not easy to penetrate and no structures were identified; again work was hampered by the risk of damage. The chest cavity was easier to visualise and was not totally collapsed. No lung tissue was identified but there were what appeared to be pleural adhesions.

5 Report from Dr Harbison on the microscopic examination of viscera received from The British Museum Conservation Laboratory on 10 January 1986. They had been kept in a cool store form the time of the autopsy on 29 August 1985:

Liver: Section showed a tendency to laminate, suggesting a loss of parenchyma with persistence of portal tracts and septae. A sizeable vessel – probably the hepatic vein – was found and viewed under the dissecting microscope. The adjacent paraenchyma was brown, soft and flecked coarsely with grey tissue suggestive of portal tract, and fine cream-coloured tissue suggestive of the presence of adipocere.

Lung: A fragment of tissue had the appearance of lung. The usual cellular structure had disappeared. Carbon particles were visible throughout. Other samples were unidentifiable.

Note: There were no signs of fire damage on the body so it is unlikely that the carbon particles in the lung were due to inhalation during a fire (see Report 6 below).

6 Histological investigations carried out by Ciaran Driver, Chief Technician, Department of Forensic Medicine, Trinity College, Dublin:

Samples of lung, liver, skin and muscle were fixed in 10% Formol-Saline before being processed for 48 hours in a Shandon Duplex Tissue Processor, followed by embedding in paraffin wax for sectioning.

Some samples were first treated prior to processing with a fabric softener as outlined by Turner and Holtom (1988, 35–8). No difference was noted in the samples treated from those that were not. From researching previous literature on bog bodies it was noted that connective tissue stains tended to give the best results.

The staining methods employed were: Haematoxylin and Eosin; Weigert's Iron Haematoxylin and Van Gieson (1889) Stain; Gomori's (1937) Reticulin; Gomori's Aldehyde Fuchsin; Alcian Blue – Elastin Van Gieson (Eskelund, 1957); Heidenhain's (1896) Iron Haematoxylin, azan variant; Weigert's Elastic Stain (Miller's modification); Gordon and Sweet's Reticulin Stain.

All staining times were increased or doubled and the slides were examined microscopically during staining at regular intervals to ensure the uptake of the dyes.

The results, in general, were disappointing. No nuclei were seen and no tissue structures were adequately identified. Bog plants were noted – they had infiltrated the skin and underlying tissue. The only feature of note was the presence of carbon in the lung sections indicating that the subject had been in a smoky atmosphere.

7 Analyses of adipocere samples performed by Dr William King, State Laboratory, Dublin 15:

Introduction

When fatty material of animal or vegetable origin is buried in soil or peat, or immersed in water, it is converted over a period of time to a material commonly known as adipocere. The length of time required for this process to take place depends on a number of factors, principally temperature. Fats will be decomposed by a variety of micro-organisms in anaerobic conditions provided there is a source of nitrogen available.

A 0.5 g sample of adipocere and 10 ml of 2% sodium hydroxide in methanol were refluxed for 20 min. 10 ml of a methanol solution of boron trifluoride was then added and the mixture refluxed for a further 5 min. After addition of heptane and some saturated sodium chloride solution, two distinct layers obtained. A portion of the heptane layer was removed and dried over sodium sulphate and then analysed by gas chromatography to determine fatty acid composition. A sample of present-day human fat was analysed in the same way. The Hewlett-Packard 5890 gas chromatograph was fitted with a DEGS column and a flame ionisation detector. The results are given in Table 17.

Discussion

The main features of the results shown in Table 17 are that the content of oleic acid (C18:1) in the Meenybraddan bog body has decreased substantially while the concentration of palmitic acid (C16:0) has increased by a similar percentage. There has also been a similar decrease in the concentration of palmitoleic acid (C16:1) while no linoleic acid (C18:2) was detected. It has been shown by Morgan *et al* (1973) that when fats transform to adipocere, the unsaturated fatty acids tend to disappear and are replaced by saturated fatty acids with two carbon atoms less. For example oleic acid (C18:1) is replaced by palmitic acid (C16:0). These observations tend to suggest similar changes in this buried fat sample to those reported elsewhere for the same type of sample.

Further analyses of adipocere from the Meenybraddan bog body are published by Evershed (1992).

8 Samples of putative gut contents were sent to Dr Camilla Dixon, Department of Botany, Glasgow University; they showed no identifiable constituents.

Table 17

FATTY ACID		MEENYBRADDAN SAMPLE (%)	PRESENT-DAY SAMPLE OF HUMAN FAT (%)
Lauric	(C12:0)	0.4	0.4
Myristic	(C14:0)	12.0	4.0
Palmitic	(C16:0)	57.0	25.0
Palmitoleic	(C16:1)	2.0	7.0
Stearic	(C18:0)	11.0	7.0
Oleic	(C18:1)	10.0	40.0
Linoleic	(C18:2)	—	8.0

9 A sample of finger nail taken by Dr Don Brothwell was examined by scanning electron microscopy and has been published in the Lindow I monograph (Brothwell and Dobney 1986, 68–70 and Fig. 36i). At high magnification it showed pre-mortem chipping.

10 *Radiocarbon dating*: A sample of bone from the left femur was submitted for radiocarbon dating in June 1985 to the Isotope Measurements Laboratory, Harwell, Oxfordshire. A preliminary date received in September 1986 yielded a result of 380 ± 90 BP (AD 1570) which seemed to confirm the date as estimated by the style of the cloak used as a shroud. However, this result, published by Ó Floinn (1988) and Evershed (1992) has since been revised. The final date received in April 1991 (Har-6909) yielded a date of 730 ± 90 BP. This gives a calibrated date range at the 68% level of AD 1190–1330 and at the 95% level of AD 1050–1410 (Stuiver and Reimer 1986).

11 *Conservation*: The conservation by freeze-drying of the Meenybraddan bog body is published by Omar, McCord and Daniels (1989).

More Recent Appearance of Body

Following the examination on 26 March 1992, Dr. M. Delaney reported as follows (see Figs 61 and 62):

The body has not changed much in appearance. The most noticeable difference is in the colour of the skin. The processes of conservation have highlighted the difference between intact and damaged skin. Where the surface of the skin is intact it is smooth and a deep, almost sepia, brown. The areas of damaged skin are rough and a dry-looking tan colour, lighter in shade than the rest. The hair is about 15–20 cm long and wavy, dark brown in colour with little or no reddish tint. It is still dull and the hairs cling to each other in tresses. It is not fragile and is quite pliable, with tiny white specks present here and there. There is no sign of hair loss due to the process of conservation. The bones are now hard and rigid but the skin and tendons are remarkably pliable. The adipocere has altered little but has become a little more friable and paler in colour. The whole body is firm. The arms and hands, which are reduced to bone, remain in position. The body can be moved and lifted with little risk of damage.

The only sign of deterioration is on the legs and back which is downmost. It must be remembered that the legs

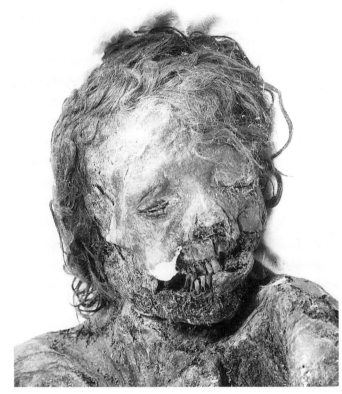

Fig. 61 Body after conservation. (*National Museum of Ireland*)

Fig. 62 Detail of the face after conservation. (*National Museum of Ireland*)

Fig. 63 Woollen cloak. (*National Museum of Ireland*)

are detached from the body at the level of the mid thigh. There is mould growing on the knee regions of both legs, more pronounced on the right. There are also some small circular white areas on the back.

The Cloak or Mantle

The woollen cloak or mantle (Reg. No. 1978:241a) is almost semicircular in shape and is reddish brown in colour (Fig. 63). A sample of wool was examined by the late Dr A. Dieck, Bremen, Germany, who reported that the fibres were of sheep's wool. The cloak measures 2.43 m in length and 1.30 m in maximum width. It is composed of four lengths of cloth sewn together along the selvedges. The main strip measures 50 cm in width and has straight ends. The second strip is 50 cm wide and the ends are cut in a curve. Two further pieces of cloth stitched together complete the curve of the cloak, one piece larger than the other, measuring 30 cm in maximum width. The smaller of the two pieces has a tear which has a stitched repair. There is evidence of a limited amount of wear along the edges and some small holes and tears are visible elsewhere. The cloak is, however, in a better condition than others of the type found in Irish bogs.

Garda Cormack's notes made shortly after the discovery indicate that the body was laid lengthwise along the centre of the long axis of the cloak, the curved edge to the left of the body, the straight edge to the right. One end of the cloak was folded down over the face. It is likely that the other end was folded up over the feet but this could not be confirmed as this end was undone at the time of finding. The curved edge was folded over the body and the straight edge over this again. The cloak was secured with a thong made of woven wool 60 cm in length. It was laced through a series of four slits roughly cut in the upper and lower layers of cloth. The upper end of the thong was knotted.

The cloak belongs to a relatively homogeneous group of homespun frieze mantles from Ireland, usually associated with male clothing (Henshall and Seaby 1961, 120–2). All are semicircular, made of two main strips of cloth cut from the same web and stitched along the selvedges with smaller pieces sewn on to complete the curve of the lower edge. They are remarkably uniform in size, the smallest being 2.20 m long (from Leigh, Co. Tipperary) and the largest 2.75 m (from Killerry, Co. Sligo). The width of the web varies from 20 cm to 60 cm. This style of cloak cannot be independently dated but a date range of the late six-

teenth to late seventeenth century has been suggested on the basis of the associated clothing (Henshall and Seaby 1961, 131–2; Dunlevy 1989, 75). The radiocarbon date of 730 ± 90 BP for the Meenybraddan find, even at the 99% probability range, is considerably earlier than the proposed date for this type of cloak based on stylistic criteria. Enquiries with the Harwell laboratory revealed that there is no reason to question the reliability of the result.

Although it is conceivable that this form of cloak was already in existence by the thirteenth century (the mean age given by the radiocarbon date) and continued to be made through the later middle ages, it is unlikely, and we must conclude that for reasons as yet unknown, the radiocarbon result is several centuries older than the true age of the body. On balance, therefore, we must accept for the moment the later sixteenth- to seventeenth-century date. The discrepancy once again highlights the problems of the radiocarbon dating of bog bodies and it is possible that the older date may derive from humic contamination as was discovered in other radiocarbon-dated Irish bog bodies (see Brindley and Lanting, pp. 133–6).

There are several recorded instances of bodies, otherwise naked, being wrapped in cloth which provide parallels for the Meenybraddan find. The body of a full-grown woman covered with a rug was found at Tintagh, Co. Derry (Briggs and Turner 1986, No. 90); a cloak and blanket found round a human body (sex unspecified) from near Nenagh, Co. Tipperary (Ti3, see gazetteer, p. 232); a body (sex unspecified) in a flexed position covered by two blankets, accompanied by a wooden plate and spoon from Dunmore, Co. Derry (Briggs and Turner 1986, No. 83) and a male body, naked, except for an oblong piece of cloth which covered the body to the waist from Cordal, Co. Kerry (Ke2, see gazetteer, p. 227). Unfortunately none of these survive today. The wooden spoon associated with the Dunmore burial was stated to have had the letter 'W' carved on it and this would suggest a date in the Late Medieval period at the earliest.

Although there have been many finds of archaeological material from Donegal bogs, few are recorded from the immediate vicinity of the Meenybraddan burial. Three polished stone axeheads and a flint arrowhead are known from Meenagran and Tullytrasna townlands respectively (Keeling 1988, Nos 19, 20). A stave-built wooden vessel and a horn spoon, both probably of late medieval date, were found in the townland of Corker More, some 4 km south-west of the bog body find (Lucas (ed) 1961, 101–3 and Fig. 32).

The position of the body at Meenybraddan and the use of a woollen cloak as a shroud indicate that this was a deliberate burial in the bog. In the absence of any other items of clothing it is not possible to establish the woman's social status and the various examinations have failed to establish a cause of death. There is no evidence from the various investigations to show that she had died in childbirth. It is not clear why the body was not buried in consecrated ground, but in a number of instances, local folklore associated with the discovery of bog bodies connect them with known suicides or with murder victims (Ó Floinn, p. 142). Hamlin and Foley (1983, 43) have documented the practice of separate burial for women and also refer to the practice of special burial outside consecrated ground which was accorded to certain categories of individuals, including suicides, shipwrecked sailors (and other victims of drowning), strangers and idiots. The practice continued into recent times and could include such out-of-the-way places as prehistoric megaliths, secular forts or disused graveyards. It is possible that the Meenybraddan woman fitted into one of the above categories.

Conclusions

Little can be learnt about either the cause of death or the way of life of the Meenybraddan woman. She may have been brought to her place of burial along the old track nearby. To date, investigation has revealed changes typical in bodies buried in a bog environment. She was plump and there was no evidence of poor nutrition. Microscopic examination of one of her fingernails indicates that she did not do rough work but probably did at least light manual tasks. The atmosphere she breathed was sooty but from the pathologist's findings it is unlikely she died in a fire. It is possible that she suffered from infection of the lungs and pleura (membranes which envelop the lungs).

This investigation was less extensive than that carried out, for example, on Lindow II and it is not certain how conservation may have affected any future biochemical analysis. Despite the fact that the cause of death could not be established, the investigations were important in that they were the first of their kind carried out on a bog body

from Ireland. The macroscopic investigations of most value in this case were the careful naked eye examination, the X-rays and the CT scan. Endoscopy proved disappointing because of the distortion of the internal organs. Autopsy might have been informative if performed before deterioration set in.

A Routine for Future Investigations

The following is an attempt to set out a framework for the future investigation of bog bodies when and if they are discovered:

1   The co-ordination of investigations is of great importance.
2   The body should undergo as little handling and disturbance as possible. The noticeable deterioration of the Meenybraddan body during her protracted storage, examination and conservation demonstrates this.
3   It is desirable that the investigating archaeologist accompanied by the appropriate medical authorities should be the first people to handle the body after discovery. This is particularly important where any clothing and grave goods remain.
4   If an excavation is to be done, the handling and description of the body should be supervised by a specialist in human remains. If this is not possible an attempt should be made to raise the body in a block of peat which is not allowed to dry out (as in Stead *et al* 1986, 13) and preferably stored at about 4°C. A sample of the water surrounding the body should be kept for analysis. The body can be removed from the peat block at a later date.
5   During the first exposure of the body most of the samples, e.g. of nails, hair, teeth, exposed tissue, and samples for botanical remains and external parasites, should be taken.
6   In future cases the X-rays, CT scan, autopsy and the taking of any further samples for analysis should ideally take place in the same institution, on the same day and in the above order.
7   Conservation should proceed as rapidly as possible after the above procedures are completed, bearing in mind that this will inevitably affect subsequent analyses and sampling in some way.

Irish Bog Bodies: the Radiocarbon Dates

A. L. Brindley   *J. N. Lanting*

Introduction

The dating of bog bodies is surrounded by considerable difficulties. Contamination of samples by humic substances of different ages from within the bog is widespread and difficult to control. Additional contamination of old finds through the use of preservatives during conservation can also cause problems. Bog bodies are rarely found with datable goods or in datable contexts but, nevertheless, the specific environment in which they occur has usually allowed the preservation of artefacts (such as clothing) and attributes (staked bodies, victims of hanging, etc.), which would not normally survive. Furthermore, the bodies themselves are of considerable interest not only as archaeological phenomena but as rarely preserved tissue remains of sometimes great antiquity. The dating of individual bog bodies is therefore of importance. The practices sometimes involved in the deposition of bodies in waterlogged environments are also of interest. Their dating is important in resolving questions such as: Are these local revivals or upsurges in morbid wetland activities, or do they belong to a wider European experience such as may have occurred during, for instance, the Late Bronze Age?

Although it is usually possible now to discriminate between finds which lie on a contemporary bog surface and those deposited in pits and therefore lying in ancient layers of peat and humic acid and those deposited in ponds, this is a complex matter. Without a correct identification of the original circumstances of deposition, the collection of sample material from the adjacent organic matter for dating purposes is useless and may yield inappropriate results. Furthermore, it will not always be apparent that the date is incorrect. To avoid this, samples of the object itself should be dated. This approach has one serious limitation, namely the large size of the sample required for conventional radiocarbon dating.

However, the development of accelerator mass spectrometry (AMS) has made it possible to circumvent this problem by allowing dating of very small samples. Even so, the impact of humic contamination and its frequency must still be taken into account. All material in the bog is or has been waterlogged and can have absorbed humic acid, either from immediately adjacent material of the same or of different age, or from higher or lower in the bog. The frequent absence of information about the age of the surrounding and possibly contaminating peat remains a source of potential problems.

The Radiocarbon Dates

Six bog bodies were dated as part of a large scale radiocarbon dating programme of Irish material (for details of context, see Ó Floinn, pp. 139–42). Three of these were dated by conventional radiocarbon methods at the Centrum voor Isotopen Onderzoek in Groningen and the remainder were dated by accelerator at the Oxford Accelerator dating unit. The results are presented here together with that of a seventh body dated at Harwell.

Meenybraddan, Co. Donegal

730 ± 90 BP $\delta^{13}C = -21.5\%o$

Har-6909   Bone

Gallagh, Co. Galway (nr. Castleblakeney)

2320 ± 90 BP $\delta^{13}C = -20.9\%o$
OxA-2923 Bone

Also:
2220 ± 90 BP $\delta^{13}C = -24.8\%o$
Har-6908 Bone

3480 ± 70 BP $\delta^{13}C = -22.7\%o$
OxA-2756 Bone
Average of OxA-2923 and Har-6908: 2270 ± 65 BP

Kinnakinelly, Co. Galway

2135 ± 35 BP $\delta^{13}C = -22.69\%o$
GrN-15374 Deer bone found with bog body

Stoneyisland, Co. Galway

5170 ± 90 BP OxA-2941 $\delta^{13}C = -21.7\%o$
5270 ± 80 BP OxA-2942 $\delta^{13}C = -21.3\%o$
5180 ± 80 BP OxA-2943 $\delta^{13}C = -20.0\%o$

Also:
6200 ± 80 BP $\delta^{13}C = -22.6\%o$
OxA-2758 Bone
Average of OxA-2941–3: 5210 ± 50 BP

Baronstown West (Clongownagh), Co. Kildare

1725 ± 30 BP $\delta^{13}C = -24.33\%o$
GrN-14758 Tissue

Derrymaquirk, Co. Roscommon

2340 ± 70 BP $\delta^{13}C = -21.79\%o$
GrN-15373 Bone

Derrydooan Middle, Co. Westmeath

1295 ± 60 BP $\delta^{13}C = -22.2\%o$
OxA-2757 Bone

The expected value of $\delta^{13}C$ for uncontaminated bone, based on measurements from 40 Irish Bronze Age burials, should fall in the range −20.7‰ to −23.1‰, with an average of −21.73‰, that is, slightly lower than the range of −19‰ to −21‰ suggested by Mook and Streurman (1983, 53).

Humic Contamination

Humic acid is produced during the decay of vegetable matter and thus the dating of objects found in bogs is complicated by the presence of humic acid of various ages.

The development of a bog is long and continuous. Over thousands of years vegetable matter producing humic acid builds up and is compressed in a wet environment. Within the resulting wet matrix, humic acids originating from different levels and ages can mingle and move with relative ease up and down through the vegetable mass, depending on the circulation pattern within the bog. Due to the nature of peat, humic acid is present in large quantities and the peat itself provides an unstable context. This leads to a high probability that the mixing of humic acids of different ages will occur at some stage.

The identification and removal of humic substances which originate from within the bog itself are therefore of vital importance. The collagen which is used for dating purposes is degraded and usually contaminated with humic material, which itself is difficult to identify. Therefore, it is essential that fractions used for dating purposes are of material which cannot have originated in the bog, e.g. peptides and amino acids. The enormous advantage of AMS dating is that it is possible to collect sufficient quantities of amino acids or peptides for dating without sacrificing a large portion of the subject matter itself (if available in the first place) and, furthermore, multiple dating of a specific sample can be contemplated.

Humic Contamination and $\delta^{13}C$

The $\delta^{13}C$ ranges of bone and humic acid are significantly different. Radiocarbon laboratories now routinely measure and report the $\delta^{13}C$ value together with the radiocarbon result. If the reading falls outside the range for the relevant sample material, it is likely that the sample is contaminated to some extent. However, humic contamination is not always reflected by the $\delta^{13}C$ measurement and, furthermore, such contamination may affect a date in either direction, depending on the age of the contaminant and, to a variable extent, depending on the movement of water in the peat. As the Gallagh and Stoneyisland bodies show, detecting humic contamination and establishing its effect are impossible without multiple datings for these bodies. The multiple dates demonstrate how different and unpredictable the effect of humic substances on samples can be.

In the case of the Gallagh dates, the necessity of further investigation was indicated by the discrepancy between the first two dates (Har-6908 and OxA-2756). The Harwell date was confirmed despite the fact that its very low $\delta^{13}C$ value indicates humic contamination. The $\delta^{13}C$ value of the initial Oxford date (OxA-2756) shows that the cleaning of the collagen had been more efficient than in the case of the Harwell sample and therefore humic contamination cannot be considered as the reason for the aberrant Oxford result. In this particular case, we may be dealing with a statistical outlier. A third attempt at removing humic matter was then made. This final Oxford date (OxA-2923) shows that the radiocarbon age of the Gallagh body was correctly indicated by the Harwell date and that the contamination which was present was of contemporary humic substances. Although the $\delta^{13}C$ measurement reliably indicated the presence of humic contamination, it did not give any indication as to the effect that contamination may have had; in this case it was nil because the humic acid was contemporary.

With the Stoneyisland body, the first sample processed (OxA-2758) was of collagen. Although on the low side, the $\delta^{13}C$ measurement still fell within the expected range. However, as humic substances cannot be isolated completely from crude collagen, three more samples were prepared by breaking down the collagen to produce samples of peptides and amino acids, i.e. substances which could not be derived from humic substances in the peat. The dates procured from these samples are internally consistent both in terms of date and $\delta^{13}C$ measurement. It is only when all four $\delta^{13}C$ measurements are compared that the presence of humic contaminants is visible and only when the four $\delta^{14}C$ dates are compared can the extent of the effect of humic contamination on the first sample be seen. The Stoneyisland bog body has been contaminated by older humic substances, but this was not apparent from the initial measurements. The Stoneyisland results indicate the necessity of dating matter which is distinguishable from humic material originating from the bog itself – collagen specific amino acids and peptides. While a low $\delta^{13}C$ measurement is a reliable indicator of humic contamination, the reverse is unfortunately not true.

A major problem in the discussion of any date (from any context) is the recognition of contamination. The $\delta^{13}C$ measurement should always be available as it gives an essential indication as to the reliability of the result and the possible source of any possible deviation. Humic acid can be identified only by its $\delta^{13}C$ measurement. Unfortunately, without additional dating, it is not possible to tell how this has affected the result.

Calibration

Calibration is the translation of radiocarbon years into calendar years. However, it does not provide a single date with a standard deviation – it provides a statistical proposition that the actual date falls within a specified range. Although calibrated dates can be read off by eye, the most accurate readings are provided now by computer analysis, such as the one used here (van der Plicht and Mook 1989, 805–15).

Although the calibrated result is in fact a date range with a calculated probability curve, it is possible to identify the most likely date either by multiple dating of the sample itself, multiple dating of the cultural phenomena or additional dendro dating or typological/stratigraphical analysis. The method works well in most circumstances. However, it is difficult if not impossible, to provide a refined calendar date for an isolated or unsupported radiocarbon date. But in this circumstance it is usually of no great importance and the uncalibrated radiocarbon date is perfectly adequate for the purposes of discussion.

Isolated bog bodies without attributes or with unique features are a good example of this. The calibrated ranges to 2 sigma (that is 95% probability that the actual calendar date falls within these) are given below. It is not possible to suggest closer dates on the basis of the available information and, for these reasons, we do not feel it necessary to use calibrated dates for the bog bodies presented here. The prefix to each entry cross refers to the gazetteer of Irish bog bodies on pp. 221–234.

Ga3 Stoneyisland, Co. Galway
Average of three dates calibrated, 5210 ± 50 BP
>   4226 cal BC ... 4196 cal BC
>   4152 cal BC ... 4056 cal BC
>   4052 cal BC ... 3958 cal BC
>   3840 cal BC ... 3826 cal BC

Ro4 Derrymaquirk, Co. Roscommon
>   762 cal BC ... 680 cal BC
>   662 cal BC ... 628 cal BC
>   602 cal BC ... 348 cal BC
>   318 cal BC ... 206 cal BC

Ga1 Gallagh, Co. Galway (near Castleblakeney)
Average of two dates calibrated, 2270 ± 65 BP
>   512 cal BC ... 434 cal BC
>   414 cal BC ... 166 cal BC
>   134 cal BC ... 126 cal BC

Ga6 Kinnakinelly, Co. Galway
>   356 cal BC ... 292 cal BC
>   250 cal BC ... 100 cal BC

Kd2 Baronstown West (Clongownagh), Co. Kildare

AD 242 cal ... AD 388 cal

Wm2 Derrydooan Middle, Co. Westmeath

AD 648 cal ... AD 874 cal

Dg7 Meenybraddan, Co. Donegal

AD 1048 cal ... AD 1090 cal

AD 1118 cal ... AD 1140 cal

AD 1156 cal ... AD 1406 cal

Discussion

Stoneyisland is one of the earliest available radiocarbon dated bog bodies from Europe. However, bog burials of Early Neolithic date are well known in Denmark where they belong to a well-documented practice of votive bog offerings of various types including 'burials' of one or sometimes two individuals often with unnatural causes of death. In a review of the bog finds of the TRB Culture, Bennike and Ebbesen (1986, 97–104) were able to list 436 Early and Middle Neolithic pots which had been found in bogs, lakes, rivers or the open sea and referred to other groups of bog finds, including mixed heaps of bones of animals and humans. On the basis of the pottery types which occur in these deposits, it appears that the practice of votive offerings declined in popularity during the Middle Neolithic (ibid. 99). Three bog bodies have slightly younger radiocarbon dates (Tauber 1979, 73–87).

Outside Denmark and much less well documented, offerings of axes (S. Jager, pers. comm.) and complete vessels, in what appear to have been similar circumstances, are known from the Netherlands and adjacent parts of Germany during the TRB Culture and probably reflect similar interests. While the Stoneyisland bog body appears at present in isolation, it could conceivably belong to an undocumented and unrecognised Irish tradition of votive bog offerings. However, very little is known of funerary or ritual activity of any kind at this date in Ireland.

In general, the results conform to the pattern anticipated on the basis of other radiocarbon-dated Irish peat phenomena – some evidence for activity from the Neolithic period onwards, an increase in the number of dates during the Late Bronze Age, and a rise in the number of dates from the Early Medieval period onwards. The temporal distribution of bog bodies is almost certainly influenced by the nature of peat exploitation in Ireland; peat which developed before the later stages of the Bronze Age in Ireland lies at a depth rarely reached by manual cutting. Some rise in the number of bodies within the bogs should be expected from the Bronze Age onwards as the extent of the peat increased.

The need for extreme caution in considering unsupported dates for bog bodies has been emphasised once again by this limited dating programme.

Recent Research into Irish Bog Bodies

R. Ó Floinn

Introduction

The *Lindow Man* monograph (1986, British Museum Publications) included a gazetteer and discussion by C. S. Briggs of bog bodies found in Ireland. In advance of the conservation by the British Museum of a complete Irish bog body from Meenybraddan, Co. Donegal in 1985, a number of specialist examinations were undertaken and are described by Delaney and Ó Floinn, pp. 123–32. As part of the research project on the Meenybraddan find, the extensive correspondence files in the National Museum of Ireland were searched for further examples of bog bodies. As a result, the total number of examples from Ireland has been almost doubled. A preliminary account of this work has already been published (Ó Floinn 1988). At the same time, a search was undertaken to find suitable samples for carbon 14 dating, as no Irish bog body had been dated by this method. The results are outlined in this volume (Brindley and Lanting, pp. 133–6). A recent study of Irish dress (Dunlevy 1989) has refined the dating for the remains of clothing found in Irish bogs and a list of clothing remains found without evidence of a body is included here.

The Gazetteer

Briggs listed 54 instances of bog bodies in his list of 1986, representing about 60 individuals. However, eight of these can be rejected on the grounds that the accounts mention only the discovery of articles of dress (Briggs and Turner 1986, Nos. 67, 70, 71, 72, 104, 107, 115, 116 – the last two, in fact, refer to the same discovery). Although items

of clothing from bogs may represent potential bog bodies, it is best to list these separately unless there is specific reference to human remains. A further two can also be rejected, as one (ibid. No. 78) refers to the discovery of intestines which are as likely to be animal as human and another (ibid. No. 81) documents a children's burial ground in an 'island' in a bog – by 'island' is meant an area of fertile ground surrounded by bog.

On the other hand, 45 new instances have been found, bringing the current total to 89, representing at least 100 individuals. Only eight of the new examples are nineteenth-century discoveries and, of these, six are found in accounts in local newspapers or archaeological journals. It is clear that the older the account of a bog body, the greater the tendency for inaccuracy in reporting and the more exaggerated is the account of certain aspects of the find, especially the dress and associated finds. Almost all of the twentieth-century discoveries have been culled from the files of the Irish Antiquities Division in the National Museum of Ireland and consist mostly of reports of discoveries of bog bodies made to the museum by local informants. The newly discovered accounts treble the number of twentieth-century examples listed by Briggs and might be expected to reflect more accurately than the nineteenth-century accounts the true pattern of discovery. However, only one of these comes from Northern Ireland – the sample of human(?) tissue from Ballycowen, Co. Antrim (An2) acquired as part of the collection of Dr Alexander D'Evelyn, of Ballymena, Co. Antrim. It is difficult to explain the absence of reports of bog burials from this area in this century. Indeed, apart from the Bally-

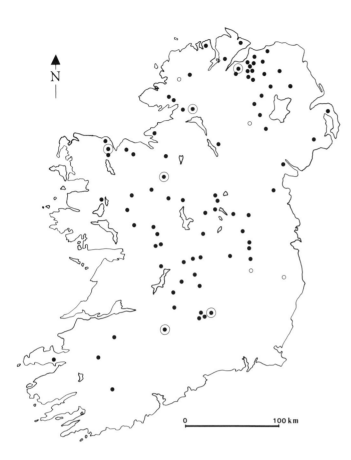

Fig. 64 Distribution of bog body finds in Ireland: ringed circles (multiple finds), open circles (county provenance only). (*After Ó Floinn 1988, with additions.*)

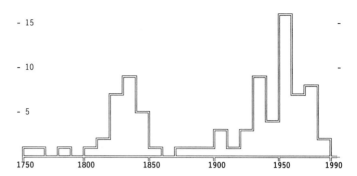

Fig. 65 The number of Irish bog bodies reported for each decade, 1750 to the present day. (*After Ó Floinn 1988, with additions.*)

Most of the new accounts consist of 'paper' bog bodies. However, it has been possible to add significantly to the number of preserved samples of human bone and tissue. There are now preserved complete or fragmentary human remains from 28 locations.

Of the eight relatively complete bodies or skeletons, six are preserved in the National Museum of Ireland:

> Meenybraddan, Co. Donegal (Dg7); Baronstown West, Co. Kildare (Kd2); Cloonbenes, Co. Galway (Ga5); Gallagh, Co. Galway (Ga1); Kilwarden, Co. Meath (Me2); Ballyrickard Beg, Co. Offaly (Of2). A body from Ardee, Co. Louth (Lh1) is preserved in the Royal College of Surgeons of Ireland and a complete skeleton from Stoneyisland Bog, Co. Galway (Ga3) is now in University College, Galway.

Fragmentary remains in the National Museum of Ireland include samples from:

> Ballycowan, Co. Antrim (An2); Rossilly Barr, Co. Donegal (Dg6); Kinnakinelly, Co. Galway (Ga6); Drinagh and Lea Beg, Co. Offaly (Of5,4); Derrymaquirk, Co. Roscommon (Ro4); Tawnamore, Co. Sligo (Sl3); Ballybeg, Co. Westmeath (Wm3).

Elsewhere there are bones from:

> Emlagh, Co. Kerry (Ke1) and skulls from Cloonsherick, Co. Limerick (Li1) in University College Cork; a skull from Derrydooan Middle, Co. Westmeath (Wm2) in University College, Galway; an incomplete skeleton from Derrinlurg, Co. Roscommon (Ro5) in Trinity College, Dublin; and a human hand from Co. Donegal (Dg3) at Newbridge House, Donabate, Co. Dublin.

It has not been possible to locate the following:

> Skulls from Co. Kildare (Kd1) and Lisnaskea, Co. Fermanagh (Fe1) in University College, Dublin;

cowen find and two Co. Tyrone finds (Ty2,3) made at the turn of the century, only the Flanders, Co. Derry costume (De15) was found this century and that was over 35 years ago. Briggs has noted the large number of accounts from Co. Derry which stem from a single source – the Ordnance Survey Memoirs of 1835–7.

In view of the variable pattern of reports, therefore, it is unlikely that the present distribution (Fig. 64) is representative of the true pattern of discoveries. The new accounts do, however, extend the distribution to include Counties Cork, Limerick, Mayo, Longford and Westmeath where previously there were no reported occurrences. The pattern of discovery dates (Fig. 65) shows significant peaks in the 1830s, the 1840s and then in the 1950s. The former can be explained by the activities of the Ordnance Survey recorders, while the latter reflects the increase in exploitation of turf as a fuel source after the Second World War, both by hand-cutting and by mechanical means, after the establishment in 1946 of Bord na Móna (the Irish Peat Board).

skulls from Co. Wicklow (Wi1) and the North of Ireland in the British Museum (Natural History), and skulls from Co. Clare (Cl1), Mount Bellew, Co. Galway (Ga4) and Cloonahinch, Co. Galway (Ga7) in the National Museum of Ireland.

There are now ten known instances of multiple burials (De6; Ga4; Kd1; Li1; Ma2; Ro2; Ro4; Sl4; Ti1; Ti2). In most cases there is little detail on the exact circumstances and, apart from the radiocarbon-dated Derrymaquirk burial (Ro4), the only other probable prehistoric multiple burial is the Cloonsherick, Co. Limerick (Li1) discovery comprising the remains of three individuals (see below). In both cases the remains were accompanied by animal bone.

There are eight instances of heads (Dg6; Ga2; Lf3; Ma1; Ro3; Of4; Wm2; Wm3) and seven of skulls (Cl1; Fe1; Ga4; Kd1; Ti1; Wi1; North of Ireland) from bogs but it is not possible to be certain in most cases whether they represent true skull burials or whether they derive from complete bodies. The same can be said of the instances where only single bones other than skulls are found (Dg3; Dg9; Ga7; Kd3; Kd4; Of5). Many of the latter come from peat-milling operations and are likely to have been part of complete skeletons. One of these, the skull from Derrydooan Middle, Co. Westmeath (Wm2) has been radiocarbon dated to the early Medieval period. In the case of the Baronstown West burial (Kd2), dated by Cl4 to the late prehistoric period, there is some evidence that the skull might have been deliberately removed prior to burial (Ó Floinn 1991).

The new discoveries vary significantly in the amount of detail recorded, as might be expected. Most were simply noted and the remains reburied. In a number of instances samples of bone and clothing were forwarded to the National Museum. With the exception of the Meenybraddan find (Dg7), only two other bodies were examined *in situ* by archaeologists: Baronstown West, Co. Kildare (Kd2) and Derrymaquirk, Co. Roscommon (Ro4). Both have been recently published (Ó Floinn, 1991; 1992) and are discussed below.

Bog Bodies and Peat Type

By correlating provenanced bog bodies with a map of Irish peat types (Hammond 1979) it can be seen that both raised and blanket bog finds are equally represented (Table 18). The absence of discoveries from fen peat should not be surprising as fenlands have been largely reclaimed in Ireland with only small patches surviving in western counties. Hammond (1979) records the Ardee,

Table 18   Bog bodies by peat type (peat types after Hammond 1979)

Raised bog (Midland Type)	35
Raised bog (Transitional Type)	7
Fen	0
Blanket bog (Atlantic Type)	4
Blanket bog (High Level Type)	36
Total	82

Co. Louth bog from which the Ardee (Lh1) burial comes as fen, but fieldwork suggests that it is in fact raised bog. The most significant point to emerge from this is that while bog bodies of medieval and later date are found in all peat types, the definite and possible prehistoric examples all come from raised bogs. Otherwise, the peatlands of Munster are considerably under-represented, as are the extensive tracts of blanket bog of Atlantic Type, especially in Counties Donegal, Mayo and Galway.

Dating of Bog Bodies

Seven Irish bog bodies have now been radiocarbon dated (Brindley and Lanting, pp. 133–6). The first two dates were obtained from Harwell, with that for the Meenybraddan, Co. Donegal body (Dg7) confirming the medieval/post-medieval date suggested by the clothing, although it is some centuries earlier than the stylistic date of the cloak in which it was wrapped would suggest (Delaney and Ó Floinn, pp. 123–32).

The reported find circumstances of the Gallagh, Co. Galway (Ga1) burial suggested parallels with prehistoric bog burials in other parts of northern Europe (Fig. 66). This was the body of an adult male found at a depth of 9½ ft (2.9 m) clothed only in a leather cape gathered at the neck with a band of sally (willow) rods. A pointed wooden post or stake was placed at each side of the body. The 'band of sally rods' around the neck may have been a rope with which the victim was strangled (Fig. 67). The original, Harwell radiocarbon date suggested that it was of late prehistoric date (Ó Floinn 1988) and this has been confirmed by further accelerator dates from Oxford.

The Harwell date for Gallagh was the first clear evidence for prehistoric bog bodies in Ireland and indicated the possibility that other Irish bog bodies might also be of prehistoric date. A search was undertaken by the writer for suitable samples for radiocarbon dating and samples were submitted to the Isotope Research Centre in Groningen. The criteria used to identify these samples were: depth in bog; position relative to base of bog; presence of animal bone or other associated artefact not obviously modern; and absence of clothing.

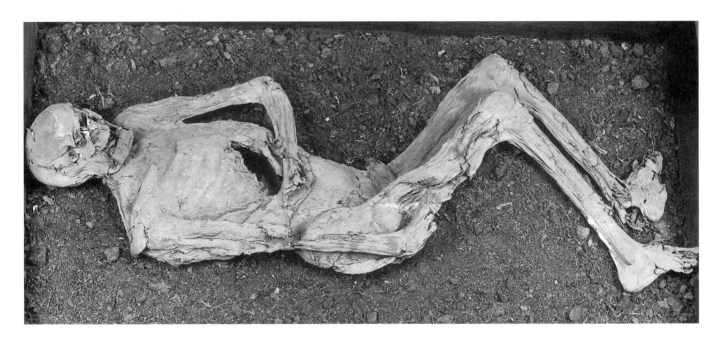

Fig. 66 Bog body found at Gallagh, Co. Galway as it is today. (*National Museum of Ireland*)

Fig. 67 Reconstruction drawing of the Gallagh, Co. Galway bog body as found. (*U. Mattenberger*)

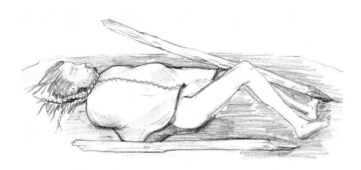

The earliest of the dated bodies is that from Stoney-island Bog, Co. Galway (Ga3) a sample of which gave a Neolithic date. This confirms the evidence of the pollen analysis undertaken at the time (Shea 1931). The skeletal remains were found at a depth of 10 ft (3 m) 'within inches of the marl at the base of the bog' (ibid., 71). The articulated skeleton was found face upwards with the arms extended, suggesting to Shea that the body had been placed in open water and had settled on the bottom. A similar explanation has been suggested for a skeleton associated with pottery of Neolithic date from Sigersdal Mose, Denmark (Bennike and Ebbesen 1986, 88).

The date of the Stoneyisland find gives added weight to the recent suggestion by Brindley and Lanting (1989/90, 6) that the Carrowkeel bowls from bogs at Lisa-lea, Co. Monaghan and Bracklin, Co. Westmeath may, in fact, be burials and not settlement deposits. The former was found in 1866 with two polished stone axeheads in an ancient fireplace resting on marl at a depth of 20 ft (6 m) – the 'fire place' perhaps being a misinterpretation of burnt bone and charcoal. The latter was found at a depth of 3 m during turf cutting. If not certainly associated with burials, the Lisalea and Bracklin finds may be interpreted as votive offerings. Such votive offerings are known from Danish bogs, in some cases associated with human remains (Bennike and Ebbesen 1986, 96–104).

Skeletal remains of a female and infant from Derryma-quirk, Co. Roscommon (Ro4; Fig. 68) were contained in a dug grave. A block of wood was placed at one end of the grave behind the head and a large stone was placed over the bones in the area of the pelvis. The burial was accompanied by bones of sheep/goat and dog and by the tip of an antler tine. A radiocarbon date of 2340 ± 70 BP suggests that the burial is of later Bronze Age or Early Iron Age date.

A wooden stave and bones of red deer were found with the skeleton of an adult at a depth of 8 ft (2.4 m) in a bog at Kinnakinelly, Co. Galway (Ga6). This also yielded a late prehistoric radiocarbon date – the 'stave' being reminiscent of the wooden posts or stakes found with the Gallagh burial.

The Baronstown West, Co Kildare (Kd2) body consisted of the remains of an adult male fully extended lying on its back. Notes made at the time of its removal are not

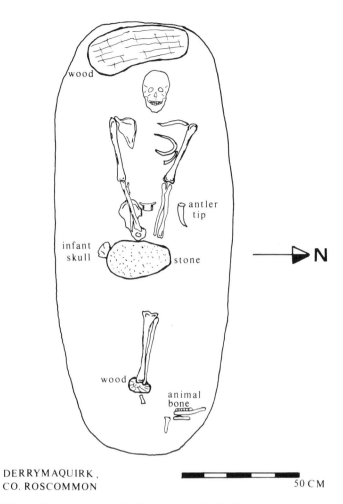

DERRYMAQUIRK,
CO. ROSCOMMON

50 CM

Fig. 68 Bog burial found at Derrymaquirk, Co. Roscommon.
(*Based on field plan by E. Prendergast.*)

fully clear but suggest that the body was covered with a woollen textile and the remains of a leather garment were also noted. The body appears to have had the skull removed but the scalp was replaced. Traces of wooden stakes and brushwood were found around the body. The leather garment does not survive but the pieces of woven wool do not make up a recognisable garment. Several small slits along one edge set at regular intervals are reminiscent of the slits made in the Meenybraddan cloak to receive a thong, converting it into a shroud. A radiocarbon date of 1725 ± 30 BP indicates a date in the Late Iron Age or Early Medieval period for the burial.

The final radiocarbon date was obtained for a human skull found at a depth of 6 ft (1.8 m) at Derrydooan Middle, Co. Westmeath (Wm2) and suggests that it was buried in the Early Medieval period.

In all but the last instance, the dates obtained confirmed the suspected prehistoric date. On the basis of this it is possible to suggest that a further ten examples may be of prehistoric date.

Three of these compare with the Gallagh find in that the accounts refer to the presence of wooden poles or stakes beside the body:

Drumcroon, Co. Derry (De10) – a skeleton 'with a pole at its side'; Ballyrickard, Co. Offaly (Of2) – a skeleton found 4 ft 9 in (1.45 m) deep with a 'hazel handle beside the skeleton' and 'a small stone about ½ cwt (25 kg) under the body'; and Newhill, Co. Tipperary (Ti9) a body found at a depth of 8 ft (2.4 m) with portions of two stakes of ash, one 46 cm in length.

The latter was examined within a few days of discovery after the remains were removed. It was noted that some portions of the body were still articulated and that soft tissue was present. There were no traces of clothing or other artefacts. Practically all the body was recovered and represents the remains of a young adult. The hair attached to the scalp was brownish in colour, long and in part it appeared to be plaited. This led to the conclusion that the remains were probably female but Glob (1969, 117–8) has pointed out that plaits and knots occur on male bodies also.

The same may be true of the Heathfield, Co. Mayo (Ma1) find where a human head with plaited hair was found wrapped in cloth. Significantly, no clothing was noted in the case of the Drumcroon, Ballyrickard and Newhill finds. As the absence of clothing has been noted on other prehistoric bog bodies this might also suggest that the latter are of prehistoric date.

Three finds refer to animal bone being found either with, or in the vicinity of, the human remains:

Cloonsherick, Co. Limerick (Li1), at a depth of 1.15 m (goat, horse, ox and pig); Melkernagh, Co. Longford (Lf2), at a depth of 10–12 ft (3–3.66 m) (pig scapula); and Ballybeg, Co. Westmeath (Wm3), found 5½ ft (1.7 m) deep at the base of the bog (jaw of cow). It is likely that animal bone found associated with human remains represents a form of food offering and is therefore another indicator of an early date.

Four further finds may be included as possibly prehistoric on the basis of their depth in the bog:

Lisnaskea, Co. Fermanagh (Fe1), 18 ft (5.5 m); Coolronan, Co. Meath (Me1), 7–12 ft (2.1–3.7 m); Drinagh, Co. Offaly (Of5), 9 ft (2.7 m); and Cloonree, Co. Roscommon (Ro3), 6 ft (1.8 m).

Samples of human bone are preserved from a number of these sites and it is hoped that further radiocarbon dates may be obtained from these.

A number of accounts speak of the presence of coffins or oak boards but in most cases it would appear that these are of relatively recent date. There are, however, two instances of wooden vessels which may in fact be coffins and which may be prehistoric in date. The first of these is the discovery at Timoney, Co. Tipperary (Ti6) of some human bones associated with a pair of oak troughs and other worked timbers underneath a trackway constructed of sandstone slabs (Lucas 1975). The precise relationship of the trackway, troughs and bones are uncertain but the human remains (unfortunately not kept or examined) were reported to have been found between the troughs which lay close together. It is possible that the troughs may have been used as coffins. A radiocarbon date of 550 ± 120 BP was obtained from a stake associated with the trackway (Lucas 1977).

The other possible example of a coffin is a wooden vessel 12 ft (3.7 m) long found at Ardragh Bog, Co. Monaghan in the 1840s (Shirley 1845, 209). It is described as a boat but it is unlike any other Irish logboat. It was made from the split trunk of an oak tree and its flattened ends, with carrying handles, combined with the fact of its discovery in a bog, rather than a river or lake, suggests the possibility that it might have been a coffin similar to those found in Denmark. Including the two coffin burials above, the current total of bog bodies likely to be prehistoric or Early Medieval in date is 18, representing some 21 individuals.

From the above analysis, it is now clear that the majority of Irish bog bodies are of Medieval or later date. Most of the clothed bodies seem to be late also. A significant number of the Irish bog costumes have recently been discussed by Dunlevy (1989) who dates the earliest to the fifteenth century and would date most to the sixteenth or seventeenth centuries. One of the distinctive features of Medieval and post-Medieval dress, both male and female, is the presence of buttons made of wool on the sleeves. This has been noted in accounts of a number of bog costumes which no longer survive and these are likely to be of a similar date: Flanders and Drumadreen, Co. Derry (De2,3) and Leitrim, Co. Donegal (Dg4).

There are 32 certain or almost certain instances of Late Medieval or modern bog bodies representing some 33 individuals. Of these, the dates of 12 are certain on the basis of radiocarbon dating (Dg7) or the style of the surviving clothing (De15; Dg2; Dg5; Dg7; Dg9; Ke1; Ma4; Sl1; Sl3; Ti4; Ti5). Descriptions of the associated clothing and artefacts of a further 14 'paper' bog bodies suggest that they are of similar date (Ar1; De1; De2; De3; De6; De11; De13; De14; Dg4; Dw1; Dw2; Ma3; Of1; Ty2). A further six instances are the remains of known suicides (An1; Co1; De12; Lh1; Of3) or murders (Dg1).

Dates can now be suggested for just over half the known Irish bog bodies and it is likely that further research of the undated specimens will assign most to the later Medieval and modern periods.

Clothing and Animal Remains from Bogs

Table 19 lists all textile remains in the National Museum of Ireland which are not known to be associated with human remains, excluding leather shoes. Examination of the records of the find associations of leather shoes from Irish bogs which are not associated with clothing shows that none are associated with bog bodies. There is therefore no reason to suppose that isolated pairs of shoes (Briggs and Turner 1986, No. 70) represent the remains of bog bodies. Where these items of bog clothing can be dated, all are of medieval or later date, confirming the pattern of clothed bog bodies. In a number of instances the clothing is described as being found rolled up and it is probable that these instances represent temporary storage. Of particular note is the otter skin cape from Derrykeighan, Co. Antrim (Fig. 69). It is undated but as it was found at a depth of 6 ft (1.8 m) and because the fine stitching used is similar to that on the cape associated with the Gallagh bog body, it may well be ancient.

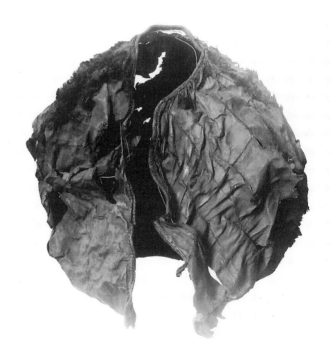

Fig. 69 Otterskin cape found at Derrykeighan, Co. Antrim. (*National Museum of Ireland*)

Only some small scraps of the woven woollen textile found wrapped around the body of a boar in a bog at Ballindine, Co. Mayo are preserved. Again, the depth of the discovery raises the possibility of it being ancient.

Other instances of domestic animal remains found in bogs have been recorded but it is likely that most of these are modern in date. A shoulder joint of bacon with the skin still attached, identified as that of a greyhound pig, was

Table 19 Bog finds of clothing in the National Museum of Ireland not associated with human remains

REGISTER NUMBER	DESCRIPTION	PROVENANCE	DEPTH
1906:14	Woollen cloth Found with horsehair tassels, socketed axehead, gouge, razor and pin – all of later Bronze Age date (Eogan 1983, No. 38)	Cromaghs, Co. Antrim	Nr. base of bog
Found in 1917	Woollen textile Used to wrap the carcase of a boar	Near Ballindine, Co. Mayo	7 ft (2.1 m)
1936:1775–7	Woollen cloth (Briggs and Turner 1986, No. 72) Three pieces of woven woollen cloth, probably a cloak	Boghil, Co. Clare	4½ ft (1.4 m)
1931:305	Woollen gown Male or female gown of 15 C. date (Dunlevy 1989, 38–9)	Moy, Co. Clare	5 ft (1.5 m)
1962:100	Felt hat Dated to the 16 or 17 C. (Dunlevy 1989, 64)	Knockfola, Co. Donegal	8–9 ft (2.4–2.7 m)
1909:66–7	Two woollen hats Dated to the 15 or 16 C. (Dunlevy 1989, 62)	Boolabaun, Co. Tipperary	—
W.4	Woollen cap Dated to the late 16 or early 17 C. (Dunlevy 1989, 62)	Ballybunnion, Co. Kerry	10 ft (3 m)
W.5	Woollen dress Dated to the late 16 or early 17 C. (Dunlevy 1989, 48–9; Briggs and Turner 1986, No. 115)	'Nr. Shinrone, Co. Tipperary'	—
W.7	Woollen textile Part of cloak or coarse rug mantle (Wilde 1861, 325–6; Briggs and Turner 1986, No. 107)	Carn, Co. Laois	—
W.6; W.8	Wool and hair fabric Fringe for a garment (Wilde 1861, 294–5)	Carrick, Co. Cavan	14 ft (4.3 m)
1944:100–1	Woollen textile	Featherbed Mt., Co. Dublin	—
1984:48	Woollen textile	Featherbed Mt., Co. Dublin	5–6 ft (1.5–1.8 m)
1939:992	Bundle of woollen textile Fragmentary, probably part of a cloak. Possibly, but not certainly, associated with a bronze cauldron of later Bronze Age date (1939:991)	Cloonta, Co. Mayo	—
1956:433	Woollen textile Fragment of woollen textile, probably a jacket	Carrignamweel, Co. Wicklow	2 ft (0.6 m)
1960:577	Piece of cotton Rectangular piece of dyed cotton – modern? (Lucas (ed.) 1962, 163)	Nr. Portarlington, Co. Laois	—
1946:416	Bale of linen	Malin More, Co. Donegal	5 ft (1.5 m)
1937:2369	Horsehair girdle	Ballindoolin or Clocharinka, Co. Kildare	—
1946:416–9	Cloak, jacket/dress Child's gown of 17 C. date (Dunlevy 1989, 71)	Owenduff, Co. Mayo	2 ft (0.6 m)
1934:5605	Goatskin cloak Fragment of leather cloak containing a seam	Corratober, Co. Cavan	—
1879:45 IA/200/52	Otterskin hood (Briggs and Turner 1986, No. 57) Leather garment	Derrykeighan, Co. Antrim Corduff, Co. Kildare	6 ft (1.8 m) 7–8 ft (2.1–2.4 m)
1874:5	Ball of wool, 2 in (51 mm) diam.	Ardragh Bog, Co. Monaghan	9 ft (2.7 m)
c. 1772	Woven coat	Nr. Edgeworthstown, Co. Longford	15 ft (4.6 m)
X.-	Woollen coat Man's coat dated to 17 C. (Dunlevy 1989, 74, 76; Briggs and Turner 1986, No. 116)	—, Co. Tipperary	—

found at a depth of 2 ft (0.6 m) in a bog at Cloondaff, Co. Mayo (N.M.I. Reg. No. 1983:103). The scapula was perforated as if for hanging. A sample of bone submitted to Groningen yielded a date of 180 ± 50 BP (Grn-13, 582).

Human Remains from Other Wetland Sites

Apart from bogs, human remains have occasionally been found in rivers and lakes, in some cases in or close to crannogs. Drainage works carried out by the Commissioners of Public Works in Ireland in the last century turned up a large quantity of artefacts including some human remains. Mulvany (1850–53) lists human skulls from river banks or river beds at Ballyduff, Co. Offaly; Borris-in-Ossory, Co. Laois; Ballycumber, Co. Offaly; Ardee, Co. Louth; a human skull and long bones from near Ferbane, Co. Offaly and a human skull found in the bed of Lough a-Claureen, Co. Galway. Some of these are now preserved in the National Museum of Ireland. In more recent times, four human skulls and other long bones were dredged from the bottom of a river at Roosky, Co. Roscommon in 1988 and human skulls have been reported from boggy ground on the shores of Rosroe Lough, Co. Clare (td. Rathlaheen South) and Bishop's Lough, Co. Westmeath (td. Froghanstown).

Bronze objects of prehistoric or Early Medieval date are rarely found with human remains despite their survival in large numbers from both dry- and wetland locations. Wilde (1861, 466) records a socketed bronze dagger found 'sticking in a human skull in Drumona Bog, Co. Armagh in 1816'. Waddell (1984) gives further details of this unique find which suggests that a complete skeleton was uncovered in the bank of a small stream, the dagger – of Early Bronze Age date – found driven through the upper part of the skull.

Wood-Martin (1886, 90) refers to fragmentary human remains being uncovered at the crannogs of Lagore, Co. Meath and Ardakillen and Clonfinlough, Co. Roscommon. He states that 'the people appear to have met with a violent end'. D'Arcy (1897, 397) discovered part of a human mandible in excavations of a crannog at Killyvilla Lake, Co. Monaghan. Near the crannog of Ardakillen, Co. Roscommon, a log boat of oak, 40 ft (12 m) long was discovered. In it were found a human skull, a spearhead and a bronze pin (Wood-Martin 1886, 237–8, Fig. 232). The skull bears the marks of some 20 sword(?) cuts, inflicted pre-mortem, and near it was found an iron fetter with an attached chain 20 ft (6 m) long.

During the course of investigations at Lagore in 1839 two skeletons lying at full length were found near the centre of the site, within two feet of the surface (Wilde 1836–40, 424). Excavations in this century at Lagore yielded some 200 human bones from levels below the crannog and from the earliest occupation levels (Hencken 1950–51, 198–203). Fourteen cut occiputs were uncovered which showed that the individuals concerned 'had evidently been put to death by having the backs of their heads partly cut off and partly broken off with a sword or axe' (ibid., 200). At least two of these skull fragments were stratified to Period Ia for which a seventh-century AD date is now accepted (Lynn 1985/6 and Warner 1985/6). Portions of more complete skeletons of both adults and children were found around the edge of the site. Parts of at least three fetters were found at Lagore, the finest coming from the same seventh-century AD Period Ia occupation from which much of the human bone came (Hencken 1950–51, 115–6).

Excavations at both crannogs in Ballinderry Lough by Hencken also uncovered human remains in the lower levels. At Ballinderry 1 a skull vault, fragment of a lower jaw and portion of a scapula were found below and in the floor timbers of House I which should date to the tenth century AD (Hencken 1936, 227–9). Although not directly associated with the human remains, the site also produced part of an iron chain (ibid., fig. 15,D) and a hinged iron ring (ibid., Fig. 24,E) which may represent parts of fetters. At Ballinderry 2, three human skulls were uncovered, apparently associated with the later Bronze Age phase on the site (Hencken 1942, 17–20). As at Lagore, two of the skulls show evidence of post-mortem cutting. Many of the so-called Bronze Age features at Ballinderry 2 are now regarded as belonging to the Early Medieval occupation at the site (Newman 1986, 63–6). Stratified under the main structure of the Early Medieval crannog, the skulls are likely to date to the sixth or seventh century, that is, roughly contemporary with those at Lagore.

Hencken interpreted the presence of human bone at Lagore as representing a massacre of the party of workers building the crannog, while the skulls at Ballinderry 1 and 2 he interpreted as foundation burials (Hencken 1950–51, 203). The growing evidence for the presence of human bone at crannog sites which show signs of pre- or post-mortem violence coupled with the association of iron fetters and cut human bone at Ardakillen, Lagore and, possibly also Ballinderry 1, may represent the ritual killing of slaves or hostages and the deposition of partial human remains in a watery environment during the Early Medieval period.

Further Work on Bog Bodies

It is certain that the number of recorded instances of bog bodies will continue to rise. However, it is unlikely that very many new bodies will come to light and most new accounts are more likely to be 'paper' bog bodies found in nineteenth-century and earlier newspaper reports and antiquarian papers.

Dr Maire Delaney has begun a PhD for University College Dublin on the subject of Irish bog bodies. This will involve a full examination of all extant human remains from Irish bogs as well as experiments on the effects of burial in bog on bone and tissue and the examination of the environs of a selected number of bog bodies. Recently a CT scan has been carried out on the bog body from Gallagh, Co. Galway (6a1) under the direction of Dr Delaney, Prof. Max Ryan and Dr John Harbison and a full autopsy has been carried out on the Ardee, Co. Louth (Lh1) body under the direction of Dr Alex Whelan. Reports on these investigations are in progress.

It is intended to submit further samples of human remains for radiocarbon dating. It is hoped that the textile and leather remains associated with the two prehistoric burials of Gallagh and Baronstown West will be examined in the near future – they are the only substantial surviving items of clothing from prehistoric contexts in Ireland.

Bog Bodies on the Continent: Developments since 1965, with Special Reference to the Netherlands

W. A. B. van der Sanden

In 1965 two monographs were published on the subject of bog bodies: P. V. Glob's *Mosefolket* (The Bog People) and A. Dieck's *Die europäischen Moorleichenfunde* (The European Bog-Body Finds). The books vary considerably in character. The latter German publication is a systematic catalogue of over 690 bog bodies, the result of several decades of intensive and obsessive data gathering. The bog bodies included in the catalogue cover the entire period from the Stone Age to the end of the Second World War. The author stresses that there is no universal explanation for the phenomenon. The message of *Mosefolket* is quite different. Basing himself on a select number of bog bodies, Glob argues in rather moving terms that the bog bodies datable to the Iron Age and the Roman period (to which periods the majority of the bodies are in his opinion to be dated) are to be interpreted as human sacrifices.

The great difference between the two books is of course partly due to the different target groups for which they were written, the Danish book being intended for the general reader and the German one for academic circles. Thanks to the numerous translations of his book, Glob and his views are now widely known all over the world, whereas Dieck's book is known to a small group of specialists only. But it cannot be said that one of the two books is more important than the other; together they give a reasonably good impression of the research that had been done until then.

The present chapter is intended to cover, in broad outline, the developments in research on the isolated bog bodies since 1965. The term 'bog bodies' is understood to include bog skeletons too, but bog bodies forming part of large finds, such as those of Thorsberg, Rappendam and Oberdorla will not be considered here. This account is limited to the north-western part of continental Europe, more specifically to the 'focal area' of bog bodies, namely Denmark, north Germany and the Netherlands. The emphasis will of course be on the results of the Dutch research.

Denmark

Since the first half of the 1950s, the period in which Tollund Man and Grauballe Man, the two protagonists of Glob's book, were found, no new bog bodies have been discovered in Denmark. The research that has been done in that country over the past years has hence concentrated on relatively old finds. The first example is 'Elling Man', one of the three bog bodies from Bjaeldskovdal (Fisher 1979; Gregersen 1979; Langfeldt and Raahede 1979). The body had dried out completely since its discovery in 1938. The fresh analysis to which the body was subjected in 1978 showed that it was not that of a man, as had originally been assumed, but that of a woman of about thirty years old. The Borremose woman, a body found in 1948, has also been re-examined. We now know that her skull was injured after she had died instead of before (Andersen and Geertinger 1984, 115). Microscopic analysis of her skin yielded a small amount of pollen, pointing to the autumn as the season of death (ibid., 113).

Another body that has recently been re-examined is the Huldremose woman, excavated in 1879. The body had been presumed lost until it turned up again in the Anthropoligical Laboratory of the University of Copenhagen around the end of the 1970s. The examination to which the body was then subjected revealed a number of wounds on the woman's arms and legs. There were also some indications suggesting that the woman's right arm had been amputated at the time of death (Liversage 1984; Brothwell *et al* 1990, 831). Analysis of the vegetable remains in her intestines showed that her last meal had presumably been a gruel prepared from mainly wheat or rye and corn spurry (Brothwell *et al* 1990, 834). A number of C14 dates have meanwhile also been obtained for these and other bog bodies (Tauber 1979; Fischer 1980; Bennike and Ebbesen 1985; Fig. 70).

The Danish Neolithic bog skeletons now constitute a special research topic. The results of the examination of four of these skeletons were published a few years ago. They are the skeletons from Bolkilde (1946; Bennike *et al* 1986) and Sigersdal (1949; Bennike and Ebbesen 1986). Those from Bolkilde were found to represent the remains of a young man of 16 and of a man of about 35 who had a deformed hip. Some remains of clothing were found in association with the last body. The rope that was found near his neck shows that he must have met a violent death. The bodies from Sigersdal are of two fairly young individuals, one between 18 and 20 and the other of 16 years; their sex can no longer be determined. There was a piece of rope around the neck of the elder of the two and a lugged vessel of the funnel-beaker culture was found between the two bodies. C14 analysis of these finds yielded dates in the local early Neolithic (Fig. 70). The results of these and other recent analyses have meanwhile been made accessible to a broad (Danish) public (Ebbesen 1986).

The investigation of the finds associated with bog bodies should also be mentioned in this survey. One of the most important publications in this field is that by Hald (1980), which discusses, among other matters, the clothing that has been recovered from Danish bogs.

Glob's sacrifice theory found wide acceptance among many Danish scholars. Fischer saw a link between bog bodies and contemporary activities in the bogs, which led

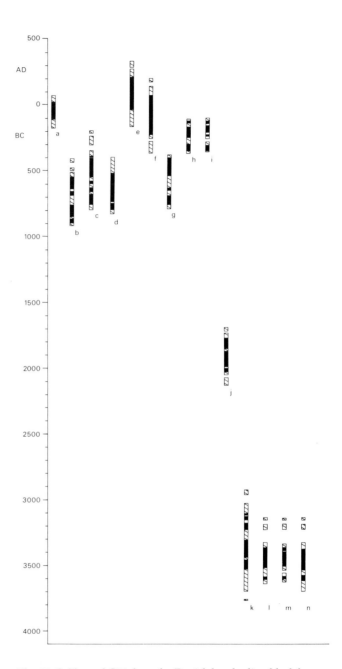

Fig. 70 Calibrated C14 dates for Danish bog bodies: black bars, 68% confidence level; hatched bars, 95% confidence level. (*Data from Bennike and Ebbesen 1985 and 1986; Bennike, personal communication; Fischer 1979; Tauber 1979. Calibration program developed by van der Plicht and Mook, University of Groningen.*) a) 1952 Grauballe; b) 1946 Borremose; c) 1947 Borremose; d) 1948 Borremose; e) 1879 Huldremose; f) 1878 Krogens Mollemose; g) 1835 Haraldskaermose; h) 1950 Tollund; i) 1938 Elling; j) 1941 Stenstrup Mose; k) 1949 Sigersdal Mose (A); l) 1949 Sigersdal Mose (B); m) Bolkilde; n) Porsmose.

him to the conclusion that bog bodies are to be interpreted as sacrifices made to the deities by way of compensation for the disturbance caused by the winning of resources from the bogs (Fischer 1979, 43). The researchers who have concentrated on the skeletons from the funnel-beaker period are also of the opinion that bog bodies are to be seen as human sacrifices. They connect the bog bodies (with a few exceptions such as the Porsmose man (Bennike and Ebbesen 1986, 101)) with the large number of objects that were deposited in the Danish bogs from the Early Neolithic until the Viking age and conclude that human lives were sacrificed to invoke good fortune, fertility and new life (Bennike *et al* 1986, 207).

Munksgaard opposes this interpretation. Basing herself on a number of common characteristics of some of the isolated bog bodies, she concludes that the bodies represent the remains of punished individuals (Munksgaard 1984); nudity and close-cropped heads are marks of disgrace, as Tacitus informs us in *Germania* 19.2. She does not altogether deny the possibility that some of the bodies may indeed be human sacrifices; the bog skeletons found in association with remains of domestic animals, pottery, parts of wagons (as at Rappendam for example; Kunwald 1970), etc. are in her opinion to be interpreted as sacrifices.

The size of the Danish bog body population is not known. Dieck (1986, 142) specifies a total of 441, while Bennike and Ebbesen (1986, 101) claim a total of some 500 bodies. There is no well-documented survey of all of the reported discoveries of bog bodies, which means that we do not know how many bodies have actually been preserved since their discovery and how many were only reported. Nor do we know how reliable the records are of the latter category of bodies. The consequence is that very little can be said about the composition of the overall population and its chronological spread (what proportion, for example, is of Medieval or Post-Medieval date?). This does not apply to the Early Neolithic portion of the bog-body population. In Bennike *et al* (1986, 203) we read that 14 of the 18 skeletons belonged to adults; nine are of men, two are of women and three are of individuals whose sex cannot be determined. Eight of these individuals died aged 16–20 years.

Germany

The publication of *Moorleichenfunde* did not mark the end of Dieck's work of compiling his inventory. On the contrary, his bog body catalogue continued to grow steadily in the years following its publication. By 1986, a few years

before his death, Dieck had reached a total of more than 1850 European bodies, half of which had been found in Germany (Dieck 1986). He never published a continuation of the catalogue of 1965, but he did publish several articles, for example, on bog bodies discovered in certain regions (Dieck 1973a; 1975a; 1984), on certain aspects of bog-body research (Dieck 1973b; 1975b) and on problems of interpretation (Dieck 1968). He never examined any bog bodies himself. His articles are the results of his worldwide inventory project. The general impression is that he did not always study the records very critically; the numbers, dates and interpretations given in his works should hence be considered with due caution.

All of the other bog body research carried out in Germany so far has taken place in the federal states of Schleswig-Holstein and Lower Saxony, where more than three-quarters of the reported discoveries were made. I will now briefly discuss the most important studies and the views that have been put forward with respect to the German bog bodies.

In 1967 Struve published an article discussing the bog body that had been discovered at Dätgen eight years earlier. The head had been found about 3 metres from the rest of the body. The body, of a man aged about 30, showed several stabs and injuries caused by blows and had been pegged down in the bog with stakes. Struve believes that some of the injuries may have been sustained after decapitation (Struve 1967, 39, 71). He regards the Dätgen man as an example of a far more common type of bog body that has nothing to do with sacrifices – the numerous bodies that have been found in contexts devoid of any other finds such as animal bones, etc. Struve's folkloristic approach led him to associate these bog bodies with *Wiedergänger*. In his opinion, they represent the remains of individuals who were considered to be too restless to be buried in a normal grave. Such persons – criminals, suicides, victims of violence or accident – were rendered 'harmless': they were abused, undressed or had their hair cut short after they had died and were then buried in the bog to ensure that they would not return to haunt the living. Seen from this point of view, the acts of physical abuse and the cutting of the hair were means of warding off evil and had nothing to do with punishments or sacrificial rites.

Martin examined the intestines of the Dätgen man (1967). Besides remains of wheat and millet, he found evidence of several weeds such as corn spurry, persicaria and fat hen. The C14 dates obtained for the peat indicate that the body ended up in the bog around the end of the

Late Iron Age. Average date: 2060 ± 35 BP (Aletsee 1967, 83), i.e. 156–146/116–34 BC (1 s.d.) or 174 BC–AD 4 (2 s.d.).

In the 1970s another body found in Schleswig-Holstein, the 13- or 14-year-old 'Windeby girl', was re-examined; the Schloss Gottorf Museum in Schleswig co-ordinated the research. One of the conclusions was that it was not altogether certain whether the body was indeed that of a girl (Caselitz 1979, 109). Pollen analysis revealed that the child had been buried in the Roman period (Gebühr 1979, 80). In interpreting various aspects of the find, such as the cut-off hair, the stone found on the body and the hair band, Gebühr let himself be influenced by the *Handwörterbuch des Deutschen Aberglaubens* (Dictionary of German Superstitions), and concluded that the body of the child had been buried in a normal grave that had presumably been dug at the edge of a large cemetery (id. 80, 96, 104). In 1981 the face of the Windeby child was reconstructed. Strangely enough, the report of the reconstruction (Helmer 1983) does not mention the uncertainty regarding the sex of the child. The author consistently refers to the body as that of a girl and hence also reconstructed the face believing that the child was a girl.

A final aspect that should be mentioned with respect to the German bog bodies is the research that has been carried out in the Textilmuseum in Neumünster into the clothing that has been found in bogs in north Germany, whether or not in association with human bodies. See Schlabow (1976) for a summary of the results.

The bog body research in Lower Saxony is indissolubly connected with the name H. Hayen. He chose the western half of the federal state as his research area (e.g. Hayen 1979; 1981; cf. Berg *et al* 1981, 10–16). In 1987 he published a review of the seven bog bodies in the Staatliches Museum für Naturkunde und Vorgeschichte at Oldenburg. In the past few years he had been preparing a monograph on the bog bodies found between the Weser and the Dutch/German border (Fig. 71), in which much attention was to be paid also to the bodies that had not been preserved after their discovery. His untimely death, in November 1991, has put a stop to this interesting project (for the time being at least). Hayen warns his readers to be very careful in answering the questions why and how the bodies ended up in the bogs; in his opinion there is no universal explanation. Each body must be considered separately to decide whether it represents the remains of a punished individual, a sacrificial victim, the victim of a sex crime, an accident or a violent attack, etc.. He approached the problem with the same degree of caution as Dieck and Gebühr.

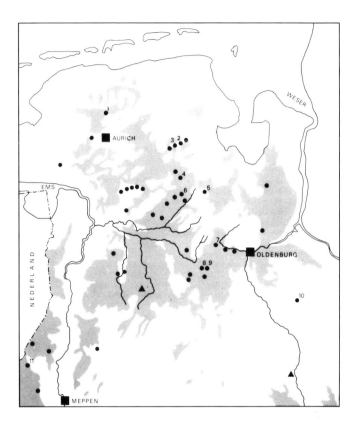

Fig. 71 Distribution of the bog bodies found in the northwestern part of Lower Saxony (*after Hayen 1964; 1987*). The triangles indicate Medieval or later bodies. See Table 20 for the reference numbers (*from van der Sanden (ed.) 1990, 211*).

The same drawback observed earlier with respect to the Danish bog bodies applies to the German bodies too; we have no well-documented survey that describes, evaluates and analyses all of the 940 find reports collected by Dieck. So for Germany, too, we have no concrete data regarding the composition of the population and the chronological spread of the bodies. No C14 dates whatsoever have been obtained so far for the German bodies. The dates that we do have are all based on the results of pollen analysis and hence are not altogether reliable. The general impression created by the data available for the western half of Lower Saxony is that a large proportion of the bodies is datable to the Late Iron Age and the Roman period (Table 20).

The Netherlands

In the past, large areas in the western and northern parts of the Netherlands and smaller areas in the southern part were covered with fens and raised bogs, of which very little remains today. The raised bogs in the western part of

Table 20   The dated pre-Medieval bog bodies from the north-western part of Lower Saxony (cf. Fig. 71). Key: M = male; Ch = child. From: van der Sanden (ed.) 1990, 212.

		NUMBER (AND SEX)	POSITION	CLOTHING	DATING
1	1907 Bernuthsfeld	1 (M)	In a pit	+	Around the beginning of our era
2	1817 Etzel	1 (M?)	In a pit, pegged down with stakes	+	Roman period
3	1861 Marx	1		+	650 BC–0
4	1954 Bentstreek	1		+	1000–800 BC
5	1934 Jührdenerfeld	1		+	400 BC–0
6	1941 Neuengland	1			Roman period
7	1922 Kayhausener Moor	1 (Ch)	Bound	+	0–AD 200
8	1931 Husbäke	1 (M)			600–200 BC
9	1936 Husbäke	1 (M)			1000–300 BC
10	1784 Bareler Moor	1 (Ch)			Around the beginning of our era
11	1900 Neu-Verssen	1 (M)			0–AD 200

the Netherlands, for example, have disappeared completely and only a fraction remains of the approximately 180 000 ha of raised bogs that used to cover the higher parts of the country (Fig. 72). These remnants, scarcely more than one per cent of the original expanse of the bogs, are now protected nature reserves that are treated with great care. No finds whatsoever are known from the bogs in the western part of the Netherlands and only very few are known from those in the south (the region known as De Peel). The situation in the northern part of the country is completely different and it is therefore this region which is dealt with here.

In the north of the Netherlands peat cutting started in the late Middle Ages but it was not until the late sixteenth and the early seventeenth century that it began on a large scale. We have hundreds of reports of discoveries made in the bogs in the nineteenth and twentieth centuries. Most of these were made in the provinces of Drenthe and Groningen (by that time peat cutting in Friesland had already started to wane). Finds came to light not only in the vast peat bogs such as Bourtanger Moor and the Smildiger bogs, but also in the smaller cauldron bogs. The human bodies were the most spectacular finds. One hundred years ago the Drents Museum in Assen, which was founded in 1854, acquired the first remains of a bog body. Since then 12 more bog bodies or parts of bodies have been put in the museum's care, the last in 1986. Surprisingly enough, the Dutch bog bodies have never received the interest they deserve. Some have been discussed in brief articles published shortly after their discovery but until recently a comprehensive survey was lacking.

The Research

In 1987 the Drents Museum launched a project for the systematic research into the Dutch bog bodies. The re-

search was prompted by a negative impulse – the poor documentation of this find category – and a positive one – the inspiring publication of *Lindow Man* by Stead *et al* in 1986. The aim of the research was to obtain the most complete and faithful possible picture of the 'bog body population', which was to cover the total number of bodies found, the sex and age of the bodies, their chronological spread and the circumstances under which they had ended up in the bogs. These data were then to serve as a basis for further interpretation. The only restriction imposed was that the investigation was to focus on the oldest bodies; the Medieval and post-Medieval specimens were to be excluded from the study.

It was clear from the very start that two separate lines of research would have to be followed. The first and main aim was a totally fresh analysis of the preserved bog bodies and all of the finds associated with them. They were to be described in a uniform manner in order to be able to verify, and where necessary correct, the observations that had been made many years ago, by several different persons. The investigation was to involve both relatively old methods that had not yet been used for these bodies, for example parasite research, analysis of pollen from the intestines and C14 analysis, and newly developed methods, such as CT scanning, DNA analysis, microscopic age determination, new methods of blood group determination, etc.

The second line of research was to comprise the study of written and oral sources for:
(a) documents and informants that may provide new, supplementary information on the preserved bog bodies, for example further details regarding the findspots, the find circumstances, the position of the body, etc;

Fig. 72 Raised bogs (1) and fen peat (2) in the Netherlands around AD 1500 (*from Casparie 1987, 38*).
A) Bourtanger Moor; B) bogs at the border between Drenthe and Overijssel; C) Smilde bogs; D) Drachten bogs.

(b) documents and oral information regarding bodies that are now lost, which will be referred to as 'paper bodies' below.

The results of this research are discussed in seven publications (van der Sanden (ed.) 1990, 1992, 1993, 1994; van der Sanden, Haverkort and Pasveer 1991/1992; Evershed 1990; Osinga, Buys and van der Sanden 1992). Before discussing these results, we will first take a look at a very important aspect of the research – the records.

The Records

The part of Dieck's catalogue (1965) that discusses the Dutch bog bodies was taken as a starting point for the study of the records. Dieck lists a total of 49 bodies but he does not specify his sources and so I had to consult his personal files. Dieck was most co-operative in supplying me with all the information I needed for my research. Close study of the records in question showed that a relatively large number of the bodies had to be removed from the list. Some of the entries in the catalogue turned out to be based on legends about drowned persons or on rather improbable tales, while a number of other, vague, unspecified entries seemed to concern bodies discussed elsewhere in the catalogue. After these had all been removed from the list about three-quarters of the original number remained. The next step was to study the files of regional newspapers and the correspondence files of the Drents Museum and the Biologisch-Archaeologisch Instituut of the University of Groningen. In addition, I made a number of announcements in regional newspapers and on regional radio stations in the hope that old peat cutters would remember any discoveries they may have made. In this way I managed to add several new, or rather forgotten, bog bodies to the Dutch catalogue, which now comprises 55 bog bodies from a total of 41 findspots, all in the north of the Netherlands (Table 21).

Some of the records on which this list is based are more reliable than others. Three main groups of bodies can be distinguished: category A comprises the bodies, or parts of bodies, that have been preserved; categories B and C comprise the bodies that are mentioned in reports that cannot be verified owing to the lack of material evidence – the paper bodies. The reports of the bodies of category B are the most reliable in that the bodies in question are mentioned in several records or were seen and reported by an experienced observer or were discussed in a newspaper. Category C comprises the bodies that are mentioned in one record only. This leads to the following division:

Category A	17 bodies from 12 findspots
Category B	14 bodies from 12 findspots
Category C	24 bodies from 17 findspots

Ten of these bog bodies, from six findspots, are of Medieval or post-Medieval date. We are hence left with a group of 45 bog bodies, from 35 findspots, which almost certainly date from before the Middle Ages. These can be categorised as follows (Fig. 73):

Category A	13 bodies from 11 findspots
Category B	13 bodies from 11 findspots
Category C	19 bodies from 13 findspots

As far as the grouping of the oldest bog bodies is concerned, we have to rely on Dieck in the case of 15 of the paper bodies from 12 findspots. The peat workers and other informants and the journals, letters and

Table 21 Catalogue of the Dutch bog bodies from a total of 41 findspots (No. 7 has been removed from the catalogue). The bodies indicated in italic type are of Medieval or later date, those indicated in bold type are the oldest bodies of which parts have been preserved. Key: Dr = Drenthe; Fr = Friesland; Gr = Groningen.

1	1791, Kibbelgaarn, mun. Veendam, Gr.
2	Ca. 1820, Zweeloo, mun. Zweeloo, Dr.
3	1822, Opwierde, mun. Appingedam, Gr.
4	Before 1830, Koeverdensche Veen, mun. Coevorden, Dr.
5	1841, Zweeloo, mun. Zweeloo, Dr.
6a–b	1844, Assen, mun. Assen, Dr.
8a–b	1858, Hooghalen, mun. Beilen, Dr.
9a–b	*Ca. 1865, Assen, mun. Assen, Dr.*
10	Ca. 1865, Nieuweroord, mun. Hoogeveen, Dr.
11	1866, Hooghalen, mun. Beilen, Dr.
12	1866, Terhaarsterveen, mun. Vlagtwedde, Gr.
13	*1868, Assen, mun. Assen, Dr.*
14a–c	1870, Westergeest, mun. Kollumerland and Nieuwkruisland, Fr.
15	1882, Sellinger Veld, mun. Vlagtwedde, Gr.
16	1891, Terhaarsterveen, mun. Vlagtwedde, Gr.
17	*1891, Smilde, mun. Smilde, Dr.*
18a–b	1897, Terhaarsterveen, mun. Vlagtwedde, Gr.
19	**1897, Yde, mun. Vries, Dr.**
20a–d	*1901, Wijster, mun. Beilen, Dr.*
21a–b	**1904, Weerdinge, mun. Emmen, Dr.**
22	**1914, Exloërmond, mun. Odoorn, Dr.**
23	**1920–30, SE-Drenthe.**
24	1921, Erica, mun. Emmen, Dr.
25a–b	Before 1922, Zeijen, mun. Vries, Dr.
26	*1927, Hooghalen, mun. Beilen, Dr.*
27	**1931, Weerdinger Aschbroeken, mun. Emmen, Dr.**
28	*1932, Hooghalen, mun. Beilen, Dr.*
29	1932, Witten, mun. Asssen, Dr.
30	Before 1937, Donderen, mun. Vries, Dr.
31	1937, Hooghalen, mun. Beilen, Dr.
32a–b	Before 1938, Witten, mun. Assen, Dr.
33	**1938, Emmer-Erfscheidenveen, mun. Emmen, Dr.**
34	1943/49, Midlaren, mun. Zuidlaren, Dr.
35	**1951, Zweeloo, mun. Zweeloo, Dr.**
36	Ca. 1910, Barger-Erfscheidenveen, mun. Emmen, Dr.
37a–b	Ca. 1914–1919, Barger-Compascuum, mun. Emmen, Dr.
38a–b	**1975, Borger, mun. Borger, Dr.**
39	1898, Emmer-Compascuum, mun. Emmen, Dr.
40	1925, Nieuw-Weerdinge, mun. Emmen, Dr.
41	**?, N-Drenthe.**
42	**1985, Buinen, mun. Borger, Dr.**

other documents which he quotes as sources can no longer be consulted. The 15 bodies in question have the catalogue numbers 11, 15 and 30 of category B; and 1, 3, 4, 5, 6a-b, 8a-b, 18a-b, 31 and 32 of category C. The following account is restricted to these oldest bog bodies.

The Findspots

The majority (35) of these 45 bog bodies were found in the province of Drenthe; seven were found in Groningen and the remaining three were discovered in Friesland. In the case of only 31 of the bodies is the findspot accurately or reasonably accurately known. Most of the bodies were found in raised bogs; in expansive bogs such as the Bour-

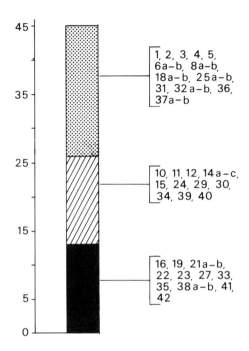

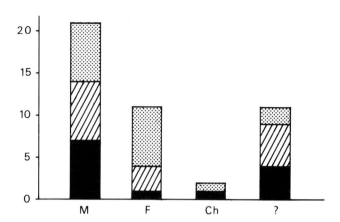

Fig. 73 (left) Dutch pre-Medieval bog bodies categorised according to the reliability of the records: black, category A; hatched, category B; dotted, category C. See text for explanation. Note the catalogue numbers.

Fig. 75 (above) Dutch pre-Medieval bog bodies grouped according to age and sex. M: males; F: females; Ch: children. The bodies of the last bar are unclassified. See Fig. 73 for explanation of symbols.

tanger Moor and the bogs at the border between the provinces of Drenthe and Overijssel but also in smaller cauldron bogs. The soft tissues of these bodies had been preserved. Of a small number of bog bodies the skeleton only had been preserved. Four of these are known to have been found in a river valley, i.e. in fen peat (38a-b, 39 and 42; Fig. 74).

Sex and Age

Figure 75 presents a summary of the results of the sex and age determinations of the bodies of each of the afore-mentioned categories A, B and C. The sex and age of the bodies of category A were scientifically determined, whereas those of the bodies of categories B and C of course had to be inferred from the contents of the records.

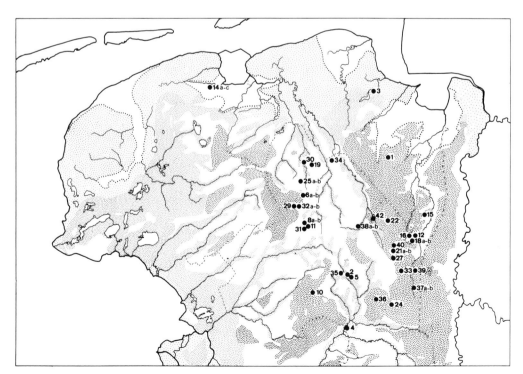

Fig. 74 Distribution of the Dutch bog bodies that are considered to be of pre-Medieval date.

We may assume that the sex of the bodies of the last two categories was in some cases incorrectly determined owing to prevailing misconceptions, for example that bodies with long hair always represented the remains of women.

The Dutch bog body population includes men, women and children. Children are very rare, while men clearly prevail. In the case of six of the preserved bodies it proved possible to obtain some indication of the age of the deceased; four adult men were found to have met their death when aged 20–45 (21b; Fig. 76), younger than 45 (22), 35–45 (27) and 30–50 (38a); one adult woman (35) was about 35. Finally, the child whose age could be determined (19) was about 16 years old.

Fig. 76 Two bog bodies from Weerdinge, discovered in 1904 (cat. nos 21a–b). Recent analysis has shown that they are not the bodies of a man and a woman but those of two men. (*Drents Museum*)

Stature

Two bodies were measured shortly after they had been excavated. Body 16 measured 1.65 m. However, as the circumference of the skull was only 0.54 m at the time when the body was discovered, we may assume that a small degree of post-mortem shrinkage had occurred and that the man was in fact slightly taller in life. Body 21b was found to measure 1.75 m in 1904. The full length of the skin of this body is much shorter now, because the body has dried out since its discovery. If we apply the regression equation of Trotter and Gleser (1958) to the preserved shin-bone, we arrive at an original height of 1.69 m, which does not differ too much from the value measured in 1904. The Trotter and Gleser method was used to determine the original stature of some of the other bog bodies. The values obtained for the girl whose remains were found at Yde (19) are 1.40–1.43 m. It is not certain whether post-mortem shrinkage has occurred in this case. Aschbroeken man (27) had a length of 1.68–1.74 m and one of the two individuals from Borger (38a) was 1.78–1.82 m tall in life. The value obtained for Zweeloo woman (35) is 1.38 m. This small stature is probably due to pathological causes.

Blood Groups and DNA

Analysis of skin samples of seven bog bodies revealed three blood types of the ABO system: A (19, 21a, 21b), B (33) and O (23 and probably also 35) (Connolly 1990). Rather noteworthy is the fact that 21a and 21b, the two bodies that are also known as the 'Weerdinge Couple', are both of blood group A.

The DNA research to which a number of skin and kidney samples were subjected yielded no useful results, not even when use was made of analytical methods with which short sequences of base pairs can be determined (Osinga and Buys 1990). In June 1992, one of the bog bodies, that from Zweeloo (35), was re-examined for the presence of DNA, this time using the relatively new polymerase chain reaction method (cf. Brown and Brown 1992, 10). Again no trace of DNA was found (Osinga, Buys and van der Sanden 1992). Apparently the DNA has decomposed completely in the peaty matrix.

Hair

The right half of the head of the Yde girl (19) had been shaven while the hair on the left half of her head still had its normal length. Research using an electron microscope showed that the hair of three other bodies of category A (22, 33, 35) had been cut around the time of death. The hair of body 16 was relatively short (about 8 cm); that of bodies 21b and 41 was a little longer (about 12 cm and 10–16 cm, respectively). Traces of moustache and/or beard growth were found in two cases (21a, 22).

The records mention four bodies with beards (11, 12, 16, 18a). In two cases the hair of the paper bog bodies is described as long (12, 15); one record mentions that the hair was tied in a knot (11) and three others report that one half of the head had been shaven (18a, 18b, 30 – right half).

Position

Relatively little is known about the position in which the body was found in the peat. The available information is summarised below:

Face downwards	3, 6b, 11, 18a?, 19?, 33?, 37a-b
Face upward	6a?, 12?, 16, 18b?, 21a-b, 22?, 35?
On one side	15
In a pit	22?, 23?, 29?, 32?, 35
Beneath branches	18, 27, 32, 33
Beneath stakes	4?, 12, 29
Pegged down with stakes	18a-b?

Clothing

The following garments were found in association with a total of 17 bodies:

CATEGORY	A	B/C
Clothing	—	2, 3, 4, 32a-b
skin cape	33	8a-b, 11, 29, 37b?
fur cap	33	—
shoe(s)	33	6a, 6b, 11, 18a, 18b
belt	—	5, 6a, 6b, 18a
woollen trousers	—	5, 15, 18a
woollen jacket	15	—
woollen undergarment	33	30?
woollen tunic	19	5? 10?, 12 15
woollen mitten	15	—
woollen band	19	—

The bodies were not all actually wearing the above garments. In some cases the clothing had been wrapped around the body (e.g. 8a-b, 11, 33) or had been placed beneath the head (10) or at the feet (5, 33). The shoes that are mentioned in the records are described as 'made from a single piece of leather'.

Other Finds

The human remains that were found at Borger (38a-b) were recovered from a context that also yielded animal bones and stones. But as the faunal remains have not been dated we do not know whether they are actually associated with the human remains.

Six of the paper bodies are reported to have been found in association with finds other than clothing, namely jewellery (2), a flint knife with a bone handle and a leather sheath decorated with notches (3), a bronze axe (5, 15), a pot (30) and the skull of a dog (30). However, we do not know how reliable these reports are. Jewellery and earthenware have been found in association with bog bodies elsewhere too, for example in Borremose (1947) and Windeby (1952). The discovery of a dog in the peat is not unusual either (Dieck 1959). The reported discovery of two bronze axes is rather questionable though, particularly as the axes are said to have been found together with a pair of trousers.

Pathology and Degenerative Changes

The amount of information available on the subject of pathology is very small. The curvature of the vertebral column of the girl from Yde (19) was first explained in terms of pseudopathology (Uytterschaut 1990). Recent CT scans, however, show wedge-shaped vertebrae and mild degenerative changes, indicating that the girl suffered from mild scoliosis (van der Sanden 1994). Aschbroeken man (27) suffered several growth arrests during his childhood. The extremely short forearms and the striking difference in size between corresponding bones of the right and the left half of the skeleton of Zweeloo (35; Fig. 77) were first explained as post-mortem changes (Uytterschaut 1990), but it is now thought more likely that they are pathological (though the nature of this disease is as yet unclear). Analysis of the intestines of this bog body revealed the presence of eggs of the parasites maw worm, *Ascaris lumbricoides* and the human whipworm, *Trichuris trichuria* (Paap 1990). It is no longer possible to determine the degree of infestation.

The record of another bog body (16) mentions that the teeth were all 'cylindrically shaped', which must undoubtedly have meant that they were badly worn.

Cause of Death

Two of the investigated bog bodies showed indications of unnatural death: one individual appeared to have been strangled (19, Fig. 78), while the other seemed to have been stabbed with a sharp object (21b). The latter's intestines were found lying on the chest of the body; they had probably already spilled from the abdomen before the body was deposited in the peat.

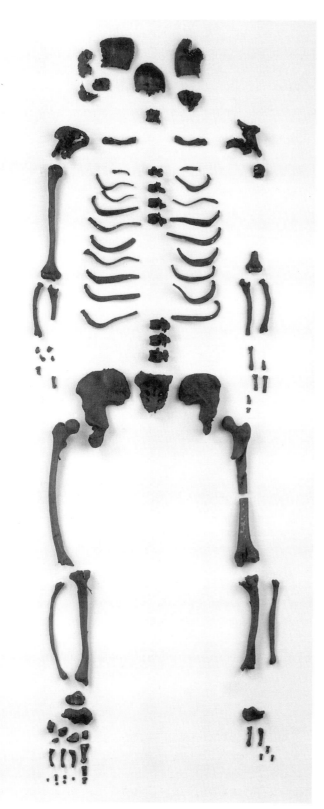

The records of the paper bodies speak of hanging with reference to two bodies (18a and 18b, which are said to have been found together in one noose) and mention a fractured skull on two other occasions (11 and 31; the latter body is said to have been bound). The 'fractured skulls' are to be interpreted with due caution as they may very well be the result of post-mortem changes.

The Last Meal and the Season of Death

The analysis of the contents of the stomach and intestines is an important part of bog body research. Of the bog bodies found in the Netherlands, only that from Zweeloo (35) could be subjected to such analysis, as it was the only body of which the intestines had been preserved. Analysis of the macroremains found in the woman's stomach and large intestine revealed the presence of remains of millet, *Panicum miliaceum* and blackberries, *Rubus fructicosus*, and smaller amounts of remains of wheat/rye, *Triticum/ Secale*, barley, *Hordeum* sp., oats, *Avena* sp., linseed, *Linum usitatissimum*, and several weeds, *Polygonum lapathifolium, Spergula arvensis, Brassica* sp., also animal hairs and fragments of a beetle, *Tenebris obscuris* (van der Sanden 1990; Hakbijl 1990; Holden 1990, 265–9).

It was concluded that the last meal that this individual had consumed must have been a fairly clean gruel that consisted largely of millet. The coarsely ground millet grains had not been dehusked. Of course, it is impossible to say whether the blackberries had been mixed in with the gruel. What is more important, though, is that they tell

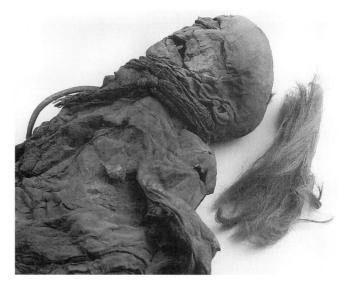

Fig. 77 Zweeloo skeleton, found in 1951 (cat. no. 35). Note the short forearms and the difference in size between corresponding bones of the left and right half of the body. (*Drents Museum*)

Fig. 78 Yde girl, discovered in 1897 (cat. no. 19); the band of sprang fabric around her neck suggests that she was strangled to death. (*Drents Museum*)

us in which season the individual died. On the assumption that fruit was not conserved in the first centuries of our era, the time of death must have been between August and October. The analysis of pollen from the stomach and intestines yielded more or less the same information. Rather surprising was the high percentage of *Triticum* pollen. It has been suggested that this pollen was inhaled during threshing (Troostheide 1990).

A different way of obtaining information on the season of death is via entomological research. The discovery of parts of a Carabid beetle, *Carabus clatratus* on the bog body from Exloërmond (22) led to the conclusion that this scavenger found its bait between April and August, the period of activity of this particular insect (Hakbijl 1990). It should be stressed, however, that this gives us no more than an *indication* of the season of death; the boundaries of the period of activity are not very sharp. When F. Netolitzky examined the body's intestines (now no longer present) in 1934 he found numerous fragments (epidermal remains and chaff) of barley, *Hordeum vulgare*, an amount of millet chaff, *Panicum miliaceum* and remains of several indeterminate vegetable and/or weed species. He also observed a concentration of fungus spores in the intestines. These observations can no longer be verified.

Dating

Of course, only the bog bodies of category A could be dated in a reliable manner. The dating was done in laboratories in Groningen (33 and 35), Oxford (16, 19, 21b, 22, 23, 27, 35, 41 and 42) and Uppsala (38a), using samples of wood, hair, skin and bone. The last two laboratories used AMS dating methods. Figure 79 shows the results of the eleven determinations. Four bog bodies date from the Middle Bronze Age (33), the end of the Middle Bronze Age/beginning of the Late Bronze Age (27) or the early part of the Iron Age (22 and 23), but the majority are datable to the centuries around the beginning of our era, in other words to the Late Iron Age and the Roman period (16, 19, 21a-b, 38a-b, 35, 41 and 42).

The information obtainable from the records of the bodies of categories B and C confirms the above picture. Only few records provide any information from which the date of the body can be inferred. The pottery found in association with body 30 and the results of pollen analysis obtained for body 34 are left out of consideration here because the dates that they yield (Bronze Age/Iron Age and Neolithic/Bronze Age, respectively) are far too uncertain to be used. The most informative are the records of bodies 5, 11, 15 and 18a-b. Three records mention the

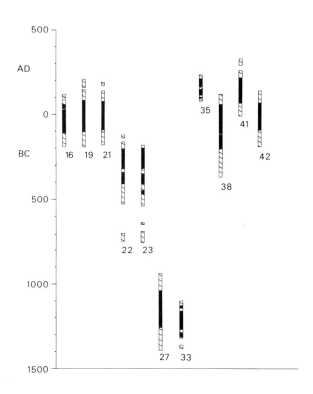

Fig. 79 Calibrated radiocarbon dates for the Dutch bog bodies. See Fig. 70 for explanation of the symbols. Numbers refer to the catalogue. No. 35 gives the pooled age of two C14 dates.

presence of a pair of trousers: one pair of knee-length breeches (5), one pair of long trousers (15) and one pair of three-quarter-length ones (18a). The trousers that have been found in bogs in north Germany and Denmark, which clearly resemble those found in the Netherlands, are definitely (Thorsberg 1858–61; Marx-Etzel 1817; Obenaltendorf 1859) or in all probability (Dätgen 1906) datable to the Roman period (Hald 1980, 328–35; Schlabow 1976, 76–80). The Swabian knot (11) should also be mentioned in this context. From classical authors like Tacitus (*Germania*, 38), ancient sculptures (Trajan's column) and a C14 date (Struve 1967, 46; Aletsee 1967, 83) we know that this particular hairstyle was in fashion in the Roman period and possibly even earlier too, in the Late Iron Age.

The C14 dates and the aforementioned information from the records of the bog bodies of categories B and C show that most of the bodies date from the last part of the Iron Age and the Roman period (we may assume that the majority of the undated bodies of groups B and C are also datable to these periods). The above information is summarised in Fig. 80.

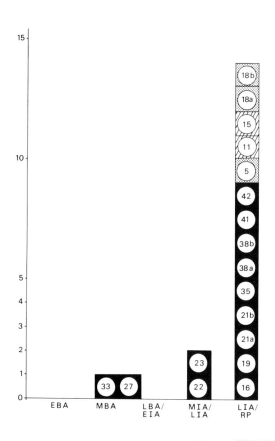

Bog Bodies and Bog Trackways

Casparie has recently published a survey of the remains of bog trackways that have been found in the northern part of the Netherlands (Casparie 1987). They are datable to the period from the Late Neolithic to the end of the sixteenth century. However, there is very little evidence of any links between these trackways and the bog bodies, as will become apparent below.

Bog trackway ıı(Bou) was observed a short distance to the south of the spot where the Aschbroeken bog body (27) was found. Casparie has his doubts about this trackway, however (ibid., 46). The same holds for 'trackway ıv(Bou)', which was found a short distance to the north of the findspot; the wood interpreted as the paving of the

Fig. 80 Dated paper bog bodies and preserved bog bodies in the Netherlands. EBA: Early Bronze Age; MBA: Middle Bronze Age; LBA/EIA: Late Bronze Age/Early Iron Age; MIA/LIA: Middle Iron Age/Late Iron Age; LIA/RP: Late Iron Age/Roman period. See Fig. 73 for symbols. Numbers refer to the catalogue.

Fig. 81 Excavation of the *Valtherbrug* in 1892.

trackway could equally well be natural wood remains (ibid., 46). The remains of the so-called *Valtherbrug*, scientifically known as I(Bou), are less ambiguous (Fig. 81). This 2.5–3 m wide and probably 12 km long bog trackway has been investigated and described at different times: by Karsten in 1819, Landweer in 1898 and Van Giffen in 1938. Casparie has summarised the information in these three sources (Casparie 1987, 41–3).

The trackway, which was paved with planks and roundwood, ran close to the remarkable concentration of bog bodies (12, 16 and 18a-b) found in the Ter Haarster bog (Fig. 82). Body 16, which has been dated to 2025 ± 65 BP, lay closest to the trackway. As already mentioned above, bodies 18a and 18b date from the same or a slightly later period. The date obtained for the trackway after calibration of the C14 date of 2295 ± 50 BP shows that there cannot be any connection between the bog bodies and the *Valtherbrug* (Fig. 83); at the time when the bodies were deposited in the bog the trackway must already have been covered with peat.

Interpretation

There are clear similarities between the bog bodies of the Netherlands that have been described above and bog corpses that have been found in the neighbouring countries Germany and Denmark. These similarities concern the positive indications of violent death (the result of hanging, strangling, stabbing or beating) observed in a number of cases; the (partly) shaven heads of some of the bodies; the fact that several of the bodies were found naked, while others were accompanied by clothing (though only a small minority was found actually wearing any); and the fact that some of the bodies had been covered with branches or pegged down with stakes. The Dutch bog body population clearly fits in the bog body population of northwest Europe as a whole.

It is virtually impossible to estimate the original size of the Dutch bog-body population. We now know of 45 bodies that were deposited in the raised bogs and fen peat in the northern part of the Netherlands in the period before the Middle Ages; we may safely assume that there were in fact many more. Peat cutting started long before 1791, the year when the Kibbelgaarn body was found, and we know nothing about any discoveries that will undoubtedly have been made in those early days. There is no mention whatsoever of any bog bodies in the literature of those times. There were no museums until that at Friesland was established in 1846, that at Drenthe in 1854 and

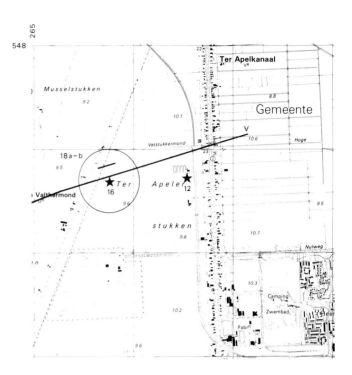

Fig. 82 Concentration of bog bodies found in the Ter Haarster bog; V = *Valtherbrug*; bog bodies 18a and 18b were found in the encircled area.

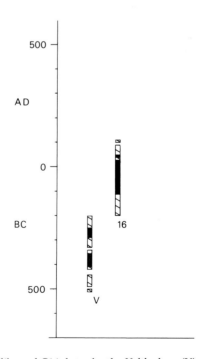

Fig. 83 Calibrated C14 dates for the *Valtherbrug* (V) and one of the bog bodies found near it (cat. no. 16). See Fig. 70 for a further explanation.

that at Groningen in 1874, and virtually no regional papers that could have reported any discoveries; the first newspaper in Groningen was published in 1743, that in Friesland in 1752 and that in Drenthe in 1823. Of course, we have no idea how many discoveries were never reported, but we may assume that several dozen bodies have disappeared without any record. This means that the distribution pattern as we know it today is seriously distorted; the areas where peat was cut first are 'empty' whereas those which were exploited at the end of the nineteenth and in the twentieth century show numerous findspots, for instance, the part of Bourtanger Moor that lies in the south-eastern part of Drenthe.

Other Finds Recovered from the Bogs

'... that this district was peculiarly close to heaven and that nowhere did the gods give more immediate audience to human prayer.' (Tacitus, *Annals* XIII–XVI, 57; tr. J. Jackson)

Bog bodies are not the only remarkable finds that have come to light in the large raised bogs and cauldron bogs in the northern part of the Netherlands. The peat-cutting activities in these areas have yielded an impressive list of objects of archaeological interest. With the exception of the bog trackways and the wooden 'temple' of Barger-Oosterveld, most of these objects are relatively small, isolated finds. Exactly how many objects have been found over the past centuries in turf cutting and dredging activities is difficult to say – once again the evidence presents a distorted picture – but they must have totalled several hundreds, at the very least. The finds recovered from the Dutch bogs have not all been preserved. The majority of those that were kept are now in the possession of the Drents Museum; their dates vary from the Neolithic to the Middle Ages.

The objects are made of wood (containers, wheels, wheel hubs, axe shafts, a 'fish swatter', a bow, ard shares), leather (shoes, a cape, a pouch), horn (a comb), wool (balls of worsted, clothing), earthenware (pots), stone (querns, whetstones, hammers), flint (axes, daggers, sickles), bronze (daggers, swords, spearheads, axes, neck-rings, bracelets, brooches), silver (coins), gold (bracelets, coins) and amber (beads). Some objects are made of several different materials, such as the string of beads from Exloo, which has beads of amber, tin and faience and a copper fastener. Two final categories of finds are cut-off human hair and animal remains (hair, antlers, horns).

This list, which is by no means complete (the finds from the bogs in the northern part of the Netherlands have never been studied systematically), shows that the majority of the finds are simple tools associated with agricultural activities, clothing, weapons and jewellery. The weapons and jewellery may be considered valuable because mostly they are made of materials that had to be imported from other regions, either because they were not available locally (copper, tin, gold) or because the quality of the available material was not good enough (flint). The gold and silver Roman and Early Medieval coins are also imports.

The odd object may of course have ended up in the peat by accident but most were without doubt deposited there deliberately. Similarly practices have also been attested in, for example, north Germany and Denmark, although the value of the finds recovered from these areas differs considerably, those from Denmark being by far the more precious. The most likely explanation for these objects is that they are votive offerings: gifts deposited by individuals or groups of people to implore the help of supernatural powers or to express their gratitude for services rendered. Similar votive gifts are known from areas further south too. In a recent study, Roymans discusses the votive offerings from the sanctuaries datable to the Late Iron Age and the early part of the Roman period in northern Gaul. The categories of finds he mentions are the same as those that have been recovered from the bogs in the north: parts of wagons, harvesting and other agricultural tools, jewellery (brooches, torcs, bracelets), weapons (spearheads, swords), coins, pottery and animal bones (Roymans 1990, 62 ff).

The objects that have been found in the Dutch large raised bogs and cauldron bogs indicate that these peculiar environments must have been regarded as liminal places – places where people could communicate directly with the supernatural world (Wait 1985, 3). The same holds for river valleys, which have also yielded many remarkable finds such as stone and bronze axes, bronze spearheads, bracelets, brooches, loose coins and hoards of coins. Like the bog finds, these 'river finds' also reflect supra-regional, European practices (Torbrügge 1970–71; Fitzpatrick 1984).

The Bog Bodies in Relation to Other Bog Finds

Seen in the context described above, the bog bodies could also be interpreted as votive offerings. It is very unlikely that such sacred environments were used for the simple dumping of undesirable social elements, as Munksgaard (1984) has suggested. The obvious question then is: Who were these people who were sacrificed in the Dutch bogs and river valleys? This question can hardly be answered in any detail. In principle, both foreigners and locals may have been sacrificed. The available information shows that it was mostly men who were sacrificed; women and children were selected less often. The victims were killed by hanging, strangulation, stabbing or possibly even blows on the head. Very little can be said about the social status of the victims. The bodies are too poorly preserved to allow any conclusion to be drawn from groomed hands and nails and noble features, if such characteristics are considered criteria at all. The clothing of the man whose body was found at Emmer-Erfscheidenveen (33), a handsome cap and an undergarment of fine wool with a beautifully embroidered hem (Fig. 84; Groenman van Waateringe 1990; Vons-Comis 1990), appears to be rather unusual and could possibly indicate that the man held a high social position in life. But unfortunately we have no material for comparison to confirm this – Bronze Age clothing is extremely rare in the Netherlands.

Three of the Dutch bodies show signs of more or less serious physical abnormalities (19, 27 and 35), however, the quality of the data does not permit us to conclude that such deviations were used as a criterion in the selection of sacrifices.

The way in which the two men whose remains were found at Weerdinge (21a-b) had been deposited in the peat – the arm of one extended affectionately behind the other's back – makes it hard to believe that they are *corpore infames* (cf. Tacitus' *Germania* 12,1). Their social position and their relationship (were they brothers, father and son or two members of the same age group?) will always be a mystery.

Then there is the paper body whose hair was tied in a Swabian knot (11). Tacitus gives a detailed description of this particular knot in *Germania*: ' ... this distinguishes the Suebi from other Germans, and the free-born of the Suebi from the slave. In other tribes, whether from some relationship to the Suebi, or, as often happens, from imitation, the same thing may be found, but it is rare and confined to the period of youth.' (Tacitus, *Germania*, ch. 38; trans. M. Hutton, Loeb Classical Library.) As the findspot Hooghalen lay outside the territory of the Suebi we may not infer from this that the above body is that of a person of high social status. It may equally well be the body of a prisoner of war.

The fact that the hair of some of the bog bodies had been cut on one side of the head may indicate that in some cases individuals who had violated the rules and regulations of their society were chosen as human sacrifices. A good example is the Yde girl (19). It cannot be purely accidental that the tunic found with her was of poor quality and showed several darned worn patches.

Equally difficult to answer is the question as to the occasion on which these sacrifices were made. It has already been mentioned that some of the other bog finds are associated with agriculture and stock-breeding. Maybe the human sacrifices were deposited in the bogs for the same purpose as some of the other finds, namely to implore agricultural success. In those rare cases in which there are indications of the season of death it seems that the individuals in question met their death before the winter. This means that the theory of a spring rite, as Glob has suggested for Denmark, does not hold for (at least some of) the Dutch bog bodies. We have far too little empirical evidence to decide whether the human sacrifices discussed here were made during cyclic (calendar) rites or whether they are to be seen as *ad hoc* sacrifices, made during rites held in times of crisis.

Another question concerns the socio-political level at which the sacrifices were made. Elsewhere this author has argued that the map showing the distribution of the bog bodies from the 'peak' period (Fig. 85) does not suggest that the sacrifices were made at a tribal level. It would seem that decisions regarding life and death were taken at a much lower – settlement – level. Other scholars who have concentrated on different regions have come to similar conclusions (Jankuhn 1967, 134).

If we take a look at the distribution of the bodies through time we arrive at the following conclusions (cf. Fig. 79):

> Neolithic bodies, which have come to light in Denmark, have not been found in the Netherlands so far.
> The oldest bog body dates from the (Middle) Bronze Age.
> Bog bodies datable to the period from the Middle Bronze Age to the end of the Middle Iron Age are relatively rare.
> Most of the bog bodies date from the last century BC and the first centuries AD.

The cause of this sudden peak is not clear. Most probably it is connected with increased social unrest but the nature of this unrest eludes us completely. We have no evidence of any links with other remarkable contemporary devel-

Fig. 84 The Emmer-Erfscheidenveen bog body was accompanied by several garments: a) a shoe; b) a calf(?)skin cape; c) parts of a woollen undergarment; d) a sheepskin cap; e) how some of these garments were worn. (*Drents Museum*)

a

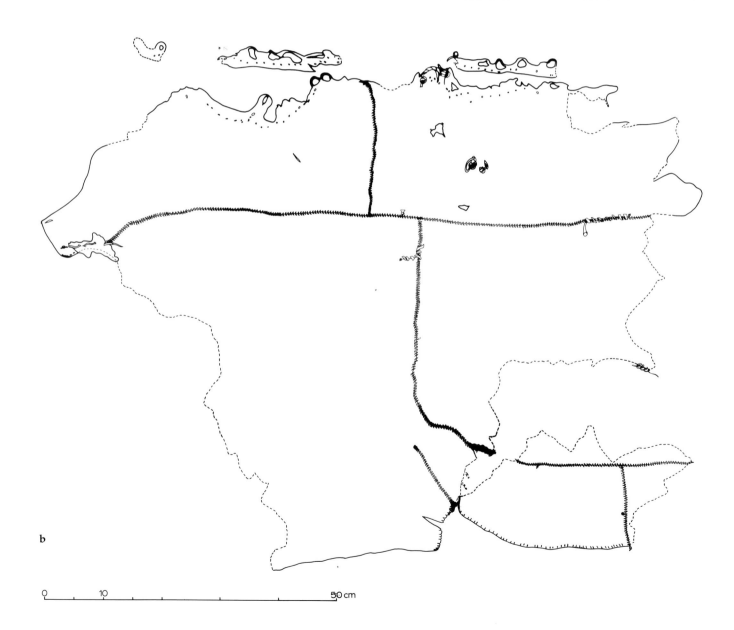

b

0   10   50 cm

c

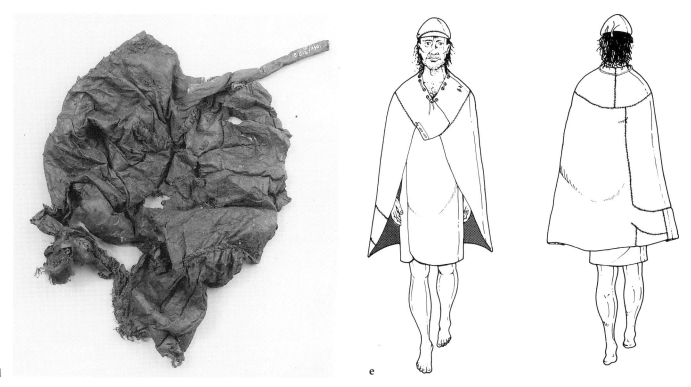

d

e

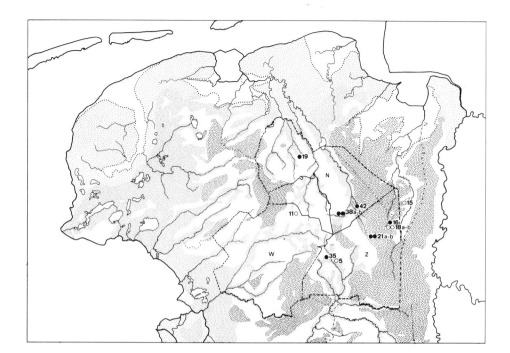

Fig. 85 Distribution of the Dutch bog bodies from the 'peak' period (LIA/RP). The open circles indicate paper bodies.

opments in the northern part of the Netherlands, such as the coming into existence of the so-called fortified settlements, which, as Waterbolk (1977, 168) has suggested, may also have served a religious purpose.

From written sources we know that the custom of sacrificing human beings in watery contexts did not die out in the Roman period in the northern half of the Netherlands. Human sacrifices were still being made in the Early Middle Ages. However, by then the socio–political organisation had changed considerably; a kingdom had been formed. Moreover, the sacrifices were no longer made in bogs but on the beach. This we know from the *Vita Wulframni*, a ninth-century text which describes the life of the seventh-century bishop Wulfram. In it we read about the bishop's experiences in the kingdom of 'Fresia' during the reign of King Radbod (Halbertsma 1984; Halbertsma 1989). The Frisian kingdom extended from the Zwin to the river Weser. When Wulfram visited the kingdom, presumably shortly before AD 690, for the purpose of converting the heathen population, he saved the lives of two children who had been appointed by lot to be sacrificed. This most probably took place in the region that is now referred to as West Friesland, in the province of North Holland. Eurinus and Ingomarus, aged five and seven, respectively, had already been bound to a stake on the beach, where they were to be engulfed by the sea. Wulfram asked King Radbod, who was also present at the ceremony, whether he considered this a proper act. The Frisian king answered that the well-being of his people

depended on this kind of sacrifice. However, he was prepared to release the children on the condition that Wulfram would perform a miracle. The king got his miracle and the children escaped sacrifice. But there was no longer any place for them in the Frisian society and so they accompanied the bishop on his journey back to France.

Finally, I would like to return to the ten Late Medieval and post-Medieval bog bodies that have been found in the north of the Netherlands (Cat. Nos. 9a-b, 13, 17, 20a-d, 26, 28). The remains of only four of these bodies have been preserved (Wijster, 20a-d); the others are paper bodies. In so far as the scarce data allow interpretation, these relatively young bodies appear to be either victims of murder and violent attacks or 'normally' buried bodies. They have nothing whatsoever to do with human sacrifices.

Future Research

Bog body research on the continent is not the most inviting of archaeological topics. It is quite probable that no new discoveries will be made in the future, but if so they will almost certainly be made by chance. Therefore, one has to concentrate on the old, now dried-out finds and the (sometimes unbelievable) reports of bog bodies in the paper record. There is, however, still considerable progress to be made.

A very important first step would be to compile reliable gazetteers of the bog bodies found in Germany and Denmark. Dieck's catalogues cannot be taken at face value, but must be reconsidered in a critical way (van der Sanden 1993). A German archaeologist has recently come to the same conclusion (Eisenbeiss 1992). A systematic search in local and regional archives will undoubtedly lead to the discovery of, as yet, unknown bog bodies. The final gazetteers will indicate the reliability of the information available for different groups within these extensive numbers of discoveries. In Germany, a beginning has been made (Eisenbeiss 1992).

The most reliable group – those bog bodies of which remains are kept in museum stores and displays – need to be analysed in a systematic way. Despite the problems encountered elsewhere, this means radiocarbon dating those bodies for which dates are not available, namely most of the Danish finds and all of the German ones. For the German bog bodies – most of which have only a vague date derived from pollen analysis – a radiocarbon dating programme has been initiated. Accelerator dates will be available in 1995 (van der Sanden, in preparation). Other lines of research regarding this group include the analysis of age, sex, trauma, pathology, treatment of the hair and fingernails, stomach contents and biochemical changes, using the latest scientific methods. Only then will different trends emerge which can be compared with the findings from bog bodies in the Netherlands, from Lindow Moss and examples from Ireland.

Well-preserved human bodies are only a part of the archaeological evidence from peat bogs. They should not be treated in isolation from the wide range of other wetland finds. The distribution of the occurrence of bog bodies needs to be compared, both in time and space, with this much larger range of material. Danish archaeologists have always paid a lot of attention to these other bog finds, but Germany and certainly the Netherlands lag far behind. Recently, the Drents Museum has begun to create an inventory of all wetland finds from the northern part of the Netherlands.

It is not before we have re-evaluated the sources and explored the contexts, that we can hope to gain further understanding of the bog-body phenomenon in continental Europe.

PART III

The Meaning and Myth of Bog Bodies

Did They Fall or Were They Pushed? Some Unresolved Questions about Bog Bodies

C. S. Briggs

Introduction

The history of curiosity as to how artefacts or bodies came to be preserved in bogs has a long pedigree in north-west Europe going back to at least as early as the seventeenth century. Great interest is aroused when bodies can be shown to have been damaged, particularly with wounds to the neck or scalp. Over the past half century it has become commonplace to regard this as deliberate, even sadistic injury, connected with dumping bodies in 'watery places'. This ritual interpretation appears to have been a brainchild of J. J. A. Worsaae during the mid-nineteenth century (1842).

Through more recent systematic catalogues of German and Danish bog clothing by *inter alia* Margarethe Hald (1950; 1980) and Lisa Bender Jørgensen (1986), catalogues of human remains by Alfred Dieck (1965), and the writings of P. V. Glob (1969), both popular opinion and prehistorians have come to associate bog bodies almost exclusively with Germanic and Celtic (Iron Age) cult practices involving head worship and a reverence for water as described in classical sources. If this cultural connection is valid, it would seem reasonable to date victim deposition between, say, *c.* 300 BC and AD 400.

Not all archaeologists favour the exclusive interpretation of ritual body disposal. Dissenters have hinted at its unlikelihood on the grounds that deliberate bogside executions or burials would have been impractical and dangerous (Andersen 1984, 117; Molleson 1986). Similarly sceptical was Connolly's proposal (1985) made at the time

of the Lindow II discovery, that this bogman might have been victim to a mugging. But the idea had a poor reception; it could hardly be believed that such bizarre corporal damage might have been inflicted other than through ritual in the Iron Age (Stead *et al* 1986, 178).

Now that more is known of Lindow and of other bodies, it does seem important to review and test alternatives to the ritual killing interpretation. Could accidental death, or death by misadventure assisted by natural causes possibly leave the same gruesome 'clues'? Does the absence of diagnostic artefacts leave open questions of dating? Are those cadavers dated by radiocarbon certainly Iron Age 'killings', or could our understanding of both date and disposal method be seriously flawed by shortcomings in the application of scientific method and of deductive logic to bogs and human behaviour? There can be no easy answers.

Many individuals have been found naked without even detached clothing, ornament or artefact indicative of date. This further adds to the mystery surrounding preserved bodies. Unassociated bog clothes and shoes can survive but are often datable only on stylistic grounds. They could have clad those unfortunates whose bodies dissolved, or whose feet wriggled free of footwear during an escape.

In recent years forensic studies have focused upon detailed pathological aspects of bog corpses (for example, Andersen *et al* 1984; Brothwell *et al* 1990; Stead *et al* 1986; van der Sanden 1990). Although these may answer questions about the state of corpses as discovered, despite some confident diagnoses of pre-mortem injury, it remains unclear how far forensic science is capable of determining precisely how, or why, or even when, the bodies came to be immersed in quagmires.

Because of the high profile, Glob in particular afforded his well-preserved antecedents – until *Lindow Man* was published in 1986, Danish archaeology appeared to possess a phenomenon which had become almost emblematic of its own antiquarian nationhood. The Lindow discoveries evoked a British reaction anxious to possess and share similarly sensational discoveries. They also provoked assertion of a contemporary excellence in British forensic archaeology. Through these reactions it was possible to detect hints of national competition. Sadly, an initial claim that Lindow II was the 'finding in Britain of the first prehistoric "bog body"' (Stead and Turner 1985, 25) merely emphasised British–Irish neglect and misunderstanding of this archaeological curiosity.

Ritual Deposition or Selective Preservation in 'Watery Places'?

Interpretation of the Lindow discoveries underlines several features in common among European bog bodies, particularly pre-immersion strangulation or garrotting and beheading. These comprise integral components of the Iron Age 'watery places' depositional ritual theory (Stead *et al* 1986, 186; Turner, pp. 108–22). Despite this common interpretation pertaining to a widespread if not diverse type of discovery, cogent objections beset the belief that most artefact discoveries from 'watery places' must be almost exclusively interpreted as 'ritual depositions' (Bradley 1990). It now seems important to list these objections.

In a sense, metal, particularly thin metal, may be considered similar to flesh in that anaerobic conditions are thought important for its preservation, although Painter (pp. 88–99) demonstrates the necessity of a *Sphagnum* decay product for the longevity of flesh. Metal deteriorates by electrolysis, oxidation, carbonisation or even sulphurisation, combined to a greater or lesser degree with bacterial action when deposited in aerated soils above the water table. Decay can be arrested completely or slowed down in an artefact only in conditions where a watery medium completely covered it *at the time of deposition, or where submersion occurred rapidly thereafter, and where water has remained continuously ever since.*

The current fashion ascribing virtually all bog finds to votive or ritual deposition fails to acknowledge that in spite of deposition in corrosive organic soils, metal hoards can and do survive in some numbers from non-watery depositions (for example Burgess and Coombs 1979, *passim*). On occasion, hoards (Briggs 1987, 186–7) as well as single finds originally buried in or upon agricultural soils subsequently overtaken by peat, can also survive (Briggs 1985). Although in Britain and Ireland the recorded incidence of Late Bronze Age bucket and cauldron, shield and trumpet finds is certainly greatest in bogs, fine sheet metalwork was also deliberately deposited in non-anaerobic conditions. Claims for the virtually exclusive deposition of 'status goods' in 'watery places' are therefore difficult to uphold.

Although references have been made to 'votive' sacrifices of prehistoric artefacts from bogs, particularly from those bogs which hosted bodies (for example by Glob 1969, 26), with two or three exceptions, datable artefacts are noticeably absent from bog bodies. Although several hundred bodies are now known, none has yet been found associated with diagnostically Bronze Age or Iron Age artefacts. Indeed, there exists no firm evidence to connect the iron object found in Somerset with either discovery or deposition of any bodies from Lindow (cf. Stead in Budworth *et al* 1986, 39; Fig. 13.2, 40). It is not demonstrably prehistoric and may even be of recent date.

To impute a motivation of ritual deposition, purely on the grounds that artefacts and bodies happen to be well preserved in bogs or anaerobic soils, is therefore to create circularity of argument by hindsight.

Bodies and Bog Growth

Many of the north-European bodies were said to have been placed in convenient old peat cuttings or within prepared holes also in working fuel bogs. For the theory of Iron Age ritual deposition to be valid it is necessary to postulate widespread peat-cutting during the later prehistoric period. Although it is indisputable that 'cutting peat for fuel has gone on in Danish bogs for over 2,000 years' (Glob 1969, 65), as incontrovertible evidence exists of its small-scale use in the Iron Age (Becker 1948) and of its industrial use in the English Fenland during Roman times (Silvester 1991), its widespread establishment for large-scale domestic and industrial exploitation in Denmark (Rasmussen 1970, 200) and elsewhere in Europe, tended to come much later. Darby and Godwin considered that the growth period in organised peat cutting came after *c*. AD 1100 (Godwin 1978, 114–15). In any case it requires very much more evidence than has so far been published, to substantiate the argument that whilst Danish Iron Age man created extensive peat cuttings at a time of probable climatic desiccation, it remained possible to accommodate contemporary bodies within strata which, because of prevailing conditions, seem unlikely to have been particularly wet until a later phase of climate history.

Another depositional interpretation suggests that ritual demanded somehow casting off bodies into quagmires. Perhaps realising how difficult this might have been and appreciating the climatic problems of maintaining a constantly high water table for anaerobia, Liversage (1985) forwards an alternative to quagmire deposition; that assured body preservation could have been achieved in graves emplaced or dug within contemporary Iron Age peat cuttings or bog surfaces with peat deliberately piled above them. Of course, this almost assumes the body to have been buried by people who anticipated body preservation, or who may have had some motive for ensuring evidence of their (alleged) dastardly ritual be preserved.

It is possible, nevertheless, that peat may have been heaped over interments, if only of necessity to prevent the escape of unpleasant odours from decomposition. However, it is difficult to find evidence for such a practice from the extensive repertory of body finds. In any event, Liversage's suggestion rather falls short because it is improbable that graves dug into relatively firm peat would have remained perpetually immersed. Also important are questions concerning mire morphology and the stratigraphic integrity of the deposit when later drained to shrink or waste (Godwin 1978, 124–33).

Flesh putrefies when constant immersion is not maintained. Carrion-eating organisms in aerobic surface parts of a bog then 'attack the body and consume important parts of it within a very short time' (Andersen *et al* 1984, 117). The body therefore has to sink quickly or be buried well below the effects of seasonal changes in water table. For these and other reasons, the Borremose girl probably soon lay 'in the mud at the bottom of a pond or bog hole' (idem).

Because the conditions demanded for survival of a complete body are so well-defined, these need reviewing, first in terms of the conditions which obtained at the time bodies were supposedly deposited – during the Iron Age and Romano-British period – and then in terms of the bog's potential powers of preservation at later dates.

Mire Types

It is first worth considering briefly what type of mire or pool is represented by the Lindow II section (Stead *et al.* Fig. 41, 80). As the literature on mire types is extensive (for example Hammond 1981, 8–15 and references), it seems unnecessary to provide technical detail of the climatic and geomorphic conditions favourable to such variety of potential drowning places. However, Hammond's *Scheme of hydroseres in stages of bog development* (Fig. 5) illustrates some general principles and indicates bog water-holding potential. Although simplified, a comprehensive series showing more diverse and widespread bog surface areas is illustrated by Bellamy (1986, 56). Both authorities indicate how many mire types could satisfy the necessary conditions for body preservation, given *Sphagnum* tanning and anaerobia.

Some bogs grow massive and unstable; within particularly large mires there may be convection of liquid peat. As bogs grow older and dry out through climatic change or drainage, overall contraction creates movement. Similarly, through continuously taking in water some bogs grow within topographical confines until forced to move or explode as 'bog flows' (discussed already in the context of bog bodies (Briggs 1986, 153)).

Unfortunately for body preservation, in the short term the most watery parts of mires are probably those least capable of long-term geomorphic stability. The more obvious consequences of mire desiccation and hydraulic expansion are probably slumping, sediment mixing and a general destruction of stratigraphic integrity. Because of wastage and peat cutting, the upper half of most bog body stories – the half which could best help us to understand surface morphology at the time the body descended or was forced through it – is almost certain to be missing. Full scientific recognition or recording of original surface morphology therefore tends to be unusual, though it survived at Lindow (see Branch and Scaife, pp. 19–30). Nevertheless, stratigraphic interpretations may be difficult if not potentially controversial.

Prior to the introduction of radiocarbon dating it was widely believed that the key to chronologies for both bog bodies and artefacts was through palynology. Certainly, characterisation of vegetation deposits from beneath a bog body can offer potential advantage. In the absence of any other method it could provide accurate *termini ante quem* for artefact or body deposition. As appreciated by Gowlett *et al* (1989) peat 'samples taken in contact with the body date the pieces of peat which happened to end up against it'. However, they felt this did not preclude the possibility that peat may have actually grown around the body (idem. 75). Although there is the possibility of peat growth around a preserved body, the existence of growing (aerobic) plants close to it when anaerobia was important to the preservation process, signals the relative improbability that peat ever grew around bodies subsequently found preserved in peat.

In reconsidering these problems, an important question which must be posed of Lindow II, is: Can we be certain from its place in the bog stratigraphy that interment in Iron Age peat would have guaranteed the body's preservation? To attempt an answer we must turn to the two original palaeoecological investigations of Lindow. In their report on the peat stratigraphy of Lindow II, Oldfield *et al* lamented that 'by the time detailed stratigraphic investigations were possible, the body had been removed from the section and the envelope of peat both depleted and disturbed'. They regretted the impossibility of being able to state categorically, 'from the stratigraphic evidence alone, that the emplacement of the body was not accompanied by some displacement of overlying peat or some sinking within the loose infill of the pool' (1986, 85). In his detailed peat report, Barber, on the other hand, concluded discussion of the Lindow II plant macrofossil analysis assuming the moment of death to have been coincident with the level in which the man was found (1986, 89).

It is therefore important to reconsider what types of sediment surrounded the body in order to establish their implications for contemporary fen hydrology and historic development of bog morphology.

When found, the Lindow II body was lying partially within *Eriophorum* peat, spanning a stratum of pool mud above it, and partially covered by fresh *Sphagnum* peat, though lying in a posture suggesting the possibility of ingress through an overlying layer of humified *Eriophorum/Calluna* peat with some *Sphagnum* (Stead *et al*, Fig. 41, 80). Due to the density of the lowest layer it is unlikely that the body could have sunk further into the lowest of these layers at any time. Apparently this deposit had been formed at some time during the later centuries before Christ, and in it pools might have formed up to 20 cm deep. It is not so easy to interpret and date the lacustrine silt, but this seems to have formed at the base of an algal pool in conjunction with the overlying *Sphagnum*. Barber felt it likely that this pool would have been at least knee deep when the body entered it. But it seems unlikely that we should be talking of dependence upon 'how far

Lindow Man's body sank into the soft peat ... [covering him in] ... a wet blanket of *Sphagna* within a few years' (Barber 1986, 89), since no body is likely to have survived intact over a matter of years under the shallow water conditions implied by this slow process.

On the face of it, this shallow pool may appear a plausible drowning place until it is appreciated that its location was over 200 m from the southern edge of a massive raised bog (Turner 1986, Fig. 2), and that its approach must have posed considerable risk for all concerned.

The depth or height of the surrounding bog during, say, the Iron Age, or even in Medieval or later times, is of interest here. In the mid-1980s, workmen digging peat at Lindow recalled that the bog was domed centrally as late as the 1960s. Although former depths for the algae pool and its surrounding peat can only be estimated, an expansion in depth by factors of two or three may be conjectured from the remaining metre or so of the *Sphagnum* deposit. But obviously an unknown amount of surface stratum is now lost through peat cutting or wastage. This particular pool must have been reasonably deep at the time the body came to rest on the bottom, since its base always remains beyond the reach of any water convection currents carrying bacteria harmful to its preservation.

Unfortunately, although there are radiocarbon dates and pollen analyses, they are of limited value in reconstructing the pool's morphological development. Because *Sphagnum*–algal pool formation is anomalous to maintaining any integrity of bog stratigraphy, these data are likely to be of limited assistance and, due to the admixture of deposit types, scientific analyses may actually mislead stratigraphic interpretation. Although radiocarbon dates were obtained from four sampling spots connected with the body, giving dates between 400 and 200 BC (Ambers *et al* 1986; Otlet *et al* 1986), the peat section above remains undated and its sequence in terms of the pool's history can only be conjectured.

We are now considering a stratigraphic succession in which Lindow II must have been inserted at a point in the Iron Age or later. But if Lindow Man had entered the peat stratigraphy in Iron Age times and national climatic trends were to be anticipated, the stratigraphy immediately above him would have formed after interment relatively slowly, during a dry period of forest clearance and agriculture (cf. Turner 1981, 261). The pollen analytical evidence from the initial investigation at Lindow only permitted discussion of the pool (which may well have had exclusively local origins), in terms of mire development and later stabilisation (Barber 1986, 89), rather than in more general climatic terms.

Here it must be asked what mechanism might successfully preserve a body in but a few centimetres of mud *before* drier Iron Age conditions set in, during times which would hardly have been suited to lasting preservation had the body been interred during the earlier part of that period. Clearly, interment into Iron Age peat during the Iron Age would have been difficult since insufficient depth would have existed for permanent waterlogging at that time and the ideal preservation conditions created by the later pool could not have then existed.

To summarise: although some have suggested that Lindow II could have survived as a well-preserved body sacrificed and submerged only in a pool of surface water (Connolly *et al* 1986, 72), a re-interpretation of the Lindow peat section prompts the suggestion that a reasonable depth of *Sphagnum* pool would be required for the body to have survived intact in that particular deposit. Development of deep pools within the mire through concentration of impeded groundwater could readily have accounted for some local mixing of earlier with later peat strata, and thus account for Iron Age radiocarbon dates from both above and below the body's resting place (cf. Buckland, pp. 47–50).

Because quite a depth of peat would be required for pool formation, it becomes difficult to escape the conclusion that Lindow II entered the Iron Age peat stratum and pool mud at a later date, only *after* the pool above had attained considerable depth. This is more consistent with earlier deductions about the body's dating relative to the peat (Otlet *et al* 1986, 30), though the contributors to Stead *et al* did not consider the geomorphic or dating implications posed by the existence of this *Sphagnum* pool.

This re-interpretation seems to point to environmental and geomorphic processes within the bog not yet properly investigated or understood, and it suggests that further radiocarbon samples might have better assisted interpretation of pool formation and dessication.

With odd exceptions, it has been found impossible to apply palaeobotany to the environments of the bog people on a scale greater than the micro or macro because so often so much of the bog has been cut away. As a general observation, it is, however, curious that no stratigraphies from around bog bodies are published showing cross-sections of the flooded cuttings or sodden holes in which the bodies are alleged to have been placed. How far it is realistic to postulate successful ritual interment of

Lindow II in this topographical situation at the base of a post-Iron Age pool, and how much more likely it is that someone accidentally fell in at a later date and was unable either to climb out or attract sufficient attention to be pulled out is now a matter of speculation.

The Problems of Radiocarbon Dating

Although production of single dates for bog-finds of the 1950s and later in multiples seemed to confirm all that was believed of supposed exclusively Iron Age ritual finds, bog bodies never lent themselves easily to the radiocarbon method. The problem of dating the bodies rather than the surrounding bog is well recognised (Bowman 1990, 52). Basic difficulties of principle were articulated by Tauber (1978, 78) when reviewing 14 dates for the best-known Danish finds in 1979:

> Accurate C14 dates of samples can only be obtained if the original carbon compounds of the sample material can be isolated and purified prior to dating. In contrast to cellulose and lignin of common plant materials, which are rather resistant to chemical reactions, proteins of animal and human tissues may react chemically with humic matter and other components in bog deposits. Moreover, during the usual purification procedure proteins gradually become hydrolysed and are transformed into water soluble amino-acids. Purification and isolation of the original carbon compounds in tissues deposited in bog deposits therefore pose serious problems.

Despite the passage of much time and gathering of experience these difficulties remain strong challenges for scientific evaluation. Also the questions remain: Are the biochemical effects of humic acid upon flesh and bone yet understood sufficiently well for there to be certainty of isolating *any* original carbon compounds from the contaminated corpse with confidence? Or can animal proteins suffer such total biochemical change that mineral compounds could take on the imprint of their immersion medium?

The original mean for radiocarbon dates of Lindow II was between AD 410 and AD 560 (Otlet *et al* 1986, 30), though some individual dates produced ranges extending into the first or second centuries BC.

Cultural problems posed by these inconsistencies were largely overlooked at the time of the first Lindow finds but have since been discussed in detail by Gowlett *et al* (1989; cf. Brindley and Lanting, pp. 133–6). Gowlett *et al* posed the central question of Lindow II: 'Should we dismiss the radiocarbon dates on the body altogether, and turn to other dating evidence – albeit indirect?' What emerged from Gowlett's team's thorough interrogation was an admission that soft tissue (the least well preserved) may have been contaminated, possibly by amino acids from the peat (1989, 72, 77). They go on to suggest the possibility that 'carbon atoms derived from the groundwater' may have been added to the biological sample. 'Potentially contaminating carbon will give a wrong date to the sample if it is of a significantly different radiocarbon age. In this case our results on different fractions suggest that the difference in age is relatively small (compare humic dates, and especially stomach contents and the stomach humics), and that such contamination is likely to make the date for the body too old rather than too young.'

Clearly controlled experimental data are required and, in the absence of comparable published evidence from recently buried bodies, we must return to the principles of Ellerman and steep animal flesh in humic peat. This should provide some idea of the rates at which atomic invasion can take place. It would indeed be strange were it to be demonstrable that flesh mineralises rapidly and its chemical content disappears completely, thereby assuming the atomic composition of the host media. Yet the absence of DNA from bog bodies (Hughes and Jones 1986) might hint that complete atomic replacement is a viable explanation. Such mineralisation could explain Neolithic radiocarbon determinations for bodies at one time thought to be Iron Age (Bennike *et al* 1988), and the Iron Age dates for some bodies thought to have been losses of nineteenth-century personalities (like Red Christian; see below and Turner, pp. 188–204).

Experimental work also needs to be undertaken immersing skin artefacts in order to help to corroborate tissue dates to support the cultural integrity of Iron Age radiocarbon dates for bodies like Derrykeighan Man (Petrie 1839; Briggs 1986; Ó Floinn 1989).

The Forensic Evidence

Although some were 'perfectly preserved', most European bog people were disinterred in a mutilated state. Damaged bodies have been interpreted almost universally as victims of violence which helped them to a watery grave (Glob 1969, *passim*). Close pathological examination of Lindow II showed him to have been so badly damaged by his alleged aggressors that even those convinced of ritual were puzzled by what seemed to amount to overkill.

At the time of discovery, the emphasis of possible injury or torture to the living tended to exclude consideration of the potential for extensive damage post-mortem.

For it to be possible to answer the more fundamental questions which may assist in distinguishing between accidental death and intentional killing, particular limbs and organs must be sufficiently well preserved for disinterested forensic examination to provide unambiguous evidence. Such questions are obviously concerned about establishing whether or not the victim expired before reaching the bog, through immediate drowning once immersed in it, or through heart attack, stroke or long exposure prior to complete immersion. Other injuries caused by 'warding off', on the one hand, or occasioned by an exhausting struggle to climb out, on the other, together with clear recognition of deliberate wounding, are obvious prerequisites if evidence is to be interrogated unequivocally.

Although mutilation is usually interpreted as deliberate wounding, it is rarely possible at considerable remove from the date of deposition to ascertain whether or not injury was occasioned before interment, or as the result of post-mortem activity. What should not be forgotten is that injuries could be incurred even in frustrated rescue attempts on weakened, dead or even mineralised bodies, and that the shapes of known bog bodies are likely to result from some degree of pressure beneath peat overburden.

Few bog bodies have been examined upon their discovery in recent times by forensic scientists experienced in both the pathology of violence and peat bog morphology. Unfortunately, it is now usually too late to subject the classic Danish finds to detailed re-examination because many or most of the internal organs were either removed to help preserve the cadaver for display, or they were subjected to destructive experimental pre-treatments prior to radiocarbon assay. This makes it impossible to address some of the most important pathological questions such as whether or not the lungs contained algae, growing vegetable matter, brackish deposits or mature peat sediment.

Re-examining the third Borremose find (a girl) during the early 1980s, pathologists sought and found tiny blood cells from the choroid and argued that it 'certainly deserve[d] to be considered whether they might be the shrunken remains of burst blood cells' (Andersen *et al* 1984, 115, 118). Experiment and reflection upon the total results seemed more to indicate 'that ... severe cranial injury occurred after death' (idem, 115, 118). Because of her exceptionally well-preserved skin, it was felt that she could scarcely have been exposed to brute force, particularly from beating with sticks, since these would have left marks on the back of the hands and forearms (idem, 118–19). This writer interprets Andersen's meticulous report to indicate that the absence of burst blood cells might reasonably be taken to indicate that the body's unnecessarily grotesque injuries most probably resulted from much later, accidental disturbance, while the cadaver lay in the bog.

However, Brothwell *et al* (1990, 174) rejected Andersen's suggestion of the probability that the apparent scalping of the Borremose girl may have been a peat-digging accident, because at the time of discovery 'a piece of scalp the size of a hand lay underneath the body'. Although citing an 'original report in [the] National Museum', no indication is given of who wrote it or what became of this vital evidence (the scalp). Neither is it explained why such evidence was omitted from the first published report. Explanation of the omission could be due to the finders' knowledge of how it came to be detached.

Further, an absence of facial blood is dismissed as merely 'negative evidence', and it is argued that: 'On the whole it seems doubtful whether a great deal should be concluded from the multiple facial injuries. It is not particulary likely that the executioners were closely observant of the exact moment of clinical death. After all, a little extra beating is only being thorough, and there may have been standers by who wanted a turn' (Brothwell *et al* 1990, 175).

Curiously, before the Iron Age ritual idea had really caught on, when, in 1913, the Vester Thorsted bog man was found clad in a leather jacket lying beneath a large branch, it was felt 'impossible to determine whether the man … died a natural death; but there [was] nothing to indicate with certainty that he [had] been subjected to violence' (Andersen *et al* 1984, 116). Even more interesting was the contemporary view that this and similar bogmen were not 'members of respectable society' … but probably represented gypsies of the sixteenth or seventeenth centuries. The possibility that Vester Thorsted man had been a certain labourer who disappeared in 1860 was felt unlikely because his patched hide jacket seemed not to reflect such recent times. This discovery stimulated the forensic pathologist Vilhelm Ellerman to conduct the first of several experiments designed to help explain how human skin might be preserved in peat (Ellerman 1916). It was Ellerman who first established that raised *Sphagnum* acid bog was required for tanning and preserving bodies;

also important was his discovery of the great rapidity with which bone decalcification could occur.

The Death of Lindow Man

How far did the Lindow II forensic investigations establish conclusively that all the damage was ante rather than post-mortem? At the time of investigation scholars felt confident that distinctions could clearly be drawn on a body in this condition (Bourke 1986; Connolly 1986; West 1986). The extremely comprehensive catalogue of injuries with which Lindow Man arrived in the laboratory have already been well described and need not be rehearsed (West 1986, 77). However, several points remain noteworthy.

First, it was impossible to examine lungs for contents or indications of drowning, since the lungs were absent (Bourke 1986, 51). Secondly, beginning with the top of the head, it is difficult to accept confidently that the wound margins on the head were swollen ante-mortem in a body so changed as this. No blood had survived on the hair and no bruising could be detected. The signs normally anticipated and detectable from a horrific injury like this were hardly present due to earth processes acting upon the buried body. It is therefore difficult to be certain that the very slight swelling around the wound margins could not have occurred post-mortem, or indeed was not actually the result of pressure put upon the head when it became contorted during its stay in the bog. It is easy to imagine the head protruding from a *Sphagnum* pool or lying just beneath its surface and being prodded from behind by someone wielding a sharp pointed stock in an attempt to ascertain the nature of a curious, foreign body.

Turning next to the neck, West himself was sceptical about the improbably thin ligature believed to have garrotted its victim (West 1986, 78). No evidence was presented of swelling on the neck wound margins, though observations were again certainly felt to be consistent with wounding ante-mortem. But here one is struck by the sheer improbability of such a mode of death.

Deterioration of the Arms

One of the most important features which none of the original investigators were drawn to discuss at length was perhaps 'the surprisingly decomposed state of the hands and forearms' (Brothwell and Dobney 1986, 66). The left hand was entirely absent (Bourke 1986, 51), its arm generally in a worse state than the right, suggesting that 'during the period immediately after death when most of the body was immersed, the left arm may have extended beyond the pool and thus been subject to decomposition' (Connolly 1986, 58). Interestingly, this exposure appears to have lasted sufficiently long for parasitic beetles to alight on the body (Girling 1986, 91), though necrophilous fauna were not generally present (Skidmore 1986, 92).

However, in common with most other investigators, neither Girling nor Skidmore felt there was sufficient evidence to suggest the body had been exposed long before being consumed entirely by the bog. This seems strange, since no estimates are offered of how long deterioration might have taken. Yet rapid putrefaction probably claimed a hand and acted effectively on both arms. So a period of days if not weeks rather than of hours, must have been involved.

Of course, this deterioration may not have taken place initially, but might have happened when the body surfaced some time after entering the bog. This could probably be considered the less likely choice, since once impregnated with humic antiseptics, the arms would have been less attractive as carrion.

In conclusion, selective approaches to both evidence and circumstances of finding have contributed to the ready dismissal of all but ritual interpretation for many bodies. Reconsideration of forensic evidence for Lindow II and for bog bodies generally leaves many questions unanswered or even unanswerable. Interpretations of Lindow II which take into account evidence for partial exposure of the body now need to be carefully addressed.

Bodies Preserved as the Result of Accidental Death

From the reckoning of Danish ritual, Glob excepted people 'who ended their days in bog by accident, such as those who went astray in fog or rain and were drowned, one dark autumn day ... those who were murdered and hidden in bogs, away from the beaten track ... several such [were] known,' he felt, 'but by far the greatest number ... bear the stamp of sacrificial offerings' (Glob 1969, 109). That people were lost traversing British and Irish bogs in Medieval and later times through accident, misadventure or even murder (Briggs 1986, 154–6), can hardly be in question. During Medieval times considerable tracts of land were well endowed with peat cover. In poor visibility it would have been easy to stumble into one of the innumerable deep cuttings which littered contemporary peat workings (Godwin 1978, 117–23). In wet conditions these cuttings would have been deceptive and

treacherous particularly if, after harvesting 'the turf removed from the top of the bank ... [had been] ... replaced, grassy side up, in the ditch at the bottom of the bank, to preserve the moor pasture for sheep' (av Skarði 1970, 72). A similar practice, following age-old traditions, known as 'making the bearing' was adopted by workmen digging peat by machine at Lindow during the 1980s.

How possible is it that some of the apparently Iron Age bodies with neck injuries – including those from Lindow Moss – may have come to these bogs other than ritually? Scholars have not been quick to consider bog bodies as possibly resulting from natural death and communal burial practice during historic or prehistoric times. But on this subject Glob was quite firm. In his view, 'clearly ... the circumstances of the bog people's depositions show nothing in common with normal burial customs' (1969, 108). Dissidents to this view like Gebühr (1981) are all too readily dismissed. He argued that the Windeby girl (whose case was felt unexceptional) had probably been a normal burial which happened to be placed in a bog. Brothwell *et al* (1990, 173) found his argument 'novel ... but ... unconvincing' ... [one which] ... 'certainly fits the evidence for bog bodies as a whole very badly'. However, no convincing lists of criteria controverting Gebühr were presented.

Notions of recent, unrecorded losses, or indeed the possibility of historic immersion or deliberate burial tend to escape consideration at the moment. But society was probably never so well organised that mechanisms existed for recording every disappearance, particularly those incurred during cross-country travel. The difficulties of long-distance movement regularly occasioned robbing and mugging, murder and disappearance. How easy is it to distinguish retrospectively between a body attacked and ditched by robbers and one deposited ritually?

Loss in Early Travel?

For a better understanding of this problem, we require an appreciation of the quality of travel over British–Irish terrains, particularly before the turnpikes. Ogilby's strip maps depict many unenclosed routes passing through 'boggy ground' or 'moorish ground' in England and Wales (e.g. Ogilby 1675, pls. 3 and pl. 51). As late as 1783 there was hardly an Irish coach road that didn't at some point pass through a bog of some size (Taylor and Skinner 1783, *passim*). Recent accounts of individuals slowly sinking unnoticed into boggy ground relatively close to settlements (*The Independent*, 10 May 1992), and of lives lost in snowdrifts around the home, demonstrate some ease of disappearance through misadventure, even at the present day.

To Glob's list of conditions potentially responsible for departure from the beaten track into a 'moorish place' might be added senility and sickness – particularly the onset of cardiac arrest or strokes, perhaps connected with initial immersion in the cold dank peat pool. Even youthful imprudence including intoxication could have contributed. From his writings it is clear that Glob (in common with many others) was confident in the ability of forensic science to establish unequivocal causes, motives and dates of decease for the bog people. Although his work acknowledges a widespread folklore chronicling historic losses of individuals from communities near the body discovery sites, is it not remarkable that science and peat cutting have failed to produce one body acceptably identifiable as historic in origin? Were there really so few accidental deaths among the several hundred bodies listed by Alfred Dieck (1965; Glob 1969, 75)? Lindow itself has produced nineteenth-century folklore of such local losses (Turner, p. 10).

Perhaps the time has now come to examine those folk stories in the light of earlier bog finds. Lindow II brought his own folklore, though he was less significant to a police Missing Persons inquiry than was a woman's head (Lindow I) found some time before (Turner 1986, 10–11; pp. 188–204). So did Grauballe man (who at first offered 'nothing in particular to provide a firm date ... only the circumstances of the find itself' (Glob 1969, 36)). It might be recalled that at the time of his discovery a controversy of national proportions raged, in which the 'scientists' were pilloried and disbelieved for failure to acknowledge the testimony of neighbours who swore the body had been that of a local character, Red Christian, a consumptive, lost, probably drunk, in 1887 or 1888. Even the place of his loss was known locally. Only publication of radiocarbon dates actually quelled protests from incredulous locals, and nationals, originally quite unsympathetic to interpretations of Iron Age ritual loss in their familiar bog (Glob 1969, 46–8).

Also well known is the sad tale of the 'Hope runaways' (a seventeenth-century master and his maidservant), at one time a most celebrated British–Irish bog couple (Briggs and Turner 1986, no. 17, 183) who died in a winter snowstorm and remained deep-frozen until their corpses were noticed in warmer weather prior to local re-burial in peat ground by the authorities (Balguy 1734). Similarly, the credentials of a naked girl alleged to have committed suicide, from Ardee bog, Co. Louth – presented from

word of mouth at her inquest – were found acceptable by the coroner at the time of her recovery in 1845 (Briggs and Turner 1986, 194, no. 105; Briggs unpublished investigation). It is interesting to speculate that in different times, without radiocarbon dating and the minutiae of forensic science, the identification of the Lindow and Grauballe bodies may have passed unquestioned as known missing persons.

What emerges from an analysis of Glob's *The Bog People* is that even before any radiocarbon or deductive dating had been undertaken, nay, even before some had been lifted from the bog, he was confident of deposition dates and mode of death. From the book's core 63 pages (pp. 21–83), a total of 63 citations can be chronicled referring to the Iron Age, 'the time of Christ' or to '2000 years ago'. Despite Glob's caveat on accidental death, few normal or recent burials are detailed. Also, for the first time and without reference to any published authority, the Irish 'Drumkeeragh lady' (from her clothing, certainly of medieval or later origin) is claimed as a Danish Viking (p. 78). Can Glob's book today actually pass muster as responsible popular scholarship?

We need to know what really did happen to those persons believed to have been lost or buried recently in Lindow, and about the nineteenth-century character who was lost at Grauballe. Do they still await recovery and recognition, or is it possible that peat bogs do age corpses so as to distort completely the usefulness of radiocarbon? Other bogs carry folklore of their victims, some losses even documented by written record. But by now radiocarbon is considered more reliable than local history, so the chances of balanced consideration being given to folklore or history are diminished. This is an interesting reversal of the situation which obtained before radiocarbon.

The Mode of Accidental Death

It hardly requires great imagination to conjecture the nature of the fate awaiting those who fell into 'moorish' ground. But for the purposes of offering alternative interpretations to ritual, it may be useful to speculate. Much of the following process derives from the writer's observations of sheep lost in *Sphagnum* bogs.

Once in, the body would slowly sink, even the arms of the unfortunate traveller being overtaken by dank pool peat, eventually leaving a head the most likely visible feature. Depending upon circumstances, cries for help might continue to be heard from the pool for maybe a couple of days, though by that time birds seeking carrion would begin to settle on the bare head, possibly even pecking off hair. The state in which the third Borremose body (a woman) was disinterred, the back of her head scalped (Glob 1969, 71) could indicate that she had been attacked in this way, probably post-mortem.

Similar deep triangular lesions on the Lindow head could be the result of post-mortem attacks by scavengers. But for a British carrion bird to penetrate the human skull without the bone first being softened by immersion would seem unlikely. To digress for a moment – driving a fence post or a wood scavenger's pole into the bog is another possibility. However, most noteworthy at Lindow were the 'two small pits ... slightly undercutting the baulk [where Lindow II lay] and containing humified grey peat ... [which] ... could have been caused by the recent peat diggers' (Turner 1986, 12). Turner went on to express relief about the close shave 'Pete Marsh' had had with these peat diggers, having already explained how the body was located only after a machine first took off his foot and a piece of lower leg (idem, 11). So the possibility of modern damage cannot be entirely excluded and helps to underline the existence of a wide variety of potential agents of post-mortem injury.

As long as the sinking victim was strong enough to shout, mutilation by animals would be less likely. On occasion, searches for missing travellers must have been made, so that cries for help and diligent searching would be rewarded by discovery, or even by successful rescue. Recovery would be of a weakened but live person, or of the corpse for burial elsewhere.

At this stage we may still be dealing with an individual whose loss was within local recall. It is arguable that, once immersed in the quagmire, bodies may have disappeared for some weeks or months, to surface only when weather conditions created warm convection currents temporarily drawing them to the surface.

Methods of Recovering Bodies from Bogs

How may rescue or recovery best be effected from a watery grave? Strong rope would be essential, and if irreparable and horrific wounding were not to be inflicted, the victim's hands would need to be free to grasp it. If it were too late for the victim to pull, the only alternative would be to lasso all that remained exposed – the head – and hope that sufficient force was available to extract the body entire. Obviously, attempts to recover softened, partially tanned bodies would easily result in extensive in-

jury, forensically almost indistinguishable from injuries inflicted by robbers or sustained in a struggle before death. Removal and decent burial (if that were intended) could be guaranteed only by sound rope.

Emergency alternatives such as leather belts or halters, thonged purse strings or withies would need to be very strong and reasonably long. Wellington boots can easily be lost through powerful bog suction. Acts of casting-in cloaks, sheets of hide, sticks, branches or even hurdles to within the victim's grasp must have been made from sheer desperation to save life. Prior to the industrial era, the limited availability of reliable rope within rural farming communities would have made the rescue hazardous. Breakages must have been commonplace, since considerable lengths would have been demanded to reach the heart of peaty pools, and this might not always have been to hand.

Bearing in mind these problems, it is curious that, in each and every case where science has most convincingly ascertained the cause of death of a bog body, injury infliction had been upon the neck, either through apparent strangulation by rope, or, in odd cases such as Grauballe, Ravnholt (Glob 1969, 31–48; 53) and Lindow II (West 1986, 77) the throat itself had been severed.

In Munck's 1956 publication of the Grauballe find, the illustration (Fig. 2) suggests less torsion *across* the neck, and more friction at right angles to the chin. This is most clearly illustrated in the well-known photographs (for example, Munck Fig. 1). Such damage could hardly be achieved from behind the cranium, but would more probably come from a rope or gag fastened more or less directly above it. There was no classic hanging mark behind the lower skull; only friction marks in front of the neck. The so-called cut-throat therefore appears not to be a straightforward slash but might well be interpreted as a worn burn-mark. Such burning could occur post-mortem by tying rope around the head with the intention of dragging out the body on to the vegetation surface. If this is not a more likely interpretation than garrotting, it might have to be argued that the original intention was to pull off, rather than to hang or garrotte the victim's head.

How do the few surviving string and leather halter pieces stand up to scrutiny as garrotting or hanging media, as opposed to hasty makeshifts for rescuing the victims of accident?

The cord believed to have garrotted Lindow II was made of fibrous strands, probably of animal sinew, only 1.5 mm in diameter. It had been overtwisted, producing backspin or crepe twist slubs. After careful study it was concluded that 'no knot-tying skill … [was] apparent; besides 'the [extremely] short ends [being puzzling, and] … [it was] not typical of a garrotte'. Furthermore, 'the use of the cord as a sliding noose [was] thought unlikely' and [the short ends of the knotted cord were also felt] not typical in a ligature used to strangle someone' (Budworth in Budworth *et al* 1986, p. 39). Although puzzled by the nature of the cord, Budworth also observed 'that most cordage clues found at contemporary scenes of crime consist of a haphazard assortment of overhand knots, not suited to the job in hand' (p. 40). Although not obviously tied with the skill of a practised executioner, he was thus prepared to accept this cord as one which might have been used with malice aforethought.

Besides the diversity of material and noose types there are other circumstances which make more difficult an easy acceptance that these had been premeditated ritual or punishment killings. The first objection to habitual bog-body ritual must be that out of several hundred known bodies only a handful or as few as perhaps one per cent have neck wounds – which, if correct, is a lamentably small statistic from which to generalise and establish a tradition of pan-European Iron Age ritual sacrifice.

It is also difficult to understand, in a peasant society where rope was a commodity of some expense, why, if those undertaking the ritual had such control over circumstances, the ropes were not detached for re-use to be saved; and why have no bodies garrotted or 'hanged' survived without cord or rope? In answer to the former, it may of course be argued that the cause of ritual knows no bounds of expense, a point amply illustrated by alleged votive offerings of artefacts. A final and most important objection must be repeated: it would be very difficult to drag bodies into bogs of the sort which were sufficiently deep to guarantee preservation, without great risk to the ritual executors.

An interesting point about both British–Irish and European finds is that, in the main, few bogs tend to have hosted more than a single cadaver. Despite claims to the contrary (at Bjælskov Dal and Borremøse, where respectively two and three bodies are recorded, with one exception separated by considerable distances (Glob 1969, 21, 23; *passim*)) there is no real evidence to show that any of these were certainly the subject of ritual.

It has already been noted that the dangers posed by the bog to its executioners should not be underestimated. And indeed, in view of the unforeseen dangers of these 'ritual bogs', it is amazing that so few multiple burials are known (Bolkide on Als (Bennike *et al* 1990) and Weerdinge Veen,

Holland (van der Sanden 1990, 108–12)). At Bolkide it seems just as likely that the first victim pulled in his would-be rescuer (Glob 1969, 72) as it is that these were demonstrably the subject of a ritual. To assert the latter interpretation (whatever the date) merely because there was a fabric belt lying between the bodies, would seem to stretch the evidence well beyond its reasonable interpretation (Bennike *et al* 1990).

Considered against the entire bog-body population, 'ritual groupings' are few and statistically almost insignificant. This observation might lead to the supposition that memories of a relative or friend accidentally falling in helped deter later would-be accidents. Most significant to criticism of the ritual argument is that contemporary artefactual 'votive deposits' are absent from those bogs hosting multiple 'ritual' victims. The connection between artefact hoard groupings and bog bodies is therefore at present extremely tenuous, if not altogether absent.

How Did Bodies Lose Their Heads?

An important tenet in the argument for ritual is the survival of heads without bodies. These need not have been cut or pulled off in ritual, but could alternatively result from accident (or even deliberate non-ritual burial). In some cases the victim's head, animal or human, sinews weakened from exposure outside the bog, would detach naturally. As to deliberately detach a live human head requires considerable force, so it is possible that decapitated bog bodies reached that state through natural causes, as well as by the alternative, rescue attempt theory, if not more remotely, by the accredited ritual method.

Some questions posed by discoveries of fragmented clothing, odd shoes or partial corpses (particularly those certainly of Medieval origin) are better answered with reference to the geomorphic behaviour of peat bogs rather than ascribable to deliberate sacrifices. Whereas headless corpses and isolated heads provoke suggestions of pre-disposal decapitation (Turner, pp. 193–4), there is usually no forensic or archaeological evidence confirming that decapitation was either the cause of death or indeed that its removal was ante rather than post-mortem.

Peat-bog convection has already been mentioned. This process may have caused animal and human bodies to be attracted or carried towards the pool core. Within more mobile deposits, limbs or items of clothing would become lost to resettle both horizontally and vertically.

Peat slumping would also break up and scatter both

bodies and artefacts. Perhaps an even better explanation for loss of limbs was the presence of the peat cutter. Again and again, accounts are given of bodies noticed incomplete during recent peat-digging (e.g. Hald 1980, 15–82), where it seems reasonably clear that a portion of the cadaver was carted away with an earlier season's fuel. This inability to distinguish between rotten timber and shrivelled bodies extends to the present day. Lindow I herself was not easy to recognise as a human likeness on the conveyor belt at the peat depot.

An example of scattering probably accounted for by processes suggested above is recorded by Richard Fenton, the Pembrokeshire Antiquary. Passing through Carmarthenshire in 1809 he noted 'that Sir Joseph Banks, who, when on a visit some 25 years ago at Edwinsford … had in digging in boggy ground on the mountain, found a Hat of felt not decayed; and that about 3 ft [0.9 m] lower, a Hilt of a sword was found; and about 2½ ft [0.8 m] lower, shoes and something like Buckles, supposed to have belonged to some person, who, crossing the mountains, had been sunk in the Bog' (Fisher 1917, 56). The absence of a body in this instance can probably be put down to its disappearance through the extreme acidity of the host bog, though the victim may have just escaped with his life.

A Place for Medieval and Later Bodies and Their Clothes

Some account of both bodies and the unaccompanied medieval and later clothing known from Ireland (McClintock 1950) has already been given (Briggs 1986, 153–6). There can be little doubt that much of this clothing, like that from Meenybradden (pp. 131–2), belonged to lost travellers or others who suffered death in bogs by accident or misadventure. One child had a belt around his neck suggesting a frustrated rescue attempt by his mother (who had accompanied him) (Briggs 1986, 156). They were certainly not victims of ritual, but descriptions of these bodies do help to pose similar questions of the many undated British and Danish examples.

The usual interpretation of European bog bodies is that their greater majority did not die through natural causes or by accident. However, it now seems reasonable to seek explanation for many of these bodies among those individuals who were regularly lost in longer or shorter journeys across fen or moor during medieval or later times. Some may have been assisted to their graves by muggers or robbers; others merely fell in and failed to get out. Some were certainly rescued, while others again were probably badly hurt or perished at the hands of their would-be rescuers. Other bodies may have suffered accidental mutilation subsequently through peat-winning or other activities on the bog.

Hurdles for Help or for Hindrance?

One of the most acceptable indicators in the theory of 'ritual' deposition has been the rare observation of pegging down or covering a victim, possibly with hurdle-like structures. More commonly there are records of odd wooden poles or stakes. Like hurdles, these, it is believed, were laid over the body with the express intention of preventing a victim's escape from the boggy grave.

The most celebrated victim of pegging down was the alleged Norwegian Queen Gunhild from Haraldskjær Møse. Apparently she was 'fastened to the underlying peat by wooden crooks, driven down tight over each knee and elbow joint … strong branches had been fixed like clamps across the chest and lower abdomen' (Glob 1969, 58; Hald 1980, 10–11, no. 32, 56). Whilst her identification was the subject of well-rehearsed contemporary controversy, it seems odd that the remarkable circumstances enabling her supposed executioners to undertake the task has attracted no comment. Yet remarkable it is to think of the control demanded by her murderers over the drowning medium. For if this was bog at the time of her interment, like those already described, it would have been unstable and dangerous. The very act of driving pegs into the base of a peatbog with any degree of accuracy from above staggers credulity. It smacks of stunt work from a sub-aqua team. However, without greater information about the original disposition of the wooden pegs and clothing fragments, it is difficult to offer any easy alternative than that she had been deliberately placed there.

'A sort of cage' appeared to surround the body found at Bunsok, Ditmarsh in 1790. It was composed of birchwood poles, three at the head and three at foot and sides, and seemed to be strengthened by three parallel horizontal sticks (Glob 1969, 79). A birch branch lay across the first Borremose man (Glob 1969, 70; Hald 1980, no. 4, 18–20); two birchwood stakes 'were associated' with the Halland, Sweden man, found in 1936 (Glob 1969, 110); a 'willow post' or 'stake' 3 ft (0.9 m) long lay obliquely across the Huldremose woman's breast (Glob 1969, 63; Hald 1980, no. 27, 47–54). Windeby Bog, Schleswig, hosted *inter alia* a man associated with eight roundels of wood and forked branches of hazel bough (Kersten 1949; Glob 1969, 85). The back of the body found at Landegge, Holland in 1861 was criss-crossed with sticks (Glob 1969, 78–9). In some cases it is claimed that crooked sticks were used to hold down the victim, for example at Auning Fen (Glob 1969, 63; Hald 1980, no. 29a, 54–5). Hald considered the possibility that a slender birch trunk lying above Vester Thorsted man could have been intended to anchor him in the bog (1980, no. 37, 66). Similarly, pronouncing upon the Ravnholt discovery in 1773, the Judge and Recorder was convinced that branches and twigs placed crosswise across the body had been intended to prevent it floating away (Hald 1980, 9; no. 46, 72).

Wooden oar finds from Aardestrup and two paddles with a handled wooden peg (possibly a primitive rowlock) from True Møse (Hald 1980, no. 13, 33; no. 23, 42), both bodyless and associated with skin cloaks could each signal the sites of successful rescue attempts in some tiny craft during which victim or rescuer lost his mantle. The three willow switches found in 1797 with a body at Undelev, Holbøl (Glob 1969, 53; Hald 1908, no. 42, 69), are of uncertain status.

Whereas with some imagination this selection of timbers could indeed have served the purposes of ritual, as a group of artefacts for execution they seem mundane. But yet they are mundane and comprise the sort of material which may still be to hand for casting in around many peat bogs today.

The question posed here is whether or not such timbers may equally be re-interpreted as having been used to assist the egress of a body from the bog. Whatever the ideal rescue agency, emergency rescue from bogs is likely to have attracted only such equipment as was immediately to hand. This might have included peat-carrying or agricultural hurdles, branches and individual or grouped poles. Branches and twigs would be plucked optimistically from those willow and birches bordering the 'drowning place' by both victim and rescuers in efforts to make safer the ground or the pool's rim. Casting in of a buoyant mass to be grasped or to be hauled over in the hope of assisting recovery, seems a likely reason for the presence of odd branches in the water.

Over the course of time all manner of flotsam could soak and sink into the pool above the body. But because wood takes some time to impregnate with water, it is difficult to see the sense or practicability of intentionally casting in wooden objects to hinder escape of a submerged body or of its spirit. Bodies and wood would sink at different rates. Bodies discovered close to or beneath hurdles or even near single branches need not require exclusive interpretation as ritual deposits. It therefore seems impossible to determine retrospectively if groups of stick or brushwood found adjacent to or above a body had been deliberately placed to hinder some ritual victim's escape. But hindrance in the way postulated by Danish scholars seems unlikely.

Accounts of peat-digging practices may offer further potentials in this respect. A variety of lightly constructed sledge types were current in North Wales before adoption of coal fuel in the mid-nineteenth century. In carrying peat at great speed from the mountain tops, these sleds would occasionally overturn, inflicting severe or mortal injury on the sledsman (Owen 1975, 316–18). Sledge-like constructions of wicker or willow would have been important for facilitating peat recovery from some softer surfaces, particularly during wet summers. Such carriages must have served well to support workers accidentally coming upon unstable ground.

During awakening interest in the archaeology of the Severn Levels in the early 1980s, one team member involved in pollen analytical investigations sank to her knees in estuarine mud. Her safety was assured only after students dragged a wooden palette some distance over the levels. With exhaustive effort and the loss of boots, she was able to clamber upon the palette before making safe her escape barefoot.

Examples of supposed wooden 'ritual' structures or wooden branches so far propounded as integral to the bog-body sacrifice theory can reasonably be re-interpreted either as peat-cutting paraphanalia left close to the findspot of the body, or as material cast into the bog during vain rescue attempts.

The Nature of Ritual: a History of Hanging

Suggestions that the few bog bodies with neck injuries corroborate those claims of barbarism in the remoter known world made by contemporary classical writers (principally Tacitus), have been well rehearsed (Glob 1969, *passim* but particularly 112 ff. and 117 ff.) and need not be repeated here. As there has always been reasonable doubt about the Iron Age dating of Lindow II, modes of punishment or of burial at a later date may now be considered.

The questions must be addressed: What is known of the history of hanging or of strangulation as a method of social control? Also, do we have archaeological evidence suggesting its longevity to remote antiquity?

Indeed, we do possess it and the sixteenth-century

London annalist and chronicler John Stow reckoned that the Britons inflicted death by drowning in a quagmire, before 450 BC (Haydn 1871, 246). But in common with his lacking incredulity at other aspects of the then accepted British History (Kendrick 1950, 159), this notion was probably of Stow's own making rather than one carrying the authority of an earlier manuscript. As there appear to be no other written assertions as early as Stow's, it seems probable that his was based upon contemporary bog discoveries for which he was providing what then must have seemed the most reasonable explanation.

Hanging, however, together with drawing and quartering, is first recorded in England only in the twenty-fifth year of Henry III's reign (1241; Haydn 1871, 357). Prior to that, beheading had been introduced by the Conqueror (ibid. 93). There is little evidence for the practice of hanging or strangulation in Anglo-Saxon (Meaney 1964), Viking or Roman Britain, though there is an abundance of literary evidence for a variety of other forms of deliberate killing from these periods (e.g. Folke Strom 1942 *passim*, for Viking punishment).

Hanging is mentioned as a distinct punishment in Biblical contexts, (Numbers xxv, 4; Second Book of Samuel xxi, 2, 9). Furthermore, strangulation is said by the rabbins to have been regarded as the most common but least severe of the capital punishments, and to have been performed by immersing the convict in clay or mud, and then strangling him by a cloth twisted round the neck (Smith 1916, 781). It is tempting to connect both circumstances of Hebrew immersion and hanging with the strangled bodies of northern Europe.

However, though there are superficial similarities between alleged practices in the two culture zones, this analogy leaves a great deal to be desired. First, the Jewish custom suggests close control of the medium of immersion, a feature which seems quite contrary to the circumstances obtaining in north and north-western Europe, where it would have been, and still can be, lethal to attempt to approach the centres of marshes of the type in which bog bodies have been so well preserved. If the northern Europeans ritually disposed of victims by casting them into bogs, dead or alive (as some feel to be acceptably documented by the classical writers), it must again be supposed that the executors of the ritual act risked their own lives to do so.

It may be argued that in northern Europe rope was a substitute for the Jewish cloth, but the Jewish ritual was one in which it was intended that the body could safely be recovered and buried.

There exist numerous classical and later sources from which it is possible to select descriptions of folk punishment and suit them to the bog-body discoveries. Few are specific in their claims and it is not until the emergence of Anglo-Saxon, and of later Medieval law, that social controls appear to evoke regular recognisable punitive responses. Only a limited number of the bog bodies possess indications of hanging, or indeed indications of any certain punitive injury, so to interpret the majority as ritual or punitive exemplars is to overstep the implications of extremely limited evidence.

Discussion and Conclusions

A significant number of those circumstances which have for long strongly supported the view that European bog bodies were deposited ritually during the Iron Age are capable of alternative interpretation. There are ample grounds upon which to question the traditional ritual or punishment explanation and offer instead the view that damage to the body is equally or more likely to have come about through frustrated rescue attempts using rope, and in some cases this may have happened a long time post-mortem. The concept of actually taking victims to dangerous saturated bogs and locating a suitable spot for the disposal of a body, dead or alive, is one which credits the executors with too great an ability to escape the very death they sought to bring about. There must have been many other punishments practised in remote antiquity far less dangerous for all concerned.

Close scrutiny is demanded of what is acceptable evidence or fact on the one hand, rather than what has evolved as strong opinion on the other. This applies not only to interpreting damaged bodies, but also to understanding the many complex environmental factors surrounding their findspots.

Future investigation requires controlled experiments in which animal flesh is immersed in *Sphaghum* peat for a matter of months and years so that the biochemical degradation of proteins by atomic or molecular displacement can be measured. A start might usefully be made upon the girl from Ardee using data from her cadaver as a control for younger, experimentally controlled protein degradation.

Concern must be expressed that little, if any, radiocarbon dating has been undertaken upon known medieval or later bodies, and that some scholars consider these not to be sufficiently important to investigate (van der Sanden 1990, 234). Testing the atomic displacement hypothesis should not be difficult, though experiments may take some years. Carbon-14 dating could readily be undertaken on other historic, clothed bodies like Meenybraddan (Lucas 1967), and upon surviving stylistically distinct bog clothing, to see if the dates behave as irregularly as did the decayed proteins at Lindow.

We are now faced with dichotomous interpretations of the evidence or with two or three types of potentially conflicting evidence. In Britain and Ireland, with a few notable exceptions (Turner, pp. 108–22), many bog people are acceptably Medieval and later in date. Many of them quite definitely fell, some appear to have been mugged and were therefore probably pushed.

A review of the palaeoecological, radiocarbon and stratigraphical aspects of Lindow II throws doubts upon his Iron Age origins. It is extremely difficult to determine whether his injuries were deliberately inflicted before death, or, along with his decayed arm, were the result of events post-mortem. His gaping neck wound may well have come from a frustrated, ill-equipped rescue attempt. But this could have happened only when Lindow Moss was sufficiently deep to preserve him at the spot where he was found, and that may well have been in medieval or later times, when nearby communities were obliged to risk life and limb to cross this deceptive tract.

Generally, there are probably still too few bodies investigated in sufficient detail to be sure precisely who was pushed and who fell. For Lindow Man, were all the circumstances of discovery, the forensic evidence and a full catalogue of unanswered questions to be offered Judge and Jury, at strongest, it could be death by accident or misadventure, though at frankest, an open verdict should be recorded.

Lindow Man: the Celtic Tradition and Beyond

J. R. Magilton

Lindow Man: The Body in the Bog (Stead *et al* 1986) contains two chapters dealing with religion and folklore. The first, by Dr Anne Ross (op. cit. 162–9), consists of three sections discussing the triple death motif, Celtic cake ceremonies and mistletoe. The second, by R. C. Turner (op. cit. 170–6), is concerned with recorded and surviving customs in (mainly) the English oral tradition, looking in particular at the Haxey Hood Game, which is still played, and beheading myths in English and Celtic legends with especial reference to Sir Gawain and the Green Knight.

At the suggestion of one of the contributors to this book, Dr P. C. Buckland, the writer has re-examined the classical and Celtic written sources in particular, which are now seen in an Indo-European rather than an insular Celtic context. This is not intended to suggest that the bodies in Lindow Moss were other than those of Celtic speakers who lived in a Celtic cultural milieu, even if perhaps under Roman political control, but as a reminder that 'Celtic', if used other than in a linguistic sense, must be used with caution.

The cauldron from Gundestrup, Jutland, Denmark, attributed to the Celtic Iron Age, provides a useful caveat. Although discovered in an area distant from Celtic influence, the cauldron portrays the drowning of a victim in a vat. This recalls the scene described by Lucan (*de Bello Civili*, I, 444–6) who relates that the Gaulish god whom he names as Teutates was propitiated through the sacrifice of victims being drowned in a tub. This, and references in the insular Celtic literature to both ritual drownings and magic cauldrons, has led some to the conclusion that the Gundestrup cauldron is the work of Celtic craftsmen, and even that it 'casts much light on pagan Celtic practice in the immediately pre-Roman period' (Ross 1986, 162). The circularity of the argument is obvious, and if some of the customs seen as peculiar to the Celts can be shown to be more widespread, so too can the possible origins of the Gundestrup cauldron, which appears to have few stylistic affinities in the Celtic world.

A Ritual Death?

It has been for so long a standing joke among archaeologists that the unusual or otherwise inexplicable must be interpreted as 'ritual' that there is perhaps a danger of rejecting this conclusion even when it best fits the facts.

Of the two individuals recovered from Lindow Moss, the death of Lindow II (better known as Lindow Man) may be seen in a ritual or judicial context. As Caesar's account of Gallic customs reminds us (*de Bello Gallico* VI, 16), there may have been little distinction between ritual and judicial deaths in Celtic society. According to Caesar, some tribes, as well as performing regular state sacrifices, actually chose to sacrifice those caught in the act of theft or some other offence on the grounds that the gods preferred such persons to innocent men although, if there were a dearth of criminals, the innocent would be sacrificed without hesitation.

Caesar's account of human sacrifice is echoed by Strabo (IV, 5) and Diodorus Siculus (V, 32). Strabo says that the victim was stabbed in the back with a dagger and the future foretold from his convulsions; others were shot down with arrows and impaled in temples, and he repeats Caesar's story of a wickerwork effigy filled with sacrificial victims which was then set alight. According to Diodorus Siculus, criminals were imprisoned for five years and then impaled in honour of the gods. Prisoners of war were also sacrificed, and even animals captured in war. Both

Caesar's and Diodorus' accounts name druids as performing the sacrifices which, according to Caesar, were intended to ward off serious diseases as well as to protect those who were exposed to the dangers of battle.

In Britain, Cassius Dio (LXX, VI, 7) states that the Britons have holy places and offer human sacrifices to Andraste in a sacred wood, and the barbarous superstitions which Tacitus (*Annals*, XIV, 30) tells us took place in the groves of Anglesey may have included human sacrifice. The *Rennes Dindshenchas* attests sacrifice by drowning among the Irish (see below), and, as noted above, the first century AD Latin poet Lucan describes sacrifices to Teutates which involved drowning the victims in a cauldron.

Sacrifice by throat-slitting is attested by Strabo (VII, 2) among the Germanic Cimbri. White-cloaked priestesses who accompanied the wives of the warriors on expeditions would utter prophecies and cut the throats of prisoners of war while the latter were suspended over huge bronze cauldrons. Other priestesses would inspect the entrails of victims to see if victory would ensue in the forthcoming battle.

The Threefold Death in Celtic Contexts

Lindow II was rendered brain-dead by two blows to the back of the head, had his throat cut and his neck broken by a garrotte. His death thus falls readily within what Rees and Rees (1961, 333) have termed the 'betwixts and betweens' category – deaths which are neither this nor that or, as a union of opposites, may be regarded as both this and that. The answer to the question 'How did he die?' is 'By strangulation/by having his throat cut/from blows to the back of the head' and the answer to the question 'Where was he buried?' is 'In a pool/on dry ground', a bog being both and neither.

Examples from the insular Celtic tradition include the death of the sixth-century King Diarmait, son of Fergus, whom St Ciarán had prophesied would be wounded, drowned and burnt. He had earlier caused the house of Flann, son of Dima, to be burnt and the wounded owner, to escape the flames, had climbed into a bath-tub and expired there. After violating various prohibitions (*gessa*) Diarmait met his end as predicted, speared by Aed Dub at the house of Banbán the Hospitaller, which was then set on fire by the Ulstermen who surrounded it. Diarmait sought refuge from the flames in an ale-vat, whereupon the ridge-pole of the burning house fell on his head and he died, thus fulfilling the prediction of a second seer who

foretold that a roof-tree would cause his end (O'Grady 1892, 86–8; II, 80–4). The answer to the question 'What caused Diarmait's death?' is thus 'He was speared/he was drowned/he was burnt' or alternatively, 'The falling ridge-pole killed him'. All this took place during the celebration of a festival, and it has been suggested that the story represents the euhemerisation of a sacrificial myth in which a king was simultaneously sacrificed to three classes of divinities (Ward 1970, 137).

A second Irish example is provided by the legend of Suibhne Geilt as recorded in the seventeenth-century *Anecdota* of Michael O'Clery (Jackson 1940, 539) and the Life of St Moling (Stokes 1906, 285–7). Grag, who has killed Suibhne and stolen some cattle, is told by the saint that he will die by a weapon, by being burnt and by drowning. Grag is understandably unperturbed by the prophecy, reasoning that a man can die but once, but meets his end when climbing an oak tree, during which he is wounded by his spear, falls from the tree into a fire and then into water where he drowns. There are brief allusions to this story in the ninth and tenth centuries (O'Keeffe 1913). A third, incomplete, account of a ritual death is the story of Aidhedh Muirchertaig mac Erca whose house is burned during a festival. He climbs into a vat of ale and half burns and half drowns (Stokes 1902, 395–437). Allusions to the hero's death in other manuscripts confirm that he was also wounded by a weapon (Ward 1970, 137, fn. 38), thus suffering the traditional threefold death.

Versions of the legend were also current in Wales. Llew Llaw Gyffes (Llew of the skilful hand – the Irish god Lug in one of his guises) in the *Mabinogion* story, Math, son of Mathonwy (Gantz 1976) is invulnerable except in very unusual circumstances. He must be killed by a spear which has taken a year to make, and has been manufactured only when people are at Sunday mass. He cannot be killed indoors or out of doors, on horse or on foot. He reveals this to his wife Blodeuedd, who with her lover Goronwy contrives his downfall on a river bank where a bath tub has been prepared beneath a thatched roof. Llew, having taken a bath, is putting on his trousers and, with one foot in the tub and the other on a buck goat which he has caused to be brought to him, is struck by the magic spear which Goronwy has made and flies away as an eagle. Thus the answer to the question 'How was Llew killed?' is 'In water/not in water/; clothed/unclothed; outdoors/indoors'.

The triple death also occurs in one of the Arthurian legends. In Geoffrey of Monmouth's *Vita Merlini*, Merlin prophesies that a youth will die in a tree, fall from a rock and drown, and indeed the youth suffers all three deaths simultaneously. Ward (1970, 138) gives two further examples of the triple death from the Welsh tradition.

Scotland provides the earliest reference to the triple-death theme although, as the source is Adhamnán's seventh-century *Vita Columbae*, the story strictly belongs to the Irish milieu. The saint informs Aedh the Black that he will die three different deaths, being wounded in the neck by a spear, falling from a tree and drowning. In fact, Aedh is wounded, falls from a boat and drowns, so the conclusion does not quite fit the prophecy.

The Triple Death as an Indo-European Phenomenon

Such deaths were not confined to the insular Celts, or to the Celtic world in general. Greek mythology provides a close parallel in the death of Agamemnon to the story of Math, son of Mathonwy, and the circumstances are so similar that the possibility of elements of the Greek myth creeping into the Welsh story cannot be discounted.

In the Greek version, Clytaemnestra conspires with her lover Aegisthus to bring about her husband's death. Agamemnon, returning from the Trojan War, goes to the bath-house in an annex to the palace, washes himself and, with one foot out of the bath, is entangled in a net woven by Clytaemnestra, which he mistakes for a towel. He is twice struck by Aegisthus, wielding a two-edged sword, and falls back into the bath where Clytaemnestra beheads him with an axe (Graves 1960, (2), 51–6). Agamemnon thus dies neither in the palace nor outside it, neither in water nor on dry land, neither clothed nor unclothed, killed by a sword/an axe/drowning.

The same motif occurs in Indian legend. The demon Namuci once captured Indra but released him on condition that he agreed not to slay him by night or by day, with a staff or a bow, with the flat of his hands or with fists, with anything wet or dry. Eventually he is slain at twilight with the foam of the waters (Śatapatha Brāhmaṇa XII, 7, quoted in Rees and Rees 1961, 333). The ambiguity about the cause of death is absent from this legend, but the either/or element about its circumstances survives.

The triple death motif survived in Central European folk traditions into relatively recent times. Green George, a character in spring-time processions, was ducked, beaten and finally burned (Frazer 1890, 84–6). It occurs also in a Finnish ballad 'Mataleena' (i.e. outside the Indo–European sphere) but it has been suggested that the story came from a German or Swedish source (Talley 1970).

The Fate Tale

In the Celtic versions of the triple death myth, death comes about usually as a consequence of a violation of taboos. If Diarmait had not rendered himself vulnerable by ignoring various prohibitions he could not have been killed and Llew, although not specifically guilty of such offences, is killed only in circumstances in which he himself knew could prove fatal. Agamemnon apparently had no such forewarning, but the myth survives in such a stylised and dramatic form that elements may have been lost.

Achilles, betrayed by his betrothed, Polyxena, to Paris, has several features in common with Llew: both were given arms as a result of a ruse by Odysseus/Gwydion, and each died as a result of his partner's treachery. Achilles has an Irish counterpart in Conganches (Horny-skin), vulnerable only on the soles of his feet, who was betrayed by his wife, and in the north-European tradition Sigurd, invulnerable after a bath in dragon blood except between the shoulder-blades, is innocently betrayed by his wife (Turville-Petre 1964, 204).

In Ireland, there is a type of myth which may be termed a 'fate tale' in which the manner of the victim's death is straightforward but which comes about as a result of the violation of prohibitions. The death of Cú Chulainn is a case in point. After a series of ill-omened events before his last battle, the hero passes three hags roasting a dog on spits of rowan. It is prohibited for him to eat his namesake, the dog, and especially prohibited for him to pass a cooking-place without eating (Rees and Rees 1963, 327). The death of Conaire stems from a violation of eight separate *gessa* before his death during the sack of Da Derga's Hostel (loc. cit.). In both cases the hero is checkmated. Conaire, for example, is forbidden by his personal *geis* to admit a lone woman to his house after sunset, but is required to do so by the rules of kingly hospitality.

It has been suggested (Ward 1970, 137) that such tales represent a degenerate version of an older myth in which the hero suffered a three-fold death. As the story becomes removed from its religious background, it is the element of predestination in the subject's death, rather than its manner, which captures the popular imagination, and in particular the conflict between personal prohibitions and the more general prohibitions of heroic society.

The Last Supper

An element of the three Irish fate tales alluded to above is the fatal feast. Cú Chulainn in effect eats himself, and

Conaire eats a black pig presented to him by Fer Caille, a monstrous black man, violating another *geis*. The best example, however, is the death of Diarmait, which follows his consumption of bacon from a pig which had never farrowed and ale brewed from a single grain of corn.

Whether these stories have any relevance to the stomach contents of the Lindow bodies is, to say the least, debatable. Mistletoe, as a plant revered by Druids, is attested by Pliny (*Nat. Hist.*, XVI) and its pollen is an unlikely substance for a normal diet. As a parasitic plant, it is a 'betwixt and between' substance, belonging neither on the earth nor in the sky nor in the water. The same objection does not, however, apply to hazel-nuts which, in the Irish story of Connla's Well, are symbols of wisdom (Ross 1967, 55), figure in personal names (MacCuill–'Son of hazel': op. cit. p. 64) and have other unusual powers (op. cit. p.89, note 56). Noísiu, in the story *The Exile of the Sons of Uisliu*, has a last drink of mead flavoured with hazel (Gantz 1981, 264). In a world where many everyday items had a supernatural aspect it is easy to read too much into what may have been a commonly consumed foodstuff.

As Ross (1986) has pointed out, the tradition of a ritual meal before sacrifice seems to have lingered on in eighteenth-century Perthshire, where a special bannock was baked for the Beltain (May Day Eve) festival. It was broken up and shared between those present, and the person unlucky enough to get a burnt portion was named 'the devoted' and was then referred to as dead. The earliest reference to this custom appears to be by Martin Martin (1703). A later account, also from Perthshire (Sinclair 1794), describes a boys' game involving a black bannock, noting that 'whoever draws the black bit ... is to be sacrificed to *Baal* ... in rendering the year productive of the sustenance of man and beast'. As one sceptic has commented, 'In one giant mental leap, a children's game of forfeit becomes the remnants of pagan human sacrifice' (Pegg 1981, 39).

A sacred meal of a sacrificed horse was part of the Irish kingship ritual according to Giraldus Cambrensis (Dillon and Chadwick 1967, 126). This is echoed in another tradition whereby a man ate of a sacrificed bull and then lay down to sleep. Four druids chanted an incantation over him, after which he dreamed of the person destined to be king (Mac Cana 1970, 119).

The Importance of Physical Perfection

In Ireland, a man who was physically blemished was ineligible for kingship (Dillon and Chadwick 1967, 126). In mythology, Nuada, King of the Tuatha Dé Danann, who lost an arm in the First Battle of Moytura, was thereby disqualified from leading the army in the second battle (op. cit. 187–8). When Edmund of Wessex invaded Strathclyde in 945 he blinded the sons of Donald, making them ineligible to reign under Gaelic law, leaving Malcolm I, king of the Scots, a free hand in disposing of the sub-kingdom (Smyth 1984, 222–3) in revenge for their grant of asylum to Olaf Cuaran, driven from York in the previous year.

According to Strabo (IV, 6) quoting Ephorus, the people of Transalpine Celtica 'try not to become stout and fat-bellied, and any young man who exceeds the standard length of the girdle is fined', perhaps a hint that the cult of physical perfection extended to the warrior class. Lindow III, with his vestigial thumb, may have been set aside on account of this abnormality. If, as Caesar states, the morally imperfect were preferred for sacrifices, this could have extended to the physically imperfect. In Norse mythology, Starkað, born with an extraordinary number of hands which Thor tore off to make him less ugly, was doomed to a cursed life (Turville-Petre 1964, 205–11).

Making the Punishment Fit the Crime

'The traitor and deserter are hanged on trees, the coward, the shirker and the unnaturally vicious are drowned in miry swamps under a cover of wattled hurdles.' (Tacitus, *Germania* 12, trans. Mattingley 1948).

The *Rennes Dindshenchas*, one of several mythological geographies of Ireland, records a ritual drowning of a captive prince and other hostages to ward off plagues (Stokes 1892, 467–516). The Pictish tribal king, Talorgen, was drowned by his overlord Óengus in 739, and in Ireland the Ui Néill high King Maelsechnaill executed one of his sub-kings by drowning him 'in a dirty stream' in 851 (Smyth 1984, 57).

In Sweden, according to Adam of Bremen, an English missionary called Wilfred who, in *c.* 1030 smashed an idol of Thor, was killed and his body sunk in a marsh, and a marginal note to his famous description of Uppsala speaks of 'a well where heathen sacrifices are commonly performed, and a living man is plunged into it. If he is not found again, it is deemed that the will of the people be fulfilled'. (Turville-Petre 1964, 93 and 244–5). Among the Langobardi and neighbouring German tribes the image of the goddess Nerthus was annually washed in a secluded lake by slaves who were immediately afterwards drowned in it, according to Tacitus (*Germania*, 40).

These may be interpreted as echoes of an Indo–European tradition in which there are three classes of deities, three classes of society and three methods of execution (usually noose, water and weapon), and it has been noted that the nature of capital punishment down to modern times has been dictated by the nature of the crime (Ward 1970). There may have been an underlying belief that the manner of death had a bearing on the soul's fate in the afterlife. Starkað, the semi-mythical figure of Norse legend, made sure he was slain by the sword, perhaps because one who died with the mark of battle on his body joined Odinn in Valhöll, whereas those who died in their beds went to Hel (Turville-Petre 1964, 211). Examples of the threefold death in Ireland, Wales and further afield given above could be seen as trifunctional sacrifices economically designed to placate three classes of divinities simultaneously. In the case of Lindow II/IV, however, adding drowning to the list creates an embarrassment of possible causes of death, and the explanation of the disposal of the body may be sought elsewhere.

One explanation, as Ross (1986) has pointed out, is that the bog itself was sacred, the place-name deriving from Welsh llyn ddu 'dark lake'; the evidence for Celtic veneration of springs, wells and pools is too well documented to require further elaboration here. From County Armagh, Ireland, there is even an example of a Late Bronze Age artificial ritual pool at the King's Stables, Tray, near to the seat of the legendary Kings of Ulster at Navan Fort, which in addition to high numbers of red deer antlers and dog bones contained the front portion of a human skull (Lynn 1977). In the same vicinity, Loughnashade, a natural lake, has yielded human skulls and other bones in addition to four well-known bronze horns of Late Iron Age date (Stuart 1819; Raftery 1987).

There may, however, be a more general explanation in that the Celtic Otherworld, often conceived as a distant island, is also to be found beneath the sea or the waters of a lake (Mac Cana 1970, 124; Rees and Rees 1961, 343). In the Welsh story Llyn y Fan, the supernatural woman has obviously emerged from beneath the lake; after a sojourn on earth she receives 'three causeless blows' and leaves (Rhys 1901). In Irish legend St Laichtin, a seventh-century patron saint of the fighting men of West Clare, would in times of battle stay immersed in cold water praying for their success (Mac Mathuna n.d., 100), perhaps to show solidarity with the warriors who, by imperilling their lives in battle, were effectively between this world and the next. In the myth *The Wasting Sickness of Cú Chulainn* and in the

Dream of Óengus (Gantz 1981), lakes figure as entry/exit points to the Otherworld.

The choice of a bog for the disposal of Lindow II may have been suggested by its known preservative properties. If ambiguity as to the cause of death meant that there was some uncertainty about whether the victim was dead or alive, circumstances which led to the physical preservation of the body may have been desirable in perpetuating the uncertainty.

Conclusions

Human sacrifice is a well-attested phenomenon of Celtic religion, and one which, according to Cassius Dio, was practised in Britain down to the time of Boudica's revolt. According to both Caesar and Strabo, druids carried out the rite. Sacrifices were carried out to ward off disease and to appease the gods so that those going into battle might be spared. The victims could be criminals, prisoners of war or, as in the *Rennes Dindshenchas*, hostages. The manner of the victim's death could be used to foretell the future. Those who were physically imperfect, if kings, brought disaster and had to be supplanted. Lower down the social scale, there can be little doubt that a supernumerary digit was, at best, unlucky.

According to Caesar, there was a Celtic belief in the transmigration of souls, and, in a sense, one whose death was rendered ambiguous because of its manner and circumstances was perhaps considered not dead at all. Llew, for example, was restored to life and slew his slayer. Another function of the triple death may have been to appease three classes of deity simultaneously. The triple death is an Indo–European rather than a specifically Celtic motif.

Ritual meals are attested in the 'fate tales', which may be degenerate versions of myths in which the victim originally suffered the threefold death, and are well attested in Celtic cake ceremonies.

Ritual drownings, as well as the more general veneration of pools and springs evidenced by votive deposits, are also attested. Drowning may have been appropriate for a certain category of crime, for a criminal of a particular social class or for a specific group of divinities. Pools and lakes were, however, regarded as liminal places, entrances and exits to the Otherworld, and the disposal of bodies, dead or alive, in such places may have been to ensure a quick translation from temporal existence. On the other hand, bogs, being neither land nor water, may have confined the victim to limbo.

The Lindow Man Phenomenon: Ancient and Modern

R. C. Turner

The Lindow Bodies

Lindow Moss has produced well-preserved human remains on four occasions between 1983 and 1988. Lindow I was an isolated head, identified initially as that of a woman. Lindow II (better known as Lindow Man) was the torso, arms and head of a young man whose right foot was discovered at the peat depot. Lindow III was the nearly complete body of a young man with all parts represented except the head. Lindow IV, found on two separate occasions, consists of the skin of the buttocks, part of the left leg, the right thigh and the ends of the right femur, from a point about 15 m from the findspot of Lindow II and in redeposited peat.

What do these four separate discoveries represent? Without doubt, Lindow IV represents the lower limbs of Lindow II cut off by the peat digging machinery in 1984 and moved about the site for the next four years before being spotted by the digger driver in his excavator's bucket. Only the left foot of this body is missing. This shows how keen-eyed the workmen at the site had become and how robust was the surviving tissue preserved by the tanning properties of the peat.

Detailed consideration has to be given to whether Lindow I and Lindow III are the same body. As with Lindow II and IV, they combine together to make a single body. The original identification of the head, Lindow I, by the forensic scientists was based on the architecture of the skull, which was soft and potentially deformed by the weight of peat above. Also, at that time, the police were expecting to find a woman, Malika Reyn-Bardt. There was no expectation that these remains were ancient. The findspots of Lindow I and Lindow III are not accurately known, because both finds were recovered from already excavated peat. The peat is dug out in 'mossrooms', up to 200 m long, and to about 1 m depth on each sweep. It is stacked alongside each mossroom so the excavated peat derives from a potential radius of about 6 m, that is, the length of reach of the excavator's arm. The findspot of Lindow I was plotted over a year after its discovery, from the memory of the workmen and their estimate of where it was likely to have been. Parts of Lindow III were found in the peat stack on site, so his estimated findspot is within a 12 m diameter circle of that point. The estimated distance between the two findspots (Fig. 5) is about 55 m, but because of the factors described above, the range might be of the order of 40–70 m apart.

There is circumstantial evidence linking the two bodies. Lindow I was discovered on the 13 May 1983. During the excavations of the area of the findspot of Lindow III, a drainage ditch was discovered running through the site, whose backfill contained a newspaper dated 24 May 1983. Given that the police activities halted production for a number of days on the peat moss, this is almost immediately after the workmen restarted. It is, therefore, very possible that the body of Lindow III was first excavated at that time and was subsequently re-excavated and moved into a new peat stack at least once, as certainly happened with the parts of the body, Lindow IV. This may explain why it was in so many pieces when first recovered and may indicate that the findspot of body and head were originally closer together than the 40–70 m range given above.

Looking at the bodies themselves, the only comparison that can now be made is by date. This is discussed by Housley *et al* (pp. 39–46) but statistically they are contemporary. No tissue survives from Lindow I, so no physiological or biochemical tests can be made to compare with results from Lindow III. A parallel does exist for the burial of the head and body of a bog corpse separately. This is the find made at Dätgen, Schleswig, Germany in 1959 (Struve 1967; van der Sanden, pp. 148–9), where the head and body of a man were found only about 3 m apart. From Britain, there is a headless bog body from Dolfawr Fair (gazetteer no. 63), and isolated heads from Worsley (26), Pilling (24), Red Moss (21), Llyn Mawr Farm (62) and Gifron (66). The most likely conclusion must be that Lindow I and Lindow III are the remains of the same young adult male body, buried close, but not very close, together.

So Lindow Moss has produced two very well-preserved young adult male bodies. They share similarities other than their remarkable preservation. Both died violent deaths and were buried naked (with the exception of Lindow II's fox-fur armband) 100–200 m from the nearest dryland, the two sand islands within the bog, in an extensive and potentially treacherous peat bog. They were of much the same age and build and there are suggestions, from the traces of body painting (Pyatt *et al*, pp. 62–75) and the fingernails, that both were people of high status. As there is no evidence for predation by insects or mammals it would appear that both bodies were thrust, or somehow buried in the peat bog, a fact confirmed by the same difference in radiocarbon date between the bodies and the layers from which they were retrieved. No structures or artefacts were found associated with either body.

There are also significant differences between the two bodies. The character of the violent death was different. In the case of Lindow II it had multiple causes, whilst with Lindow III it seems just to have consisted of beheading. The depositional environment was different, Lindow II being found in a layer indicating a bog pool and Lindow III on a peat surface. The components of the last meals were very different in macrobotanical content (see Holden, pp. 76–82) though similar when comparing the pollen evidence (see Scaife, pp. 83–5). There may also be significant differences in date. The calibrated date range for Lindow II with 95% confidence limits, based on the Oxford radiocarbon dates is 2 BC–AD 119, while the equivalent unified Oxford and Harwell date range for

Lindow III is AD 25–230, so the two bodies may be broadly contemporary or deposited up to 200 years apart.

In this author's opinion the most likely explanation for these two bodies is that they represent ritual sacrifices, probably for religious reasons, just before or during the first half of the Roman occupation of Britain. As such, they belong to a phenomenon well established across northern Europe and now well documented in Britain and Ireland (van der Sanden, pp. 146–65; Turner, pp. 205–20; Ó Floinn, pp. 221–34).

Despite these discoveries, Lindow Moss does not seem to be a special place in other ways. The bodies came from the remotest part of what was originally an extensive peat bog. Lindow Moss is similar to the many bogs formed in periglacial hollows across Lancashire, Cheshire and modern Humberside. It has been quite well documented by eighteenth- and nineteenth-century antiquarians and historians, but the only other antiquities reported are a wooden trackway (probably prehistoric in date) and the well-preserved body of a wild boar (Norbury 1884). There is no evidence for other human remains or votive hoards of metalwork or other objects. This cannot be taken as absolute proof for there has been peat-digging at Lindow Moss since at least the fifteenth century. However, handdigging continued well into the 1970s and some of the men who have been working at the present peat extraction site since the early 1960s, have reported no unusual finds other than the bodies.

The Cultural Context of the Lindow Bodies

It is impossible to address the cultural context of the Lindow bodies without resolving the dating question. This relies on the radiocarbon dating of the bodies and the consideration of the stratigraphic positions in which they were found. Both have been considered in some detail by other authors in this volume. It is now generally accepted by those working on the Lindow bodies that the calibrated date range of 2 BC–AD 119 for Lindow II and AD 25–230 for Lindow III are correct. This differs from the conclusion reached by Stead in the *Lindow Man* monograph (Stead 1986, 180) who then favoured the stratigraphic date of the Middle Iron Age for Lindow II. It is clear from other papers in this volume that the radiocarbon dating of human bodies from peat bogs presents special problems because of the biochemical processes involved in the interaction between the peat and human tissue. However,

Lindow III has produced repeatable radiocarbon dates from two laboratories and the extensive range of dates performed by Oxford on Lindow II are internally consistent.

Buckland and Barber (pp. 47–51) have presented a variety of mechanisms by which the radiocarbon dates and stratigraphic positions may be resolved. Peat bogs do not follow exactly the same rules of stratigraphy as traditional dryland archaeological sites. Their layers grow rather than accumulate, whilst on dryland sites they are dumped or dug away. However, an age difference of up to 400 years between the body dates and stratigraphic position is probably beyond the limits of the presently accepted models of peat-bog formation. Certainly the dated peat column analysed by Branch and Scaife (pp. 19–30) and the results of the excavations in 1987 do not suggest that bog pools at Lindow were that long-lived, so there must have been some attempt at burial within the peat that was not represented in the undisturbed levels recorded above Lindow II (Oldfield *et al* 1986). The problem of the depositional environment and the discrepancies in dates have recently been reconsidered for some of the famous Danish and German finds (Brothwell *et al* 1990) and the Dutch bodies (van der Sanden 1990). The Lindow bodies are therefore not alone in having this difference in date, though the evidence for peat-digging – a possible explanation – is not established in northern England as early as the beginning of the Romano-British period (for a review of such evidence in Britain see Innes and Shennan 1991, 16).

Having decided on the most likely dates for the Lindow bodies, it is possible to explore their cultural context. Both date ranges span the Roman conquest of north-west England, with the mean date of Lindow II being around that specific time. Following the invasion of Britain in AD 43, Roman control quickly spread across lowland England and south Wales with an informal frontier forming along the Fosse Way running across the Midlands. To protect this frontier, the Romans reached an arrangement with the Brigantes, the main tribal grouping of northern England led by their queen, Cartimandua. The Lindow area would have been under Brigantian control. Unrest in north Wales seems to have led to the establishment of the first fort at Chester in the AD 50s (Petch 1987) and was followed by the famous punitive raid led by Suetonius Paulinus in AD 60 to crush the Druids in their headquarters on Anglesey. Relationships with the Brigantes began to break down during the AD 60s when a succession of rebellions was suppressed by military activity in the south Pennines (Dudley and Webster 1965). The conquest of Brigantia was begun by the governor, Petilius Cerialis (AD 71–4) and completed by Agricola (AD 77–84).

In Cheshire, this conquest led to the establishment of the legionary fortress at Chester and auxiliary forts at Northwich and Middlewich, and to the north of Lindow at Manchester. All these remained garrisoned through the second century, but the auxiliary forts and the Roman site at Wilderspool became increasingly devoted to a wide range of crafts and industries manufacturing goods for the Roman army and local consumption. Archaeological evidence shows that the size of garrisons varied in these auxiliary forts due to operational demands elsewhere. The constant rebuilding and refining of the military frontiers of Hadrian's and the Antonine Wall implies that native rebellion was a constant threat further north. However, there is no evidence for unrest within the southern Brigantes until the governor Clodius Albinus (AD 191–6) took away some of the British garrison to further his own political ambitions on the continent. The result was predictable, for his successor Virius Lupus (AD 197–201) had to 'buy off' the northern tribes and was heavily involved in rebuilding forts in the Pennines (Shotter 1984).

Lindow Moss is rather remote from these Roman centres (Fig. 86), being 19 km north-east of Northwich and 17 km south of Manchester. Cheshire remained within the military zone of Roman Britain. The only evidence for some form of local government in the north-west comes from the large civilian settlements at Chester and Carlisle. Local Brigantian landowners did not, or were not allowed to, adopt Romanised ways. The small Roman villa at Eaton-by-Tarporley (Petch 1987, 210–1) is the only one known in Cheshire and the only other in the north-west is at Kirk Sink, Gargrave, Yorkshire. The two men from Lindow Moss were therefore drawn from the existing pre-Roman native population.

Whilst the Roman invasion completely changed the political organisation of the region, the basic pattern of economic and social life probably continued largely unchanged. The Roman army provided new roads, a market for agricultural produce, and a source of consumer goods, such as pots and metalwork. It would levy and collect taxes, but the pattern of small dispersed settlements or farmsteads probably continued. In Brigantian territory this pattern of settlement is well established in Cumbria and north Lancashire (Higham and Jones 1975; Higham 1980), where the population remained thin, though with concentrations of new settlements occurring around Roman forts. Much less well-known, is the pattern of settlement in south Lancashire and Cheshire in and

Fig. 86 Map of Roman Cheshire showing the relationship of known sites to Lindow Moss. (*After Petch 1987*)

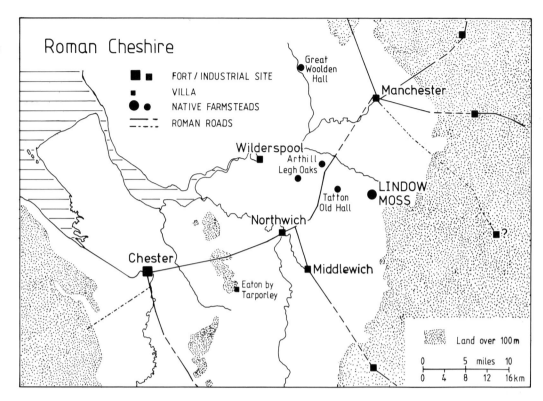

around the extensive mosslands, no doubt because of the differences in later land use.

Around Lindow Moss itself, the evidence for Late Iron Age and Romano-British settlement is very thin indeed. Stray finds are limited to a collection of coins from Alderley Edge and the second century Roman head of a maenad found at Over Alderley (Petch 1987). Simple farmsteads have been identified lower down the Bollin Valley from Lindow at Tatton Old Hall, Legh Oaks Farm and Arthill Heath Farm (Higham 1985; Nevell 1989 and 1988), though the nearest of these is 5 km away. Cheshire's ten hillforts are concentrated on the central sandstone ridge. They are modest in size and have simple defences, and what little excavation has taken place does not suggest Late Iron Age or Romano-British occupation (Longley 1987). Perhaps the most recently discovered site in the region which shows best how the Lindow men and women may have lived is at Great Woolden Hall, Greater Manchester (Nevell 1991). This site lies on a low promontory overlooking the Glaze Brook and on the western fringe of the formerly very extensive Chat Moss. It shows a period of occupation from the Late Iron Age well into Romano-British times and is positioned to exploit both dryland and wetland resources.

Peat bogs can provide a variety of resources. Perhaps the most important at this period is bog iron, concretions

of iron ore formed by solution through the peat on tree stumps and other solid objects towards the base of the bog. These concretions can be the only natural source of high grade iron ore in many regions. Peat also provided fuel. What is perhaps an early peat spade was recovered at Tytherington near Macclesfield (Sainter 1898, 64–5), but there is little stratigraphic evidence for late prehistoric or Romano-British peat extraction locally. In historic times Cheshire peat bogs provided a source of safe lighting, men probed for the large pine trunks at the base of the peat bogs. When split into spills these provided lights that burnt without ash (King 1656, 17). *Sphagnum* peat was well known as an antiseptic and was used as recently as the First World War for field dressings.

Peat bogs offered a variety of animal and plant foodstuffs. They are a haunt of wildfowl and snipe. Bilberry (*Vaccinium myrtillus*) and cranberry (*Vaccinium oxycoccus*) can be collected in season. During dry summers, raised bogs, including Lindow Moss, were used to graze cattle. Potentially important were intoxicants and stimulants. Bog myrtle (*Myrica gale*) was used to flavour Celtic beer. The sundew (*Drosera rotundifolia*) was used to make a celebrated liqueur (Grigson 1956, 193). From the birch woodlands which formed on the sandy margins around the peat bogs, comes the hallucinogenic fungus fly agaric (*Amanita muscaria*), widely used across northern Europe to

Fig. 87 The modern distribution of mistletoe with the records on oak shown below. (*Biological Records Centre, Monks Wood Experimental Station*)
- 1950 onwards (GB 684, Ir 2, Ch Is 1)
- before 1950 (GB 58, Ir 0, Ch Is 1)

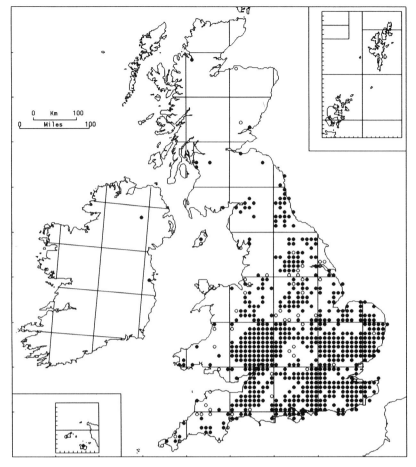

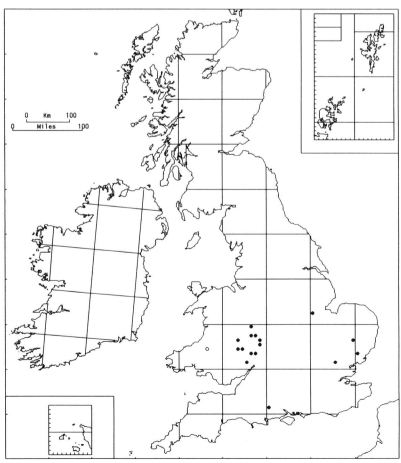

induce altered states of mind (Phillips 1981, 15, for example).

Various natural phenomena occur on peat bogs, of which will-o'-the-wisp, jack-o'-lantern or *ignis fatuus* is the most remarkable. The cause of these is methane produced from the decay of peat which can ignite spontaneously to form pale flames playing across the bog surface. So peat bogs provided a range of resources to supplement those from dryland, in a setting that could be both treacherous and mysterious.

The Lindow bodies are best interpreted as the victims of ritual sacrifice probably associated with a religious ceremony. It is notoriously difficult to reconstruct ritual and religious practices from archaeological evidence alone, but for the Celtic religions there is documentary evidence from Graeco-Roman commentators and the vernacular Celtic legends (Green 1986; Magilton, pp. 183–7). The Lindow bodies potentially provide much more evidence of the ritual practice involved because of their remarkable preservation. With Lindow II, much has been made of his 'triple death'. 'Triplism' is one of the commonest Celtic religious symbols (Magilton, pp. 184–5; Green 1986) but Ross has gone further in linking the triple death to the appeasement of three Celtic gods, Esus, Taranis and Teutates (Ross 1986; Ross and Robins 1989). These three gods are mentioned together only once, by the Roman poet Lucan, who describes the propitiation of these gods in Gaul by human sacrifice. It is only later commentators who relate Esus to hanging, Taranis to burning, and Teutates to drowning (Green 1986, 27).

Four grains of mistletoe (*Viscum album*) pollen were recovered from Lindow II's gut contents (Scaife 1986). This has been taken as a possible link to the Druids (e.g. Ross 1986). Pliny's famous passage describing the Druids states that they hold nothing more sacred than the mistletoe when it is found growing on the oak tree where it is gathered by a gold sickle (Pliny, *Nat. Hist.*, xvi, 95). Mistletoe is on the limit of its range in midland England and Wales. None of the Cheshire floras record it as occurring in the county, though since the publicity surrounding Lindow Man, over eight sites have now been reported, all on apple trees. It is almost unknown in north Wales and has never been recorded on Anglesey. In Britain it is most commonly found on apple, lime, popular and hawthorn but it is very rare on oak (less than twenty trees in a survey carried out in 1969/70), with colonies largely restricted to Herefordshire (Perring 1973), (Fig. 87). Mistletoe is dioecious, i.e. it has male and female flowers, with the pollen deriving from only the male flower. It is not a pollen common in the archaeological record. Godwin (1975, 217) gives only seven records for the Flandrian all within the main area of distribution except for Kirkby Thore in Westmoreland. So it could only have been swallowed in some mixture to have got into Lindow II's stomach. Mistletoe has been used widely in herbal remedies, and the berries can induce nervous paralysis. Culpepper states it is useful for convulsive fits, palsy and vertigo. An eighteenth-century recipe in the Dyfed County Record Office for a cure for epilepsy consisted of the ground skull of a man who had died a violent death added to some mistletoe of the oak gathered in the wane of the moon (ref. HDX/382/1).

The classical authors link Druidic practices with human sacrifice. However, Green notes that:

> The main fascination of Graeco-Roman historians for the Druids was their role in human sacrifice, an emphasis which may have been designed deliberately to disgust their readers as a practice typical of outlandish barbarians. The literature makes it clear that as far as the Druids themselves were concerned, the main aim of human sacrifice was not so much the propitiation or appeasement of the gods, but divination (Green 1986, 27).

So, the body of Lindow Man seen by Ross as the evidence for the propitiation of powerful gods, could also have been dumped following its sacrifice for divination purposes.

Lindow III suffered a different death and has no evidence for mistletoe within the gut. However, beheading is also a central part of Celtic mythology and religious practice. The cult of the head has been explored in considerable detail by Ross, who concludes:

> The cult of the human head thus constitutes a persistent theme throughout all aspects of Celtic ·life, spiritual and temporal, and the symbolism of the severed head may be regarded as the most typical and universal of their religious attitudes (Ross 1967, 126).

Lindow III has a number of local parallels in the heads from Worsley, Red and Pilling Mosses. The stone Celtic heads with their schematised features are a feature of the Romano-Celtic period. In Britain, the majority of British finds come from the Brigantian region (Fig. 88a) where a plethora of local indigenous deities are recorded (Green 1986, 218). Very few of these finds can be confidently dated to the Romano-British period. This tradition of carving schematic heads and mounting them on

Fig. 88a A probable Romano-British Celtic head found in Cuppin Street, Chester. (*Manchester Museum*)

Fig. 88b A modern 'Celtic head' set into a wall at Yarrow Reservoir, near Bolton. (*Manchester Museum*)

buildings, the keystones of bridges or other prominent places (Fig. 88b) continued to be practised throughout the post-medieval and into the modern period in the Pennine regions (Jackson 1973).

The violent suppression of the Druidical cult was followed by a steady assimilation of the Celtic pantheon by their appropriate Roman gods so that their names are often twinned on inscriptions. These gods tend to have a localised distribution and only appear in a human form under Roman influence. A striking and perhaps relevant example of this is a Roman altar from Chester, dedicated to *I(ovi) O(ptimo) M(aximo) Tanaro* (Green 1983). The altar was erected in AD 154 by a legionary soldier of Spanish origin and is dedicated to Jupiter and the Celtic god of thunder Tanarus or Taranis, one of the three deities mentioned by Lucan in connection with the triple death. It is one of only seven known epigraphic dedications to Taranis, with three from France, two from Germany and one from Yugoslavia. This altar shows that the cult of Taranis was sufficiently powerful in Cheshire for a non-native legionary soldier to publicly dedicate an altar to him in the mid-second century.

There are, therefore, a number of possible links between the Lindow bodies and what is known of Celtic religious practices to confirm the likelihood that they were ritual sacrifices. Both were probably men of status, the neatly trimmed hair, beard and fingernails of Lindow II and the evidence of body-painting on both bodies are suggestive of membership of the warrior or bardic classes. The changing political climate within the date range of these bodies provides a number of possible motives for such sacrifices.

The Bog Body Phenomenon

Having considered the Lindow bodies in detail it is now time to consider the wider phenomenon of bog bodies. Various papers in this volume have shown that bog bodies have a very wide distribution across Northern Europe. The extent and numbers of these discoveries was first recognised by Alfred Dieck, who showed that they could occur from a very wide date span, ranging from the Mesolithic to modern times; and resulted from a whole range of causes – inhumation, accidental death, murder and ritual. If some of the items were included in his catalogue uncritically, it does not detract from the overall distribution he established. However, the bog body phenomenon is best known to archaeologists and the general public through P. V. Glob's very successful book *Mosefolket* (The Bog

People). The spectacular discoveries with which he was associated, Tollund and Grauballe Man, were presented with a carefully selected group of other bodies from Denmark, northern Germany and isolated examples from further afield. These bodies formed the basis of his very attractive theory of ritual sacrifice as an offering to a Mother Goddess.

The study has been taken forward by further work in Denmark (Fischer 1979; Brothwell *et al* 1990) and Germany (Hayen 1987). More detailed reconsideration has been given to the whole assemblages from the Netherlands, Ireland and Britain (van der Sanden, pp. 146–54; Ó Floinn, pp. 137–45; Turner, pp. 108–22). Radiocarbon dating has begun to be applied quite widely to bog bodies since its early use in proving the antiquity of Grauballe Man. Only rarely were there diagnostic artefacts found with these bodies to provide an independent source for the date.

Nevertheless, groupings within the spans of the radiocarbon dates are beginning to appear. There are Neolithic dates for bog skeletons from Denmark (Bennike and Ebbesen 1986) and isolated Neolithic dates from Hartlepool, England and Stoneyisland, Ireland. From the Fenland, England, are a number of sites in Methwold parish producing potentially contemporary burials of Early Bronze Age date. There is a Middle Bronze Age body from Emmer-Erfschidenveen, Holland, where the tissue survived extensively and the body is clothed and wrapped in an elaborate cape. Though there is no other radiocarbon date of this period, the reported stratigraphic position of the bodies from Scaleby Moss (also wrapped in a cape) and Whixall Moss might be broadly contemporary.

The best preserved and most celebrated bodies have produced dates from throughout the Iron Age and Roman periods (more accurately the Roman Iron Age in countries not conquered by the legionaries). Table 10 shows the calibrated dates of bodies from Denmark, Holland, and those from Britain and Ireland. In general terms, the Danish bodies span the whole of the Iron Age, those from Holland come from the later Iron Age and early Roman period, while those from Britain are probably Roman in date. The Irish finds range quite widely from the later Iron Age well into the Roman period. The preferred explanation for the death of these bodies is as the result of ritual sacrifice, though this may not be the only explanation (Briggs, pp. 168–82).

The sample of dated bodies remains small and the dates themselves are fraught with difficulties. However, there does seem to be a trend, where this practice of ritual sacrifice moved slowly from east to west and continues in Britain and Ireland when it had ceased on the continent. In moving from east to west, it crossed racial and cultural boundaries. The Germanic peoples of Denmark, Germany and Holland shared little direct contact with the Celts of Britain and Ireland. British Celtic finds in Denmark are limited to two gold coins of the Catevellauni of south-east England (Parker-Pearson 1986). What they do share is the tradition of depositing votive objects, pottery, metalwork, wooden images and objects, and human bodies into peat bogs and other watery places.

This tradition was recognised by Glob, who observed a trend beginning with the deposition of both pottery and metal vessels in the Late Bronze Age and Early Iron Age. There are two famous cauldrons from Rynkeby and Gunderstrup. The imagery on the panels of the Gunderstrup cauldron is seen by some to be Celtic (Olmsted 1979), though the vessel is probably central European in origin and imported and ultimately deposited by Germanic peoples; associated with some of these vessels, or in isolation, were wooden images of gods. From the end of the Iron Age and to the Roman Iron Age, the cauldrons are superseded by vast hoards of weaponry and other war booty, like the finds from the site at Illerup, near Skanderborg, Denmark. Here, three separate deposits of military equipment have been found, two dating to *c.* AD 200 and the third to AD 400 (Ilkjaer 1977; Jensen 1982).

A similar pattern of deposition can be found in Britain. Taking Wales as an example, there are hoards of single objects from lakes and peat bogs which span the same period. From the Late Bronze Age are two unusual vessels, the Caergwrle Bowl, a small carved shale boat inlaid with gold leaf, and the Arthog bucket, a bronze vessel of Hallstatt 'B' type, found in a marsh on the sea-shore. Two large sheet-metal bronze cauldrons form the basis of the Llynfawr hoard found in peat at the centre of a former lake in Glamorgan (Fig. 89). However, the hoard also contained five socketed axes, socketed sickles, gouges, harness fittings, a razor, belt-hook, and an iron sword and spearhead. This mixture of vessels, tools and weapons conflicts with the simpler progression put forward by Glob. Also from the Late Bronze Age are three sheet-bronze shields found in peat bogs (Savory 1980).

From the Late Iron Age in Wales comes the famous Llyn Cerrig Bach hoard of La Tène metalwork and other objects, found in the peat margins of a lake in Anglesey in 1942–3, when 138 metal objects were retrieved from mechanically excavated peat being used in airfield construction. There were weapons – swords, part of a dagger, spears and a shield-boss – metal fittings from chariots,

Fig. 89 Part of one of the cauldrons with a representative collection of tools, weapons, and ornaments from the hoard at Llyn Fawr, Glamorgan. (*National Museum of Wales*)

Fig. 90 A selection of items from the Llyn Cerrig Bach hoard, Anglesey. (*National Museum of Wales*)

horse-trappings – and other items such as gang-chains, currency bars, cauldrons, tools, a bronze trumpet and some finely decorated bronze fittings (Fig. 90). Associated with the metalwork were also large numbers of animal bones.

Few finds were made in context but they appear to have been thrown into the lake from a rocky eminence. Many of the objects showed evidence for damage in antiquity. The objects from the hoard belong to the period between 200 BC and AD 100 implying that it accumulated over many years. Whilst there are possible associations with the Druids because of its date and location, there were no human bones found here as have been recovered at the type site of La Tène (Fox 1947; Savory 1976).

Something of this pattern of deposition occurs across Britain and Ireland. The vast majority of certain classes of object are known from watery places; of the 32 findspots of Late Bronze Age shields found in Britain and Ireland, 8 were found in rivers, 13 in peat bogs, 5 during drainage works, one in an earthen mound and for the other 5, the findspots are unknown (Coles 1962). Three shields were found vertically and the five or six shields from Luggtonridge, Ayrshire were placed in a ring. Musical instruments, which also potentially have ritual significance, are also commonly found in groups in bogs. The Irish side-blown horns of the Late Bronze Age have been found often in groups in bogs, such as the 15 or 16 instruments from a bog between Cork and Mallow. Rarely are they found in mixed hoards such as the Dowris or Whigsborough hoard of Co. Offaly, whose contents otherwise parallel those at Llynfawr. England has similar finds of instruments from Tattershall, Lincolnshire (Davey 1971), and the great lurer from Denmark are found exclusively in bogs, and usually in pairs (Brøndsted 1958, 181–3).

So the phenomenon of the deposition of metalwork objects and hoards in peat bogs and watery places was well established in the Late Bronze Age in Britain and Ireland and the practice continued through the Iron Age. The newly discovered material from the post-alignment at Flag Fen (Pryor 1991) shows that some sites had long periods of deposition extending from the Late Bronze Age to the Middle Iron Age. Later in the Iron Age, deposition seems to have become concentrated in rivers rather than bogs. The Thames has produced a series of remarkable objects (Fitzpatrick 1984; Stead 1985) as well as a lot of human skeletal material (Bradley and Gordon 1988). The Witham in Lincolnshire can be compared with the Thames and the fourth or third century BC finds from alongside a timber alignment or jetty at Fiskerton, including three

swords, one with a coral-encrusted handle, were made in context (Field 1984).

Britain and Ireland have also produced a number of anthropomorphic wooden figurines paralleling those illustrated by Glob from Denmark and north Germany. These have recently been re-assessed and radiocarbon dated (Coles 1990). Six could be dated directly and in the case of the Somerset Levels God-Dolly, by association. The range of dates is surprising, with the limits of the calibrated time span being 3000–430 BC, with two figures dating to the Neolithic, one Early Bronze Age, one Late Bronze Age and three Early Iron Age (Fig. 91).

The long tradition of the deposition of a wide variety of objects in watery places in Britain and Ireland, may have had origins in the Neolithic, but there is a peak of

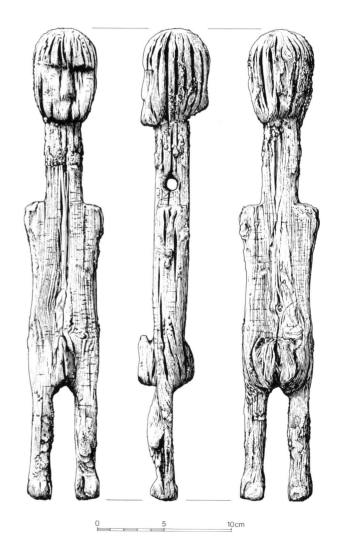

Fig. 91 The Kingsteignton Iron Age wooden figure, Devon. (*M. Rouillard*)

activity in terms of the numbers and quality in the Late Bronze Age, i.e. in a pre-Celtic period. Bradley puts the British evidence alongside a European tradition of the deposition of valuable objects in wet places, often in formalised groups, from which they could be recovered only with difficulty (Bradley 1990). This type of site commonly produces human remains and these tend to be most frequent in periods with few identifiable formal burials.

Where the dated British bog bodies stand apart is that they seem as a group to post-date the rest of this depositional activity. The same is not true in Denmark and Holland, where contemporary deposition of objects does occur. However, well-preserved bog bodies do not occur with, or in close association to, valuable metalwork. They are often naked, or with simple clothing and occasionally a few personal adornments. However, to the communities which deposited them, they may have been of great value or status. Lindow II's unabraded fingernails and the delicate unabraded fingerprint of Grauballe Man suggest men who did not take part in manual work. The body painting traced on Lindow II and III also suggest status. One of the Dutch bodies had the distinctive knotted hairstyle of a Swabian warrior and so may have been a prisoner of war, though a beheaded victim with the same hairstyle was also recovered from his native territory (van der Sanden 1990, 53–4; Glob 1969, 117).

Holden (pp. 76–82) argues that the mixture of weed seeds which constituted the last meals of the bodies from Tollund, Grauballe and Borre Fens is typical of a famine diet, where all that is left is the waste fraction of the harvest, after all the grain has been eaten. Glob took this combination of seeds as a symbolic attempt to purge the fields of these weeds. However, the meals of the bog bodies as a whole are varied and, with the exception of the blackberries from Zweeloo Man, are not indicative of particular seasons.

Even though it has to be accepted that the numbers of bog bodies reported from Britain, Ireland and Holland are probably a small proportion of those who have been uncovered over the centuries, there are insufficient bodies to argue for the sacrifices here being on an annual or cyclical basis. The two bodies from Lindow Moss may have been buried up to two hundred years apart. In the absence of systematic studies of the much larger numbers of finds from Denmark (up to 500) and Germany (over 900) it is impossible to assess their chronological distribution or their likely causes of death.

What evidence there is, for those bodies seen as human sacrifices, argues that their deaths were in response to crisis. These crises could be political: attack, invasion or failure of succession; or economic: famine, disease or failure of trade. The Druids performed human sacrifice not as offerings but for divination, perhaps seeking guidance on how to react to these crises. As many of the bodies seem to have died from hanging or strangulation, it may have been their death throes which were as important as the later deposition of the body within the bog.

However, no single explanation is sufficient to explain the bog-body phenomenon. The execution of criminals and their subsequent burial in bogs among the Germans in the first century AD are recorded by Tacitus. Sacrifices could be made in celebration or as thank offerings to the gods as favoured by Glob and Fischer. Other bodies of this period could have been the victims of accidental death or unfamiliar funerary practices, as can be demonstrated with bog bodies of other dates. Perhaps the explanations offered tell more about the explainer than the phenomenon itself.

Myth, Legend and Bog Bodies

The practice of ritual sacrifice seems to have ceased in the middle of the Roman period with those dated bodies from Britain. Nevertheless, the Lindow Man phenomenon appears to have continued on, spanning the gap between the period of the sacrifices and the modern reports of their rediscovery. Within the oral tradition and its earliest transcriptions into written form, is a wealth of imagery concerned with human sacrifice, magic cauldrons, watery places and incorruptibility.

On pages 183–7, Magilton explores the Welsh and Irish myths which appear to incorporate elements which can also be interpreted from the archaeological evidence. The imagery within these myths stresses the essential ambiguity of the bog body phenomenon. Peat bogs are neither wet nor dry. The bodies are dead but do not decay. Victims die, only to be reborn. This author has shown that beheading myths and watery places were incorporated into a number of the most celebrated early English tales (Turner 1986). The combination of English and Celtic strands occurs in the legend of St Winefrid. She has an English name, but her uncle St Beuno and her attacker Caradoc are Celts. Whilst the saint's legend is full of pagan imagery, it was enthusiastically adopted and promoted by the Christian church.

Another early English saint, St Guthlac, late in the seventh century, set out to seek solitude in the 'hideous fen of a huge bigness' in Lincolnshire. Accompanied by a boatman Tatwin and a servant named Beccelm he landed on the island of Croyland, to take on the forces of the devil in his homeland. His legend also records that his servant Beccelm tried to cut Guthlac's throat while shaving him. Somehow the forces of evil seemed to reside in the peat bogs and early Christian heroes felt the need to overcome them there.

One of the attributes of early saints was that their bodies remained incorrupt after death. It is the apparent incorrupt nature of bog bodies which so excites the sense of wonder in those who now behold them. The unusual quality of the preservation seems to give rise to the need to seek an equally unusual explanation for the presence of these bodies. These explanations are often very exact and linked to historical events. Antiquarians and archaeologists seeking to prove their antiquity have had to fight hard to overcome what are often very attractive stories.

In the case of St Edmund, King of East Anglia, murdered by the Danes in 869, it is the later recorded history of his body that is of interest. Edmund refused to surrender to the Danes (led by the appropriately named Inguar the Boneless) and was taken from his hall, bound to a tree and shot full of arrows. During this dreadful ordeal, he expressed his love of Christ. In the end, his head was cut off and hidden, separately from the body, in a wood. Eventually, the king's followers found both the head and body. Miraculously, on being brought together, they rejoined. Abbo's life of the saint, written in 986–7, emphasised the remarkably incorrupt condition of the corpse, and says there was no trace of the wounds or scars, except for a tenuous red crease, like a scarlet thread around his neck. As late as 1198, Abbot Samson examined the body in the company of 18 monks and found it still incorrupt and supple (Scarfe 1970). This author has argued elsewhere that the relics of St Edmund were in fact the remains of England's earliest recorded bog body and, in this case, the remarkable preservation was linked to a royal martyrdom (Turner 1986, 175).

The case of Queen Gunhild in Denmark provides a striking parallel. From a bog on the ancient estate of Haraldskjaer, south of the former royal seat of Jelling in East Jutland, in 1835, came the well-preserved and clothed body of a woman found staked down within the peat (Glob 1969, 69–79). A professor and other eminent scholars concluded, largely from an early place name for the area of 'Gunnelsmose', that this was the body of Queen Gunhild, the cruel consort of King Erik Bloodaxe. There was a legend that she had been drowned in a bog by King Harald Blue-tooth. Set against his attractive explanation was J. J. A. Worsaae, then a young student, but later a key figure in the development of archaeology. He showed that there was no historical basis for the legend and argued that this should be seen as one of a group of Iron Age finds. The controversy raged, and the body was laid to rest in a special chapel of the church of St Nicholas, Vejle. King Frederick VI himself presented the oak coffin in which she can still be seen in her unconserved state (Fig. 92).

Several bog bodies from Scotland have been explained as Covenanters, men persecuted during the reign of James II for their Protestant beliefs, whilst the find from Mulkeeragh, Co. Derry was seen as a Highland Soldier (Turner and Briggs 1986). The woman's head, wearing a jet and amber necklace, found deep beneath the peat in Pilling Moss in 1824, was wrapped in a coarse woollen cloth. A local doctor, W. Birch, reported on the discovery and sought to link this find to the infamous 'baby farm' at the nearby Bone Hill Farm, where, in the eighteenth century, illegitimate children of wealthy families were left to be reared or disposed of according to the fee paid (Lawrenson undated).

P. V. Glob faced a problem when first exhibiting Grauballe Man, for an old farmer's wife identified the body as Red Christian, a peat cutter who had disappeared from the district in 1887. The story was picked up and stoked up by the local and national press, dividing the citizens of Aarhus into factions for and against the archaeologists. The controversy was eventually quelled when a very early

Fig. 92 'Queen Gunhild' in her chapel, St Nicholas Church, Vejle, Denmark.

radiocarbon date demonstrated the body's antiquity (Glob 1969, 37–62). The links between the Reyn-Bardt murder and the Lindow bog bodies echo this story in reverse.

Unfortunately, Lindow Man has not escaped the desire to seek a historical and spectacular explanation for his death. Despite all the problems over his date, and the fact that he is one of two or more bodies from Lindow Moss and many hundreds from Britain and across Northern Europe, two authors seek to name him, reconstruct his history and even give the day and year of his death. In their book, *The Life and Death of the Druid Prince*, Anne Ross and Don Robins select some facts, confuse others and pile supposition upon supposition to produce the story of Lovernios, an Irish druid, sacrificed on 1 May AD 60 (Ross and Robins 1989). Stirred into the pot for good measure are Boudicca, the Llyn Cerrig Bach hoard, the East Anglian gold torcs and a group of Celtic temples. The book is presented as reputable archaeological interpretation but is no more than poorly written, historical fiction.

This explanation does a disservice to archaeology, which can only ever partially reconstruct and explain the events of the past from the material evidence. An archaeologist should present the most probable explanation of the facts available and be willing to modify or change that explanation as new evidence is gathered. To give names to these discoveries and attempt to link them to our very partial knowledge of the Roman conquest and occupation, defuses the sense of wonder which one gets from gazing on a face from late prehistory and detracts from, rather than sheds light on, the complex ritual which must have surrounded the death of many of these bog bodies.

The Relics of Bog Bodies

The remains of bog bodies exert a special fascination. They are analogous to the holy relics which were traded and jealously guarded by the medieval church. Indeed, in the case of St Edmund and perhaps of St Winefrid, the relics may have been bog bodies. Their remains were translated to major abbey churches by ambitious clerics, St Edmund to Bury St Edmunds in 1013 and St Winefrid to Shrewsbury Abbey in 1138. The cults were carefully orchestrated and pilgrims brought great prosperity to both abbeys (Farmer 1978).

A number of bodies were re-interred in Christian churchyards as a more appropriate location for well-preserved human remains. This is true of Grewelth-

orpe Man, Amcotts Woman, the bodies from Whitaside, Grinton-in-Swaledale, Dol Fawr Fair, Whixall Moss and the two bodies from Hope, Derbyshire. In the last case, the reburial was intended to stop them being used as a public spectacle. In 1674, a man and women died from exposure on the moors near Hope. It was several months before their bodies were found in a snowdrift, and as they had begun to decay they were buried on the spot, which happened to be a peat bog. Twenty-eight years later,

> … some countrymen, having observed, I suppose, the extraordinary quality of this soil in preserving dead bodies from corrupting, were curious enough to open the ground to see if these persons had been so preserved and found them no way altered … They were afterwards exposed for a sight 20 years, though they were much changed in this time … The woman, by some rude people had been taken out of the ground, to which one may well impute her greater decay … (Balguy 1734, 414).

So these bodies had become something of a rather macabre local attraction until the man's grandson paid for a decent funeral in Hope churchyard. A deposition concerning this reburial is shown as Fig. 93.

Another common practice was for onlookers to take away clothing, artefacts or even parts of the body as trophies. In the case of the Drumkeeragh body, Co. Down, the peasants took away the clothing for re-use, as it was in such good condition. It was only the efforts of Lady Moira in gathering together fragments that allowed her to make

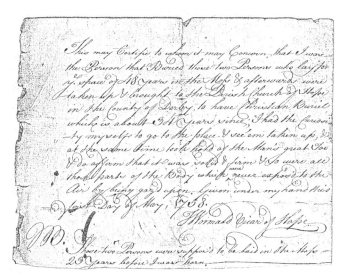

Fig. 93 Deposition made by Revd Thomas Wormald regarding the bog bodies from Hope. (*By kind permission of the Derbyshire Record Office.*)

a full and accurate description of this unusual find (Moira 1783). Unfortunately, the remarkable clothing of GrewelthorpeMan, North Yorkshire, 'the toga of a green colour, while some portions of the dress were of a scarlet hue, the stockings were of yellow cloth and the sandals of a finely artistic shape', was taken away by local people, leaving the local constable to recover the sandals and part of a stocking (Turner *et al* 1991). Whilst most of these items must have been taken as souvenirs, they did have a resale value, for the coat recovered from a body found at Drumadreen, Co. Derry, was sold for 2*s*. 6*d*. and taken to Belfast (Briggs and Turner 1986, 190–1).

Human remains were also collected by interested antiquarians. The arm of a body found in *c*. 1645, in the Isle of Axholme, was in the possession of the local antiquarian, Dr Nathaniel Johnson. Dr Stovin, who excavated a woman's body from nearby Amcotts in 1747, sent one of her hands and one of her shoes to the Society of Antiquaries for comment. Though these are now lost, the other shoe has been rediscovered in the collections of the second oldest antiquarian society in Britain, the Spalding Gentlemen's Society, and is the subject of a re-evaluation (Turner and Rhodes 1992). The body, wrapped in an animal skin cape, from Scaleby, Cumbria was found in 1845 (Turner 1988). The local rector, Revd J. Hill, obtained part of the skull with its black hair, other bones and some of the cape. These he passed to a friend, the Revd Isaacson, who passed them on to the great Derbyshire antiquarian, Thomas Bateman, where they are noted in the catalogue of his collection in 1855. They were sold when this huge collection was auctioned in 1893, where they appeared as part of a miscellaneous lot, which also included a piece of oak from the *Mary Rose*. The lot fetched £4 14*s*.

So finds from bog bodies have a long history of being treated as curiosities. Several museums in the late nineteenth and early twentieth centuries made collections of skeletal material from peat sites, with the Sedgwick Museum, Cambridge and the British Museum (Natural History), South Kensington having the largest groups. There was considerable interest in the demineralised character of the bone and some speculation that people living close to bogs were of a distinctive racial type.

The idea that these human remains should be displayed for public interest and spectacle seems to be a more modern idea. Though this clearly happened in the late seventeenth century on the open moors above Hope, Derbyshire, the first complete bog body to be put on public display was that found at Castle Blakeney, Gallagh, Co. Galway, in 1821. After reburial, this body and its deerskin cape were dug up on several occasions before being passed to the Royal Dublin Society and in 1860 to the Royal Irish Academy where they were put on public display. They now survive in their unconserved state in the National Museum of Ireland (Ó Floinn, pp. 137–45). A bog body from Rendswuhren Fen, North Germany, found in 1871 was displayed by an enterprising man in a local barn where visitors helped themselves to parts of the body and the clothing as souvenirs (Glob 1969, 106–7). Indeed, P. V. Glob had to display Grauballe Man in his unconserved state at the Museum of Prehistory at Moesgard, Aarhus, to satisfy the immediate public demand to view the body and raise sufficient money to cover the cost of conservation and investigation.

The discovery of Lindow Man has raised the questions of who owns human bodies and whether it is right to display them to the public gaze and to raise money. The Lindow bodies had to be retrieved, or they would have been totally destroyed by the peat-digging machinery. When Lindow Man was taken from the bog it was under the jurisdiction of the coroner and the police, because of its potential links to the Reyn-Bardt case. On proving that the body was ancient, did the coroner have the right to grant it to the British Museum? Or if the body were to be considered an object, was the peat company right to pass it to a scientific institution? The detailed investigations of Tollund, Grauballe and Lindow Man have contributed an enormous amount to our knowledge of man's appearance and his diet, living conditions and ritual practices in late prehistory. However, due to modifications in the tissue chemistry following their conservation, they are now no more than objects for display. Mr Ben Stocker and Dr Joan Taylor discussed the sanctity of the excavation and the future display of Lindow Man in the letter columns of *The Times* soon after his discovery. The World Archaeological Congress debated the issue in 1989, but as yet no code has emerged for British archaeologists to follow.

Well-preserved human remains and those of famous people have a talismanic quality. The trade in and display of holy relics is well known, but remains of persons other than saints have frequently been treated in the same way. The bodies of English kings and queens were sometimes dismembered and distributed for burial in the key cathedrals and abbeys of the country as symbols of the extent of their jurisdiction. Some humanists have been kept as talismans, for the finger of Galileo is an important exhibit in the Museum of the History of Science in Florence, and the smoked head of Jeremy Bentham forms part of a figure in the Senate House of London University.

Corruptions based on Lindow Man:

Lindoman	Man in the Mud
Lindo Man	Mudman
Litho Man	Cheshire Man
Indo Man	Swamp Man
Limo Man	Boggy Man
Ludlow Man	Shropshire Man
Lyndhurst Man	
Linden Man	**Corruptions based on condition**
Lansdowne Man	**when found and preservation**
Loden Man	**process:**
Linlo Man	Petrified Man
Lidlow Man	Kipper Man
Limus Man	Skin Man
Early Lithgo Man	Plastic Pete

Corruptions based on Pete Marsh:

Pete Bog	**Corruptions based on similar**
Pete-in-the-Bog	**finds elsewhere:**
Old Pete the Bog	Piltdown Man
Pete Bog in Marsh	Pitman Excavations
John Marsh	Tollund Man
Pete Moss	
Peter Marsh	**Corruptions based on ?:**
Bill Bog	That Man
Stone-Age Pete	Ludlow Bog in the
Pete Gentleman	Architecture Exhibition
Pete's Body	Body in the Bag
Pete the Bog	Brit Man
Peter Marns	That Old Man
Wilmslow Pete	Irish Man
	Pink Man
	Sludge Man
Corruptions based on where	Elephant Man
he was found:	Lake Man
Wisley man	Body in the Box
Bog Mummy	Man in the Toilet
Marsh Man	The Bog Lady
Moor Man	The Mock Body
	Merman
	Stuffed Pygmy

Fig. 94 List of names given by members of the public for Lindow Man. (*British Museum Enquiry Desk*)

In 1987, Venice launched a campaign to have the bones of the city's most infamous son, Casanova, returned from Czechoslovakia to add to its tourist attractions. With the collapse of the Soviet Union, the future of the mummified body of Lenin is now uncertain.

Underlying this trade in human remains is an economic motive. Following the discovery of Lindow Man and his investigation at the British Museum, Mrs Barbara O'Brien of Altrincham launched a 'Keep Lindow Man in the North Campaign'. This campaign was enthusiastically supported by local MPs, local councillors, the chairman of the North-West Tourist Board and, a little more guardedly, local museum staff. Its publicity rested heavily on the 'North–South divide'. Here was London taking away another potential source of wealth from the North West. The concept that a national museum should be responsible for collecting and conserving material across the whole country was lost. What the Celtic Lindow Man would have made of this tug-of-war for his remains between London and Manchester, two cities owing their origins to the Roman invaders, would have been most interesting. Ultimately a compromise was reached in which he has twice been displayed at the Manchester Museum.

Lindow Man is now an international archaeological celebrity; he was the subject of political cartoons, an article in *Punch*, and the star of two television programmes, which had an audience of over 10 million in Britain and have since been distributed worldwide. In 1987, there was a Christmas song produced about him; he features in an Australian primary school reader; referring to the problem over his radiocarbon dating, Cardinal Hume implied that the radiocarbon dates of the Turin shroud were open to question. However, many of the public have only a partial grasp of the full facts, as illustrated by the list of variations on his name collected by staff on the British Museum Enquiry Desk (Fig. 94).

Strangely, Lindow III has largely passed unnoticed. At the press conference to announce his discovery, the journalists failed to see his importance in confirming the ritual significance of Lindow Moss and as comparative evidence for the data produced by Lindow Man. As he was not the first British bog body, he was not news. His only claim to fame was a passing mention on the 'Wogan' television programme.

Perhaps the most surprising response to the bog body phenomenon in modern times has been literary. Its beginnings seemed to have followed the discovery of Queen Gunhild. Worsaae's friend, C. Hostrup, wrote a whimsical play entitled *A Sparrow among Hawks*, in which Gunhild was released from the bog by a tailor Peter Raven. Based originally on the academic feud which surrounded this discovery, it was edited for performance in the Royal Danish Theatre with the personal allusions cut out. A poem about Queen Gunhild followed in 1841 written by Steen Steensen Blicher (Glob 1969, 72–3). The first newspaper report of the discovery of the body in Seascale Moss in 1834 ended with a stanza drawn from a poem (Turner 1989, 21).

The publication of *The Bog People* in English was to foster another wave of poetry. Seamus Heaney wrote a number of fine poems drawing on the Danish bog bodies (Heaney 1975). In the 'Tollund Man', the violence of his death is compared to the violence of Northern Ireland. The poem 'Grauballe Man', explores the colours and textures of this body:

> Who will say "corpse"
> to his vivid cast?
> who will say "Body"
> to his opaque repose

while the 'Bog Queen' rages at the disturbance and lifting of the body from the timeless bog. Geoffrey Grigson in his poem 'Tollund Man' regrets the loss of mystery that scientific investigation induces and compares the suburban setting of the Silkeborg museum to the sanctity of the bog (Grigson 1980):

> No consolation after millenia, my friend,
> sacrificed for a future, to stir in this way
> by your shiny, silky-black shape; your
> fluidity hardened, more natural than
> Lenin; your stomach post-mortem'd; head cut from
> your body: like ours, your finger-prints taken

Not only these ancient sacrifices have prompted poems. The seventeenth-century body found at Clayton Hill, Scotland in 1975 inspired Irene Bell-Fause to write an unpublished poem now in the National Museums of Scotland's archives. She took a less pessimistic view of our scientific age:

> Many now quest the answers of antiquity
> Seek thus by science, art or fantasy.
> Yet rest in peace, young spirit, rest ye still
> This vigorous probing age bears thee no ill

The appearance of Lindow Man in 1984 caused a new flurry of literary activity which continues to the present day. The news coverage of his discovery led to a rather laconic piece by Michael Bywater in *Punch*. The problem of Lindow Man's date has shaped the literary response. Bywater's article had 'Pete Marsh' as a union leader of the Wilmslow Bronze Movement, superseded by the new technology of the Iron Age, promoted by government sources. After months of leading the bronze industry on strike, he is garotted in a boggy revolution (Bywater 1984).

In time, Lindow Man has become a literary hero. The *New York Times Book Review* of 2 June 1991 had a lead item on the fiction of bog bodies. Sarah Boxer of *The Times* had already noticed the new genre of bog-stories starring 'the limp silent type' (Chippendale 1991). In Margaret Drabble's novel *A Natural Curiosity*, the fate of Lindow Man provides a subtext to the lives of the modern characters (Drabble 1988). Three short stories have been published, *The Preserved Woman* (Lawrence Millman 1988), *Lindow Man* (Richard Seltzer, 1990) and finally *Bogman* by Margaret Atwood, published in *Playboy*.

Raymond Williams' novel *People of the Black Mountains – The Beginning*, attempts to write a prehistory of the area in which he was born, in a series of episodes. 'The Wise One and The Slave' deals with the invasion of a warrior class into the Black Mountains in *c.* 250 BC. The local population is enslaved by the new La Tène lords. One of the slaves, Karan, outwits and ultimately defies one of the lords, Lugon. His punishment was to be garotted in the manner of Lindow Man and his body given to the water (Williams 1989, 309).

Finally, a bogman has a novel of his own. Michael Cadnum's *Sleepwalker* is a bogman excavated on a site in York. He proves to be a vengeful Anglo-Saxon king who is seen moving about the site trying to reach down the throats of the archaeologists to pull their hearts out. Tiring of this no doubt amusing pastime he ends the novel begging to be reburied. This bogman, if a little confused in time and place, is perhaps taking revenge on all the indignities that his fellows have suffered at the hands of archaeologists, anatomists, conservators, peat diggers and publicists.

Ultimately, scientific analysis is insufficient to understand the bog-body phenomenon. While it can detail the facts and analyse the data, it can only go a little way in reconstructing the motives and manner of death. Where ritual sacrifice has been proposed, the problems are at their greatest, for religious belief and religious ceremony leave little tangible remains in the archaeological record. The other strands of evidence come from the written and oral descriptions of these beliefs and ceremonies. In the past, undue weight has been given to the very few surviving classical descriptions of the Celtic and German peoples. Many of these derive from even fewer direct observations and all are written from an outsider's viewpoint. They comment on an aspect of these cultures, human sacrifice, which they found abhorrent despite the similar brutalities being inflicted in the Roman world. Perhaps this undue weight results from the classical training received by most archaeologists in the past.

Greater sympathy and knowledge of the rituals concerned are to be expected in the oral traditions of our own culture. These tales would have been learned and transmitted by constant repetition, and formed the core of an illiterate society's history and myth. They may have undergone little change over centuries but they are available to us in written forms, which are easier to manipulate and embellish, and where new elements can be more easily introduced into the texts. These sources too must be treated with great care.

The modern literary response to the discovery of bog bodies is, therefore, not unexpected. The sense of wonder they conjure up is combined with the feeling that they have in some way cheated death, to live again. The forces behind the violent and often complex deaths they suffered are beyond mere scientific enquiry to convey. That they have stirred the imagination of so many novelists and poets ensures that the bog bodies are perhaps the most evocative discoveries from European prehistory. Despite the recent discovery of the 'Iceman', the fear remains that almost all the levels within European peat bogs which preserve bog bodies have been consumed. Future generations may not share the thrill of finding another Lindow Man.

PART IV

Gazetteer of Bog Bodies in the British Isles

1 Britain

R. C. Turner

This first part of the gazetteer is an attempt to list all the evidence for human remains from peat deposits in England, Wales and Scotland. It follows earlier catalogues published by Dieck (1965) and Briggs and Turner (1986) in trying to list any form of human remains from any type of peat deposit and of any date. But it differs from that of 1986 by presenting the information in a tabulated form. This allows for easier quantification, assessment of the quality of the data, and referencing. The extensive extracts from eyewitness accounts and early descriptions have been omitted as many would just duplicate those published in 1986 or in a succession of articles published since then. However, only by a detailed study of these sources can a critical assessment of any individual find be made.

The information has been ordered into groups of finds from particular peat bogs or more accurately defined sites. These are listed by county or region within each country. Old counties have been favoured for England, modern counties or regions for Wales and Scotland. Where fields have been left empty, no definite information can be gleaned from the sources.

There seems to be no logical system for cataloguing this shifting body of data, and a concordance list is provided on page 220. Ten records have been rejected from Dieck's list as they can be shown not to come from peat deposits, or involve human remains or cannot be corroborated. Two records from Briggs and Turner's list have been rejected for the same reasons. The author would be very interested to hear of any additional finds or references known to readers.

ENGLAND

Record number: 1/1 *NGR:*
Date of discovery: 1870 *Date of first report:*
Findspot: Bottisham Fen *Parish:* Bottisham
County: Cambridgeshire *Country:* England
Sex: Unknown *Age:* Adult
Preservation: Cranium
Assoc. artefacts: None
Date:
Present location: British Museum (Natural History)
Ms. refs: BM Sub-dept of Anthropology: SK3123
Published refs: None

Record number: 2/1 *NGR:*
Date of discovery: pre 1971 *Date of first report:* 1971
Findspot: Burwell Fen *Parish:* Burwell
County: Cambridgeshire *Country:* England
Sex: Male *Age:* Adult
Preservation: Full body standing upright in canoe
Assoc. artefacts: Long leather jacket
Date:
Present location:
Ms. refs:
Published refs: J. W. Day, in Clarke 1971

Record number: 2/2–3 *NGR:*
Date of discovery: 1884 *Date of first report:* 1911
Findspot: Burwell Fen *Parish:* Burwell
County: Cambridgeshire *Country:* England
Sex: Male *Age:* Adult
Preservation: Two skulls and one mandible, humerus
Assoc. artefacts: None
Date:

Present location: Sedgewick Museum, Cambridge
Ms. refs: Sedgewick Mus. catalogue D33838, 40, 42, 32
Published refs: Duckworth and Shore 1911

Record number: 2/4   *NGR:*
Date of discovery: 1890   *Date of first report:* 1980
Findspot: Burwell Fen   *Parish:* Burwell
County: Cambridgeshire   *Country:* England
Sex: Unknown   *Age:* Adult
Preservation: Mandible
Assoc. artefacts: None
Date:
Present location: Sedgewick Museum, Cambridge
Ms. refs: Sedgewick Mus. catalogue D33828
Published refs:

Record number: 2/5   *NGR:*
Date of discovery: 1898   *Date of first report:* 1911
Findspot: Burwell Fen   *Parish:* Burwell
County: Cambridgeshire   *Country:* England
Sex: Female   *Age:* Adult
Preservation: Skull
Assoc. artefacts: None
Date:
Present location: Sedgewick Museum, Cambridge
Ms. refs: Sedgewick Mus. catalogue D33837
Published refs: Duckworth and Shore 1911

Record number: 2/6   *NGR:*
Date of discovery: 1901   *Date of first report:* 1980
Findspot: Burwell Fen   *Parish:* Burwell
County: Cambridgeshire   *Country:* England
Sex: Unknown   *Age:* Adult
Preservation: Six skull fragments
Assoc. artefacts: None
Date:
Present location: Sedgewick Museum, Cambridge
Ms. refs: Sedgewick Mus. catalogue D33824
Published refs:

Record number: 2/7   *NGR:*
Date of discovery: pre 1911   *Date of first report:* 1911
Findspot: Burwell Fen   *Parish:* Burwell
County: Cambridgeshire   *Country:* England
Sex: Female   *Age:* Adult
Preservation: Mandible
Assoc. artefacts: None
Date:
Present location: Sedgewick Museum, Cambridge
Ms. refs: Sedgewick Mus. catalogue D33841
Published refs: Duckworth and Shore 1911

Record number: 2/8–9   *NGR:*
Date of discovery: pre 1911   *Date of first report:* 1911
Findspot: Burwell Fen   *Parish:* Burwell Fen
County: Cambridgeshire   *Country:* England
Sex: Unknown   *Age:* Adult
Preservation: Two mandibles
Assoc. artefacts:
Date:
Present location: Sedgewick Museum, Cambridge
Ms. refs: Sedgewick Mus. catalogue D33830–1
Published refs: Duckworth and Shore 1911

Record number: 3/1   *NGR:*
Date of discovery: 1989   *Date of first report:* 1991
Findspot: Fengate Power   *Parish:* Peterborough
    Sta. site   *Country:* England
County: Cambridgeshire   *Age:* Adult
Sex: Unknown
Preservation: Partly articulated skeleton
Assoc. artefacts: Wide range of Late Bronze Age/Early Iron
    Age metalwork and adornments
Date: Late prehistoric probably Early Iron Age
Present location: Fenland Archaeological Trust
Ms. refs:
Published refs: Pryor 1991

Record number: 3/2   *NGR:*
Date of discovery: 1989   *Date of first report:* 1991
Findspot: Fengate Power   *Parish:* Peterborough
    Sta. site   *Country:* England
County: Cambridgeshire   *Age:*
Sex: Unknown
Preservation: Two femurs
Assoc. artefacts: As above
Date: Late prehistoric, probably Early Iron Age
Present location: Fenland Archaeological Trust
Ms. refs:
Published refs: Pryor 1991

Record number: 3/3   *NGR:*
Date of discovery: 1989   *Date of first report:* 1991
Findspot: Fengate Power   *Parish:* Peterborough
    Sta. site   *Country:* England
County: Cambridgeshire   *Age:*
Sex: Unknown
Preservation: Collection of bones
Assoc. artefacts: In same pit as broken shale bracelet
Date: Late prehistoric, probably Iron Age
Present location: Fenland Archaeological Trust
Ms. refs:
Published refs: Pryor 1991

Record number: 4/1–2 *NGR:* TL 64 74
Date of discovery: 1952 *Date of first report:* 1965
Findspot: Isleham Fen *Parish:* Isleham
County: Cambridgeshire *Country:* England
Sex: Unknown *Age:* Unknown
Preservation: Two individuals reported
Assoc. artefacts:
Date:
Present location:
Ms refs:
Published refs: Dieck 1965

Record number: 5/1 *NGR:*
Date of discovery: 1874 *Date of first report:* 1874
Findspot: Isle of Ely *Parish:*
County: Cambridgeshire *Country:* England
Sex: Male *Age:* Adult
Preservation: Skull, demineralised
Assoc. artefacts: None
Date:
Present location:
Ms. refs:
Published refs: Marshall 1874

Record number: 6/1 *NGR:* TL 56 66
Date of discovery: 1891 *Date of first report:* 1980
Findspot: Reach Fen *Parish:* Reach
County: Cambridgeshire *Country:* England
Sex: Unknown *Age:* Child
Preservation: Mandible
Assoc. artefacts: None
Date:
Present location: Sedgewick Museum, Cambridge
Ms. refs: Sedgewick Mus. Catalogue D33826
Published refs:

Record number: 6/2 *NGR:* TL 56 66
Date of discovery: 1901 *Date of first report:* 1980
Findspot: Reach Fen *Parish:* Reach
County: Cambridgeshire *Country:* England
Sex: Unknown *Age:* Unknown
Preservation: Radius
Assoc. artefacts: None
Date:
Present location: Sedgewick Museum, Cambridge
Ms. refs: Sedgewick Mus. Catalogue D33833
Published refs:

Record number: 7/1 *NGR:*
Date of discovery: 1911 *Date of first report:* 1916
Findspot: Shippea Hill *Parish:* Littleport
     Farm *Country:* England
County: Cambridgeshire *Age:* Adult

Sex: Male
Preservation: Skeleton
Assoc. artefacts: None
Date: Bronze Age stratigraphically
Present location: Sedgewick Museum, Cambridge
Ms. refs: Sedgewick Mus. Catalogue D33928–30
Published refs: Hughes 1916; Clark 1933

Record number: 8/1 *NGR:* TL 54 75
Date of discovery: 1918 *Date of first report:* 1980
Findspot: Barway Fen *Parish:* Soham
County: Cambridgeshire *Country:* England
Sex: Unknown *Age:* Adult
Preservation: Facial bones and mandible
Assoc. artefacts: None
Date:
Present location: Sedgewick Museum, Cambridge
Ms. refs: Sedgewick Mus. Catalogue D33834
Published refs:

Record number: 8/2 *NGR:*
Date of discovery: pre 1923 *Date of first report:* 1923
Findspot: Soham Fen *Parish:* Soham
County: Cambridgeshire *Country:* England
Sex: Unknown *Age:* Adult
Preservation: Skeleton
Assoc. artefacts: Jet beads and plates from necklace
Date: Bronze Age
Present location: Artefacts, British Museum
Ms. refs:
Published refs: Fox 1923

Record number: 9/1 *NGR:* TL 53 70
Date of discovery: pre 1911 *Date of first report:* 1911
Findspot: *Parish:* Upware
County: Cambridgeshire *Country:* England
Sex: Male *Age:* Adult
Preservation: Skull and lower jaw
Assoc. artefacts: None
Date:
Present location: Sedgewick Museum, Cambridge
Ms. refs: Sedgewick Mus. Catalogue D33835
Published refs: Duckworth and Shore 1911

Record number: 9/2 *NGR:* TL 53 70
Date of discovery: pre 1911 *Date of first report:* 1911
Findspot: *Parish:* Upware
County: Cambridgeshire *Country:* England
Sex: Unknown *Age:* Adult
Preservation: Jaw (fragment), molar, metacarpal
Assoc. artefacts: None
Date:

Present location: Sedgewick Museum, Cambridge
Ms. refs: Sedgewick Mus. Catalogue D33829
Published refs: Duckworth and Shore 1911

Record number: 9/3   *NGR:* TL 53 70
Date of discovery: pre-1980   *Date of first report:* 1980
Findspot: Fen near Upware   *Parish:* Upware
County: Cambridgeshire   *Country:* England
Sex: Unknown   *Age:* Adult
Preservation: Mandible
Assoc. artefacts: None
Date:
Present location: Sedgewick Museum, Cambridge
Ms. refs: Sedgewick Mus. Catalogue D33825
Published refs:

Record number: 10/1   *NGR:*
Date of discovery: pre 1911   *Date of first report:* 1911
Findspot: Cambridgeshire   *Parish:*
    Fens   *Country:* England
County: Cambridgeshire   *Age:* Adult
Sex: Male
Preservation: Skull
Assoc. artefacts: None
Date:
Present location: Sedgewick Museum, Cambridge
Ms. refs: Sedgewick Mus. Catalogue D33839
Published refs: Duckworth and Shore 1911

Record number: 11/1   *NGR:* SJ 2290
Date of discovery: pre 1863   *Date of first report:* 1863
Findspot: Dove Point   *Parish:* Meols
County: Cheshire   *Country:* England
Sex: Unknown   *Age:* Unknown
Preservation: Skeletons in whole or part
Assoc. artefacts: Wide range from late prehistory to Norman
    Conquest
Date: Unknown
Present location:
Ms. refs:
Published refs: Hume 1863, 348

Record number: 12/1   *NGR:* SJ 2692
Date of discovery: 1864   *Date of first report:* 1864
Findspot: Leasowe   *Parish:* Leasowe
    Embankment   *Country:* England
County: Cheshire   *Age:* Adult
Sex: Male
Preservation: Extended skeleton
Assoc. artefacts: None
Date: Prehistoric on stratigraphy
Present location: Unknown

Ms. refs:
Published refs: Cust 1864; Busk 1866

Record number: 13/1   *NGR:* SJ 8219 8066
Date of discovery: 1983   *Date of first report:* 1984
Findspot: Lindow Moss   *Parish:* Mobberley
County: Cheshire   *Country:* England
Sex: Male?   *Age:* Young adult
Preservation: Calvarium, hair, brain and left eyeball
Assoc. artefacts: None
Date: 1740±80 BP (OxA-114)
Present location: British Museum
Ms. refs:
Published refs: Brothwell 1986; this volume pp. 100–3

Record number: 13/2   *NGR:* SJ 8202 8057
Date of discovery: 1984   *Date of first report:* 1984
Findspot: Lindow Moss   *Parish:* Mobberley
County: Cheshire   *Country:* England
Sex: Male   *Age:* Young adult
Preservation: Tissue and demineralised bone of torso and
    right foot
Assoc. artefacts: Fox-fur armband, sinew garotte
Date: Calibrated radiocarbon date, 2 BC–AD119; other
    dates see ref.
Present location: British Museum
Ms. refs:
Published refs: Stead *et al* 1986. This volume

Record number: 13/3   *NGR:* SJ 8219 8073
Date of discovery: 1987   *Date of first report:* 1987
Findspot: Lindow Moss   *Parish:* Mobberley
County: Cheshire   *Country:* England
Sex: Male   *Age:* Young adult
Preservation: Tissue and demineralised bone, whole body
    less head
Assoc. artefacts: None
Date: Calibrated radiocarbon date, AD25–230
Present location: British Museum
Ms. refs:
Published refs: This volume

Record number: 13/4   *NGR:* SJ 8201 8057
Date of discovery: 1988   *Date of first report:* 1988
Findspot: Lindow Moss   *Parish:* Mobberley
County: Cheshire   *Country:* England
Sex: Male   *Age:* Young adult
Preservation: Tissue and demineralised bone of buttocks
    and legs
Assoc. artefacts: None
Date: As 13/2
Present location: British Museum

Ms. refs:
Published refs: This volume

Record number: 14/1   *NGR:* NZ 5206 3145
Date of discovery: 1972   *Date of first report:* 1975
Findspot: Hartlepool Bay   *Parish:* Hartlepool
County: Cleveland   *Country:* England
Sex: Male   *Age:* Adult
Preservation: Disarticulated skeleton
Assoc. artefacts: None
Date: 4680±60 BP (HV-5220)
Present location: Unknown
Ms. refs:
Published refs: Tooley 1978b; Innes *et al* 1991

Record number: 15/1   *NGR:* NY 596 765
Date of discovery: c. 1850   *Date of first report:* 1873
Findspot: Murchie's C'n,   *Parish:* Bewcastle
    Hessilgil   *Country:* England
County: Cumbria   *Age:* Adult
Sex: Male
Preservation: Skeleton with some skin and hair
Assoc. artefacts: None
Date: Unknown
Present location: Unknown
Ms. refs:
Published refs: Maughan 1873

Record number: 16/1   *NGR:* NY 43 63
Date of discovery: 1845   *Date of first report:* 1845
Findspot: Scaleby Moss   *Parish:* Scaleby
County: Cumbria   *Country:* England
Sex: Female   *Age:* Adult
Preservation: Skeleton with hair, brain, intestines and
    ligaments
Assoc. artefacts: Deerskin Cape
Date: Bronze Age or earlier stratigraphically
Present location: Unknown
Ms. refs: See Turner 1988
Published refs: Turner 1988

Record number: 17/1   *NGR:* NY 34 69
Date of discovery: pre 1772   *Date of first report:* 1786
Findspot: Solway Moss   *Parish:* Longtown
County: Cumbria   *Country:* England
Sex: Male   *Age:* Adult
Preservation: Whole skeleton
Assoc. artefacts: Suit of armour and skeleton of horse
Date: 1542
Present location: Unknown
Ms. refs:
Published refs: Gilpin 1786; Lyell 1838

Record number: 17/2   *NGR:* NY 34 69
Date of discovery: pre 1777   *Date of first report:* 1777
Findspot: Solway Moss   *Parish:* Longtown
County: Cumbria   *Country:* England
Sex: Unknown   *Age:* Unknown
Preservation: Human bones frequently dug up
Assoc. artefacts: None
Date: Unknown
Present location: Unknown
Ms. refs:
Published refs: Nicholson and Burn 1777

Record number: 18/1   *NGR:* NY 05 01
Date of discovery: 1834   *Date of first report:* 1834
Findspot: Seascale Moss   *Parish:* Gosforth
County: Cumbria   *Country:* England
Sex: Male   *Age:* Adult
Preservation: Full tissue body, bones dissolved
Assoc. artefacts: Hazel walking stick
Date: Unknown
Present location: Unknown
Ms. refs: Cumberland Pacquet 3.6.1834
Published refs: Turner 1989

Record number: 19/1   *NGR:*
Date of discovery: 1702   *Date of first report:* 1734
Findspot: Hope Moors   *Parish:* Hope
County: Derbyshire   *Country:* England
Sex: Male   *Age:* Adult
Preservation: Full body with tissue and bone
Assoc. artefacts: Broad cloth coat
Date: 1674
Present location: Hope Churchyard
Ms. refs: Derbyshire Record Office D1828A/PI449/1
Published refs: Balguy 1734

Record number: 19/2   *NGR:*
Date of discovery: 1702   *Date of first report:* 1734
Findspot: Hope Moors   *Parish:* Hope
County: Derbyshire   *Country:* England
Sex: Female   *Age:* Adult
Preservation: Full body with tissue and bone
Assoc. artefacts: None mentioned
Date: 1674
Present location: Hope Churchyard
Ms. refs: Derbyshire Record Office D1828A/PI449/1
Published refs: Balguy 1734

Record number: 20/1   *NGR:* SD 33 15
Date of discovery: 1872   *Date of first report:* 1874
Findspot: Gloucester Road   *Parish:* Birkdale
County: Lancashire   *Country:* England
Sex: Unknown   *Age:* Unknown

Preservation: Skull
Assoc. artefacts: Red deer bone
Date: Prehistoric
Present location: Cast in Sedgewick Museum, Cambridge
Ms. refs:
Published refs: Busk 1874; Reade 1883

Record number: 21/1   *NGR:* SD 6315 1035
Date of discovery: 1942   *Date of first report:* 1955
Findspot: Red Moss,   *Parish:* Bolton
   Horwich   *Country:* England
County: Lancashire   *Age:* Adult
Sex: Female
Preservation: Skull with red hair
Assoc. artefacts: None
Date: Unknown
Present location: Rep. with Alderman Williams, Chorley
   Arch. Soc.
Ms. refs: OS Record Card SD 61NW28, Bolton Mus.
   archives
Published refs: Smith, 1988

Record number: 22/1   *NGR:* SJ 328 958
Date of discovery: 1911   *Date of first report:* 1913
Findspot: Gladstone Dock,   *Parish:* Liverpool
   Seaforth   *Country:* England
County: Lancashire   *Age:* Adult
Sex: Unknown
Preservation: Incomplete skeleton, arm and leg missing
Assoc. artefacts: None
Date: Prehistoric stratigraphically
Present location: Unknown
Ms. refs:
Published refs: Travis 1913

Record number: 23/1   *NGR:*
Date of discovery: pre 1700   *Date of first report:* 1700
Findspot: Meols   *Parish:* Southport
County: Lancashire   *Country:* England
Sex: Unknown   *Age:* Unknown
Preservation: A body entire and uncorrupted
Assoc. artefacts: None
Date:
Present location:
Ms. refs:
Published refs: Leigh 1700

Record number: 24/1   *NGR:* SD 441 462
Date of discovery: 1824   *Date of first report:* 1824
Findspot: Kentucky Farm   *Parish:* Pilling
County: Lancashire   *Country:* England
Sex: Female   *Age:* Young adult

Preservation: Skull with abundance of plaited auburn hair
Assoc. artefacts: Woollen cloth, two strings of cylindrical jet
   beads, one amber bead
Date: Bronze Age from artefact description
Present location: Unknown
Ms. refs: Preston Chronicle, 4 Jun 1824 and 5 Feb 1825
Published refs: Baines 1868; Edwards 1969; Lawrenson
   undated

Record number: 25/1   *NGR:* SD 5423 5735
Date of discovery: 1973   *Date of first report:* 1973
Findspot: Jubilee Tower   *Parish:* Quernmore
   c/park   *Country:* England
County: Lancashire   *Age:* Unknown
Sex: Unknown
Preservation: Hair and nails only
Assoc. artefacts: Woollen shroud, three white feathers
Date: AD 610 ± 110 (Birm-430); AD 650 ± 100 (Birm-474)
Present location: Lancaster Museum
Ms. refs: Lancaster Museum archives
Published refs: Edwards 1973; Ryder 1977

Record number: 26/1   *NGR:* SD 70 SW
Date of discovery: 1958   *Date of first report:* 1958
Findspot: Worsley Moss   *Parish:* Worsley
County: Lancashire   *Country:* England
Sex: Male   *Age:* Adult
Preservation: Head and upper two vertebrae, tissue and
   skin attached
Assoc. artefacts: Cord garrotte around the neck
Date: 1800 ± 70 BP (OxA-1430)
Present location: Manchester Medical School
Ms. refs: Leigh, Tyldesley and Atherton Journal, 24.10.1958
Published refs: Garland, pp. 104–7

Record number: 27/1   *NGR:* SJ 91 98
Date of discovery: pre 1900   *Date of first report:* 1911
Findspot: Ashton Moss   *Parish:*
County: Lancashire   *Country:* England
Sex: Male   *Age:* Adult
Preservation: Skull
Assoc. artefacts:
Date:
Present location: Museum of Biological Anthropology,
   Cambridge
Ms. refs:
Published refs: Duckworth and Shore 1911; Nevell 1992

Record number: 27/2   *NGR:*
Date of discovery: pre 1911   *Date of first report:* 1911
Findspot: *Parish:*
County: Lancashire   *Country:* England
Sex: Male   *Age:* Adult
Preservation: Skull

Assoc. artefacts:
Date:
Present location: Mus. of Biological Anthropology, Cambridge
Ms. refs:
Published refs: Duckworth and Shore 1911

Record number: 28/1 *NGR:*
Date of discovery: pre 1911 *Date of first report:* 1911
Findspot: *Parish:* Bracebridge
County: Lincolnshire *Country:* England
Sex: Male *Age:* Adult
Preservation: Skull
Assoc. artefacts:
Date:
Present location: Sedgewick Museum, Cambridge
Ms. refs: Sedgewick Mus. Catalogue D33836
Published refs: Duckworth and Shore 1911

Record number: 29/1 *NGR:*
Date of discovery: 1724 *Date of first report:* 1724
Findspot: Asby Moor *Parish:* Brigg
County: Lincolnshire *Country:* England
Sex: Male *Age:* Adult
Preservation: Skeleton and skin of an upright man
Assoc. artefacts:
Date:
Present location:
Ms. refs: Spalding Gents. Soc. Min. Book 1724, f. 80
Published refs: Turner and Rhodes 1992

Record number: 30/1 *NGR:*
Date of discovery: 1747 *Date of first report:* 1747
Findspot: Amcotts Moor *Parish:* Crowle
County: Lincolnshire *Country:* England
Sex: Female *Age:* Adult
Preservation: Body with skin and nails
Assoc. artefacts: Pair of sandals
Date: Late third or fourth century AD from shoe
Present location: Shoe in Spalding Gents. Society Museum
Ms. refs: Spalding Gents Soc. Min. Book 1747, f. 122 and 1757, f. 37
Published refs: Stovin 1747; Peck 1815; Stonehouse 1839; Tomlinson 1882; Gough 1789; Turner and Rhodes 1992

Record number: 31/1 *NGR:*
Date of discovery: 1901 *Date of first report:* 1981
Findspot: Feltwell Fen *Parish:* Feltwell
County: Norfolk *Country:* England
Sex: Unknown *Age:* Unknown
Preservation: Mandible
Assoc. artefacts: None
Date: Bronze Age stratigraphically

Present location: Norwich Castle Museum
Ms. refs: Norfolk SMR, PRN 5302
Published refs:

Record number: 31/2 *NGR:*
Date of discovery: pre 1911 *Date of first report:* 1921
Findspot: Feltwell Fen *Parish:* Feltwell
County: Norfolk *Country:* England
Sex: Male *Age:* Adult
Preservation: Skull
Assoc. artefacts: None
Date:
Present location: Museum of Biological Anthropology, Cambridge
Ms. refs: Norfolk SMR, PRN 5301
Published refs: Duckworth 1921

Record number: 32/1 *NGR:* TL 745 992
Date of discovery: 1956 *Date of first report:* 1956
Findspot: Borough Fen *Parish:* Foulden
County: Norfolk *Country:* England
Sex: Unknown *Age:* Unknown
Preservation: Calvarium
Assoc. artefacts: None
Date:
Present location: Norwich Castle Museum
Ms. refs: Norfolk SMR, PRN 4735
Published refs:

Record number: 33/1 *SGR:*
Date of discovery: 1983 *Date of first report:* 1983
County: West Harling *Parish:* Harling
County: Norfolk *Country:* England
Sex: Unknown *Age:* Unknown
Preservation: Frontal part of skull
Assoc. artefacts: None
Date:
Present location: Norwich Castle Museum
Ms. refs: Norfolk SMR, PRN 19697
Published refs:

Record number: 34/1 *NGR:*
Date of discovery: pre 1869 *Date of first report:* 1869
Findspot: *Parish:* Hickling
County: Norfolk *Country:* England
Sex: Male *Age:* Adult
Preservation: Skeleton in slanting semi-vertical position
Assoc. artefacts: None
Date:
Present location: British Museum (Natural History)
Ms. refs: BM (Natural History) Catalogue SK1574
Published refs:

Record number: 35/1
Date of discovery: 1721
Findspot: West Tofts
County: Norfolk
Sex: Unknown
Preservation: Bones
Assoc. artefacts: Monoxylous coffin, beads, gold funnel, shale obj.
Date: Early Bronze Age from artefact description
Present location:
Ms. refs: Tom Martin's Church Notes, in Norfolk SMR, PRN5137
Published refs: Clarke 1971

NGR: TL 837 929
Date of first report: 1721
Parish: Lynford
Country: England
Age: Adult

Record number: 36/1
Date of discovery: pre 1945
Findspot: Broad Fen
County: Norfolk
Sex: Unknown
Preservation: Skull
Assoc. artefacts: None
Date:
Present location:
Ms. refs: Norfolk SMR PRN2547
Published refs:

NGR:
Date of first report: 1945
Parish: Methwold
Country: England
Age: Unknown

Record number: 37/1
Date of discovery: 1967
Findspot: Hemplands Farm
County: Norfolk
Sex: Woman
Preservation: Truncated skeleton
Assoc. artefacts: Regular setting of wood below body
Date: 3840 ± 80 BP (OxA-2868)
Present location: Norwich Castle Museum
Ms. refs: Norfolk SMR PRN 1550
Published refs: Healy and Housley 1992

NGR: TL 6856 9591
Date of first report: 1967
Parish: Methwold
Country: England
Age: Adult

Record number: 38/1
Date of discovery: 1958
Findspot:
County: Norfolk
Sex: Woman
Preservation: Skeleton
Assoc. artefacts: Flint flake, bone awl
Date: 3760 ± 80 BP (OxA-2860)
Present location: Norwich Castle Museum
Ms. refs: Norfolk SMR PRN 2585
Published refs: Healy and Housley 1992

NGR:
Date of first report: 1958
Parish: Methwold
Country: England
Age: Adult

Record number: 38/2
Date of discovery: 1958
Findspot:

NGR: TL 631 941
Date of first report: 1958
Parish: Methwold

County: Norfolk
Sex: Unknown
Preservation: Skeleton
Assoc. artefacts: Flint flake, bone awl
Date: 3540±80 (OxA-2861)
Present location: Norwich Castle Museum
Ms. refs: Norfolk SMR, PRN 2585
Published refs: Healy and Housley 1992

Country: England
Age: Child

Record number: 38/3
Date of discovery: 1958
Findspot:
County: Norfolk
Sex: Unknown
Preservation: Skeleton
Assoc. artefacts: Flint flake, bone awl
Date: Early Bronze Age (see above)
Present location: Norwich Castle Museum
Ms. refs: Norfolk SMR, PRN 2585
Published refs: Healy and Housley 1992

NGR: TL 631 941
Date of first report: 1958
Parish: Methwold
Country: England
Age: Child

Record number: 39/1
Date of discovery: 1960
Findspot: N. of Catsholm Island
County: Norfolk
Sex: Unknown
Preservation: Mandible
Assoc. artefacts: Unfinished bronze rapier near by
Date:
Present location: Norwich Castle Museum
Ms. refs: Norfolk SMR, PRN 2540
Published refs:

NGR: TL 6885 9712
Date of first report: 1981
Parish: Methwold
Country: England
Age: Unknown

Record number: 39/2
Date of discovery:
Findspot:
Sex: Unknown
Preservation: Calvarium, mandible, femur
Assoc. artefacts:
Date:
Present location: British Museum (Natural History)
Ms. refs: BM (Natural History) SK3121
Published refs:

NGR:
Date of first report:
Parish: Methwold
Country: England
Age: Adult

Record number: 40/1
Date of discovery: 1967
Findspot: Methwold Severals
County: Norfolk
Sex: Unknown
Preservation: Femur

NGR: TL 6505 9685
Date of first report: 1968
Parish: Methwold
Country: England
Age: Adult

Assoc. artefacts:
Date: Early Bronze Age (see below)
Present location: Norwich Castle Museum
Ms. refs: Norfolk SMR, PRN 2542
Published refs: Healy and Housley 1992

Record number: 40/2   *NGR:* TL 6505 9685
Date of discovery: 1968   *Date of first report:* 1968
Findspot: Methwold   *Parish:* Methwold
   Severals   *Country:* England
County: Norfolk   *Age:* Adult
Sex: Male
Preservation: Partly articulated skeleton
Assoc. artefacts: Early Bronze Age awl
Date: 3580±80 BP (OxA–2862)
Present location: Norwich Castle Museum
Ms. refs: Norfolk SMR, PRN 2542
Published refs: Healy and Housley 1992

Record number: 40/3   *NGR:* TL 6505 9685
Date of discovery: 1968   *Date of first report:* 1968
Findspot: Methwold   *Parish:* Methwold
   Severals   *Country:* England
County: Norfolk   *Age:* Adult
Sex: Female
Preservation: Partly articulated skeleton
Assoc. artefacts: Early Bronze Age awl
Date: 3670±80 BP (OxA–2863)
Present location: Norwich Castle Museum
Ms. refs: Norfolk SMR, PRN 2542
Published refs: Healy and Housley 1992

Record number: 40/4   *NGR:* TL 6505 9685
Date of discovery: 1968   *Date of first report:* 1968
Findspot: Methwold   *Parish:* Methwold
   Severals   *Country:* England
County: Norfolk   *Age:* Adult
Sex: Female
Preservation: Fragmentary skeleton
Assoc. artefacts: Early Bronze Age awl
Date: Early Bronze Age
Present location: Norwich Castle Museum
Ms. refs: Norfolk SMR, PRN 2542
Published refs: Healy and Housley 1992

Record number: 40/5   *NGR:* TL 6505 9685
Date of discovery: 1968   *Date of first report:* 1968
Findspot: Methwold   *Parish:* Methwold
   Severals   *Country:* England
County: Norfolk   *Age:* Child
Sex: Unknown
Preservation: Skeleton
Assoc. artefacts: Early Bronze Age awl

Date: 3650±80 BP (OxA-2864)
Present location: Norwich Castle Museum
Ms. refs: Norfolk SMR PRN 2542
Published refs: Healy and Housley 1992

Record number: 40/6   *NGR:* TL 6505 9685
Date of discovery: 1968   *Date of first report:* 1968
Findspot: Methwold   *Parish:* Methwold
   Severals   *Country:* England
County: Norfolk   *Age:* Child
Sex: Unknown
Preservation: Skeleton
Assoc. artefacts: Early Bronze Age awl
Date: Early Bronze Age
Present location: Norwich Castle Museum
Ms. refs: Norfolk SMR, PRN 2542
Published refs: Healy and Housley 1992

Record number: 40/7   *NGR:* TL 6505 9685
Date of discovery: 1968   *Date of first report:* 1968
Findspot: Methwold   *Parish:* Methwold
   Severals   *Country:* England
County: Norfolk   *Age:* Infant
Sex: Unknown
Preservation: Skeleton
Assoc. artefacts: Early Bronze Age awl
Date: Early Bronze Age
Present location: Norwich Castle Museum
Ms. refs: Norfolk SMR, PRN 2542
Published refs: Healy and Housley 1992

Record number: 41/1   *NGR:* TL 6510 9684
Date of discovery: 1971   *Date of first report:* 1971
Findspot: Methwold   *Parish:* Methwold
   Severals   *Country:* England
County: Norfolk   *Age:* Adult
Sex: Male
Preservation: Skeleton
Assoc. artefacts: Two flint scrapers
Date: 3760±80 BP (OxA-2865)
Present location: Norwich Castle Museum
Ms. refs: Norfolk SMR, PRN 2542
Published refs: Healy and Housley 1992

Record number: 41/2   *NGR:* TL 6510 9684
Date of discovery: 1971   *Date of first report:* 1971
Findspot: Methwold   *Parish:* Methwold
   Severals   *Country:* England
County: Norfolk   *Age:* Child
Sex: Unknown
Preservation: Skeleton
Assoc. artefacts: Two flint scrapers
Date: 3600±80 BP (OxA-2866)

Present location: Norwich Castle Museum
Ms. refs: Norfolk SMR, PRN 2542
Published refs: Healy and Housley 1992

Record number: 41/3   *NGR:* TL 6510 9684
Date of discovery: 1971   *Date of first report:* 1971
Findspot: Methwold   *Parish:* Methwold
Severals   *Country:* England
County: Norfolk   *Age:* Child
Sex: Unknown
Preservation: Skeleton
Assoc. artefacts: Two flint scrapers
Date: 3640±80 BP (OxA-2867)
Present location: Norwich Castle Museum
Ms. refs: Norfolk SMR, PRN 2542
Published refs: Healy and Housley 1992

Record number: 42/1   *NGR:* TL 6300 9425
Date of discovery: 1933   *Date of first report:* 1933
Findspot: Southery Fen   *Parish:* Methwold
County: Norfolk   *Country:* England
Sex: Female   *Age:* Young adult
Preservation: Skeleton
Assoc. artefacts: Eight jet beads and bronze pin/awl
Date: Early Bronze Age
Present location: Camb. Univ. Mus. of Arch. and Ethnology
Ms. refs: Norfolk SMR, PRN 2546
Published refs: Clark 1933; Godwin 1940; Clarke 1971; Healy
and Housley 1992

Record number: 43/1   *NGR:*
Date of discovery: pre 1864   *Date of first report:* 1864
Findspot: *Parish:* Ridlington
County: Norfolk   *Country:* England
Sex: Unknown   *Age:* Adult
Preservation: Cranium and some post-cranial material
Assoc. artefacts:
Date:
Present location: British Museum (Natural History)
Ms. refs: BM (Natural History) SK 1575
Published refs: White 1864

Record number: 44/1   *NGR:* TF 6948 1102
Date of discovery: 1954   *Date of first report:* 1954
Findspot: Mere Plot   *Parish:* Shouldham
County: Norfolk   *Country:* England
Sex: Unknown   *Age:* Unknown
Preservation: Skull
Assoc. artefacts: None
Date:
Present location: Norwich Castle Museum
Ms. refs: Norfolk SMR, PRN 3464
Published refs:

Record number: 45/1   *NGR:* TG 3470 2480
Date of discovery: pre 1864   *Date of first report:* 1864
Findspot: Wayford Bridge   *Parish:* Smallburgh
County: Norfolk   *Country:* England
Sex: Unknown   *Age:* Adult
Preservation: Cranium with remains of other skeleton
Assoc. artefacts:
Date:
Present location: British Museum (Natural History)
Ms. refs: BM (Nat. Hist.) SK 1576 : Norfolk SMR, PRN 8282
Published refs: White 1864

Record number: 46/1   *NGR:* TL 629 950
Date of discovery: 1968   *Date of first report:*
Findspot: Black Bank   *Parish:* Southery
Drove   *Country:* England
County: Norfolk   *Age:* Adult
Sex: Unknown
Preservation: Occipital bone
Assoc. artefacts: None
Date:
Present location:
Ms. refs: Norfolk SMR, PRN 16017
Published refs:

Record number: 47/1   *NGR:* TG 3029 1816
Date of discovery: 1959   *Date of first report:* 1959
Findspot: Bank of River   *Parish:* Wroxham
Bure   *Country:* England
County: Norfolk   *Age:* Unknown
Sex: Unknown
Preservation: Skull
Assoc. artefacts: None
Date:
Present location: Norwich Castle Museum 473.959
Ms. refs: Norfolk SMR, PRN 8424
Published refs:

Record number: 48/1   *NGR:* TG 0954 0296
Date of discovery: 1961   *Date of first report:* 1961
Findspot: Sewage works   *Parish:* Wymondham
County: Norfolk   *Country:* England
Sex: Unknown   *Age:* Unknown
Preservation: Part of skull
Assoc. artefacts: Roman sherds and leather
Date:
Present location: Norwich Castle Museum 183.961
Ms. refs: Norfolk SMR, PRN 8901
Published refs:

Record number: 49/1   *NGR:*
Date of discovery: pre 1866   *Date of first report:* 1866
Findspot: *Parish:*

County: Northamptonshire *Country:* England
Sex: Unknown *Age:* Unknown
Preservation: Frontal and parietal bones of cranium
Assoc. artefacts:
Date:
Present location:
Ms. refs:
Published refs: Flower 1907, 63

Record number: 50/1 *NGR:*
Date of discovery: pre 1880 *Date of first report:* 1880
Findspot: River Blyth *Parish:* Blyth
County: Northumberland *Country:* England
Sex: Unknown *Age:* Adult
Preservation: Cranium with teeth
Assoc. artefacts:
Date:
Present location: British Museum (Natural History)
Ms. refs: BM (Natural History) SK 3115
Published refs:

Record number: 50/2 *NGR:*
Date of discovery: pre 1880 *Date of first report:* 1880
Findspot: River Blyth *Parish:* Blyth
County: Northumberland *Country:* England
Sex: Unknown *Age:* Adult
Preservation: Cranium with teeth
Assoc. artefacts:
Date:
Present location: British Museum (Natural History)
Ms. refs: BM (Natural History) SK 3116
Published refs:

Record number: 51/1 *NGR:*
Date of discovery: 1889 *Date of first report:* 1889
Findspot: Whixall Moss *Parish:* Whixall
County: Shropshire *Country:* England
Sex: Male *Age:* Adult
Preservation: Bones with some hair and flesh attached
Assoc. artefacts: None
Date: Neolithic/Bronze Age stratigraphically
Present location: Whixall Churchyard
Ms. refs: *Whitchurch Herald* 7 Sep 1889
Published refs: Turner and Penney 1996

Record number: 51/2 *NGR:*
Date of discovery: 1868 *Date of first report:* 1889
Findspot: Whixall Moss *Parish:* Whixall
County: Shropshire *Country:* England
Sex: Male *Age:* Young adult
Preservation: Bone and tissue
Assoc. artefacts: Leather apron and three-legged wooden
    stool

Date:
Present location: Whitchurch Churchyard
Ms. refs: *Whitchurch Herald* 7 Sep 1889
Published refs: Turner and Penney 1996

Record number: 51/3 *NGR:*
Date of discovery: 1876 *Date of first report:* 1889
Findspot: Whixall Moss *Parish:* Whixall
County: Shropshire *Country:* England
Sex: Female *Age:* Adult
Preservation: Unspecified but tissue implied
Assoc. artefacts:
Date:
Present location: Whitchurch Churchyard
Ms. refs: *Whitchurch Herald* 7 Sep 1889
Published refs: Turner and Penney 1996

Record number: 52/1 *NGR:*
Date of discovery: 1869 *Date of first report:* 1869
Findspot: Burnt Fen *Parish:* Mildenhall
County: Suffolk *Country:* England
Sex: Unknown *Age:* Adult
Preservation: Calvarium
Assoc. artefacts:
Date:
Present location: British Museum (Natural History)
Ms. refs: BM (Natural History) SK 3122
Published refs:

Record number: 53/1 *NGR:*
Date of discovery: *Date of first report:*
Findspot: *Parish:* Moredon
County: Wiltshire ? *Country:* England
Sex: Unknown *Age:* Unknown
Preservation: Imperfect calvarium
Assoc. artefacts:
Date:
Present location: British Museum (Natural History)
Ms. refs: BM (Natural History) SK 3113
Published refs:

Record number: 54/1 *NGR:* SD 76 69
Date of discovery: 1846 *Date of first report:* 1871
Findspot: Austwick *Parish:* Clapham
    Common *Country:* England
County: Yorkshire *Age:* Young adult
Sex: Female
Preservation: Skeleton
Assoc. artefacts: Pair of one-piece shoes near by
Date: Romano-British from shoe description
Present location:
Ms. refs:
Published refs: Denny 1871

Record number: 55/1
Date of discovery: 1850
Findspot: Grewelthorpe Moor
County: Yorkshire
Sex: Male
Preservation: Full body preserved by adipocere
Assoc. artefacts: Full suit of clothes retaining colour
Date: Romano-British
Present location: Sock and shoe in Yorkshire Museum
Ms. refs: Heslington 1867
Published refs: Sheahan 1871; Grainge 1892; Tinsley 1974; Turner *et al* 1991

NGR: SE 170 758
Date of first report: 1867
Parish: Kirby Malzeard
Country: England
Age: Adult

Record number: 56/1
Date of discovery: 1797
Findspot: Whitaside Moor
County: Yorkshire
Sex: Unknown
Preservation: Described as a body
Assoc. artefacts:
Date:
Present location: Grinton-in-Swaledale Churchyard
Ms. refs: Parish register, 18 Jun 1797
Published refs: Anon 1909

NGR:
Date of first report: 1797
Parish: Grinton-in-Swaledale
Country: England
Age: Unknown

Record number: 57/1
Date of discovery: pre 1880
Findspot:
County: Yorkshire
Sex: Unknown
Preservation: Cranium
Assoc. artefacts:
Date:
Present location: British Museum (Natural History)
Ms. refs: BM (Natural History) SK 3120
Published refs:

NGR:
Date of first report: 1880
Parish: Riccall
Country: England
Age: Child

Record number: 58/1
Date of discovery: 1645
Findspot: Hatfield Chase
County: Yorkshire
Sex: Male
Preservation: Body with skin intact
Assoc. artefacts:
Date:
Present location:
Ms. refs:
Published refs: de la Pryme 1694; Gough 1789; Peck 1815; Tomlinson 1882

NGR:
Date of first report: 1694
Parish: Hatfield
Country: England
Age: Adult

Record number: 58/2
Date of discovery: pre 1600

NGR:
Date of first report: 1828

Findspot: Hatfield Chase
County: Yorkshire
Sex: Unknown
Preservation: Body
Assoc. artefacts: Leather sandals similar to Amcotts, 30/1
Date:
Present location:
Ms. refs:
Published refs: Hunter 1828

Parish: Hatfield
Country: England
Age: Unknown

Record number: 58/3
Date of discovery: pre 1720
Findspot: Hatfield Chase
County: Yorkshire
Sex: Male
Preservation: Perfect body
Assoc. artefacts: Ancient 'Saxon' costume
Date:
Present location:
Ms. refs:
Published refs: Bakewell 1833

NGR:
Date of first report: 1833
Parish: Hatfield
Country: England
Age: Adult

Record number: 59/1
Date of discovery: pre 1700
Findspot:
County: Yorkshire
Sex: Unknown
Preservation: Part of a body
Assoc. artefacts:
Date:
Present location:
Ms. refs:
Published refs: Stovin 1747

NGR:
Date of first report: 1747
Parish: Goole
Country: England
Age: Unknown

Record number: 60/1
Date of discovery: 1740
Findspot: Thorne Moor
County: Yorkshire
Sex: Unknown
Preservation: Body with hair, teeth and nails
Assoc. artefacts: None
Date:
Present location:
Ms. refs:
Published refs: Stovin 1747

NGR:
Date of first report: 1747
Parish: Thorne
Country: England
Age: Adult

Record number: 83/1
Date of discovery: pre 1868
Findspot:
County: Nottinghamshire
Sex: Unknown
Preservation: Cranium
Assoc. artefacts:

NGR:
Date of first report: 1868
Parish:
Country: England
Age: Young person

Date:
Present location:
Ms. refs:
Published refs: Flowers 1907, 63

WALES

Record number: 61/1   *NGR:*
Date of discovery: pre 1924   *Date of first report:* 1924
Findspot: *Parish:* Prestatyn
County: Clwyd   *Country:* Wales
Sex: Female   *Age:* Adult
Preservation: Skeleton
Assoc. artefacts: None
Date:
Present location:
Ms. refs: Ann. Rep. Mus. R. Coll. Surg. 1924
Published refs:

Record number: 61/2   *NGR:*
Date of discovery: 1984   *Date of first report:* 1989
Findspot: Melyd Avenue   *Parish:* Prestatyn
County: Clwyd   *Country:* Wales
Sex: Unknown   *Age:* Infant
Preservation: Partial skeleton
Assoc. artefacts: Enclosed by a fence of 8 oak stakes
Date: Late Iron Age stratigraphically; 1980±60 BP
  (CAR-827)
Present location: Clwyd-Powys Archaeological Trust
Ms. refs:
Published refs: Blockley 1989

Record number: 62/1   *NGR:* SN 510 159
Date of discovery: 1848   *Date of first report:* 1893
Findspot: Commins, Llyn   *Parish:* Llandarog
  Mawr Farm   *Country:* Wales
County: Dyfed   *Age:* Unknown
Sex: Unknown
Preservation: Human skull
Assoc. artefacts:
Date:
Present location:
Ms. refs:
Published refs: Anon 1893

Record number: 63/1   *NGR:* SN 711 670
Date of discovery: 1811   *Date of first report:* 1813
Findspot: Dolfawr Fair,   *Parish:* Ystrad Meurig
  Gwnnws   *Country:* Wales
County: Dyfed   *Age:* Adult
Sex: Unknown
Preservation: Body consisting of bones and skin, missing
  head
Assoc. artefacts: None

Date:
Present location: Ystrad Meurig Churchyard
Ms. refs: Nat. Lib. of Wales, 1755B/15/1475
Published refs:

Record number: 64/1   *NGR:*
Date of discovery: 1684   *Date of first report:* 1695
Findspot: Mownog   *Parish:*
  Ystratgwyn   *Country:* Wales
County: Gwynedd   *Age:* Adult
Sex: Unknown
Preservation: Skeleton
Assoc. artefacts: Wooden coffin with gilding
Date:
Present location:
Ms. refs:
Published refs: Gibson 1695, 794

Record number: 65/1   *NGR:*
Date of discovery: pre 1910   *Date of first report:* 1910
Findspot: Dock   *Parish:* Aberavon
County: Mid-Glamorgan   *Country:* Wales
Sex: Unknown   *Age:* Adult
Preservation: Part of the calotte of skull
Assoc. artefacts: Sacrum of Irish elk
Date: Neolithic stratigraphically
Present location: British Museum (Natural History)
Ms. refs: BM (Natural History) SK 1640
Published refs: Keith 1925, 58–9

Record number: 66/1   *NGR:*
Date of discovery: 1858   *Date of first report:* 1858
Findspot: Gifron   *Parish:* Nantmel
County: Powys   *Country:* Wales
Sex: Unknown   *Age:* Unknown
Preservation: Skull with full complement of hair
Assoc. artefacts: None
Date:
Present location:
Ms. refs:
Published refs: Williams 1858

SCOTLAND

Record number: 67/1–2   *NGR:*
Date of discovery: pre-1905   *Date of first report:* 1905
Findspot: *Parish:* Longside
County: Grampian   *Country:* Scotland
Sex: Unknown   *Age:* Unknown
Preservation: No human remains
Assoc. artefacts: Two monoxylous wooden coffins
Date:
Present location:

Ms. refs:
Published refs: Abercromby 1905

Record number: 68/1   *NGR:*
Date of discovery: 1927   *Date of first report:* 1927
Findspot: Dava Moor   *Parish:* Cromdale
County: Highland   *Country:* Scotland
Sex: Unknown   *Age:* Young adult
Preservation: Skeleton
Assoc. artefacts: Woollen clothing, broad bonnet, and birch stick
Date: Late C.16 or C.17 from clothing
Present location:
Ms. refs:
Published refs: Anon 1927; Henshall 1952

Record number: 69/1–6   *NGR:*
Date of discovery: 1880   *Date of first report:* 1952
Findspot: *Parish:* Culrain
County: Highland   *Country:* Scotland
Sex: Unknown   *Age:* Unknown
Preservation: Six skeletons
Assoc. artefacts: Fully clothed, wool garments and leather shoes
Date: Post-Medieval from clothing fragments
Present location: National Museums of Scotland NA 4–5
Ms. refs:
Published refs: Henshall 1952

Record number: 70/1   *NGR:* NG 332 634
Date of discovery: 1975   *Date of first report:* 1985
Findspot: Clayton Hill   *Parish:* Keiss
County: Highland   *Country:* Scotland
Sex: Male   *Age:* Young adult
Preservation: Skeleton nearly complete, tissue on legs
Assoc. artefacts: Sleeved woollen jacket
Date: Mid C.17 from clothing
Present location: National Museums of Scotland
Ms. refs: Nat. Mus. of Scotland archives
Published refs:

Record number: 71/1   *NGR:*
Date of discovery: 1920   *Date of first report:* 1921
Findspot: Quintfall Hill   *Parish:* Barrock
County: Highland   *Country:* Scotland
Sex: Male   *Age:* Adult
Preservation: Skeleton
Assoc. artefacts: Suit of woollen clothes, purse with coins
Date: Late C.17 from coins
Present location: National Museum of Scotland NA 416
Ms. refs: Nat. Mus. of Scotland archives
Published refs: Orr 1921; Henshall 1952

Record number: 72/1   *NGR:*
Date of discovery: 1875   *Date of first report:* 1875
Findspot: Springhill, Knockan   *Parish:* Rogart
County: Highland   *Country:* Scotland
Sex: Unknown
Preservation: Decayed extended skeleton
Assoc. artefacts: Stone cist, linen clothing, shoes
Date: Medieval?
Present location: National Museums of Scotland L 1981, 40–4
Ms. refs: Nat. Mus. of Scotland archives
Published refs: Henshall 1952

Record number: 73/1   *NGR:*
Date of discovery: 1881   *Date of first report:* 1882
Findspot: *Parish:* Birsay
County: Orkney   *Country:* Scotland
Sex: Female   *Age:* Child
Preservation: Skeleton
Assoc. artefacts: Worn and patched woollen clothing
Date: C.17 from clothing
Present location:
Ms. refs:
Published refs: Anon 1882; Henshall 1952

Record number: 74/1   *NGR:* HY 3490 1815
Date of discovery: 1968   *Date of first report:* 1969
Findspot: Huntsgarth   *Parish:* Harray
County: Orkney   *Country:* Scotland
Sex: Unknown   *Age:* Infant
Preservation: Few hairs
Assoc. artefacts: Woollen cloth and bonnet
Date: C.18 from clothing
Present location: Orkney Museum ?
Ms. refs: Nat. Mus. of Scotland archives
Published refs: Henshall 1969

Record number: 75/1   *NGR:*
Date of discovery: 1864   *Date of first report:* 1864
Findspot: *Parish:*
County: Orkney   *Country:* Scotland
Sex: Female   *Age:* Adult
Preservation: Body with hair and brain, bones soft
Assoc. artefacts: Coarse woollen clothing
Date:
Present location:
Ms. refs: Orcadian May 1864
Published refs: Brothwell 1986, 10

Record number: 76/1   *NGR:* HU 328 732
Date of discovery: 1951   *Date of first report:* 1952
Findspot: Gunnister   *Parish:* Northmaine

County: Shetland Country: Scotland
Sex: Male Age: Adult
Preservation: Decalcified bone, hair and nails
Assoc. artefacts: Woollen clothing, leather clothing, purse
Date: Late C.17 from coins
Present location: National Museums of Scotland NA 1050/1
Ms. refs: Nat. Mus. of Scotland archives
Published refs: Henshall and Maxwell 1952

Record number: 77/1 NGR:
Date of discovery: 1849 Date of first report: 1854
Findspot: Norsewick Parish: Mainland
County: Shetland Country: Scotland
Sex: Male Age: Adult
Preservation: Skeleton with some hair
Assoc. artefacts: Tunic and piece of wood
Date:
Present location: Nat. Mus. Scotland NA6, hair and woollen
  cloth
Ms. refs:
Published refs: Anon. 1854; Henshall 1952

Record number: 77/2 NGR:
Date of discovery: 1849 Date of first report: 1854
Findspot: Norsewick Parish: Mainland
County: Shetland Country: Scotland
Sex: Female Age: Adult
Preservation: Skeleton with some hair
Assoc. artefacts: Tunic and piece of wood
Date:
Present location: as 77/1
Ms. refs:
Published refs: as 77/1

Record number: 78/1–12 NGR:
Date of discovery: 1866 Date of first report: 1866
Findspot: Parish: Bressay
County: Shetland Country: Scotland
Sex: Unknown Age: Unknown
Preservation: Fatty substances, fingernail
Assoc. artefacts: Sawn pine coffins, carved stone
Date: Post-Medieval
Present location:
Ms. refs:
Published refs: Hunt 1866

Record number: 79/1 NGR:
Date of discovery: pre-1810 Date of first report: 1810
Findspot: Ards Moss Parish:
County: Strathclyde Country: Scotland
Sex: Unknown Age: Adult
Preservation: Some bodies
Assoc. artefacts: Clothing implied
Date:
Present location:
Ms. refs:
Published refs: Rennie 1810, 520

Record number: 80/1 NGR:
Date of discovery: 1932 Date of first report: 1937
Findspot: Greenhead Moss Parish: Cambusnethan
County: Strathclyde Country: Scotland
Sex: Male Age: Adult
Preservation:
Assoc. artefacts: Full suit of clothes, sticks across body
Date: C.18 or early C.19 from clothing
Present location:
Ms. refs:
Published refs: Mann 1937

Record number: 81/1 NGR:
Date of discovery: pre-1879 Date of first report: 1879
Findspot: Parish: Oban
County: Strathclyde Country: Scotland
Sex: Unknown Age: Unknown
Preservation: No remains recorded
Assoc. artefacts: Log coffin in wooden setting
Date:
Present location:
Ms. refs:
Published refs: Mapleton 1879; Abercromby 1905

Record number: 82/1 NGR: NB 386 300
Date of discovery: 1964 Date of first report: 1964
Findspot: Arnish Moor Parish: Lewis
County: Western Isles Country: Scotland
Sex: Male Age: Young adult
Preservation: Hair, nails and demineralised skeleton
Assoc. artefacts: Full suit of clothes, purse
Date: Late C.17 early C.18 from clothing
Present location: National Museum of Scotland
Ms. refs: Nat. Mus. of Scotland archives
Published refs: Anon. 1964; Bennett 1975

Table 22 Concordance for British bog bodies

TURNER 1995	BRIGGS & TURNER 1986	DIECK 1965	TURNER 1995	BRIGGS & TURNER 1986	DIECK 1965
1/1		1870a Bottisham Fen	40/2	33	
2/1	1		40/3	33	
2/2–3	1	1884c Burwell Fen	40/4	33	
2/4			40/5	33	
2/5	1	1898d Burwell	40/6	33	
2/6	1		40/7	33	
2/7	1	Vor 1911h Burwell Fen	41/1	33	
2/8–9	1	Vor 1911l Burwell Fen	41/2	33	
3/1			41/3	33	
3/2			42/1	34	Vor 1933a Southery Fen
3/3			43/1		1948g Ridlington
4/1–2	2	1952c-d, Isleham Fen	44/1	35	1954c Shouldham
5/1	3		45/1	36	1948h-j Wayford Br.
6/1	4		46/1	37	
6/2	4		47/1	38	
7/1	5	1911c Shippea Hil	48/1	39	
8/1	6		49/1	40	1866c Northants
8/2	7	Vor 1923a Soham Fen	50/1		Vor 1961b R. Blyth
9/1	8	Vor 1911e Upware	50/2		Vor 1961c R. Blyth
9/2	8		51/1		
9/3			51/2		
10/1	9	Vor 1911g Cambs	51/3		
11/1	10		52/1		
12/1	11		53/1		Vor 1961a Moredon
13/1	12		54/1	41	
13/2	12		55/1	42	1850a Grewelthorpe
13/3			56/1	43	
13/4			57/1		Vor 1961d Riccall
14/1	13		58/1	45	
15/1	14		58/2	45	
16/1	15	1843c Scaleby	58/3	45	
17/1	16		59/1	45	Vor 1836b Hatfield
17/2	16		61/1	45	1700a Axholm
18/1			61/1	46	1740a Axholm
19/1	17	1703a Hope	61/2	46	
19/2	17	1703b Hope	62/1	47	
20/1	18		63/1	48	
21/1	19		64/1	49	
22/1	20		65/1		
23/1	21		66/1	50	Vor 1910e Aberavon
24/1	22		67/1–2	52	
25/1	23		68/1	53	
26/1	24		69/1–6	54	1927a Dava Moor
27/1	25	Vor 1911i Lancs	70/1	55	1879d-j Culrain
27/2	25	Vor 1911j Lancs	70/1	56	
28/1	26	Vor 1911f Bracebridge	72/1		1920d Quintfall Hill
29/1	27		73/1	57	
30/1	45	1747a Axholm	74/1	58	1881a Birsay
31/1	28	1901f Feltwell Fen	75/1		
31/2	28	Vor1911k Feltwell Fen	76/1	61	
32/1	29	1956b Foulden	77/1	62	1951a Gunnister
33/1	30		77/2	62	1849a Norsewick
34/1			78/1–12	59	1849b Norsewick
35/1	31	1720a West Tofts	79/1	63	
36/1	32		80/1	64	
37/1	32		81/1	64	1932b Greenhead Moss
38/1	32		81/1	65	
38/2	32		82/1	66	
38/3	32				
39/1	32				
39/2					
40/1	33				

2 Ireland

R. Ó Floinn

This second part of the gazetteer, covering 89 sites (96+ individuals), builds on C. S. Briggs' list of Irish bog bodies in *Lindow Man* (1986). Primary references cited in the latter are not repeated here. The majority of new sites are gathered primarily from a systematic search of the correspondence files of the Irish Antiquities Division of the National Museum of Ireland which are complete from 1928 onwards. Most surviving bog bodies and associated finds are preserved in the National Museum of Ireland and their registration numbers, where known, are given here. A reference to 'NMI files' indicates that the primary information is contained in the topographical files of the Irish Antiquities Division of the National Museum of Ireland. I am grateful to my colleague, Mary Cahill, for bringing the Moanflugh, Co. Cork (Co1) find to my attention and to Mr John Bradley, Dept of Archaeology, University College Dublin, for information on two Co. Mayo finds, from Heathfield (Ma1) and Breaghwy (Ma2). I would also like to acknowledge the assistance of Dr Maire Delaney for information on some of the surviving skeletal material.

The information is arranged alphabetically by county and within each county by year of discovery. The use of abbreviated county codes should make new finds easier to incorporate into such a system. The summary format adopted here means that the primary source cannot be cited in full but all significant details are recorded under each heading. It must be remembered that some details, especially age and sex, must be treated with caution as few bog bodies have been examined by qualified personnel. Where fields have been left empty, no definite information can be gleaned from the sources. The most significant new finds are discussed in Chapter 16, pp. 137–45.

ANTRIM

An1
Date of discovery: 1827
Findspot: Rasharkin par.
County: Antrim
NGR: C 9713
Depth:
Sex: Male
Age:
Preservation: 'Body … without the smallest signs of decomposition'
Assoc. artefacts:
Remarks: Body of man who had committed suicide in 1776
Present location:
Reference: Briggs and Turner 1986, No. 68

An2
Date of discovery: 1927
Findspot: Ballycowan td., Connor par.
County: Antrim
NGR: J 1299
Depth:
Sex:
Age:
Preservation: Soft tissue and skeleton
Assoc. artefacts:
Remarks:
Present location: NMI 1934:1012a,b
Reference: NMI file

ARMAGH

Ar1
Date of discovery: 1816
Findspot: Charlemont td., Loughgall par.
County: Armagh
NGR: H 8555
Depth:

Sex: Male?
Age:
Preservation: 'Body'
Assoc. artefacts: Clothes and spurs of reign of Elizabeth I
Remarks: Post-Medieval?
Present location:
Reference: Briggs and Turner 1986, No. 69

CLARE
Cl1
Date of discovery: pre-1935
Findspot:
County: Clare
NGR:
Depth:
Sex: Male
Age:
Preservation: Skull
Assoc. artefacts:
Remarks:
Present location: NMI (Not located)
Reference: Briggs and Turner 1986, No. 73

CORK
Co1
Date of discovery: 1838
Findspot: Moanflugh td., Clondrohid par.
County: Cork
NGR: W 3280
Depth: '5½ sods deep'
Sex: Male
Age:
Preservation: Body 'in perfect state'
Assoc. artefacts: Not mentioned. Nine or ten irregularly placed upright sticks and a large stone about half a hundredweight placed over the body, which was placed on its back at full length
Remarks: Reputed to be the remains of one Denis Looney who had committed suicide *c.* 200 years earlier
Present location:
Reference: Newspaper cutting dated Bandon, 10 August 1838, p. 34 of Windle MS 12 C 10 RIA Dublin

DERRY
De1
Date of discovery: 1753
Findspot: Mulkeeragh td., Dungiven par.
County: Derry
NGR: C 7016
Depth: 2 ft (0.6 m)
Sex: Male
Age:

Preservation: 'Human body ... little change or decay'
Assoc. artefacts: Tartan military dress and cloak
Remarks: Found 'stretched at full length'. Post-Medieval?
Present location: Re-buried, stone raised over grave
Reference: Briggs and Turner 1986, No. 88

De2
Date of discovery: 1804
Findspot: Flanders td., Dungiven par.
County: Derry
NGR: C 6711
Depth: 'Some feet under the surface'
Sex: Male
Age:
Preservation: 'Body'
Assoc. artefacts: Long woollen coat with buttons. Dagger and other weapons found nearby
Remarks: Body stretched full length, head severed from body. Local lore suggests the body to be that of a drover, the victim of robbers
Present location: Re-buried nearby
Reference: Briggs and Turner 1986, No. 84

De3
Date of discovery: 1813
Findspot: Drumadreen td., Bovevagh par.
County: Derry
NGR: C 6915
Depth: 'Several feet'
Sex: Male?
Age:
Preservation: Bones, locks of hair
Assoc. artefacts: Woollen jacket with wool buttons
Remarks: Garment found fully stretched with hair at top or neck. Post-Medieval date likely
Present location:
Reference: Briggs and Turner 1986, No. 79

De4
Date of discovery: 1820
Findspot: Knocknakeeragh td., Ballinderry par.
County: Derry
NGR: C 8932
Depth: 3 ft (0.9 m)
Sex:
Age:
Preservation: Skeleton
Assoc. artefacts:
Remarks:
Present location:
Reference: Briggs and Turner 1986, No. 87

De5
Date of discovery: 1825
Findspot: Tintagh td., Lissan par.
County: Derry
NGR: H 8186
Depth: 2 ft (0.6 m)
Sex: Female
Age: 'Full grown'
Preservation: 'Body'
Assoc. artefacts: Rug or 'caddy' over body
Remarks:
Present location:
Reference: Briggs and Turner 1986, No. 90

De6
Date of discovery: 1831
Findspot: Ballygudden td., Dungiven par.
County: Derry
NGR: C 6810
Depth: 'Some feet'
Sex: Female and infant
Age:
Preservation: Skin, hair, adipose tissue
Assoc. artefacts: Leather strap with small buckle around child's neck
Remarks: Medieval or post-Medieval date likely
Present location:
Reference: Briggs and Turner 1986, No. 75

De7
Date of discovery: 1832
Findspot: Terrydremont South td., Balteagh par.
County: Derry
NGR: C 6918
Depth: 3 ft (0.9 m)
Sex: Female
Age:
Preservation: Bones, hair
Assoc. artefacts: Shoes and wooden crutch
Remarks: Medieval or post-Medieval?
Present location: Reburied nearby
Reference: Briggs and Turner 1986, No. 89.

De8
Date of discovery: 1833
Findspot: Drumard td., Maghera par.
County: Derry
NGR: C 9701
Depth: 6 ft (1.8 m)
Sex:
Age:
Preservation: Skeleton
Assoc. artefacts:

Remarks:
Present location: Reburied nearby
Reference: Briggs and Turner 1986, No. 80

De9
Date of discovery: 1834
Findspot: Camnish td., Bovevagh par.
County: Derry
NGR: C 6812
Depth:
Sex: Female
Age:
Preservation:
Assoc. artefacts:
Remarks:
Present location: Reburied. Stones raised over head and foot of grave
Reference: Briggs and Turner 1986, No. 77

De10
Date of discovery: pre-1835
Findspot: Drumcroon td., Aghadowey par.
County: Derry
NGR: C 8425
Depth:
Sex:
Age:
Preservation: Skeleton, hair adhering to scalp
Assoc. artefacts: Pole at side of skeleton
Remarks:
Present location:
Remarks: Briggs and Turner 1986, No. 82

De11
Date of discovery: 1835
Findspot: Ballygroll td., Comber par.
County: Derry
NGR: C 5215
Depth: 'Several feet'
Sex:
Age: Child
Preservation: Skeleton
Assoc. artefacts: In coffin wrapped in paper
Remarks: Post-Medieval or modern?
Present location:
Reference: Briggs and Turner 1986, No. 74

De12
Date of discovery: 1835
Findspot: Boghill td., Coleraine par.
County: Derry
NGR: C 8734
Depth:

Sex: Male
Age:
Preservation:
Assoc. artefacts: Coffin boards only, of a suicide, a man called McMurray
Remarks: Modern?
Present location:
Reference: Briggs and Turner 1986, No. 76

De 13
Date of discovery: 1837
Findspot: Gortnamoyagh td., Ballinascreen par.
County: Derry
NGR: C 8013
Depth:
Sex: Male (?)
Age:
Preservation: 'Body'
Assoc. artefacts: Armour, spears, trunks with embroidered cloth, horse trappings, stirrups
Remarks: Post-Medieval or modern?
Present location:
Reference: Briggs and Turner 1986, No. 86

De14
Date of discovery: 1881
Findspot: Dunmore bog, Lissan par.
County: Derry
NGR: H 7685
Depth: '3 spits in depth'
Sex:
Age:
Preservation: Skeleton
Assoc. artefacts: Body flexed, covered by two blankets, one coarse, one fine; wooden bowl placed over face and spoon, latter engraved with letter W
Remarks: Post-Medieval or modern?
Present location:
Reference: Briggs and Turner 1986, No. 83

De15
Date of discovery: 1956
Findspot: 'The Hill', Flanders td., Dungiven par.
County: Derry
NGR: C 677116
Depth:
Sex: Male
Age:
Preservation: No body preserved
Assoc. artefacts: Woollen cloak, jacket, trews, leather shoes
Remarks: Clothing dated to 17 C. (Dunlevy 1989, 77–8)
Present location: Ulster Museum A356.1956
Reference: Briggs and Turner 1986, No. 85

DONEGAL
Dg1
Date of discovery: 1840
Findspot: Ballykinard bog, Clondavaddog par.
County: Donegal
NGR: C 2138
Depth: 'near the surface'
Sex: Female
Age:
Preservation: 'Perfectly preserved'
Assoc. artefacts: Dark 'stuff' gown; flannel petticoat and scarlet handkerchief
Remarks: Throat cut, left arm broken. Inquest identified her as a Betty Thompson, who disappeared in May 1811
Present location:
Reference: Donegal Annual, 2, 2, (1952), 434.

Dg2
Date of discovery: 1845
Findspot: Inver par.
County: Donegal
NGR:
Depth: 10½ ft (3.2 m)
Sex: Female
Age:
Preservation:
Assoc. artefacts: Clothing, shoes with buckles
Remarks: Buckles of 17 or 18 C. date
Present location: Buckles in National Museum of Ireland IA/68/52
Reference: Hill 1847, 39

Dg3
Date of discovery: 1849
Findspot:
County: Donegal
NGR:
Depth:
Sex:
Age:
Preservation: Mummified hand
Assoc. artefacts:
Remarks: Part of the collection of Thomas Cobbe, Newbridge House, Donabate, Co. Dublin. There is some doubt as to whether the Donegal provenance is correct
Present location: Museum Room, Newbridge House, Co. Dublin
Reference: NMI file

Dg4
Date of discovery: c. 1870
Findspot: Leitrim td., Culdaff par.
County: Donegal

NGR: C 5744
Depth: 8 ft (2.4 m)
Sex: Male
Age:
Preservation: 'Body'
Assoc. artefacts: Woollen garment fragments including portion of sleeve with woollen buttons
Remarks: Probably post-Medieval
Present location: Woollen garment fragments in NMI 1886: 270–1
Reference: Briggs and Turner 1986, No. 92

Dg5
Date of discovery: 1960
Findspot: Carnamoyle td., Muff par.
County: Donegal
NGR: C 3340
Depth: 2½ ft (0.7 m)
Sex: Female
Age: 45–60
Preservation:
Assoc. artefacts: Woollen garments; bodice, dress, cloak, kerchief, bag, tassels
Remarks: Clothing dated to 17 C. (Dunlevy 1989, 71–2)
Present location: NMI (clothing) 1960: 571–3
Reference: Briggs and Turner 1986, No. 91

Dg6
Date of discovery: 1976
Findspot: Rossilly Barr td., Drumhome par.
County: Donegal
NGR: G 9873
Depth:
Sex:
Age: Over 60
Preservation: Skull
Assoc. artefacts:
Remarks:
Present location: NMI 1976:651
Reference: NMI file

Dg7
Date of discovery: 1978
Findspot: Meenybraddan td., Inver par.
County: Donegal
NGR: G 793869
Depth: 3 ft (0.9 m)
Sex: Female
Age: 25–35
Preservation: Skin, bones, hair, adipose tissue
Assoc. artefacts: Cloak
Remarks: C14 date of 730 ± 90 BP. Cloak indicates 16 or 17 C. date

Present location: NMI 1978: 340–1
Reference: Briggs and Turner 1986, No.93; Ó Floinn 1988; Delaney and Ó Floinn, pp. 123–32

Dg8
Date of discovery: 1978
Findspot: Craghy td., Conwal par.
County: Donegal
NGR: C 0510
Depth: 3½ ft (1 m)
Sex:
Age:
Preservation:
Assoc. artefacts: Clothing and rope
Remarks: Body reported as being crouched/flexed
Present location: Reburied
Reference: NMI file

Dg9
Date of discovery: 1989
Findspot: Mossy Glen td., Moville Lower par.
County: Donegal
NGR: C 625438
Depth: >4 ft (1.2 m)
Sex:
Age:
Preservation: Foot only found in mechanical peat extraction, part of complete body
Assoc. artefacts: Knitted sock
Remarks: Sock of 17 or 18 C. date (pers. comm. M. Dunlevy)
Present location: NMI
Reference: NMI file

DOWN
Dw1
Date of discovery: 1780
Findspot: Drumkeeragh td., Dromara par.
County: Down
NGR: J 3346
Depth: 11 ft (3.3 m)
Sex: Female
Age: Adult
Preservation: Skin, bone
Assoc. artefacts: Clothing: shroud, cloak, dress and ornaments
Remarks: Post-Medieval?
Present location: NMI R. 2028 (hair); R. 2029–34 and 1921:4 (cloth samples)
Reference: Briggs and Turner 1986, No. 94

Dw2
Date of discovery: 1824
Findspot: Loughriscouse td., Newtownards par.
County: Down

NGR: J 5274
Depth: 23 ft (6.7 m)?
Sex: Male?
Age:
Preservation: 'Body in good state of preservation'
Assoc. artefacts: 'Dress of Highlander
Remarks: Post-Medieval?
Present location:
Reference: Briggs and Turner 1986, No. 95

FERMANAGH

Fe1
Date of discovery: pre-1935
Findspot: Lisnaskea par.
County: Fermanagh
NGR:
Depth: 18 ft (5.4 m)
Sex: Male
Age:
Preservation: Skull
Assoc. artefacts:
Remarks: Lay very near marl below the peat
Present location: Museum of University College Dublin, No.101 (Not located)
Reference: Briggs and Turner 1986, No. 96

GALWAY

Ga1
Date of discovery: 1821
Findspot: Gallagh td., Killosolan par.
County: Galway
NGR: M 6843
Depth: 10 ft (3 m)
Sex: Male
Age: Adult
Preservation: Skeleton and skin
Assoc. artefacts: Leather cape, body otherwise naked, rope around neck, pointed wooden stake on either side
Remarks: C14 dates of 3840 ± 70 BP; 2320 ± 90 BP; 2220 ± 90BP. Latter date incorrectly quoted in Ó Floinn 1988 and wrongly attributed to Groningen
Present location: National Museum of Ireland, W.5 and R.207
Reference: Briggs and Turner 1986, No. 100; Ó Floinn 1988

Ga2
Date of discovery: pre-1920
Findspot: Cloonascragh td., Tuam par.
County: Galway
NGR: M 4350
Depth:
Sex:
Age:
Preservation: Human head

Assoc. artefacts: Two leather shoes 'not far from it'
Remarks: Located not far from an ancient togher or bog road composed of timber beams, 5 ft (1.5 m) deep in bog
Present location:
Reference: Briggs and Turner 1986, No. 97

Ga3
Date of discovery: pre-1931
Findspot: Stonyisland Bog, par. Lickmolassy
County: Galway
NGR: M8104
Depth: 10 ft (3 m)
Sex: Male
Age: c.40
Preservation: Skeleton
Assoc. artefacts:
Remarks: Arms outstretched, head in contact with marl C14 dates of 6200 ± 80 BP; 5170 ± 90 BP; 5270 ± 80 BP; 5180 ± 80 BP
Present location: University College Galway 118
Reference: Briggs and Turner 1986, No. 101

Ga4
Date of discovery: 1934
Findspot: Near Mount Bellew (6 miles N. of)
County: Galway
NGR: M 6957
Depth: 4–5 ft (1.2–1.5 m)
Sex: Male
Age:
Preservation: Skull
Assoc. artefacts:
Remarks: Banks of R. Shiven. Fragment of another skull found in same locality
Present location: NMI (Not located)
Reference: Briggs and Turner 1986, No. 99; NMI file

Ga5
Date of discovery: 1936
Findspot: Cloonbenes td., Grange par.
County: Galway
NGR: M 6628
Depth: 4½ ft (1.4 m)
Sex:
Age: c.12 years
Preservation: Skeleton and hair
Assoc. artefacts: Fragments of patched woollen clothing
Remarks:
Present location: NMI 1936:1990
Reference: Briggs and Turner 1986, No. 98

Ga6
Date of discovery: 1952
Findspot: Kinnakinelly td., Addergoole par.

County: Galway
NGR: M 435670
Depth: 8 ft (2.4 m)
Sex:
Age: Adult
Preservation: Skeleton found, mandible only preserved
Assoc. artefacts: Wooden stave, bones of red deer
Remarks: Oriented north/south. C14 date of 2135 ± 35 BP obtained from red deer bone
Present location: NMI 1952:5
Reference: NMI file

Ga7
Date of discovery: 1972
Findspot: Cloonahinch td., Killaan par.
County: Galway
NGR: M 6932
Depth: 4 ft (1.2 m)
Sex:
Age: Adult
Preservation: Foot only – bone and soft tissue
Assoc. artefacts:
Remarks: Found in bog hole
Present location: NMI (Not located)
Reference: NMI file

KERRY
Ke1
Date of discovery: 1950
Findspot: Emlagh td., Cloghane par.
County: Kerry
NGR: Q 658044
Depth: c. 3 ft (0.9 m)
Sex: Indeterminate, possibly male
Age: 6–8
Preservation: Bones, hair
Assoc. artefacts: Long pinafore dress, poss. cloak, fragments of two other garments, boxwood comb, leather purse containing flax fibres and ball of woollen thread
Remarks: clothing dated to 17 C. (Dunlevy 1989, 72)
Present location: University College Cork
Reference: Briggs and Turner 1986, No. 102

Ke2
Date of discovery: 1952
Findspot: Kilquane or Cordal East td., Ballincuslane par.
County: Kerry
Depth: 2½ ft (0.7 m)
NGR: R 0909
Sex: Male
Age:
Preservation: Soft tissue, no bone
Assoc. artefacts: Square or oblong piece of woollen cloth (cloak?)

Remarks: Body extended, naked except for wool found over body covering upper body to waist
Present location: Reburied in local cemetery. Cloth in NMI
Reference: NMI file

KILDARE
Kd1
Date of discovery: pre-1935
Findspot:
County: Kildare
NGR:
Depth:
Sex: 1 male; 1 female
Age:
Preservation: 2 skulls
Assoc. artefacts:
Remarks:
Present location: Museum of University College Dublin, Nos 32; 105 (Not located)
Reference: Briggs and Turner 1986, No. 103

Kd2
Date of discovery: 1953
Findspot: Baronstown West td., Rathernan par.
County: Kildare
NGR: N 755184
Depth: 6 ft (1.8 m)
Sex: Male
Age: Adult
Preservation: Articulated skeleton, skin, hair
Assoc. artefacts: Woven wool and leather (?) garment, cut stakes
Remarks: Covered with brushwood. Oriented east/west with head in west. C14 date of 1725 ± 30 BP.
Present location: NMI F72/53
Reference: Ó Floinn 1991

Kd3
Date of discovery: 1959
Findspot: Timahoe bog
County: Kildare
NGR:
Depth:
Sex:
Age:
Preservation: 'Human forearm'
Assoc. artefacts:
Remarks:
Present location:
Reference: NMI file

Kd4
Date of discovery: 1981

Findspot: Ballynakill Lower/Drummond td., Kilpatrick par.
County: Kildare
NGR: N 7330
Depth:
Sex:
Age:
Preservation: Femur, vertebrae with soft tissue
Assoc. artefacts:
Remarks:
Present location:
Reference: NMI file

LIMERICK
Li1
Date of discovery: 1959
Findspot: Cloonsherick td., Killeedy par.
County: Limerick
NGR: R 289285
Depth: 1.15 m
Sex: 1 male; 2 females
Age: 30–40 (male); 35–40 and late adolescent (females)
Preservation: Skeletal; 3 skulls only recovered, more bones left at site
Assoc. artefacts: Animal bones, including skull of young goat, jaws of horse, ox and pig, as well as ribs and other bones of the above
Remarks: Pieces of roots and branches of thorn trees above bones
Present location: Skulls in Anatomy Dept, University College Cork
Reference: NMI file

LONGFORD
Lf1
Date of discovery: pre-1857
Findspot: Castlewilder td., Agharra par.
County: Longford
NGR: N 2561
Depth:
Sex: Female
Age:
Preservation: 'Body', hair
Assoc. artefacts: Leather shoes, woollen garment, gold ornaments
Remarks: Not Co. Roscommon as in Wilde 1861, 283, and Briggs and Turner 1986, 194
Present location: One shoe in NMI W.23
Reference: Briggs and Turner 1986, No. 109

Lf2
Date of discovery: 1965
Findspot: Melkernagh td., Granard par.
County: Longford
NGR: N 365763

Depth: 10–12 ft (3.0–3.6 m)
Sex: Male?
Age: Adult?
Preservation: Portion of human fibula
Assoc. artefacts: Pig scapula found at same spot
Remarks: Found in digging grave
Present location: Human and animal bones disposed
Reference: NMI file

Lf3
Date of discovery: 1970
Findspot: Melkernagh bog, Cooldoney td., Abbeylara par.
County: Longford
NGR: N 375763
Depth: 4 ft (1.2 m)
Sex:
Age:
Preservation: Skull, hair and soft tissue
Assoc. artefacts:
Remarks: Found in the upcast from a drain
Present location: Reburied in Granardkill cemetery
Reference: NMI file

LOUTH
Lh1
Date of discovery: 1895
Findspot: Ardee par.
County: Louth
NGR:
Depth:
Sex: Female
Age:
Preservation: Skin, adipose tissue, bone
Assoc. artefacts:
Remarks: Body of known individual buried in 18 C.
Present location: Royal College of Surgeons Museum, Dublin
Reference: Briggs and Turner 1986, No. 105

Lh2
Date of discovery: 1939–45
Findspot: Edentober td., Ballymascanlan par.
County: Louth
NGR: J 0818
Depth:
Sex: Female
Age: 'Young'
Preservation: 'Body'
Assoc. artefacts: 'Moleskin coat'
Remarks: Said to have been found standing upright, bog trackway nearby
Present location: Removed by local Gardaí
Reference: NMI file

MAYO

Ma1
Date of discovery: 1840
Findspot: Heathfield, near Ballycastle
County: Mayo
NGR: G 1336
Depth: 2–3 ft (0.6–0.9 m)
Sex: Female
Age: 17–18
Preservation: Head only
Assoc. artefacts: 'Coarse canvas cloth'
Remarks: Head found rolled in cloth, hair plaited
Present location:
Reference: Ballina Advertiser, 22 May 1840

Ma2
Date of discovery: 1843
Findspot: Breaghwy td., Kilfian par.
County: Mayo
NGR: G 0929
Depth:
Sex: 3 individuals, 1 female, 2 male
Age:
Preservation: 'Bodies'
Assoc. artefacts: Male clothing – 'looked vaguely military'
Remarks: Woman's hair in ringlets. Post-Medieval or modern?
Present location:
Reference: Ballina Advertiser, 14 April 1843

Ma3
Date of discovery: 1939
Findspot: Cloonkee td., Kilfian par.
County: Mayo
NGR: G 1721
Depth: 3½ ft (1 m)
Sex: Male
Age: 'Old'
Preservation:
Assoc. artefacts: Wrapped in canvas, leather boot with nails. Two loads of stones placed on top of body.
Remarks: In grave with lime. Local tradition identifies the body as that of a Mr Connel or Connolly, a pedlar who died in 1846 or 1847
Present location:
Reference: NMI file

Ma4
Date of discovery: 1954
Findspot: Derrindaffderg td., Ballintober par.
County: Mayo
NGR: M 1075
Depth: 1 ft 4 in (0.4 m)
Sex: Male?
Age: Adult
Preservation: Skeleton, hair
Assoc. artefacts: Woollen clothing consisting of gown, stocking, felt hat and leather shoe
Remarks: Clothing dated to 17 C. (Dunlevy 1989, 71–2).
Present location: NMI 1954: 34–8
Reference: NMI file

Ma5
Date of discovery: 1955
Findspot: Cloonfaughna td., Knock par.
County: Mayo
NGR: M 4180
Depth: 3½ ft (1 m)
Sex: Male
Age: Adult
Preservation: Bones, skin
Assoc. artefacts:
Remarks: No trace of clothing. Examined by local doctor
Present location: Reburied in Castlebar
Reference: NMI file

MEATH

Me1
Date of discovery: 1952
Findspot: Coolronan td., Killaconnigan par.
County: Meath
NGR: N 6658
Depth: 7–12 ft (2.1–3.6 m)
Sex:
Age:
Preservation: Bones, hair (human?)
Assoc. artefacts: Textile, leather
Remarks: Textile found rolled up into a ball
Present location: NMI 1952:10
Reference: NMI file

Me2
Date of discovery: 1978
Findspot: Kilwarden td., Clonard par.
County: Meath
NGR: N 624473
Depth: 1½ ft (0.4 m)
Sex:
Age:
Preservation: Skin, bones, hair
Assoc. artefacts: Woollen clothing
Remarks: Body extended east–west with head in west. Hands crossed over head and bound. Left leg broken
Present location: NMI 1978: 149 (body); 1978: 150 (clothing)
Reference: Briggs and Turner 1986, No. 106

Offaly

Of1
Date of discovery: 1828
Findspot: Cloghan Castle, Cloghan Demesne td., Lusmagh par.
County: Offaly
NGR: M 9712
Depth: 40 ft (12 m) (?)
Sex: Male
Age:
Preservation: Skeleton
Assoc. artefacts: Leather boot and spur on one leg. EBA dagger found nearby
Remarks:
Present location:
Reference: Briggs and Turner 1986, No. 108

Of2
Date of discovery: 1941
Findspot: Ballyrickard Beg td., Aghancon par.
County: Offaly
NGR: S 1394
Depth: 4¾ ft (1.4 m)
Sex:
Age:
Preservation: Skeleton
Assoc. artefacts: Hazel handle beside body and small stone under it
Remarks: Extended, supine, head in east
Present location: NMI 1941:1139
Reference: NMI file.

Of3
Date of discovery: 1962
Findspot: Ballykean td., Ballykean par.
County: Offaly
NGR: N 4820
Depth: 2 ft (0.6 m)
Sex: Male
Age:
Preservation: Body
Assoc. artefacts: In modern plank coffin
Remarks: Body was of known suicide of 19 C
Present location: Reburied
Reference: NMI file

Of4
Date of discovery: 1969
Findspot: Lea Beg td., Wheery or Killagally par.
County: Offaly
NGR: N 170187
Depth:

Sex:
Age:
Preservation: Frontal portion of skull with skin attached
Assoc. artefacts:
Remarks: In milled peat, precise depth unknown
Present location: NMI 1969:837
Reference: Lucas (ed.) 1972, 14

Of5
Date of discovery: 1982
Findspot: Drinagh td., Eglish par.
County: Offaly
NGR: N 105162
Depth: 9 ft (2.7 m)
Sex:
Age:
Preservation: Femur only
Assoc. artefacts:
Remarks:
Present location: NMI 1982:71
Reference: NMI file

Roscommon

Ro1
Date of discovery: 1945
Findspot: Mountdillon td., Lissonuffy par.
County: Roscommon
NGR: N 0176
Depth: 3½–6 ft (1–1.8 m)
Sex:
Age:
Preservation: Bones
Assoc. artefacts: Two rectangular pieces of woven woollen textile sewn together, probably portion of a cloak
Remarks: Bog road in vicinity
Present location: NMI 1945:146.
Reference: Ó Floinn 1992, 72

Ro2
Date of discovery: 1953
Findspot: Sheegeeragh td., Killukin par.
County: Roscommon
NGR: M 8578
Depth:
Sex: Male? and 2nd individual
Age: 40–50 and child
Preservation: Bones of two individuals
Assoc. artefacts: Deer antler found nearby
Remarks: Jaw bone brought to Dental Hospital, Dublin, for identification
Present location:
Reference: Ó Floinn 1992, 72

Ro3
Date of discovery: 1955
Findspot: Cloonree td., Kilkeevin par.
County: Roscommon
NGR: M 676825
Depth: 6 ft (1.8 m)
Sex: Male
Age: 22 ± 3
Preservation: Skull only, skin, hair
Assoc. artefacts: None
Remarks: Skull found upright. Examined in Medical Dept, University College Dublin. No evidence for beheading
Present location: Re-buried
Reference: Ó Floinn 1992, 72

Ro4
Date of discovery: 1959
Findspot: Derrymaquirk td., Boyle par.
County: Roscommon
NGR: G 743007
Depth: 5 ft (1.5 m)
Sex: Female and infant
Age: c.25 and infant
Preservation: Skeleton
Assoc. artefacts: Antler point, animal bone
Remarks: In dug grave, extended, supine, wooden block at head, stone over pelvis, oriented east/west, head in west. Examined by local doctor. C14 date of 2420 ± 70 BP
Present location: NMI 1959:24–5
Reference: Lucas (ed.) 1961, 88–9; Ó Floinn 1992

Ro5
Date of discovery: 1942/44
Findspot: Derrinlurg td., Tisrara par.
County: Roscommon
NGR:
Depth:
Sex: Male
Age:
Preservation: Incomplete skeleton
Assoc. artefacts:
Remarks:
Present location: Anatomy Dept, Trinity College Dublin
Reference:

Sligo
Sl1
Date of discovery: 1824
Findspot: Killerry par.
County: Sligo
NGR: G 7732
Depth: 6 ft (1.8 m)
Sex: Male

Age:
Preservation: 'Perfect ... body'
Assoc. artefacts: Jacket, trews, leather shoes, sheepskin cap, leather bag containing ball of thread and silver coin, long staff under body
Remarks: Clothing dated to early 17 C. (Dunlevy 1989, 72–7)
Present location: NMI Clothing: W.1–3; shoes: W.16–7
Reference: Briggs and Turner 1986, No. 111

Sl2
Date of discovery: pre-1901
Findspot: Benbulben Mountain
County: Sligo
NGR: G 6946
Depth:
Sex: Female
Age:
Preservation: 'Body'
Assoc. artefacts: 'Clad in antique costume'
Remarks:
Present location:
Reference: Briggs and Turner 1986, No. 110

Sl3
Date of discovery: 1969
Findspot: Tawnamore td., Kilmacshalgan par.
County: Sligo
NGR: G 3926
Depth: 3 ft (0.9 m)
Sex: Male
Age: Adult
Preservation:
Assoc. artefacts: Woollen clothing: hat, coat, jacket, breeches, stockings, garters, shoes
Remarks: Supine on birch twigs. Head in SSE, feet to NNW. Clothing dated to late 17 C. (Dunlevy 1989, 82)
Present location: NMI 1969: 706a–k
Reference: Briggs and Turner 1986, No. 112

Sl4
Date of discovery: 1969
Findspot: Trasgarve td., Kilmacshalgan par.
County: Sligo
NGR: G 452245
Depth: 44 in (1.1 m)
Sex:
Age:
Preservation: Two skeletons
Assoc. artefacts: None
Remarks: Parts only of skeletons found. Both supine, one above the other. Oriented east–west, head in west. No clothing or associated finds. Age and sex not determined by Coroner.

Present location: Reburied locally
Reference: NMI file; *Sligo Champion* 25 July 1969

TIPPERARY

Ti1
Date of discovery: 1763
Findspot: Bog of Cullen
County: Tipperary
NGR: R 8140
Depth:
Sex: Male?
Age:
Preservation: Skulls
Assoc. artefacts:
Remarks: 'Several skulls of men'
Present location:
Reference: Briggs and Turner 1986, No. 113

Ti2
Date of discovery: 1834
Findspot: nr. Longfordpass
County: Tipperary
NGR: S 2560
Depth:
Sex:
Age:
Preservation: Skeletons
Assoc. artefacts:
Remarks:
Present location:
Reference: J. R. Soc. Antiq. Ir., 3 (1854–5), 132

Ti3
Date of discovery: pre-1838
Findspot: near Nenagh
County: Tipperary?
NGR:
Depth:
Sex:
Age:
Preservation: 'Body'
Assoc. artefacts: Cloak and blanket
Remarks: 'Ancient cloak and blanket found round a human body out of a bog near Nenagh, Co. Limerick (*sic*)'
Present location:
Reference: Ms. Register in NMI entitled 'Royal Dublin Society Museum, List of Donors'

Ti4
Date of discovery: 1946
Findspot: Gortmahonoge td., Toem par.
County: Tipperary
NGR: R 935575

Depth: 3 ft (0.9 m), almost on bottom of bog
Sex: Male
Age: Adult
Preservation: Nails, hair
Assoc. artefacts: Woollen suit of clothes
Remarks: Oriented east/west, head in west. Not Kilcommon td. as Briggs and Turner 1986, 195. Clothing dated to late 16 or early 17 C. (Dunlevy 1989, 56–8)
Present location: NMI 1946: 359–366
Reference: Briggs and Turner 1976, No. 114

Ti5
Date of discovery: 1955
Findspot: Leigh td., Twomileborris par.
County: Tipperary
NGR: S 233560
Depth:
Sex: Male
Age: 20–30
Preservation:
Assoc. artefacts: Woollen coat and cloak
Remarks: Clothing dated to 17 C. (Dunlevy 1989, 73–7)
Present location: NMI 1955: 93–4
Reference: NMI file

Ti6
Date of discovery: 1958
Findspot: Timoney td., Corbally par.
County: Tipperary
NGR: S 177849
Depth: 1.5 m
Sex:
Age:
Preservation: 'Fragments of a skull and pelvis and arm and leg bones'
Assoc. artefacts: Located between two wooden troughs (coffins?) below trackway
Remarks: C14 date of 550 ± 120 BP for trackway above bones
Present location:
Reference: Lucas 1975, 1977

Ti7
Date of discovery: 1961
Findspot: Leigh td., Twomileborris par.
County: Tipperary
NGR: S 232574
Depth: 2½ ft (0.7 m)
Sex:
Age:
Preservation: Fragmentary bones: humeri
Assoc. artefacts: Fragment of hide, non-human
Remarks: Found 100 m south of weaver's sword

Present location: Bones and hide disposed of
Reference: NMI file

Ti8
Date of discovery: 1969
Findspot: near Cloghjordan
County: Tipperary
NGR: R 9888
Depth:
Sex: Female
Age:
Preservation: Bones, skin
Assoc. artefacts: Clothing
Remarks:
Present location:
Reference: NMI file

Ti9
Date of discovery: 1971
Findspot: Newhill td., Twomileborris par.
County: Tipperary
NGR: S 212548
Depth: c. 8 ft (2.4 m)
Sex: Female?
Age: Adult
Preservation: Bone and soft tissue, complete; hair plaited
Assoc. artefacts: An assortment of wood fragments were acquired by the National Museum of Ireland, including at least two stakes of ash, one 46 cm long and cut to a blunt point
Remarks: Body was naked, sex identified only on basis of plaited hair
Present location: NMI 1971:1128 (wood fragments only)
Reference: NMI file.

TYRONE
Ty1
Date of discovery: c. 1858
Findspot: Gleneely Valley
County: Tyrone
NGR:
Depth:
Sex: Male?
Age:
Preservation: 'Lock of a man's hair'
Assoc. artefacts: Woollen coat
Remarks:
Present location: Armagh Museum. Lock of hair and wool fragment 15–60
Reference: Briggs and Turner 1986, No. 117; Weatherup 1975, 16

Ty2
Date of discovery: 1900

Findspot: Kildress td., Kildress par.
County: Tyrone
NGR: H 7777
Depth:
Sex: Male
Age:
Preservation: Body
Assoc. artefacts: Dressed in coachman's coat with brass buttons
Remarks: Body crouched, appears murdered, head split with spade. Post-Medieval or modern?
Present location:
Reference: Briggs and Turner 1986, No. 118

Ty3
Date of discovery: pre-1901
Findspot: Thornhill parish church
County: Tyrone
NGR:
Depth: 'Some feet'
Sex: Female
Age:
Preservation: 'Body'
Assoc. artefacts:
Remarks: Fracture in skull
Present location:
Reference: Briggs and Turner 1986, No. 119

WESTMEATH
Wm1
Date of discovery: 1916
Findspot: Barbavilla Demesne td., St. Feighin's par.
County: Westmeath
NGR: N 5265
Depth:
Sex:
Age:
Preservation: Skeleton, skin, nails
Assoc. artefacts: Sheepskin cape
Remarks:
Present location: NMI 1916:127 (cape). Bones interred in Kilmany cemetery
Reference: NMI file

Wm2
Date of discovery: 1929
Findspot: Derrydooan Middle td., Rathaspick par.
County: Westmeath
NGR: N 285675
Depth: 6 ft (1.8 m)
Sex: Male?
Age: Young adult
Preservation: Skull and hair

Assoc. artefacts:
Remarks: C14 date of 1295 ± 60 BP
Present location: University College Galway 116
Reference: NMI file

Wm3
Date of discovery: 1940
Findspot: Ballybeg td., Kilcumreragh par.
County: Westmeath
NGR: N 2239
Depth: 5½ ft (1.7 m), just over gravel bottom of bog
Sex: Male
Age: 45–50
Preservation: Skull
Assoc. artefacts: Lower jaw of 2-year-old cow found 6 ft
    (1.8 m) away at same level
Remarks:
Present location: NMI 1940:82
Reference: NMI file.

WICKLOW
Wi1
Date of discovery: pre-1935
Findspot:
County: Wicklow

NGR:
Depth:
Sex: Female
Age:
Preservation: Skull
Assoc. artefacts:
Remarks:
Present location: Museum of Royal College of Surgeons,
    London No. 4982 (now BM Nat. Hist.) (Not located)
Reference: Briggs and Turner 1986, No.120

NORTH OF IRELAND
Date of discovery: pre-1935
Findspot:
County:
NGR:
Depth:
Sex: Male
Age:
Preservation: Skull
Assoc. artefacts:
Remarks:
Present location: Museum of Royal College of Surgeons,
    London, No. 4.9825 (now BM Nat. Hist.) (Not located)
Reference: Martin 1935, 155

Bibliography

The bibliography is arranged by chapter. In the case of the two-part gazetteer, the references have been included in the chapter dealing with the recent research into the bog bodies of Britain and Ireland. To save space, contributions to I. M. Stead, J. B. Bourke and D. Brothwell (eds), 1986, *Lindow Man: The Body in the Bog*, British Museum Publications, London, have been abbreviated to Stead *et al*, with the page numbers of the individual contributions following.

Chapter 1

Barber, K., 1986 'Peat macrofossil analyses as indicators of the bog palaeoenvironment and climatic change', in Stead *et al* 86–90.

Dodgson, J. McN., 1970 *The Placenames of Cheshire*. EPNS (I).

Moore, P. D. and Bellamy, D., 1974 *Peatlands*, London.

Norbury, W. H., 1884 'Lindow Common as a peat bog: its age and its people', *Trans. Lancs. & Ches. Antiq. Soc.* (2) 59–75.

Smith, A. G., 1981 'The Neolithic', in Simmons, I. G. and Tooley, M. J. (eds), *The Environment in British Prehistory*, 125–209.

Turner, R. C., 1986 'Discovery and excavation of the Lindow bodies', in Stead *et al* 10–13.

Worthington-Barlow, T., 1853 'History of Wilmslow Parish – Lindow Common', *Lancs. & Ches. Hist. Collector* (I), 42–6.

Chapter 2

Andersen, S. Th., 1970 'The relative pollen productivity and pollen representation of north European trees, and correction factors for tree pollen spectra'. *Danm. Geol. Unders.* II, 96, 1–99.

Andersen, S. Th., 1973 'The differential pollen productivity of trees and its significance for the interpretation of a pollen diagram from a forested region', in Birks, H. J. B. and West, R. G. *Quaternary Plant Ecology* 109–15. Blackwell, Oxford.

Barber, K. E., 1981 *Peat Stratigraphy and Climatic Change. A Palaeoecological Test of the Theory of Cyclic Peat Bog Regeneration*. Balkema, Rotterdam.

Barber, K. E., 1982 'Peat-bog stratigraphy as a proxy climatic record', in Harding, A. (ed.) *Climatic Change in Later Prehistory*, 103–14. University Press, Edinburgh.

Barber, K. E., 1986 'Peat macrofossil analyses as indicators of the bog palaeoenvironment', in Stead *et al* 86-9.

Birks, H. J. B., 1965 'Pollen analytical investigations at Holcroft Moss, Lancashire and Lindow Moss, Cheshire'. *J. Ecol.* (53) 299–314.

Blytt, A., 1876 *Essay on the Immigration of the Norwegian Flora During Alternating Rainy and Dry Periods*. Kristiana, Norway.

Clapham, A. R., Tutin, T. G. and Moore, D. M., 1987 *Flora of the British Isles*, 3rd edn Cambridge University Press.

Eckblad, F. E., 1975 '*Tilletia sphagni, Heliotum schimperi*, or what', *Pollen et spores* (17) 423–7.

Granlund, E., 1932 'De svenska Högmossarnas geologi', *Sver. Geol. Unders. Afh.* (C26) 1–193.

Greig, J. R. A., 1982 'Past and present lime woods of Europe', in Bell, M. and Limbrey, S., *Archaeological Aspects of Woodland Ecology*. British Archaeological Reports, International Series 146, 23–55.

Moore, P. D. and Webb, J. A., 1978 *An Illustrated Guide to Pollen Analysis*. Hodder and Stoughton, London.

Oldfield, F., Higgitt, S. R., Richardson, N. and Yates, G., 1986 'Pollen, charcoal, rhizopod and radiometric analyses', in Stead *et al* 82–5.

Scaife, R. G., 1980 *Late-Devensian and Flandrian Palaeoecological Studies in the Isle of Wight*. PhD thesis, University of London, King's College.

Sernander, R., 1910 *Die schwedischen Torfmoore als Zeugen postglazialer Klimaschwankungun*. Stockholm.

Stead, I. M., Bourke, J. B. and Brothwell, D., 1986 *Lindow Man: The Body in the Bog*. British Museum Publications.

Tauber, H., 1965 'Differential pollen dispersion and the interpretation of pollen diagrams', *Danm. Geol. Unders.* II, 89, 1–69.

Troels-Smith, J., 1955 'The characterisation of unconsolidated sediments', *Danm. Geol. Unders.* IV Raekke, 3, No. 10.

Turner, J., 1962 'The *Tilia* decline: an anthropogenic interpretation', *New Phytologist* (61) 328–41.

Van Geel, B., 1978 'A palaeoecological study of Holocene peat bog sections in Germany and the Netherlands', *Rev. Palaeobot. & Palynol.* (25) 1–120.

Chapter 3

Angus, R. B., 1978 'The British species of *Helophorus*', *Balfour-Browne Club Newsletter* (11) 2–15.

Balfour-Browne, F., 1940 *British Water Beetles I*. Ray Society, London.

Balfour-Browne, F., 1950 *British Water Beetles II*. Ray Society, London.

Balfour-Browne, F., 1958 *British Water Beetles III*. Ray Society, London.

Bilton, D. T., 1984 'Four water beetles (Col., Dytiscidae) new to Cumberland, including *Hydroporus scalesianus* Stephens', *Entomologists' Monthly Magazine* (120) 251.

Buckland, P. C., 1979 *Thorne Moors: A Palaeoecological Study of a Bronze Age Site. A contribution to the history of the British insect fauna*. Occasional publication No. 8, Geography Department, University of Birmingham.

Coope, G. R. and Osborne, P. J., 1968 'Report on the Coleopterous fauna of the Roman Well at Barnsley Park, Gloucestershire', *Trans. Bristol & Gloucs. Archaeol. Soc.* (86) 84–7.

Foster, G. N., 1982 'Notes on rare Dytiscidae (Coleoptera) in Norfolk', *Trans. Norfolk and Norwich Natur. Soc.* (26) 3–10.

Fowler, W. W., 1890 *The Coleoptera of the British Isles* (4). Reeve, London.

Franz, H., 1971 'Tribus Scydmaenini', in Freude *et al* (3) 302–3.

Freude, H., Harde, K. W. and Lohse, G. A. (eds) *Die Käfer Mitteleuropas*. Goeke & Evers, Krefeld.

Friday, L. E., 1988 *A Key to the Adults of British Water Beetles*. Field Studies Council 189.

Girling, M., 1976 'Fossil Coleoptera from the Somerset Levels: the Abbot's Way', *Somerset Levels Papers* (2) 28–33.

Girling, M., 1984 'Aquatic Coleoptera in the fossil insect assemblages from archaeological sites in the Somerset Levels', *Balfour-Browne Club Newsletter* (3) 1–11.

Girling, M., 1986 'The insects associated with Lindow Man', in Stead, *et al* 90–91.

Guignot, F., 1933 *Hydrocanthares de France*. Toulouse.

Hansen, M., 1987 'The Hydrophiloidea (Coleoptera) of Fennoscandia and Denmark', *Fauna Entomologica Scandinavica* (18). Scandinavian Science Press, Leiden.

Harde, K. W., 1984 *A Field Guide in Colour to Beetles*. Octopus, London.

Hoffman, A., 1950 *Coléoptères Curculionides. Faune de France* (59) Lechevalier, Paris.

Horsfield, D. and Foster, G. N., 1985 '*Hydroporus scalesianus* Stephens and *Laccobius oblongus* (Stephens) (Col. Dytiscidae) in Hart Bog, County Durham', *Entomologists' Monthly Magazine* (119) 62.

Joy, N. H., 1932 *A Practical Handbook of British Beetles*. Witherby, Edinburgh.

Kenward, H. K., 1975 'Pitfalls in the environmental interpretation of insect death assemblages', *J. Archaeol. Sci.* (2) 85–94.

Kloet, G. S. and Hinks, W. D., 1977 *A Check List of British Insects, 4, Coleoptera*. Royal Entomological Society, London.

Lindner, E., 1959 'Beitrage zur Kenntnis der Larven der Limoniidae (Diptera)', *Z. Morph. Okol. Tiere.* (48) 209–319.

Lindroth, C. H., 1974 *Carabidae. Handbooks for the Identification of British Insects, 4* (2). Royal Entomological Society, London.

Lindroth, C. H., 1986 'The Carabidae (Coleoptera) of Fennoscandia and Denmark', *Fauna Entomologica Scandinavica* (15) 2. Scandinavian Science Press, Leiden.

Lohse, G. A., 1964 'Fam. Staphylinidae (Micropeplus bis Tachyporinae', in Freude *et al* (4).

Lohse, G. A., 1967 'Fam. Cryptophagidae', in Freude *et al* (7) 110–58.

Lohse, G. A., 1983a 'U. Fam. Barinae' in Freude *et al* (11) 171–8.

Lohse, G. A., 1983b 'U. Fam. Ceutorhynchinae', in Freude *et al* (11) 180–253.

Mohr, K. H., 1966 'Fam. Chrysomelidae', in Freude *et al* (9) 95–280.

Osborne, P. J., 1972 'Insect faunas of Late Devensian and Flandrian age from Church Stretton, Shropshire', *Phil. Trans. R. Soc. Lond.* (B 263) 327–67.

Palmer, M., 1981 'Relations between species richness of macrophytes and insects in some water bodies in the Norfolk Breckland', *Entomol. Monthly Mag.* (117) 35–46.

Pearce, E. J., 1974 'Coleoptera: Pselaphidae', *Handbooks for the Identification of British Insects, 4* (9). Royal Entomological Society, London.

Peez, A. V., 1971 'Fam. Leiodidae', in Freude *et al* (3) 243–65.

Reitter, E., 1916 *Fauna Germanica, Die Käfer des Deutschen Reiches*, 4. Lutz, Stuttgart.

Skidmore, P., 1986 'The dipterous remains', in Stead *et al* 92.

Smith, E., Lee, J. and Lazenby, A., 1985 'Beetles (Coleoptera)', in Whiteley, D. (ed.) *The Natural History of the Peak District*, 152–66. Sorby Natural History Society, Sheffield.

Stainforth, T., 1944 'Reed-beetles of the genus *Donacia* and its allies in Yorkshire (Col. Chrysomelidae)', *Naturalist* (810), 81–91.

Tottenham, C. E., 1954 'Staphylinidae section (a) Piestinae to Euaesthetinae', *Handbook for the Identification of British Insects* 4 (8a). Royal Entomological Society, London.

Vogt, H., 1967 'Fam. Cucujidae', in Freude *et al* (7) 83–104.

Chapter 4

Gowlett, J. A. J., Gillespie, R., Hall, E. T. and Hedges, R. E. M., 1986 'Accelerator radiocarbon dating of ancient human remains from Lindow Moss', in Stead *et al* 22–4.

Gowlett, J. A. J., Hedges, R. E. M. and Law, I. A., 1989 'Radiocarbon accelerator (AMS) dating of Lindow Man', *Antiquity* (63) 71–9.

Healy, F. and Housley, R. A., 1992 'Nancy was not alone: human skeletons of the Early Bronze Age from the Norfolk peat fen', *Antiquity* (66) 948–55.

Hedges, R. E. M., Law, I. A., Bronk, C. R. and Housley, R. A., 1989 'The Oxford Accelerator Mass Spectrometry Facility: technical developments in routine dating', *Archaeometry* (31) 2, 99–113.

Klinken, G. J. van, and Hedges, R. E. M., 1992 'Experiments on ^{14}C dating of contaminated bone using peptides resulting from enzymatic cleavage of collagen', *Radiocarbon* (34) 3, 292–5.

Otlet, R. L., 1979 'An assessment of laboratory errors in liquid scintillation methods of ^{14}C dating', in Berger, R. and Suess, H. E. (eds) *Int. Radiocarbon Conf., IXth Proc.*, 256–67. University of California Press.

Otlet, R. L., Huxtable, G., Evans, G. V., Humphreys, D. G., Short, T. D. and Lonchie, S. J., 1983 'Development and operation of the Harwell small counter facility for the measurement of ^{14}C in very small samples', *Radiocarbon* (25) 2, 565–75.

Otlet, R. L., Sanderson, D. C. W. and Walker, A. J., 1986 'Miniature gas counter dating techniques based on two years experience', in Olin, J. S. and Blackman, M. J. (eds) *Int. Archaeometry Symp. 24th Proc.*, 507–17. Smithsonian Institution Press, Washington.

Otlet, R. L., Walker, A. J. and Dadson, S. M., 1986 'Report on radiocarbon dating of the Lindow Man by AERE, Harwell', in Stead *et al* 27–30.

Stead, I. M., Bourke, J. B. and Brothwell, D., 1986, *Lindow Man: The Body in the Bog*. British Museum Publications.

Stuiver, M. and Becker, B., 1986 'High-precision decadal calibration of the radiocarbon time scale', AD 1950–2500 BC', *Radiocarbon* (28) 2B, 863–910.

Stuiver, M. and Reimer, P. J., 1986 'A computer program for radiocarbon age calibration', *Radiocarbon* (28) 2B, 1022–30.

Tauber, H., 1979 'Kulstoff-14 datering af møselig', *Kuml* 73–8.

Vogel, J. S., Nelson, D. E. and Southon, J. R., 1987 '^{14}C background level in an accelerator mass spectrometry system', *Radiocarbon* (29) 3, 323–33.

Ward, G. K. and Wilson, S. R., 1978 'Procedures for comparing and combining radiocarbon age determinations: a critique', *Archaeometry* (20) 1, 19–31.

Weber, C. A., 1900 'Uber die Moore, mit besonderer Berucksichtigung, der zwischen Unterweser und Unterelbe liegenden', *Jahres-Bericht der Männer von Morgenstern* (3) 3–23.

Chapter 5

Ambers, J. C., Matthews, K. J. and Bowman, S. G. E., 1986 'Radiocarbon dates for two peat samples', in Stead *et al* 25–6.

Backeus, I., 1991 'The cyclic regeneration on bogs – a hypothesis that became an established truth', *Striae* (31) 33–5.

Barber, K. E., 1981 *Peat Stratigraphy and Climatic Change: A Palaeoecological Test of the Theory of Cyclic Peat Bog Regeneration*. Balkema, Rotterdam.

Barber, K. E., 1986 'Peat macrofossil analyses as indicators of the bog palaeoenvironment and climatic change', in Stead *et al* 86–9.

Barber, K. E., 1994 'Deriving Holocene palaeoclimates from peat stratigraphy: some misconceptions regarding the sensitivity and continuity of the record', *Quaternary Newsletter* (72) 1–9.

Barber, K. E., Chambers, F. M., Maddy, D., Stoneman, R. E. and Brew, J. S., 1994 'A sensitive high-resolution record of Late Holocene climatic change from a raised bog in Northern England', *The Holocene* (4) 198–205.

Boatman, D. J., 1983 'The Silver Flow National Nature Reserve, Galloway, Scotland', *J. Biogeogr.* (10) 163–274.

Buckland, P. C., Pyatt, F. B. and Housley, R., 1994 'Paints, dates, bog stratigraphy and murder: some comments on Lindow Men', in Luff, R. and Rowley-Conwy, P. (eds) *Whither Environmental Archaeology?* 7–12. Oxbow Monograph 38.

Casson, W., 1829 *The History and Antiquities of Thorne*. Thorne.

Clymo, R. S., 1991 'Peat growth', in Shane, L. C. K. and Cushing, E. J. (eds) *Quaternary Landscapes*. 76–112. Belhaven Press, London.

Dayton, J. A., 1986 'Animal remains – the Cladocera and

Chironomidae', in Stead *et al* 93–8.

Dickson, J. H., 1973 *Bryophytes of the Pleistocene. The British Record and its Chorological and Ecological Implications.* Cambridge University Press.

Eversham, B., Skidmore, P. and Buckland, P. C., 1995 'Invertebrates as indicators of lowland bogs in eastern England: some British bogs in a European context', in Harding, P. and Valovirta, I. (eds) *9th Coll. European Invertebrates Survey: Bioindicators at a pan-European Level.* Institute of Terrestrial Ecology, Abbots Ripton.

Foster, D. R. and Wright, H. E. Jr., 1990 'Role of ecosystem development and climate in bog formation in central Sweden', *Ecology* (71) 450–63.

Girling, M. A., 1986 'The insects associated with Lindow Man', in Stead *et al* 90–91.

Goreham, E., 1953 'Some early ideas concerning the nature, development and origins of peatlands', *J. Ecol.* (41) 257–74.

Gowlett, J. A. J., Gillespie, R., Hall, E. T. and Hedges, R. E. M., 1986 'Accelerator radiocarbon dating of ancient human remains from Lindow Moss', in Stead *et al* 22–4.

Gowlett, J. A. J., Hedges, R. E. M. and Law, I. A., 1989 'Radiocarbon accelerator (AMS) dating of Lindow Man', *Antiquity* (63) 71–9.

Hatfield, C. V., 1866 *Historical Notices of Doncaster 1.* Doncaster.

Johnson, L. C. and Damman, A. W. H., 1991 'Species-controlled *Sphagnum* decay on a south Swedish raised bog', *Oikos* (61) 234–42.

Limbert, M., 1987 'Some notes on the landscape history of Thorne Moors', *Thorne Moors Papers* (1) 29–41.

Lindsay, R. A., Charman, D. J., Everingham, R., O'Reilly, R. M. and Rowell, T. A., 1988 *The Flow Country: Peatlands of Caithness and Sutherland.* Nature Conservancy Council, Peterborough.

McIntire, W. T., 1940 'Solway Moss', *Trans. Cumb. & Westmorland Antiq. & Archaeol.* (41) 1–14.

Moore, P. D., 1977 'Stratigraphy and pollen analysis of Claish Moss, north-west Scotland: significance for the origin of surface pools and forest history', *J. Ecol.* (65) 373–97.

Moore, P. D., 1991 'Ups and downs in peatland', *Nature* (353) 299–300.

Moore, P. D. and Bellamy, D., 1974 *Peatlands.* Elek, London.

Oldfield, F., Higgett, S. R., Richardson, N. and Yates, G., 1986 'Pollen, charcoal, rhizopod and radiometric analyses', in Stead *et al* 82–5.

Osvald, H., 1923 'Die vegetation des Hochmoores Komosse', *Svenske. Växtsoc. Sallsk. Handl.* 1.

Otlet, R. L., Walker, A. J. and Dadson, S. M., 1986 'Report on radiocarbon dating of the Lindow Man by AERE, Harwell', in Stead *et al* 27–30.

Parsons, H. F., 1877 'The alluvial strata of the Lower Ouse Valley', *Proc. Geol. & Polytech. Soc. West Riding Yorks.* (4, new ser.) 203–38.

Parker Pearson, M., 1986 'Lindow Man and the Danish connection', *Anthropology Today* (2) 15–18.

Skidmore, P., 1986 'The dipterous remains', in Stead *et al* 92.

Smith, B. M., 1985 *A palaeoecological study of raised mires in the Humberhead Levels.* PhD thesis, University of Wales (Cardiff).

Smith, K. G. V., 1986 *A Manual of Forensic Entomology.* British Museum (NH), London.

Stead, I. M., 1986 'Summary and conclusions', in Stead *et al* 177–80.

Stead, I. M., Bourke, J. B. and Brothwell, D., 1986 *Lindow Man: The Body in the Bog.* British Museum Publications.

Stoneman, R., Barber, K. and Maddy, D., 1993 'Present and past ecology of *Sphagnum imbricatum* and its significance in raised peat-climate modelling', *Quaternary Newsletter* (70) 14–22.

Walker, D. and Walker, P. M., 1961 'Stratigraphic evidence of regeneration in some Irish bogs', *J. Ecol.* (49) 165–85.

Wimble, G. A., 1986 *The palaeoecology of lowland coastal raised mires of south Cumbria.* PhD thesis, University of Wales (Cardiff).

Chapter 6

Boom, R., Sol, A., Salimans, M., Jansen, C., Wertheim-van Dillen, P. and van der Noordaa, J., 1990 'Rapid and simple method for purification of nucleic acid', *J. Clin. Microbiol.* (28) 495–503.

Brothwell, D., 1986 'The remains of Lindow Women', in Stead *et al* 52–3.

Fricker, E. J. and Fricker, C. R., 1994 'Application of the polymerase chain reaction to the identification of *E. coli* and coliforms in water', *Letters in Appl. Microbiol.* (19) 44–6.

Holden, T. G., 1986 'Plant remains from Lindow Man's last meal', in Stead *et al* 117–25.

Holden, T. G., 1990 'The rehydration of coprolites using trisodiumphosphate: colour reaction and smell', *Paleopathology Newsletter* (71) 9–12.

Hoskins, G. and Bandler, R., 1987 'Identification of mammalian faeces by coprostanol thin-layer chromatography: method development', *J. Assoc. Official Anal. Chemists*, 496–8.

Hoss, M., Kohn, M., Paabo, S., Knauser, S. and Schroder, W., 1992 'Excrement analysis by PCR', *Nature* (359) 199.

Hoss, M. and Paabo, S., 1993 'DNA extraction from Pleistocene bones by a silica-based purification method', *Nucleic Acids Res.* (21) 3913–4.

Jones, A., 1983 'A coprolite from 6–8 Pavement', in Hall *et al Environment and Living Conditions at Two Anglo-Scandinavian Sites. The Archaeology of York: The Past*

Environment of York (14/4) 225–30.

Mullis, K. and Faloona, F., 1987 'Specific synthesis of DNA *in vitro* via a polymerase catalysed chain reaction', *Methods Enzymology* (155) 335–50.

Musgrave, J. H. and Harneja, N. K., 1978 'The estimation of adult stature from metacarpal bone length', *Am. J. Phys. Anthrop.* (48) 113–20.

Ortner, D. J. and Putschar, W. G. J., 1981 *Identification of Pathological Conditions in Human Skeletal Remains.* Smithsonian Institution Press, Washington.

Ostinga, C. H. *et al.* 'DNA and the Dutch bog bodies 1993', *Ancient DNA Newsletter* (1) 2, 21–2.

Rafi, A., Spigelman, M., Stanford, J., Lemma, E., Donaghue, H. and Zias, J., 1994 '*Mycobacterium leprea* DNA from ancient bone detected by PCR', *Lancet* 28 May 1994.

Salo, W. L., Aufterheide, A. C., Buikstra, J. and Holcomb, T. A., 1994 'Identification of *Mycobacterium tuberculosis* DNA in a pre-Columbian Peruvian mummy', *Proc. Natn. Acad. Sci. USA* (91) 2091–4.

Scaife, R. G., 1986 'Pollen in human palaeofaeces: and a preliminary investigation of the stomach contents of Lindow Man', in Stead *et al* 127–35.

Spigelman, M. and Lemma, E., 1993 'The use of the polymerase chain reaction to detect *Mycobacterium tuberculosis* in ancient skeletons', *Int. J. Osteoarchaeol.* (3) 137–43.

Van Bonin, G., 1931 'Preliminary study of the Northern Chinese hand', *Anthrop. Anz.* (70) 241–56.

Chapter 7

Antonie, S. E., Dresser, P. Q., Pollard, A. M. and Whittle, A. W. R., 1988 'Bone chemistry and dietary reconstruction in Prehistoric Britain: examples from Wessex', in Slater, E. A. and Tate, J. O. (eds) *Science and Archaeology Glasgow 1987*. British Archaeological Reports, British Series 196, 369–80.

Barber, K. E., 1986 'Peat macrofossil analyses as indicators of the bog palaeoenvironment and climatic change', in Stead *et al* 1988, 86–9.

Beaumont, E. H., 1977 'Cranial morphology of the Loxommatidae (Amphibia: Labyrinthodontia)', *Phil. Trans. R. Soc. Lond.* (B 280) 29–101.

Bede, The Venerable, 731 *Historia Ecclesiastica Gentis Anglorum.*

Bethell, P. H. and Carver, M. O. H., 1987 'Detection and enhancement of decayed inhumations at Sutton Hoo', in Boddington, A., Garland, A. N. and Janaway, R. C. (eds) *Death, Decay and Reconstruction: Approaches to Archaeology and Forensic Science* 10–21. Manchester.

Biek, L., 1982 'Appendix II. Pigments', in Davey, N. and Ling, R. *Wall-Painting in Roman Britain*, 220–22. Gloucester.

Bourke, J. B., 1986 'The medical investigation of Lindow Man', in Stead *et al* 46–51.

Caesar, *De Bello Gallico.* English translation by Handford, S. A. (1951), *Caesar: The Conquest of Gaul.* Penguin, Harmondsworth.

Carlon, C. J., 1979 *The Alderley Edge Mines.* Altrincham.

Carus-Wilson, E. M., 1967 *Medieval Merchant Venturers.* London.

Connolly, R. C., Evershed, R. P., Embery, G., Stanbury, J. B., Green, D., Beahan, P. and Shortall, J. B., 1986 'The chemical composition of some body tissues', in Stead *et al* 72–6.

Cornelius, R., 1973 'Neutron activation analysis of human hair, failure of a mission', *J. Radioanal. Chem.* (15) 305–16.

Craddock, P. T. and Gale, D., 1988 'Evidence for early mining and extractive metallurgy in the British Isles: problems and potentials', in Slater, E. A. and Tate, J. O. (eds) *Science and Archaeology Glasgow 1987*, British Archaeological Reports, British Series 196, 167–92.

Cunliffe, B. W., 1975 *Iron Age Communities in Britain.* London.

Dayton, J., 1986 'Animal Remains – the Cladocera and Chironomidae', in Stead *et al* 93–8.

Eastman, R. D., 1985 *Biomedical Values in Clinical Medicine.* J. Wright, Bristol.

Ekwall, E., 1960 *The Concise Oxford Dictionary of English Place-names*, 4th edn. Oxford.

Francalacci, P., 1989 'Dietary Reconstruction at Arene Candide Cave (Liguria, Italy) by Means of Trace Element Analysis', *J. Archaeol. Sci.* (16) 109–24.

Gantz, J. (trans), 1981 *Early Irish Myths and Sagas.*

Gilbert, R. I. Jnr., 1985 'Stress palaeonutrition and trace elements', in Gilbert, R. I. Jr. and Mielke, J. H. (eds), *The Analysis of Prehistoric Diets*, 339–58, London.

Gildas, *De Excidio Britorum.*

Girling, M. A., 1986 'The insects associated with Lindow Man', in Stead *et al* 90–1.

Glob, P. V., 1969 *The Bog People.* Faber & Faber, London.

Godwin, H., 1978 *Fenland: Its Ancient Past and Uncertain Future.* Cambridge.

Golding, A. (trans), 1565 *The Eyght Bookes of C. J. Caesar.*

Goodyear, F. R. D., 1970 *Tactitus.*

Gowlett, J. A. J., Hedges, R. E. M. and Law, I. A., 1989 'Radiocarbon accelerator (AMS) dating of Lindow Man', *Antiquity* (63) 71–9.

Haffner, A., 1974 *Die keltisch-romanische Graberfeld von Wederath-Belginum*, II.

Hall, A. R., 1992 'Archaeological records of woad (*Isatis tinctoria*) from medieval England and Ireland', *Beiträge zur Waidtagung.* 21–2, figs 1–2. Arnstadt.

Hancock, R. G. V., Grynpas, M. D. and Pritzner, K. P. H., 1989 'The abuse of bone analysis for archaeological dietary studies', *Archaeometry* (31) 169–79.

Hanford, S. A. (trans), 1951 *Caesar. The Conquest of Gaul.*

Harmondsworth.

Holmboe, J., 1927 'Nytteplanter og ugraes i Osebergfundet', in Brogger, A. W. and Shetelig, H. (eds), *Osebergfundet*, 5. Oslo.

Höpfel, F., Platzer, W. and Spindler, K. (eds), 1992 *Der Man im Eis*. Innsbruck.

Jackson, K., 1953 *Language and History in Early Britain*.

Jackson, R., 1985 'Cosmetic sets from Late Iron Age and Roman Britain', *Britannia* (16) 165–92.

Jones, J. M., 1987 'Chemical fractionation of copper, lead and zinc in ombrotrophic peat', *Environ. Pollut.* (48) 131–44.

Killeen, J. F., 1976 'Ireland in the Greek and Roman Writers', *Proc. R. Ir. Acad.* (C76) 207–15.

Knorber-Grohne, U., 1987 *Nutzpflanzen in Deutschland*. Stuttgart.

Lambert, J. B., Simpson, S. V., Szpunar, C. B. and Buikstra, J. E., 1984 'Copper and barium as dietary discriminants: The effects of diagenesis', *Archaeometry* (26) 131–8.

Lambert, J. B., Liang, Xute and Buikstra, J. E., 1989 'Physical removal of contaminative inorganic material from buried human bone', *J. Archaeol. Sci.* (16) 427–36.

Linnaeus, C., 1753 *Systema Naturae. Species Plantarum*.

Livett, E. A., Lee, J. A. and Tallis, J. H., 1979 'Lead, zinc and copper analyses of British blanket bogs', *J. Ecol.* (67) 865–91.

Lucas, M. L. and Mathan, V. I., 1989 'Jejunal surface pH measurements in tropical spue', *Trans. R. Soc. Trop. Med. Hyg.* (83) 138–43.

McCord, M., 1986 'The arm band', in Stead *et al* 40.

McKenzie, J. M., 1979 'Contents of zinc in serum, urine, hair and toenails of New Zealand adults', *Am. J. Clin. Nutr.* (32) 570–9.

Moore, P. and Bellamy, D., 1976 *Peatlands*. Elek, London.

Needham, S. P. and Bimson, M., 1988 'Late Bronze Age Egyptian blue at Runnymede', *Antiq. J.* (68) 314–15.

Newton, R. G. and Renfrew, C., 1970 'British faience beads reconsidered', *Antiquity* (44) 199–206.

O'Connor, T. P., Hall, A. R., Jones, A. K. G. and Kenward, H. K., 1984 'Ten years of environmental archaeology at York', in Addyman, P. V. and Black, V. E. (eds) *Archaeological Papers from York Presented to M. W. Barley*, 166–72. York Archaeological Trust.

O'Grady, S. H., 1892 (trans. and ed.) *Silva Gadelica*. London.

Oldfield, F., Higgett, S. R., Richardson, N. and Yates, G., 1986 'Pollen, charcoal, rhizopod and radiometric analyses', in Stead *et al* 1986, 82–5.

Ovid, *Amores*.

Pliny, *Naturalis Historia*. English translation by Rackham, H. (1942–63). Loeb.

Pomponius Mela, *Chorographia*.

Price, T. D., Schoeninger, M. J. and Armelagos, C. J., 1985 'Bone chemistry and past behaviour: an overview',

J. Hum. Evol. (14) 419–47.

Priston, A. V., 1986 'Observations: the Arm Band', in Stead *et al* 40.

Pyatt, F. B. and Lacy, D., 1988 'An appraisal of atmospheric pollution by aluminium fumes emanating from smelter works in western Norway', *Environ. Int.* (14) 407–16.

Pyatt, F. B., Beaumont, E. H., Lacy, D., Magilton, J. R. and Buckland, P. C., 1991a *'Non Isatis sed Vitrum* or The colour of Lindow Man', *Oxford J. Archaeol.* (10) 1, 61–73.

Pyatt, F. B., Beaumont, E. H., Buckland, P. C., Lacy, D. and Storey, D. M., 1991b 'An examination of the mobilisation of elements from the skin and bone of the bog body Lindow ıı and a comparison with Lindow ııı', *Environ. Geochem. & Health* (13) 3, 153–9.

Rivet, A. L. F. and Smith, C., 1979 *The Place-Names of Roman Britain*. London.

Robins, D. and Ross, A., 1989 *The Life and Death of a Druid Prince: The Story of an Archaeological Sensation*. London.

Rudenko, S. I., 1970 *The Frozen Tombs of Siberia*. London.

Ryder, M. L., 1993 'Wood at Danebury', *Oxford J. Archaeol.* (12) 3, 305–20.

Skidmore, P., 1986 'The dipterous remains', in Stead *et al* 92.

Stead, I. M., 1967 'A la Tène ııı burial at Welwyn Garden City', *Archaeologia* (101) 1–62.

Stead, I. M., 1979 *The Arras Culture*, York.

Stead, I. M., 1985 *Celtic Art*. British Museum Publications.

Stead, I. M., Bourke, J. B. and Brothwell, D., 1986 *Lindow Man: The Body in the Bog*. British Museum Publications.

Stead, I. M., and Rigby, V., 1989 *Excavations at King Harry Lane, St Albans*. London.

Tacitus, *Historiae*.

Taylor, G. W., 1986 'Tests for dyes', in Stead *et al* 41.

Taylor, G. W., 1989 'Colour with a contribution on the detection and identification of dyes', in Walton, P. *Textiles, Cordage and Raw Fibre from 16–22 Coppergate*. 397–403. (Archaeology of York 17/5). London.

Thirsk, J., 1985 'The agricultural landscape: fads and fashions', in Woodell, S. R. J. (ed.) *The English Landscape Past, Present and Future*, 129–47. Oxford.

Thomas, A. C., 1963 'The interpretation of the Pictish symbols', *Archaeol. J.* (120) 31–97.

Thompson, J. O., 1948 *History of Ancient Geography*. Cambridge University Press.

Veen, M. van der, Hall, A. R. and May, J., 1993 'Woad and the Britons painted blue', *Oxford J. Archaeol.* (12) 3, 367–71.

Vegetius, *De re militaria*.

Venugopal, B. and Luckey, T. D., 1978 *Metal Toxicity in Mammals*. Plenum Press, London.

Vergil, *Aeneid*.

Vergil, *Georgics*.

Waldron, T., 1987 'The potential of analysis of chemical

constituents of bone', in Boddington, A., Garland, A. N. and Janaway, R. C. (eds) *Death, Decay and Reconstruction: Approaches to Archaeology and Forensic Science*, 149–59. Manchester.

Webster, G. W., 1980 *The Roman Invasion of Britain*. London.

Whitwell, J. B., 1970 *Roman Lincolnshire*. History of Lincolnshire II. London.

Wild, J. P., 1970 *Textile Manufacture in the Northern Roman Provinces*. Cambridge University Press.

Wreschener, E. E., 1976 'The Red Hunters: further thoughts on the evolution of speech', *Curr. Anthrop.* (17) 717–19.

Chapter 8

Brandt, J., 1950 'Planterester fra et moselig fra aeldre jernalder: Borremose (Plant remains in the body of an early Iron Age man from Borre Fen)'. *Årbøger for Nordisk Oldkyndighed og Historie* (1950), 348–50.

Brothwell, D. R., Holden, T. G., Liversage, D., Gottlieb, B., Bennike, P. and Bosen, J., 1990a 'Establishing a minimum damage procedure for the gut sampling of intact human bodies: the case of the Huldremose Woman', *Antiquity* 65 (245), 830–5.

Brothwell, D. R., Liversage, D., and Gottlieb, B., 1990b 'Radiographic and forensic aspects of the Huldremose body', *J. Danish Archaeol.* (9) 157–78.

Clapham, A. R., Tutin, T. G. and Moore, D. M., 1987 *Flora of the British Isles*, 3rd edn. Cambridge University Press.

Dickson, C., 1987 'The Identification of Cereals from Ancient Bran Fragments', *Circaea* 4(2), 95–102.

Dickson, C., 1989 'The Roman Army diet in Britain and Germany', *Archaobotanik Dissertationes Botanicae* (133) 135–54.

Fry, G. F., 1985 'Analysis of fecal material', in Gilbert, R. and Mielke, J. I. (eds) *The Analysis of Prehistoric Diets*. 127–48. Academic Press, New York.

Green, F. J., 1981 'Iron-Age, Roman and Saxon Crops: the archaeological evidence from Wessex', in Jones, M. and Dimbleby, G. (eds) *The Environment of Man: The Iron Age to the Anglo-Saxon Period*, 129–55. British Archaeological Reports, British Series 87.

Helbaek, H., 1950 'Tollundmandens sidste måltid (The Tollund Man's last meal)', *Årbøger for Nordisk Oldkyndighed og Historie* 328–41.

Helbaek, H., 1958 'Grauballemandens sidste måltid (The Grauballe Man's last meal)', *Kuml* 83–116.

Hillman, G. C., 1986 'Plant foods in ancient diet: the archaeological role of palaeofaeces in general and Lindow Man in particular', in Stead *et al* 99–115.

Holden, T. G., 1986 'Preliminary report on the detailed analysis of the macroscopic remains from the gut of Lindow Man', in Stead *et al* 116–25.

Holden, T. G., 1990 'Taphonomic and methodological problems in reconstructing diet from ancient human gut and faecal remains'. PhD thesis, Institute of Archaeology, University of London.

Holden, T. G., 1994 Dietary evidence from the intestinal contents of ancient humans with particular reference to desiccated remains from South America', in Mather, J. G. (ed.) *Tropical Archaeology: Applications and New Developments* 66–85. Routledge, London and New York.

Holden, T. G., forthcoming 'Food remains from the gut of the Huldremose bog body.'

Jones, F. W., 1910 'Mode of burial and treatment of the body', in Elliot-Smith, G. and Jones, F. W. (eds) *Report on the Human Remains – Archaeological Survey of Nubia, Volume II for 1901–1908*.

Jones, M., 1981 'The development of crop husbandry', in Jones, M. and Dimbleby, G. (eds) *The Environment of Man: The Iron Age to the Anglo-Saxon Period*. British Archaeological Reports, British Series 87, 85–129.

Liversage, D., 1985 'La femme de Huldremose', in Bocquet, A. *et al* (eds) *Eléments de Pré- et Protohistoire Européenne: Hommages à Jacques-Pierre Millotte, Ann. Litt. de l'Univ. de Besançon* 639–47. Les Belles Lettres, Paris.

Martin, O., 1967 'Bericht über die Untersuchung der Speisereste in der Moorleiche von Dätgen', *Offa* (24) 77–8.

Netolitzky, F., 1911 'Nahrungs und Heilmittel der Uragypter (Food and medication of the ancient Egyptians)', *Die Umschau* (46) 953–6.

Netolitzky, F., 1936 'Speisereste in einer Moorleiche', *Forschungen und Fortschritte* (22) 269–70.

Robins, D., Sales, K., Oduwole, D., Holden, T. and Hillman, G., 1986 'Postscript: last-minute results from E.S.R. spectroscopy concerning the cooking of Lindow Man's last meal', in Stead *et al* 140–2.

Sales, K. D., Oduwole, A. D., Robins, G. V., Hillman, G. C. and Holden, T. G., 1991 'An analysis of the stomach contents of Lindow Man with ESR spectroscopy', in Renfrew, J. (ed.) *New Light on Early Farming: Recent Developments in Palaeoethnobotany*. 51–8. Edinburgh University Press.

Sanden, W. A. B., van der (ed.), 1990a *Mens en Moeras: Veenlijken in Nederland van de Bronstijd tot en met de Romeinse Tijd*. Drents Museum, Assen.

Sanden, W. A. B. van der, 1990b 'De laaste maaltijd (2): de macro-resten', in Sanden, W. A. B. van der (ed.) 151–7.

Stead, I. M. and Turner, R. C., 1985 'Lindow Man', *Antiquity* (59) 25–9.

Stead, I. M., Bourke, J. B. and Brothwell, D. R., 1986 *Lindow Man: The Body in the Bog*. British Museum Publications.

Warren, S. H., 1911 'On a prehistoric interment near Walton-on-the-Naze', *Essex Naturalist* (16) 198–208.

Wilke, P. J. and Hall, H. J., 1975 'Analysis of ancient feces: a discussion and annotated bibliography'. Unpublished report from the Archaeological Research Facility, Department of Anthropology, University of California, Berkeley.

Young, B. H., 1910 *The Prehistoric Men of Kentucky*. Filson Club Publication 25, Louisville.

Chapter 9

Clapham, A. R., Tutin, T. G., and Moore, D. M. 1987 *Flora of the British Isles*. 3rd edn. Cambridge University Press.

Greig, J. R. A., 1981 'The investigation of a medieval barrel-latrine from Worcester', *J. Archaeol. Science* (8), 265–82.

Hillman, G., 1986 'Plant foods in ancient diet: the archaeological role of palaeofaeces in general and Lindow Man's gut contents in particular', in Stead *et al* 99–115.

Holden, T. G., 1986 'Preliminary report on the detailed analyses of the macroscopic remains from the gut of Lindow Man', in Stead *et al* 116–25.

Jones, A. K. G., 1986 'Parasitological investigations on Lindow Man', in Stead *et al* 136–9.

Laudermilk, J. C. and Munz, P. A., 1938 'Plants in the dung of *Nothotherium* from Rampart Caves, Arizona', *Carnegie Inst. Washington, Publ.* (487) 271–8.

Martin, P. S. and Sharrock, F. W., 1964 'Pollen analysis of prehistoric human faeces: a new approach to ethnobotany', *Am. Antiq.* (30) 168–80.

Pike, A. W. and Biddle, M., 1966 'Parasite eggs in medieval Winchester', *Antiquity* (40) 293–7.

Scaife, R. G., 1986 'Pollen in human palaeofaeces: and a preliminary investigation of the stomach and gut contents of Lindow Man', in Stead *et al* 126–35.

Chapter 10

Allen, A. K. and Neuberger, A., 1973 'The purification and properties of the lectin from potato tubers, a hydroxyproline – containing glycoprotein', *Biochem. J.* (135) 307–14.

Andresen, K., Grasdalen, H., Holsen, K. A. and Painter, T. J., 1987 'Structure, properties and potential applications of *Sphagnum* holocellulose', in Stivala, S. S., Crescenzi, V. and Dea, I. C. M. (eds), *Industrial Polysaccharides: The Impact of Biotechnology and Advanced Methodologies*. Gordon and Breach, London.

Andrews, H. N., 1961 *Studies in Paleobotany*. Wiley, New York.

Barber, K., 1986 'Peat macrofossil analyses as indicators of the bog palaeoenvironment and climatic change', in Stead *et al* 86–9.

Bourke, J. B., 1986 'The medical investigation of Lindow Man', in Stead *et al* 46–51.

Brehm, K., 1970 'Kationenaustausch bei Hochmoorsphagnen: Die Virkung von an den Austauscher gebunden Kationen in Kulturversuchen', *Beitr. Biol. Pflanzen* (47) 91–116.

Brehm, K., 1971 'Ein *Sphagnum*-Bult als Beispiel einer natürlichen Ionenaustauschersäule', *Beitr. Biol. Pflanzen* (47) 287–312.

Clapham, A. R., Tutin, J. G. and Moore, D. M., 1987 *Flora of the British Isles*, 3rd edn. Cambridge University Press.

Clark, R. C. and Courts, A., 1977 'The chemical reactivity of gelatin', in Ward, A. G. and Courts, A., *The Science and Technology of Gelatin*. Academic Press, London.

Clymo, R. S., 1963 'Ion-exchange in *Sphagnum* and its relation to bog ecology', *Ann. Bot.* (27) 309–24.

Clymo, R. S., 1984 '*Sphagnum*-dominated peat bog: a naturally acid ecosystem', *Phil. Trans. R. Soc. Lond.* (B305) 487–99.

Clymo, R. S. and Hayward, P. M., 1982 'The ecology of *Sphagnum*', in Smith, A. J. E. (ed.) *Bryophyte Ecology*. Chapman and Hall, London.

Colberg, P. J., 1988 'Anaerobic microbial degradation of cellulose, lignin, oligolignols, and monoaromatic lignin derivatives', in Zehnder, A. J. B. (ed.) *Biology of Anaerobic Microorganisms*. Wiley, New York.

Coles, B. and Coles, J., 1989 *People of the Wetlands*. Guild Publishing, London.

Connolly, R. C., 1986 'The anatomical description of Lindow Man', in Stead *et al* 54–62.

Connolly, R. C., Evershed, R. P., Embery, G., Stanbury, J. B., Green, G., Beahan, P. and Shortall, J. B., 1986 'The chemical composition of some body tissues', in Stead *et al* 72–6.

Czapek, F., 1913 *Biochemistry of Plants*, (1) 644–5. Fischer, Jena.

Ellis, G. P., 1959 'The Maillard reaction', *Adv. Carbohydr. Chem.* (14) 63–134.

Foster, T. V., Hayes, M. H. B. and Wase, D. A. J., 1991 'Effects of naturally-occurring iron-carriers on continuously cultivated *Escherichia coli*', *J. Biotechnol.* (17) 233–46.

Fuchsman, C. H., 1980 *Peat: Industrial Chemistry and Technology*. Academic Press, New York.

Gowlett, J. A. J., Gillespie, R., Hall, E. T. and Hedges, R. E. M., 1986 'Accelerator radiocarbon dating of ancient human remains from Lindow Moss', in Stead *et al* 22–4.

Gustavson, K. H., 1956 *The Chemistry of Tanning Processes*. Academic Press, New York.

Harmer, R. M., 1979 'Embalming, burial and cremation', *Encyclopædia Britannica*, 15th edn. Macropaedia (6) 735–41.

Hegnauer, R., 1962 *Chemotaxonomy of Plants*, (1) 181–3; 347–50. Birkhäuser Verlag, Basel and Stuttgart.

Hegnauer, R., 1963 *ibid.* (2) 128; 1966 *ibid.* (4) 69, 90.

Kononova, M. M., 1961 *Soil Organic Matter*. Pergamon, Oxford.

Lamport, D. T. A., 1973 'The glycopeptide linkages of extensin: o-D-galactosyl serine and o-L-arabinosyl hydroxyproline', in Loewus, F. (ed.) *Biogenesis of Plant Cell-Wall Polysaccharides*, Academic Press, New York.

Maga, J. A., 1988 *Smoke in Food Processing*. CRC Press, Boca Raton.

Maillard, L. C., 1916 'Synthesis of humic substances', *Ann. Chim. (Paris)* (5) 258–317.

Maillard, L. C., 1917 *Ann. Chim. (Paris)* (7) 113–52.

Mattson, S. and Koutler-Andersson, E., 1955 'Geochemistry of a raised bog', *Kgl. Lantbrukhögskolans Ann.* (21) 321–66.

McInerney, M. J., 1988 'Anaerobic hydrolysis and fermentation of fats and proteins', in Zehnder, A. J. B. (ed.) *Biology of Anaerobic Microorganisms*. Wiley, New York.

Nayudamma, Y., 1975 'Leather and Hides', *Encyclopædia Britannica*, 15th edn, Macropaedia (10) 759–64.

Omar, S., and McCord, M., 1986 'The handling and conservation of Lindow Man', in Stead *et al* 17–20.

Omar, S., McCord, M. and Daniels, V., 1989 'The conservation of bog bodies by freeze-drying', *Stud. Conserv.* (34) 101–9.

Painter, T. J., 1983a 'Residues of D-*lyxo*-5-hexosulo-pyranuronic acid in *Sphagnum* holocellulose, and their role in cross-linking', *Carbohydr. Res.* (124) C18–C21.

Painter, T. J., 1983b 'Carbohydrate origin of aquatic humus from peat', *Carbohydr. Res.* (124) C22–C26.

Painter, T. J., 1991 'Lindow Man, Tollund Man and other peat-bog bodies: the preservative and antimicrobial action of sphagnan, a reactive glycuronoglycan with tanning and sequestering properties', *Carbohydr. Polymers* (15) 123–42.

Painter, T. J., and Sørensen, N. A., 1978 'The cation-exchanger of *Sphagnum* mosses: an unusual form of holocellulose', *Carbohydr. Res.* (66) C1–C3.

Prakash, A., Jensen, A. and Rashid, M. A., 1973 'Humic substances and aquatic productivity', in Povoledo, D., and Golterman, H. L. (eds) *Humic Substances: Their Structure and Function in the Biosphere*. Centre for Agricultural Publishing and Documentation, Wageningen.

Puustjärvi, V., 1976 'On the tolerances of nutrient contents in fertilized peat', *Proc. 5th Int. Peat Congr.*, Poznań, Poland (3) 155–8.

Ridgway, G. L., Powell, M. and Mirza, N., 1986 'The microbiological monitoring of Lindow Man', in Stead *et al* 21.

Ross, A. and Robins, D., 1989 *The Life and Death of a Druid Prince*. Guild Publishing, London.

Rudolph, H., 1972 'Identifikation der Czapekschen Sphagnolkristalle', *Biochem. Physiol. Pflanzen* (163) 110–12.

Rudolph, H. and Engmann, B., 1967 'Neue Ergebnisse zur Konstitution des Sphagnols', *Ber. Deut. Bot. Ges.* (80) 114–18.

Schnitzer, M. and Khan, S. V., 1972 *Humic Substances in the Environment*, Dekker, New York.

Schwarzmaier, U. and Brehm, K., 1975 'Detailed characterisation of the cation exchanger in *Sphagnum magellanicum* Brid.', *Z. Pflanzenphysiol.* (75) 250–5.

Sharp, A. J., 1979 'Bryopsida', *Encyclopædia Britannica*. 15th edn. Macropaedia (3) 351–4.

Smidsrød, O. and Painter, T. J., 1984 'Contribution of carbohydrates to the cation-exchange selectivity of aquatic humus from peat-bog water', *Carbohydr. Res.* (127) 267–81.

Steinberg, C. and Muenster, U., 1985 'Geochemistry and ecological role of humic substances in lake water', in Aiken, G. R., McKnight, D. M., Wershaw, R. L. and MacCarthy, P. (eds) *Humic Substances in Soil, Sediment and Water*. Wiley-Interscience, New York.

Thomson, W. A. R., 1984 *Black's Medical Dictionary*, 746–7.

Turner, R. C., 1988 'A Cumbrian bog body from Scaleby', *Trans. Cumb. & Westmorland Antiq. & Archaeol. Soc.* (88) 1–7.

Varley, S. J. and Barnett, S. E., 1987 '*Sphagnum* moss and wound healing', *Clinical Rehabilitation* (1) 147–60.

Waksman, S. A., 1930 'Chemical composition of peat and the role of micro-organisms in its formation', *Am. J. Sci.* (19) 32–54.

Waksman, S. A. and Stevens, K. R., 1929 'The role of micro-organisms in peat formation and peat decomposition', *Soil Sci.* (28) 315–38.

Wilschke, J., Sprengel, B., Wolff, C. and Rudolph, H., 1989 'A hydroxybutenolide from *Sphagnum* species', *Phytochemistry* (28) 1725–7.

Chapter 11

Baker, A. S., 1990 'Two new species of *Lardoglyphus oudemans* (Acari: Lardoglyphidae) found in the gut contents of human mummies', *J. Stored Prod. Res.* (26), 139–47.

Brothwell, D., Holden, T., Liversage, D., Gottlieb, B., Bennike, P. and Boesen, J., 1990 'Establishing a minimum damage procedure for the gut sampling of intact human bodies: the case of the Huldremose Woman', *Antiquity* (64) 830–5.

Brothwell, D., Liversage, D. and Gottlieb, B., 1990 'Radiographic and forensic aspects of the female Huldremose body', *J. Danish Archaeol.* (9) 157–78.

Evershed, R. P. and Connolly, R. C., 1988 'Lipid preservation in Lindow Man', *Naturwissenschaften* (75) 143–5.

Hagelberg, E., Gray, I. C. and Jeffreys, A. J., 1991 'Identification of the skeletal remains of a murder victim by DNA analysis', *Nature* (352) 427–9.

Hansen, H. E. and Gürtler, H., 1983 'HLA types of

mummified Eskimo bodies from the 15th century', *Am. J. Phys. Anthrop.* (61) 447–52.

Holden, T. G., 1986 'Preliminary report on the detailed analyses of the macroscopic remains from the gut of Lindow Man', Stead *et al* 116–25.

Holden, T. G., 1991 'Unusual sources of dietary evidence from the gut contents of three ancient Chilean bodies', *Bioantropologia* (1) 4–8.

Höpfel, F., Platzer, W. and Spindler, K. (eds), 1992 *Der Man im Eis*. University of Innsbruck Press.

Lawlor, D. A., Dickel, C. D., Hauswirth, W. W. and Parham, P., 1991 'Ancient HLA genes from 7500-year-old archaeological remains', *Nature* (349) 785–8.

Moore, J. G., Straight, R. C., Osborne, D. N. and Wayne, A. W., 1985 'Olfactory gas chromatographic and mass-spectral analysis of fecal volatiles traced to ingested licorice and apple', *Biomed. Biophys. Res. Commun.* (131) 339–46.

Nedden, D. Zur and Wicke, K., 1992 'Der Eismann aus der Sicht der radiologischen und computertomographischen Daten', in Höpfel, F. *et al*, 131–48.

Needham, S. and Evans, J., 1987 'Honey and dripping: Neolithic food residues from Runnymede Bridge', *Oxford J. Archaeol.* (6) 21–8.

Nelson, D. A. and Sauer, N. J., 1984 'An evaluation of post-depositional changes in the trace element content of human bone', *Am. Antiq.* (49) 141–7.

Ó Floinn, R., 1991 'A prehistoric bog burial at Baronstown West', *J. Co. Kildare Archaeol. Soc.* (17) 148–50.

Ó Floinn, R., 1992 'A bog burial from Derrymaquirk and other related finds from County Roscommon', *Co. Roscommon Hist. & Archaeol. Soc. J.* (4) 71–2.

Pääbo, S., 1986 'Molecular genetic investigations of ancient human remains', *Cold Spring Harbor Symposia on Quantitative Biology* (51) 441–6.

Pahl, W. M., Parsche, F. and Ziegalmayer, G., 1988 'Innovationen in der Computertomographie (CT): Software-Routinen und ihre Relevanz für Mumienforshung und Anthropologie', *Anthrop. Anzeiger* (46) 17–25.

Price, T. D. (ed.), 1989 *The Chemistry of Prehistoric Human Bone*. Cambridge University Press.

Pyatt, F. B., Beaumont, E. H., Buckland, P. C., Lacy, D. and Storey, D. M., 1991 'An examination of the mobilisation of elements from the skin and bone of the bog body Lindow II and a comparison with Lindow III', *Environ. Geochem. & Health* (13) 153–9.

Pyatt, F. B., Beaumont, E. H., Lacy, D., Magilton, J. R. and Buckland, P. C., 1991 '*Non isatis sed vitrum*, or the colour of Lindow Man', *Oxford J. Archaeol.* (10) 61–73.

Rothhammer, F., Standen, V., Nunez, L., Allison, M. J. and Arriaza, B., 1984 'Origin y dessarrallo de las Tripanosomiasis en el área Centro-Sur Andina', *Revista*

Chungara (12) 155–60.

Sanden, W. A. B. van der (ed.), 1990 *Mens en Moeras: Veenlijken in Nederland van de Bronstijd tot en met de Romeinse Tijd*. Drents Museum, Assen.

Smith, G. J., forthcoming 'Green fluorescence from the hair of Lindow Man'.

Smith, P. R. and Wilson, M. T., 1990 'Detection of haemoglobin in human skeletal remains by ELISA', *J. Archaeol. Sci.* (17) 255–68.

Smith, S. and Fiddes, F. S. 1955 *Forensic Medicine*. Churchill, Edinburgh.

Spindler, K., 1994 *The Man in Ice*. Weidenfeld & Nicolson, London.

Vannier, M. W., Conrey, G. C., Marsh, J. L. and Knapp, R., 1985 'Three-dimensional cranial surface reconstructions using high-resolution computed tomography', *Am. J. Phys. Anthrop.* (67) 299–311.

Wales, S. and Evans, J., 1988 'New possibilities of obtaining archaeological information from coprolites', in Slater, E. and Tate, J. (eds) *Science and Archaeology, Glasgow 1987*, 403–12. British Archaeological Reports, British Series 196.

Wei, Ou., 1973 'Internal organs of a 2100-year-old female corpse', *Lancet* (1198) 24 Nov.

Yamada, T. K., Kudou, T. and Takahashi-Iwanaga, H., 1990 'Some 320-year-old soft tissue preserved by the presence of mercury', *J. Archaeol. Sci.* (17) 383–92.

Chapter 12

Garland, A. N., 1989a 'The development of a new rehydration technique – its applicability to palaeopathology and forensic science'. Paper presented at *Science and Archaeology* conference, University of Bradford, September 1989.

Garland, A. N., 1989b 'Fossil bone: the microscopical structure', *Applied Geochemistry* (4) 215–29.

Krogman, W. M. and Isçan, M. Y., 1986 *The Human Skeleton in Forensic Medicine*. C. C. Thomas, Illinois.

Workshop of European Anthropologists, 1980 'Recommendations for age and sex diagnosis of skeletons', *J. Hum. Evol.* (9) 517–49.

Chapter 13 and Gazetteer Part 1

Abercromby, J., 1905 'Report on excavations at Fethaland and Trowie Rowe, Shetland; and of the exploration of a cairn on Dumglow, one of the Cleish Hills, Kinrosshire', *Proc. Soc. Antiq. Scotland* (39) 181.

Anon., 1854 *Proc. Soc. Antiq. Scotland* (1) 95.

Anon., 1882 *Proc. Soc. Antiq. Scotland* (16) 11.

Anon., 1893 *Archaeologia Cambrensis* (x) 142.

Anon., 1909 *Proc. Yorks. Parish Register Soc.* 376.

Anon., 1927 *Proc. Soc. Antiq. Scotland* (63) 22.

Anon., 1964 *Proc. Soc. Antiq. Scotland* (98) 328.

Baines, E., 1868 *The History of Lancashire* (I).

Bakewell, R., 1833 *An Introduction to Geology*. London.

Balguy, C., 1734 'An account of the dead bodies of a man and woman which were preserved 49 years in the moors in Derbyshire', *Phil. Trans. R. Soc.* (38) 413–5.

Barber, K., 1986 'Peat macrofossil analyses as indicators of bog palaeoenvironment and climatic change', in Stead *et al* 86–9.

Bell, M. (ed.) 1991 *Annual Report of the Severn Estuary Levels Research Committee*. Lampeter.

Bennett, H., 1975 'A murder victim discovered: clothing and other finds from an early 18th century grave on Arnish Moor, Lewis', *Proc. Soc. Antiq. Scotland* (106) 172–83.

Blockley, K., 1989 'Prestatyn 1984–5, an Iron Age farmstead and Romano–British industrial settlement in North Wales', *British Archaeological Reports, British Series* 210.

Briggs, C. S. and Turner, R. C., 1986 'The bog burials of Britain and Ireland', plus Gazetteer, in Stead *et al* 144–62 and 181–96.

Brothwell, D., 1986 *The Bog Man and the Archaeology of People*. British Museum Publications, London.

Burleigh, R., Matthews, K. and Ambers, J., 1982 *Radiocarbon* (24) 237.

Busk, G., 1866 'An account of the discovery of a human skeleton beneath a bed of peat on the coast of Cheshire', *Trans. Ethnol. Soc.* (4) 101–4.

Busk, G., 1874 'Human skull and fragments of bones of the red deer, etc., found at Birkdale, near Southport, Lancashire', *J. Anthrop. Inst.* (3) 104–5.

Clark, J. G. D., 1933 'Report on an early Bronze Age site in the south-eastern Fens', *Antiq. J.* (13) 278–9.

Clarke, D. V., Cowie, T. G. and Foxan, A. (eds), 1985 *Symbols of Power*. Edinburgh.

Clarke, R. R., 1971 *East Anglia*, 2nd edn. London.

Coombs, D., 1992 'Flag Fen Platform and Fengate Power Station post alignment – the metalwork', *Antiquity* (66) 252, 504–17.

Cust, E., 1864 'The prehistoric man of Cheshire', *Trans. Hist. Soc. Lancs. & Ches.* (4) 193–201.

de la Pryme, A., 1694 'Of trees underground in Hatfield Chase', *Phil. Trans. R. Soc.* no. 275.

Denny, H., 1871 'Notice of the discovery of a pair of ancient shoes and a human skeleton in the peat moss on Austwick Common, near Clapham, Yorkshire', *Proc. Geol. & Polytech. Soc. West Riding Yorks.* (5) 162–78.

Dieck, A., 1963 'Zum Problem der Hominidenmoorfunde', *Neue Ausgrabungen und Forschungen in Niedersächsen*, 105–12.

Dieck, A., 1965 *Die europäischen Moorleichenfunde*. Neumünster.

Dieck, A., 1972 'Stand und Aufgarben der Moorleichenforschung', *Archäologisches Korrespondenzblatt* (2) 365–8.

Dieck, A., 1986 'Der Stand der europäischen Moorleichenforschung im Jahr 1986 …', *Telma* (16) 131–58.

Duckworth, W. H., 1921 *J. R. Archaeol. Inst.* (51) 358.

Duckworth, W. L. H. and Shore, L. R., 1911 'Report on human crania from peat deposits in England', *Man* (11) 134–40.

Edwards, B. J. N., 1969 'Lancashire archaeological notes', *Trans. Hist. Soc. Lancs. & Ches.* (121) 101–3.

Edwards, B. J. N., 1973 'A canoe burial near Lancaster', *Antiquity* (43) 298–301.

Flower, W. H., 1907 *Catalogue of the Specimens illustrating Osteology and Dentition of Vertebrated Animals Recent and Extinct, contained in the Museum of the RCS of England, Part I, Man*, 2nd edn.

Fox, C., 1923 *The Archaeology of the Cambridge Region*. Cambridge.

Gibson, E., 1695 *Camden's Britannia*, 1st edn London.

Gilpin, W., 1786 *Observations in the Mountains and Lakes of Cumberland and Westmorland*.

Godwin, H., 1940 *Phil. Trans. R. Soc.* (273) 281.

Gough, R., 1789 *Camden's Britannia* (II) 280.

Grainge, W., 1892 *The Ripon Millenary*, preface to part II. Ripon.

Groenman-van Waateringe, W., 1991 'Wederom prehistorisch schoeisel vit Drenthe', *Niewe Drentse Volksalmanak* (109) 34–41.

Hald, M., 1972 *Primitive Shoes: An Archaeological–Ethnological Study Based upon Shoe Finds from the Jutland peninsula*. Copenhagen.

Hald, M., 1980 *Ancient Danish Textiles from Bogs and Burials*. Copenhagen.

Healy, F. and Housley, R., 1992 'Nancy was not alone: skeletons of the early Bronze Age from the Norfolk peat fen', *Antiquity* (66), 948–55.

Henshall, A. S., 1952 'Early textiles found in Scotland: Part 1 (locally made)', *Proc. Soc. Antiq. Scotland* (86) 1–30.

Henshall, A. S., 1969 'Clothing found at Huntsgarth, Harray, Orkney', *Proc. Soc. Antiq. Scotland* (101) 150–9.

Henshall, A. S. and Maxwell, S., 1952 'Clothing and other articles from a late 17th century grave at Gunnister, Shetland', *Proc. Soc. Antiq. Scotland* (86) 30–42.

Heslington, T., 1867 *Roman Camps in The Neighbourhood of Ripon*, quoted in Sheahan, J. J., 1871 *The History and Topography of The Wapentake of Claro*, 212.

Hughes, T. McK., 1896 *Archaeologia* (LV) 129–30.

Hughes, T. McK., 1916 *Notes on The Fenland with a Description of the Shippea Man*. Cambridge.

Hume, A., 1863 *Ancient Moels: or Some Account of the Antiquities Found Near Dove Point on the Sea-coast of Cheshire*. London.

Hunt, J., 1866 'On the influence of some kinds of peat in destroying the human body, as shown by the discovery

of human remains buried in peat in the Zetland Islands',
Mems. Anthrop. Soc. Lond. (2) 364–72.

Hunter, J., 1828 *South Yorkshire: the History and Topography
of the Deanery of Doncaster in the Diocese and the County of
York*, 154. London.

Innes, J., Tooley, M., Daniels, R. and Tann, G., 1991
'Excavation of the intertidal "submerged forests" at
Hartlepool Bay, Cleveland, north-east England',
Newswarp (10) 14–7.

Keith, A., 1925 *The Antiquity of Man*. London.

Lawrenson, W. H., undated, 'Bone Hill Farm', *Over-Wyre
Hist. J.* (1) 20–2.

Leigh, C., 1700 *The Natural History of Lancashire, Cheshire
and the Peak of Derbyshire*. Oxford.

Mann, L. McL., 1937 'Notes on the discovery of a body in a
peat moss at Cambusnethan', *Trans. Glasg. Archaeol. Soc.*
(9) 44–5.

Mapleton, J., 'Notice on the discovery of an old canoe in a
peat bog at Oban', *Proc. Soc. Antiq. Scotland* (13) 336–8.

Marshall, W., 1874 'Note', *J. Anthrop. Inst.* (3) 497.

Maughan, J., 1873 'The runic inscription on Hessilgil Crags:
Murchie's Cairn', *Trans. Cumb. & Westmorland Antiq. &
Archaeol. Soc.* (1) 320–1.

Munksgaard, E. and Ostergaard, E., 1988 'Textiles and
costume from Lønne Hede: an early Roman Iron Age
burial', in Bender Jørgensen, L., Magnus, B. and
Munksgaard, E. (eds), *Archaeological Textiles: Rep. from
2nd NESAT Symp. 1–4, v. 1984*, Arkaeologiske Skrifter (2)
53–64.

Nevell, M., 1992 *Tameside before 1066*. Tameside
Metropolitan Borough Council, Manchester.

Nicholson, J. and Burn, R., 1777 *The History and Antiquities
of Westmorland and Cumberland* (2) 473.

Nockert, M.,1985 *Bockstensmannen Och Hans Dräkt*.
Halmstad and Varberg.

Orr, S., 1921 'Clothing found on a skeleton discovered at
Quintfall Hill, Barrock Estate, near Wick', *Proc. Soc.
Antiq. Scotland* (55) 213–21.

Pearce, H., 1990 *Focus on Peatlands in Peril*. RSNC.

Peck, W., 1815 *A Topographical Account of the Isle of Axholme*,
(I). Doncaster.

Pryor, F., 1991 *Flag Fen: Prehistoric Fenland Centre*. English
Heritage.

Pryor, F., 1992 'Discussion: The Fengate/Northey
landscape', *Antiquity* (66) 251, 518–31.

Reade, T. M., 1883 'The human skull found near
Southport', *Geol. Mag.* (10) 547–8.

Rennie, R., 1810 *Essay on The Natural History and Origin of
Peat-Moss*. Edinburgh.

Ryder, M., 1977 'Some miscellaneous ancient fleece
remains', *J. Archaeol. Sci.* (4) 177–81.

Sanden, W. A. B. van der (ed.), 1990 *Mens en Moeras:
Veenlijken in Nederland van de Bronstijd tot en met Romeinse*

Tijd. Drents Museum, Assen.

Sheahan, J. J., 1871 *The History and Topography of the
Wapentake of Claro*, 212.

Smith, M. D., 1988 *About Horwich*. Chorley.

Stonehouse, W. B., 1839 *The History and Topography of the
Isle of Axholme*. London.

Stovin, G., 1747 'A letter … concerning the body of a
woman, and an antique shoe, found in a morass in The
Isle of Axholme in Lincolnshire', *Phil. Trans. R. Soc.* (44)
571–6.

Tinsley, H. M., 1974 'A record of preserved human remains
from blanket peat in West Yorkshire', *Naturalist* (931)
134.

Tooley, M. J., 1978a *Sea-level Changes in North-West England
during the Flandrian Stage*. Oxford.

Tooley, M. J., 1978b 'The history of Hartlepool Bay', *Int. J.
Naut. Arch. & Underwater Explor.* (7.1) 71–87.

Tomlinson, J., 1882 *The Level of Hatfield Chase and Parts
Adjacent*. Doncaster.

Travis, C. B., 1913 'Geological notes on recent dock
excavations at Liverpool and Birkenhead', *Proc. L'pool.
Geol. Soc.* (11) 273.

Turner, R. C., 1988 'A Cumbrian bog body from Scaleby',
Trans. Cumb. & Westmorland Antiq. Archaeol. Soc. (88) 1–7.

Turner, R. C., 1989 'Another Cumbrian bog body from
Seascale', *Trans. Cumb. & Westmorland Archaeol. Soc.* (89)
21–3.

Turner, R. C. and Penney, S., 1996 'Three bog bodies from
Whixall Moss, Shropshire', *Shropshire Hist. & Archaeol.
Soc.* (71).

Turner, R. C. and Rhodes, M., 1992 'A bog body and its
shoes from Amcotts, Lincolnshire', *Antiq. J.* (72) 76–90.

Turner, R. C., Rhodes, M. and Wild, J. P., 1991 'The Roman
body found on Grewelthorpe Moor in 1850: a
reappraisal', *Britannia* (xxii) 191–201.

Twigger, S. N. and Haslam, C. J., 1991 'Environmental
change in Shropshire during the last 13,000 years', *Field
Studies* (7) 743–58.

White, W., 1864 *History, Gazetteer and Directory of Norfolk*.

Wilkinson, T. J. and Murphy, P., 1986 'Archaeological
survey of an intertidal zone: the submerged landscape of
the Essex Coast, England', *J. Field Archaeol.* (13) 2, 177–94.

Williams, J., 1858 'A history of Radnorshire: Hundred of
Knighton', *Archaeologica Cambrensis* (12) 469–614.

Chapter 14

Briggs, C. S. and Turner, R. C., 1986 'Appendix: A gazetteer
of bog burials from Britain and Ireland', in Stead *et al*
181–95.

Brothwell, D. and Dobney, K., 1986 'Studies on the hair and
nails of Lindow Man and comparative specimens', in
Stead *et al* 66–70.

Dunlevy, M., 1989 *Dress in Ireland*. London.

Evershed, R. P., 1992 'Chemical composition of a bog body adipocere', *Archaeometry* (34) 253–65.

Hamlin, A. and Foley, C., 1983 'A women's graveyard at Carrickmore, County Tyrone, and the separate burial of women', *Ulster J. Archaeol.* (46) 41–6.

Henshall, A. and Seaby, W. A., 1961–2 'The Dungiven Costume', *Ulster J. Archaeol.* (24–5) 119–42.

Keeling, D., 1988 'Neolithic and early Bronze Age artefacts from south-west Donegal', *Donegal Annual* (40) 55–74.

Lucas, A. T. (ed.), 1961 'National Museum of Ireland: archaeological acquisitions in the year 1959', *J. R. Soc. Antiq. Ir.* (91) 43–107.

Morgan, E. D., Cornford, C., Pollock, D. R. J. and Isaacson, P., 1973 'The transformation of fatty material buried in soil', *Sci. & Archaeol.* (10) 9–10.

Ó Floinn, R., 1988 'Irish bog bodies', *Archaeol. Ir.* (2) No. 3, 94–7.

Omar, S., McCord, M. and Daniels, V., 1989 'The conservation of bog bodies by freeze-drying', *Stud. Conserv.* (34) 101–9.

Stuiver, M. and Reimer, P. J., 1986 'A computer program for radiocarbon age calibration', *Radiocarbon* (28) No. 2B, 1022–9.

Turner, P. J. and Holton, D. B., 1988 'The use of a fabric softener in the reconstitution of mummified tissue prior to paraffin wax sectioning for light microscopical examination', *Stain Technol.* (56) No. 1, 35–8.

Chapter 15
Bennike, P. and Ebbesen, K., 1986 'The bog find from Sigersdal: human sacrifice in the early Neolithic', *J. Danish Archaeol.* 1986 (5) 77–84.

Mook, W. G. and Streurman, H. J., 1983 'Physical and chemical aspects of radiocarbon dating', in Mook, W. G. and Waterbolk, H. T. (eds), *14C and Archaeology. Proc. 1st Int. Symp.* Groningen 1981, PACT 8, 31–56.

Plicht, J. van der and Mook, W. G., 1989 'Calibration of radiocarbon ages by computer', *Radiocarbon* (31) 805–16.

Tauber, H., 1979 'Kulstof-14 datering af moselig', *Kuml* 1979, 73–8.

Chapter 16 and Gazetteer Part 2
Bennike, P. and Ebbesen, K., 1986 'The bog find from Sigersdal', *J. Danish Archaeol.* (5) 85–115.

Briggs, C. S. and Turner, R. C., 1986 'Appendix: a gazetteer of bog burials from Britain and Ireland', in Stead *et al* 181–95.

Brindley, A. L. and Lanting, J. N., 1989/90 'Radiocarbon dates for Neolithic single burials', *J. Ir. Archaeol.* (V) 1–7.

D'Arcy, S. A., 1897 'A Crannog near Clones', *J. R. Soc. Antiq. Ir.* (27) 389–403.

Dunlevy, M., 1989 *Dress in Ireland*. London.

Eogan, G., 1983 *The Hoards of the Irish Later Bronze Age*. Dublin.

Glob, P. V., 1969 *The Bog People*. Faber & Faber, London.

Hammond, F., 1979 'Peat', Map 26 in *Atlas of Ireland*, Royal Irish Academy, Dublin.

Hencken, H., 1936 'Ballinderry Crannog No. 1', *Proc. R. Ir. Acad.* (43C) 103–238.

Hencken, H., 1942 'Ballinderry Crannog No. 2', *Proc. R. Ir. Acad.* (47C) 1–76.

Hencken, H., 1950–51 'Lagore crannog: an Irish royal residence of the 7th to 10th centuries A.D.', *Proc. R. Ir. Acad.* (53C) 1–247.

Hill, Lord G., 1847 *Useful Hints to Donegal Tourists*. Dublin.

Lucas, A. T. (ed.), 1962 'National Museum of Ireland: archaeological acquisitions in the year 1960', *J. R. Soc. Antiq. Ir.* (92) 139–73.

Lucas, A. T., 1975 'A stone-laid trackway and wooden troughs, Timoney, Co. Tipperary' *North Munster Antiq. J.*, (17) 13–20.

Lucas, A. T., 1977 'A stone-laid trackway and wooden troughs, Timoney, Co. Tipperary: a further note', *North Munster Antiq. J.* (19) 69.

Lynn, C. J., 1985/6 'Lagore, County Meath and Ballinderry No. 1, County Westmeath Crannogs: some possible structural reinterpretations', *J. Ir. Archaeol.* (3) 69–73.

Martin, C. P., 1935 *Prehistoric Man in Ireland*. Dublin.

Mulvany, W. T., 1850–53 'Collection of Antiquities presented to the Royal Irish Academy', Appendix V in *Proc. R. Ir. Acad.* (5) xxxi–lxv.

Newman, C., 1986 *The Archaeology of Ballinderry Lough, Co. Westmeath*. MA thesis, University College, Dublin.

Ó Floinn, R., 1988 'Irish bog bodies', *Archaeol. Ir.* (2) No. 3, 94–7.

Ó Floinn, R., 1991 'A prehistoric bog burial at Baronstown West', *J. Co. Kildare Archaeol. Soc.* (17) 148–50.

Ó Floinn, R., 1992 'A bog burial from Derrymaquirk and other related finds from County Roscommon', *J. Co. Roscommon Archaeol. Hist. Soc.* (4) 71–2.

Shea, S., 1931 'Report on the human skeleton found in Stoney Island Bog, Portumna', *J. Galway Archaeol. Hist. Soc.* (15) 73–9.

Shirley, E. P., 1845 *Some Account of the Territory or Dominion of Farney in the Province and Earldom of Ulster*. London.

Stead, I. M., Bourke, J. B. and Brothwell, D., 1986 *Lindow Man: The Body in the Bog*. British Museum Publications.

Waddell, J., 1984 'Bronzes and bones', *J. Ir. Archaeol.* (2) 71–2.

Warner, R. B., 1985/6 'The date of the start of Lagore', *J. Ir. Archaeol.* (3) 75–7.

Weatherup, D. R. M., 1975 'Armagh County Museum, Archaeological Acquisitions, 1960–74', *J. R. Soc. Antiq. Ir.* (105) 5–20.

Wilde, W., 1836–40 'Animal remains and antiquities

recently found at Dunshaughlin, in the county of Meath', *Proc. R. Ir. Acad.* (1) 420–6.

Wilde, W., 1861 *A Descriptive Catalogue of the Antiquities of Animal Materials and Bronze in the Museum of the Royal Irish Academy.* Dublin.

Wood-Martin, W. G., 1886 *The Lake Dwellings of Ireland.* Dublin.

Chapter 17

Aletsee, L., 1967 'Datierungsversuch der Moorleichenfunde von Dätgen 1959/1960', *Offa* (24) 79–83.

Andersen, S. R. and Geertinger, P., 1984 'Bog bodies investigated in the light of forensic medicine', *J. Danish Archaeol.* (3) 111–19.

Bennike, P. and Ebbesen, K., 1985 'Stenstrupmanden', *Fra Holbaek Amt* 28–39.

Bennike, P. and Ebbesen, K., 1986 'The bog find from Sigersdal: human sacrifice in the early Neolithic', *J. Danish Archaeol.* (5) 85–115.

Bennike, P., Ebbesen, K. and Bender Jørgensen, L., 1986 'Early neolithic skeletons from Bolkilde bog, Denmark', *Antiquity* (60) 199–209.

Berg, S., Rolle, R. and Seemann, H., 1981 *Der Archäologie und der Tod: Archäologie und Gerichtsmedizin.* München and Luzern.

Brothwell, D., Holden, T., Liversage, D., Gottlieb, B., Bennike, P. and Boesen, J., 1990 'Establishing a minimum damage procedure for the gut sampling of intact human bodies: the case of Huldremose Woman', *Antiquity* (64) 830–5.

Brown, T. A. and Brown, K. A., 1992 'Ancient DNA and the archaeologist', *Antiquity* (66), 10–23.

Casparie, W. A., 1987 'Bog trackways in the Netherlands', *Palaeohistoria* (29) 35–65.

Caselitz, P., 1979 'Aspekte zur Ernährung in der römischen Kaiserzeit, dargestellt an der Moorleiche von Windeby-I', *Offa* (36) 108–15.

Connolly, R. C., 1990 'Bloedgroepen', in Sanden, W. A. B. van der (ed.) 144–50.

Dieck, A., 1959 'Die Hundemoorleiche von Burlage im Emsland und das Problem der Hundemoorleichen', *Der Grafschafter* (77) 624–6.

Dieck, A., 1965 *Die europäischen Moorleichenfunde (Hominidenmoorfunde).* Neumünster.

Dieck, A., 1968 'Das Problem der niedersächsischen Moorleichen', *Die Kunde* (19) 102–21.

Dieck, A., 1973a 'Vorläufige Mitteilung über Moorleichen in Bayern', *Archäologisches Korrespondenzblatt* (3) 463–8.

Dieck, A., 1973b 'Moorleichen als Belege für Mädchentötung; archäologische Materialien sowie naturkundliche und kulturgeschichtliche Anmerkungen zu einer alten Strafrechtssitte', *Die Kunde* (24) 107–42.

Dieck, A., 1975a 'Die bronzezeitlichen Moorleichen von Rübke und Wistedt im Kreis Harburg', *Harburger Kreiskalender* 69–78.

Dieck, A., 1975b 'Darmuntersuchungen bei europäischen Moorleichen', in *Moor und Torf in Wissenschaft und Wirtschaft: Siegfried Schneider zum 70. Geburtstag,* 33–42. Bad Zwischenahn.

Dieck, A., 1984 'Moorleichen und Haaropfer in Bremen und Bremerhaven', *Bremisches Jahrbuch* (62) 123–38.

Dieck, A., 1986 'Der Stand der europäischen Moorleichenforschung im Jahr 1986 sowie Materialvorlage von anthropologischen und medizinischen Sonderbefunden', *Telma* (16) 131–58.

Ebbesen, K., 1986 *Døden i Mosen.* Copenhagen.

Eisenbeiss, S., 1992 *Berichte über Moorleichen aus Niedersächsen im Nachlass von Alfred Dieck.* Magisterarbeit University of Hamburg.

Evershed, R. P., 1990 'Lipids from samples of skin from seven Dutch bog bodies: preliminary report', *Archaeometry* (32) 139–53.

Fischer, Chr., 1979 'Moseligene fra Bjaeldskovdal', *Kuml* 7–44.

Fischer, Chr., 1980 'Bog bodies of Denmark', in Cockburn A., and Cockburn, E. (eds) *Mummies, Disease and Ancient Cultures,* 177–93. Cambridge.

Fitzpatrick, A. P., 1984 'The deposition of La Tène Iron Age metalwork in watery contexts in Southern England', in Cunliffe, B., and Miles, D. (eds) *Aspects of the Iron Age in Central Southern Britain,* 178–90. Oxford.

Gebühr, M., 1979 'Das Kindergrab von Windeby. Versuch einer "Rehabilitation"', *Offa* (36) 75–107.

Glob, P. V., 1969 *The Bog People.* Faber & Faber, London.

Gregersen, M., 1979 'Moseliget fra Elling. En retsmedicinsk undersøgelse', *Kuml* 45–57.

Groenman van Waateringe, W., 1990 'De kledingstukken van leder en bont', in Sanden, W. A. B. van der (ed.) 174–80.

Hakbijl, T., 1990 'Insekten', in Sanden, W. A. B. van der (ed.) 168–73.

Halbertsma, H., 1984 'Het heidendom waar Liudger onder de Friezen mee te maken kreeg', in Sierksma, K. (ed.) *Liudger 742–809: de confrontatie tussen heidendom en christendom in de Lage Landen,* 21–43. Muiderberg.

Halbertsma, H., 1989 'Herinneringen aan St. Willibrord in Friesland', in Kiesel G., and Schroeder, J. (eds) *Willibrord, Apostel der Niederlande, Gründer der Abtei Echternach,* 42–68. Luxembourg.

Hald, M., 1980 *Ancient danish textiles from bogs and burials.* Copenhagen.

Hayen, H., 1964 'Die Knabenmoorleiche aus dem Kayhausener Moor 1922', *Oldenburger Jahrbuch* (63) 19–42.

Hayen, H., 1979 'Funde aus dem Vehne Moor – Linie Edewecht-Bösel (Teil 1)', *Archäologische Mitteilungen aus Nordwestdeutschland* (2) 39–55.

Hayen, H., 1981 'Funde aus dem Vehne Moor – Linie Edewecht-Bösel (Teil 2)', *Archäologische Mitteilungen aus Nordwestdeutschland* (4) 23–41.

Hayen, H., 1987 *Die Moorleichen im Museum Am Damm.* Oldenburg.

Helmer, R., 1983 'Die Moorleiche von Windeby: Versuch einer plastischen Rekonstruktion der Weichteile des Gesichtes auf dem Schädel', *Offa* (40) 345–52.

Holden, T. G., 1990 *Taphonomic and Methodological Problems in Reconstructing Diet from Ancient Human Gut and Faecal Remains.* Thesis. London.

Jankuhn, H., 1967 *Archäologische Beobachtungen zu Tier- und Menschenopfern bei den Germanen in der römischen Kaiserzeit.* Göttingen.

Kunwald, G., 1970 'Der Moorfund im Rappendam, Seeland, Dänemark', in Jankuhn, H. (ed.) *Vorgeschichtliche Heiligtümer und Opferplätze in Mittel- und Nordeuropa*, 100–118. Göttingen.

Langfeldt, B. and Raahede, J., 1979 'Møseliget fra Elling, Røntgenundersøgelse', *Kuml* 59–66.

Liversage, D., 1984 'La femme de Huldremose', in Bocquet, A. *et al Eléments de Pré- et Protohistoire Européenne: Hommages à Jacques-Pierre Millotte, Ann. Litt. de l'Univ. de Besançon*, 639–47. Les Belles Lettres, Paris.

Martin, O., 1967 'Bericht über die Untersuchung der Speisereste in der Moorleiche von Dätgen', *Offa* (24) 77–8.

Munksgaard, E., 1984 'Bog bodies – a brief survey of interpretations', *J. Danish Archaeol.* (3) 120–3.

Osinga, J. and Buys, C. H. C. M., 1990 'DNA-onderzoek', in Sanden, W. A. B. van der (ed.) 125–8.

Osinga, J., Buys, C. H. C. M. and Sanden, W. A. B. van der, 1992 'DNA and the Dutch bog bodies', *Ancient DNA Newsletter* (1) nr. 2, 21–2.

Paap, N. A., 'Parasieten', in Sanden, W. A. B. van der (ed.) 162–7.

Roymans, N., 1990 *Tribal societies in Northern Gaul: an anthropological perspective.* Amsterdam.

Sanden, W. A. B. van der, 1990 'De laatste maaltijd (1): de macro-resten', in Sanden, W. A. B. van der (ed.) 151–7.

Sanden, W. A. B. van der, (ed.), 1990 *Mens en Moeras: Veenlijken in Nederland van de Bronstijd tot en met de Romeinse Tijd.* Drents Museum, Assen.

Sanden, W. A. B. van der, 1992 'Mens en moeras: het vervolg', *Nieuwe Drentse Volksalmanak* (109) 140–54.

Sanden, W. A. B. van der, 1993 'Alfred Dieck und die niederländischen Moorleichen: einige kritische Randbemerkungen', *Die Kunde* (44) 127–139.

Sanden, W. A. B. van der, 1994 *Het meisje van Yde, Assen.* Drents Museum, Assen.

Sanden, W. A. B. van der, Haverkort, C. and Pasveer, J. 1991/92 'Een menselijk skelet uit de Aschbroeken bij Weerdinge (Drenthe); reconstructie van een

misverstand', *Palaeohistoria* (33–34) 155–63.

Schlabow, K., 1976 *Textilfunde der Eisenzeit in Norddeutschland.* Neumünster.

Stead, I. M., Bourke, J. B. and Brothwell, D. (eds) 1986 *Lindow Man: The Body in the Bog.* British Museum Publications.

Struve, K. W., 1967 'Die Moorleiche von Dätgen: ein Diskussionsbeitrage zur Strafopferthese', *Offa* (24) 33–76.

Tauber, H., 1979 'Kulstof-14 datering af møselig', *Kuml* 73–8.

Torbrügge, W., 1970–71 'Vor- und frühgeschichtliche Flussfunde; zur Ordnung und Bestimmung einer Denkmälergruppe', *Bericht der Römisch-Germanischen Kommission* (51–2) 1–146.

Troostheide, C. D., 1990 'De laatste maaltijd (2): de stuifmeelkorrels', in Sanden, W. A. B. van der (ed.) 158–61.

Trotter, M. and Gleser, G. C., 1958 'A re-evaluation of estimation of stature based on measurements of stature taken during life and long-bones after death', *Am. J. Phys. Anthrop.* (16) 79–123.

Uytterschaut, H. T., 1990 'Trauma en pathologie', in Sanden, W. A. B. van der (ed.) 129–35.

Vons-Comis, S. Y., 1990 'De wollen kleding', in Sanden, W. A. B. van der (ed.) 181–97.

Wait, G. A., 1985 *Ritual and Religion in Iron Age Britain.* Oxford.

Waterbolk, H. T., 1977 'Walled enclosures of the Iron Age in the north of the Netherlands', *Palaeohistoria* (19) 97–172.

Chapter 18

Ambers, J. C., Matthews, K. J. and Bowman, S. G. E., 1986 'Radiocarbon dates from two peat samples', in Stead *et al* 25–6.

Andersen, S. R, and Geertinger, P., 1984 'Bodies investigated in the light of forensic medicine', *J. Danish Archaeol.* (3) 111–19.

Balguy, C., 1734 'An account of the dead bodies of a man and woman which were preserved 49 years in the moors of Derbyshire', *Phil. Trans. R. Soc.* (38) no. 434, 413–15.

Barber, K., 1986 'Peat macrofossil analyses as indicators of the bog palaeoenvironment and climatic change', in Stead *et al* 86–9.

Becker, C. J., 1948 'Tørvegravning i ældre jernalder', *Fra Nationalmuseets Arbejdsmark*, 92–100.

Bellamy, D., 1986 *Bellamy's Ireland: the Wild Boglands.* Country House, Dublin.

Bender Jørgensen, L., 1986 *Forhistoriske Textiler I Skandinavien: Prehistoric Scandinavian Textiles.* Copenhagen.

Bennike, P., Ebbesen, K. and Jørgensen, L. B., 1986 'Early Neolithic skeletons from Bolkide bog, Denmark', *Antiquity* (60) 199–209.

Bourke, J. B., 1986 'The medical investigation of Lindow Man', in Stead *et al* 46–51.

Bradley, R., 1990 *The Passage of Arms*. Cambridge University Press.

Briggs, C. S., 1985 'Some problems of survey and study in prehistoric Ireland: Highland and lowland distributions in Central Ulster, *c*. 3600–1800 BC', in Burgess, C. B. and Spratt, D. A. (eds) *Upland Settlement in Britain*, 351–63. British Archaeological Reports, British Series 143.

Briggs, C. S., 1986 'The bog burials of Britain and Ireland: history and Irish finds', in Stead *et al* 144–61.

Briggs, C. S., 1987 'Buckets and cauldrons in the Late Bronze Age of north-west Europe: a review, with appendix on buckets by M. Holland', in Blanchet, J. C. *et al* (eds) *Les Rélations entre le Continent et les Iles Britanniques a l'Age du Bronze: Actes du colloque de Lille dans le cadre du 22ième Congrès Préhistorique de France, Séptèmbre, 1984*, 161–86. Supplément Revue Archéologique de Picardie. Socièté Préhistorique, Française. Amiens.

Briggs, C. S. and Turner, R. C., 1986 'A gazetteer of bog burials from Britain and Ireland', in Stead *et al* 181–95.

Briggs, C. S. 'The Ardee Lady'. Unpublished investigation.

Brothwell, D., 1986 *The Bog Man and the Archaeology of People*. British Museum Publications, London.

Brothwell, D. and Dobney, K., 1986 'Studies on the hair and nails of Lindow Man and comparative specimens', in Stead *et al* 66.

Brothwell, D., Liversage, D. and Gottlieb, B., 1990 'Radiographic and forensic aspects of the female Huldremøse body', *J. Danish Archaeol.* (9) 157–78.

Budworth, G., McCord, M. E. A., Priston, A. V. and Stead, I. M., 1986 'The Artefacts, in Stead *et al* 38–40.

Burgess, C. B. and Coombs, D., 1979 *Bronze Age Hoards: Some Finds Old and New*, British Archaeological Reports, British Series 67.

Connolly, R. C., 1985 'Lindow Man: Britain's prehistoric bog body', *Anthrop. Today* (1.5) 15–17.

Connolly, R. C., 1986 'The anatomical description of Lindow Man', in Stead *et al* 54–62.

Dieck, A., 1965 *Die europäischen Moorleichenfunde (Hominidenmoorfunde)*. Neumünster.

Fisher, J., 1917 *Fenton's Tours*. Cambrian Archaeological Association, Cardiff.

Gebühr, M., 1981 'Das Kindergrab von Windeby. Versuch einer "Rehabilitation"', *Offa* (36) (1979), 75–107.

Girling, M. A., 1986 'The insects associated with Lindow Man', in Stead *et al* 90–91.

Glob, P. V., 1956 'Jernaldermaned fra Grauballe', *Kuml* 99–113.

Glob, P. V., 1969 *The Bog People*. Faber & Faber, London.

Godwin, H., 1978 *Fenlands: Its Ancient Past and Uncertain Future*. Cambridge University Press.

Gowlett, J. A. J., Hedges, R. E. M. and Law, I. A., 1989 'Radiocarbon accelerator AMS dating of Lindow Man', *Antiquity* (63) 71–9.

Hald, M., 1980 *Ancient Danish Textiles from Bogs and Burials: A Comparative Study of Costume and Iron Age Textiles*. National Museum of Denmark.

Hammond, R. F., 1981 *The Peatlands of Ireland*. An Foras Taluntas, Dublin.

Haydn, J., 1871 *Dictionary of Dates*. London.

Hughes, M. A. and Jones, D. S., 1986 'Body in the bog but no DNA', *Nature* (323) 208.

Jørgensen, S., 1956 'Grauballemandens fundsted', *Kuml* 1956, 114–30.

Kendrick, T. D., 1950 *British Antiquity*. Methuen, London.

Liversage, D., 1985 'La Femme de Huldremøse', in Bocquet, A. *et al*, *Eléments de Pré- et Protohistoire Européenne: Hommages à Jacques-Pierre Millotte, Ann. Litt. de l'Univ. de Besançon*, 639–44. Les Belles Lettres, Paris.

Lucas, A. T., 1972 'National Museum of Ireland Acquisitions in the year 1969', *J. R. Soc. Antiq. Ir.* (102), 181–223.

McClintock, H. F., 1950 *Old Irish and Highland Dress*, 2nd edn. Dundealgan Press, Dundalk.

Meaney, A., 1964 *A Gazetteer of Early Anglo-Saxon Burial Sites*. London.

Molleson, T., 1986 'Visitors from the Past', Review of *Lindow Man, Nature* (322) 602.

Munck, A. W., 1956 'Patologisk-anatomisk og Retsmedicinsk undersøgelse af Møseliget fra Grauballe', *Kuml* 131–7.

Munksgaard, E., 1984 'Bog bodies – a brief survey of interpretations', *J. Danish Archaeol.* (3) 120–3.

Ó Floinn, R., 1988 'Irish Bog Bodies', *Archaeol. Ir.* (2) 2, 94–8.

Ogilby, J., 1675 *Britannia, Volume the First: or an Illustration of the Kingdom of England and Dominion of Wales: By a Geographical and Historical Description of the Principal Roads thereof*. Reprinted 1939. Duckham, London.

Oldfield, F., Higgitt, S. R., Richardson, N. and Yates, G., 1986 'Pollen, charcoal, rhizopod and radiometric analyses', in Stead *et al* 82–5.

Otlet, R. L., Walker, A. J. and Dadson, A. M., 1986 'Report on radiocarbon dating of the Lindow Man by AERE, Harwell', in Stead *et al* 27–30.

Owen, T., 1975 'Historical aspects of peat-cutting in Merioneth', *J. Merioneth Hist. Soc.* (7) 308–21.

Rasmussen, H., 1970 'Peat cutting in Denmark', 200–10, in Gailey, A. and Fenton, A. (eds) *The Spade in Northern and Atlantic Europe*. Ulster Folk Museum, Queen's University, Belfast.

Sanden, W. A. B. van der (ed.) 1990 *Mens en Moeras: Veenlijken in Nederland van de Bronstijd tot en met de Romeinse Tijd*. Drents Museum, Assen.

Silvester, R. J., 1991 *The Wissey Embayment and the Fen

Causeway, Norfolk. East Anglian Archaeology 52, Norwich.

Skarði, J., av, 1970 'Faroese cultivating and peat spades', in Gailey, A. and Fenton, A. (eds) *The Spade in Northern and Atlantic Europe*, 67–72. Ulster Folk Museum and Institute for Irish Studies, Queen's University, Belfast.

Skidmore, P., 1986 'The dipterous remains', in Stead *et al* 92.

Smith, W., 1916 *A Dictionary of the Bible, Comprising its Antiquities, Biography, and Natural History.* Hertford, Conn.

Stead, I. M., Bourke, J. B. and Brothwell, D., 1986 *Lindow Man: The Body in the Bog.* British Museum Publications.

Stead, I. M. and Turner, R. C., 1985 'Lindow Man', *Antiquity* (59) 25–9.

Strom, F., 1942 *On the Sacred Origin of The Germanic Death Penalties, Kungl. Vitterlets Historie och Antikvitets Akademien Handlinger*, Del 52. Wahlstrom and Widsrand, Stockholm.

Tauber, H., 1979 'Kulstof-14 datering af møselig', *Kuml* 73–8.

Taylor, G. and Skinner, A., 1783 *Maps of the Roads of Ireland.* Longman, London. Reprinted with introduction by J. H. Andrews, 1969. Irish University Press, Shannon.

Thorvildsen, K., 1947 'Møseliget fra Borremøse i Himmerland', *National Museets Arbejdsmark*, 57–66.

Thorvildsen, K., 1951 'Møseliget fra Tollund', *Aarbøger for Nordisk Oldkyndighed og Historie*, 303–41.

Turner, J., 1981 'The Iron Age', in Simmons, I. and Tooley, M. (eds) *The Environment in British Prehistory*, 250–81. Duckworth, London.

Turner, R. C., 1986 'Discovery and excavation of the Lindow bodies', in Stead *et al* 10–13.

Turner, R. C. and Briggs, C. S., 1986 'The burials of Britain and Ireland', in Stead *et al* 144–61.

West, I. E., 1986 'Forensic aspects of Lindow Man', in Stead *et al* 77–80.

Worsaae, J. J. A., 1842 [untitled], in *Historisk Tidsskrift* (3) 249–92.

Chapter 19

Dillon, M. and Chadwick, N. 1967 *The Celtic Realms.* Weidenfeld & Nicolson, London.

Frazer, J. G., 1890 *The Golden Bough*, vol. I.

Gantz, J. (ed.) 1976 *The Mabinogion.* Penguin, Harmondsworth.

Gantz, J. (ed), 1981 *Early Irish Myths and Sagas.* Penguin, Harmondsworth.

Graves, R. (ed.), 1960 *The Greek Myths*, 2 vols. Penguin, Harmondsworth.

Jackson, K., 1940 'The motive of the three-fold death in the story of Suibhne Geilt', in J. Ryan (ed.) *Essays and Studies presented to Eoin Mac Neil*, 535–50. Dublin.

Lynn, C. J., 1977 'Trial excavations at the King's Stables,

Tray Townland, County Armagh', *Ulster J. Archaeol.* (40) 42–62.

Mac Cana, P., 1970 *Celtic Mythology.* Hamlyn, London.

Mac Mathuna, S. [no date] *Kilfarboy: A History of a West Clare Parish.*

Martin, M., 1703 *A Description of the Western Islands of Scotland.* London. (Republished Stirling 1934).

O'Grady, S. (ed.), 1892 *Silva Gadelica.* London.

O'Keefe, J. G., 1913 *Buile Suibhne, Being the Adventures of Suibhne Geilt.* Irish Texts Society XII, London.

Pegg, B., 1981 *Rites and Riots. Folk Customs of Britain and Europe.* Poole.

Raftery, B., 1987 'The Loughnashade Horns', *Emania* (2) 21–4.

Rees, A. and Rees, B., 1961 *Celtic Heritage.* Thames & Hudson, London.

Rhys, J., 1901 *Celtic Folklore, Welsh and Manx.* Oxford.

Ross, A., 1967 *Pagan Celtic Britain.* London.

Ross, A., 1986 'Lindow Man and the Celtic Tradition', in Stead *et al* 162–9.

Sinclair, J. (ed.), 1794 *The Statistical Account of Scotland*, 21 vols, 1791–9.

Smyth, A. P., 1984 *Warlords and Holy Men: Scotland AD 80–1000.* Edinburgh University Press.

Stead, I. M., Bourke, J. B. and Brothwell, D., 1986 *Lindow Man: The Body in the Bog.* British Museum Publications.

Stokes, W., 1892 'The Bodleian Dinnshenchas', *Folk-Lore* (3) 467–516.

Stokes, W., 1902 'The death of Muirchertach Mac Erca', *Revue Celtique* (23) 395–437.

Stokes, W., 1906 'The birth and life of St Moling', *Revue Celtique* (27) 285–7.

Stuart, J., 1819 *Historical Memoirs of the City of Armagh.* Armagh.

Talley, J. E., 1970 'The threefold death in Finnish lore', in Puhvel, J. (ed.) *Myth and Lore Among the Indo-Europeans*, 143–6. University of California Press.

Turner, R. C., 1986 'Boggarts, bogles and Sir Gawain and the Green Knight: Lindow Man and the oral tradition', in Stead *et al* 170–6.

Turville-Petre, E. O. G., 1964 *Myth and Religion of the North. The Religion of Scandinavia.* Weidenfeld & Nicolson, London.

Ward, D. J., 1970 'The threefold death: an Indo-European trifunctional sacrifice ?', in Puhvel, J. (ed.) *Myth and Lore Among the Indo-Europeans*, 123–42. University of California Press.

Ancient Sources

Adhamnán, *Vita Columbae* Ed. Reeves, W. (1874).

Caesar, *De Bello Gallico.* English translation by Handford, S. A. (1951), *Caesar: The Conquest of Gaul.* Penguin, Harmondsworth.

Cassius Dio, Books LXI–LXX. English translation by Cary, E. (1925). Loeb.

Geoffrey of Monmouth, *Vita Merlini*. Ed. Parry, J. (1925). Illinois.

Lucan, *De Bello Civili*. English translation by Duff, J. D. (1928). Loeb.

Pliny, *Naturalis Historia*, Books XII–XVI. English translation by Rackham, H. (1968). Loeb.

Diodorus Siculus, Books IV–VIII. English translation by Oldfather, C. H. (1935). Loeb.

Strabo, *Geographicon*, Books III–V. English translation by Jones, H. L. (1923). Loeb.

Tacitus, *Annales*. English translation by Grant, M. *The Annals of Imperial Rome*. Penguin, Harmondsworth.

Tacitus, *Germania*. English translation by Mattingley, H. (1948) *Tacitus on Britain and Germany*. Penguin, Harmondsworth.

Chapter 20

Balguy, C., 1734 'An account of the dead bodies of a man and woman which were preserved 49 years in the moors in Derbyshire', *Phil. Tran. R. Soc.* (38) no. 434, 413–5.

Bennike, P. and Ebbesen, K., 1986 'The bog find from Sigersdal: human sacrifice in the early Neolithic', *J. Danish Archaeol.* (5) 85–115.

Bradley, R., 1990 *The Passage of Arms*. Cambridge.

Bradley, R. and Gordon, K., 1988 'Human skulls from the River Thames, their dating and significance', *Antiquity* (62) 236, 503–9.

Brøndsted, J., 1958 *Danmarks Oldfid II: Bronzealderen*. Glyendal.

Brothwell, D., Liversage, D. and Gottlieb, B., 1990 'Radiographic and forensic aspects of the female Huldremose body', *J. Danish Archaeol.* (9) 157–78.

Bywater, M., 1984 'Bog standards', *Punch*, 17 Oct 1984.

Chippendale, C., 1991 'Editorial', *Antiquity* (65) 248, 443.

Coles, B., 1990 'Anthropomorphic wooden figurines from Britain and Ireland', *Proc. Prehist. Soc.* (56) 315–34.

Coles, J. M., 1962 'European Bronze Age shields', *Proc. Prehist. Soc.* (28) 156–91.

Davey, P. J., 1971 'Distribution of later Bronze Age metalwork from Lincolnshire', *Proc. Prehist. Soc.* (37) 96–112.

Drabble, M., 1988 *A Natural Curiosity*. London.

Dudley, D. R. and Webster, G., 1965 *The Roman Conquest of Britain*. London.

Farmer, D. H., 1978 *The Oxford Dictionary of Saints*. Oxford University Press.

Field, N., 1984 'Fiskerton', *Current Archaeology*.

Fischer, C., 1979 'Moseligene fra Bjaeldskovdal', *Kuml* (1979), 7–44.

Fitzpatrick, A. P., 1984 'The deposition of La Tène Iron Age metalwork in watery contexts in southern England', in

Cunliffe, B. and Miles, D. (eds) *Aspects of the Iron Age in Central Southern England*, 178–90. Oxford University Comm. Archaeology Series (2).

Fox, C., 1947 *A Find of the Early Iron Age from Llyn Cerrig Bach, Anglesey*. Cardiff.

Glob, P. V., 1969 *The Bog People*. Faber & Faber, London.

Godwin, H., 1975 *The History of the British Flora* 2nd edn. Cambridge.

Green, M., 1983 'Tanarus, Taranis and the Chester Altar', *J. Chester Archaeol. Soc.* (65) 37–44.

Green, M., 1986 *The Gods of the Celts*. Gloucester.

Grigson, G., 1955 *An Englishman's Flora*. London.

Grigson, G., 1980 *Collected Poems 1963–80*. London.

Haylen, H., 1987 *Die Moorleichen im Museum am Damm*. Oldenburg.

Heaney, S., 1975 *Selected Poems 1965–1975*. London.

Higham, N. J., 1980 'Native settlements west of the Pennines', in Branigan, K. (ed.) *Rome and the Brigantes* 41–7. Sheffield.

Higham, N. J., 1985 'Tatton Park – deserted village', *Cheshire Archaeol. Bull.* (10) 75–82.

Higham, N. J. and Jones, G. D. B., 1975 'Frontier, forts and farmers', *Archaeol. J.* (132) 16–53.

Ilkjaer, J., 1977 'Illerup adal: Udgravnigen 1976', *Kuml*, 105–17.

Innes, J. B. and Shennan, I., 1991 'Palynology of archaeological and mire sediments from Dud, Border Regions, Scotland', *Archaeol. J.* (148) 1–45.

Jackson, S., 1973 *Celtic and Other Stone Heads*. Shipley.

Jensen, J., 1982 *The Prehistory of Denmark*. London.

King, D., 1656 *The Vale Royall of England*. London.

Lawrenson, W. H., undated, 'Bone Hill Farm', *Over-Wyre Hist. J.* (1) 20–2.

Longley, D. M. T., 1987 'Prehistory', in Harris, B. (ed.) *A History of the County of Chester* (1) 36–114.

Moira, Lady, 1783 'Particulars relative to a human skeleton etc.' *Archaeologia* (7) 90–110.

Nevell, M., 1988 'Arthill Heath Farm', *Manchr. Archaeol. Bull.* (3) 5–13.

Nevell, M., 1989 'Legh Oaks Farm', *Manchr. Archaeol. Bull.* (4) 44–52.

Nevell, M., 1991 'Great Woolden Hall Farm, excavations on a late prehistoric/Romano–British native site', *Manchr. Archaeol. Bull.* (6) 35–44.

Norbury, W., 1884 'Lindow Common as a peat bog – its age and people', *Trans. Lancs. & Ches. Antiq. Soc.* (II) 60–75.

Oldfield, F., Higgitt, S. R., Richardson, N. and Yates, G., 1986 'Pollen, charcoal, rhizopod and radiometric analyses', in Stead *et al* 82–5.

Olmsted, G., 1979 'The Gundestrup Cauldron', *Collection Latomus* (162).

Parker-Pearson, M., 1986 'Lindow Man and the Danish

connection – further light on the mystery of the Bogman', *Anthrop. Today* (2,1) 15–18.

Perring, F., 1973 'Mistletoe', in Green, P. S. (ed.) *Plants: Wild and Cultivated* 139–46. Middlesex.

Petch, D. F., 1987 'The Roman period', in Harris, B. (ed.) *A History of the County of Chester*, 115–236. Oxford University Press.

Phillips, R., 1981 *Mushrooms and other fungi of Great Britain and Europe*. London.

Ross, A., 1967 *Pagan Celtic Britain*.

Ross, A., 1986 'Lindow Man and the Celtic tradition', in Stead *et al* 162–9.

Ross, A. and Robins, D., 1989 *The Life and Death of a Druid Prince*. London.

Sainter, J. D., 1898 *Scientific Rambles around Macclesfield*. Macclesfield.

Sanden, W. A. B. van der (ed.), 1990 *Men en Moeras: Veenlijken in Nederland van de Bronstijd tot en met de Romeinse Tijd*. Drents Museum, Assen.

Savory, H., 1976 *Guide Catalogue of the Early Iron Age Collections*. National Museum of Wales.

Savory, H., 1980 *Guide Catalogue of the Bronze Age Collections*. National Museum of Wales.

Scarfe, N., 1970 'The body of St. Edmund: an essay in necrobiography', *Proc. Suffolk Inst. Archaeol.* (31) 303–17.

Shotter, D. C. A., 1984 'Roman North-West England', *Centre for North-West Regional Studies* (14).

Stead, I. M., 1985 *Celtic Art*. British Museum Publications.

Stead, I. M., 1986 'Summary and conclusions', in Stead *et al* 177–80.

Struve, K. W., 1967 'Die Moorleiche von Dätgen: ein Diskussionsbetreige zur Stafopferthese', *Offa* (24) 33–76.

Turner, R. C., 1986 'Boggarts, bogles and Sir Gawain and the Green Knight: Lindow Man and the oral tradition', in Stead *et al* 170–6.

Turner, R. C., 1988 'A Cumbrian bog body from Scaleby', *Trans. Cumb. & Westmorland Antiq. & Archaeol. Soc.* (88) 1–7.

Turner, R. C., 1989 'Another Cumbrian bog body, found in Seascale Moss in 1843', *Trans. Cumb. & Westmorland Antiq. & Archaeol. Soc.* (89) 21–3.

Turner, R. C., Rhodes, M. and Wild, J. P., 1991 'The Roman body found on Grewelthorpe Moor in 1850: a reappraisal', *Britannia* xxii, 191–201.

Turner, R. C. and Rhodes, M., 1992 'A bog body and its shoes from Amcotts, Lincolnshire', *Antiq. J.* (72) 76–90.

Williams, R., 1989 *People of the Black Mountains – The Beginning*. London.

Index to Chapters